The
Difficult
Road to Peace
Netanyahu, Israel and the Middle East Peace Process

INTERNATIONAL POLITICS OF THE MIDDLE EAST SERIES

The
Difficult
Road to Peace

Netanyahu, Israel and the Middle East Peace Process

Neill Lochery

ITHACA
PRESS

THE DIFFICULT ROAD TO PEACE
Netanyahu, Israel and the Middle East Peace Process

Ithaca Press is an imprint of Garnet Publishing Limited

Published by
Garnet Publishing Limited
8 Southern Court
South Street
Reading
RG1 4QS
UK

First Edition

ISBN 0 86372 248 2

British Library Cataloguing-in-Publication Data
A catalogue record for this book is available from the British Library

Jacket design by David Rose
Typeset by Samantha Abley

Printed in Lebanon

*Dedicated to those who continue
the search for peace*

Contents

PART III
ISRAELI RELATIONS WITH THE ARAB STATES
AND THE WIDER MIDDLE EAST

PART IV
EXTERNAL ACTORS IN THE PEACE PROCESS:
THE CASE OF THE UNITED STATES

PART V
APPLICABLE LESSONS OF THE MIDDLE EAST
PEACE PROCESS FOR OTHER CONFLICTS

APPENDICES

FIGURES

TABLES

Acknowledgements

There are a number of individuals and organisations who have made contributions to this book: As well as expressing gratitude to all of them, the author also wishes especially to thank the following: the British Academy, who helped finance the fieldwork stage of this project in Israel; the Elie Kedourie Memorial Fund Prize, which helped with a generous contribution to fieldwork studies; John Levy and the Academic Study Group, who helped support a trip to Israel during the first stages of this project; the Moshe Dayan Centre at Tel Aviv University, for the prize and award that helped with research related to, and originating from, this project; Professor Efraim Karsh at Kings College London for support; Professor John Klier at University College London for all his efforts on the author's behalf; Dr Rosemary Hollis at Chatham House for her enthusiasm and help; Dr Michael Dumper for reading parts of the manuscript and making valuable suggestions; as always, Professor Niblock for his support and teachings; and Dean Godson for his seemingly endless enthusiasm for the subject.

At Ithaca the author wishes to thank the editors for all their support during the various stages of the writing of this book and his previous book on the Israeli Labour Party; and in general to all the members of staff who make it such a pleasant company to deal with.

In Israel, the author wishes to thank all those who agreed to be interviewed, particularly those who are currently serving in the Netanyahu-led government and who trusted the author with information that was invaluable to the project. A special acknowledgement must go to David Bar-Ilan, Netanyahu's Director of Communications and Policy, for talking candidly about the domestic difficulties of the Netanyahu government. In addition, the author wishes to express his immense gratitude to the staff of the Knesset Records; Labour Party Archives at Beit Berl; Likud Archives in Tel Aviv; Labour Party Headquarters in Tel Aviv; Likud Headquarters in Tel Aviv; Meretz Headquarters in Tel Aviv;

the Government Press Office in Jerusalem; and Dan Meridor (Likud MK) and Yossi Beilin (MK) for their continued help and support. In addition, the author would like to thank the Palestinian individuals who helped to arrange meetings during visits to East Jerusalem and the Gaza Strip.

On a personal note, thanks to my mother for all her support and encouragement; and to my friends who gave me ideas and were willing to read and check the manuscript and to put up with me during the writing-up stage of this project.

Neill Lochery
London 1999

Preface

Israel has been at the centre of conflict with the Arab world since its creation some 50 years ago. During this time the Middle East has experienced five major Arab–Israeli wars: the war of 1948, the Suez War 1956, the Six Day War 1967, the October War 1973 and the Lebanon War 1982. In addition, the periods between these wars were characterised by a series of low to medium intensity conflicts, guerrilla attacks on Israeli targets and the near total isolation of the Jewish state in the region. However, the Camp David agreement with Egypt in 1977 and, more recently, Israel's peace accords with the Palestinian Liberation Organisation (PLO) and peace settlement with Jordan have transformed the political landscape of the Middle East.

The period of the last Labour-led governments of Yitzhak Rabin and Shimon Peres in Israel (1992–6) seemingly offered new hope and impetus to a peace process that had stagnated during the 1980s. The major concessions offered by Rabin and, subsequently, Peres to the Arabs appeared to pave the way for a permanent ending to the conflict in the region. However, both Rabin's death at the hands of a Jewish zealot in November 1995 and the deepening complexities of securing a lasting peace have meant that it appears unlikely that a full and comprehensive political settlement can be reached in the Middle East in the near future. It should be made clear that Rabin's death, while itself a major tragedy for the prospects of peace, cannot obscure the fact that many of the current difficulties that dog the peace process would have occurred even if he had lived and been re-elected in 1996.

In the event, Binyamin Netanyahu became Israel's first directly elected prime minister after securing a narrow but decisive victory in the election for prime minister in May 1996. Following his election there was widespread international concern about the future of the Middle East peace process given Netanyahu's publicly stated opposition to the Oslo Accords signed by the late Yitzhak Rabin. However, during the election campaign Netanyahu had pledged to continue the process outlined in the Oslo agreements. Consequently, during his first years in office the prime minister has attempted to implement the parts of Oslo that were agreed prior to his coming to power as well as continuing, albeit at a slower pace, the peace process with the PLO. During this period the Middle East peace process as a whole has experienced a growing number of difficulties, which have led many commentators and participants to conclude that it is doomed to eventual failure. This is in stark contrast to the feelings of optimism that defined the period immediately following the signing of the Israeli–Palestinian Accords in Washington in 1993 and 1994.

This book has one principal aim: to analyse and chronicle the development of the various tracks of the peace process under the Likud-led government in Israel. Its secondary aim is to examine any useful lessons, both positive and negative, that can be drawn from the Middle East peace process and applied to other regions of conflict. With regards the first, the book examines the key issues that have determined the state of the peace process since the historic breakthrough in Oslo. As a result, the study aims to provide a comprehensive guide to the Middle East peace process under the Likud-led government in Israel.

Part I provides a detailed account of the rise of Netanyahu, his background and an assessment of his beliefs. Little has hitherto been written in English on what Israel's youngest prime minister stands for or the profound changes in the Israeli political system of which his election is a direct product. The second part will examine perhaps the most complex issue of the Middle East peace process, the Israeli–Palestinian negotiations from Oslo towards a final status agreement. Part III examines Israel's relations with the Arab states and the wider Middle East. It will be argued that there appears little chance of a comprehensive Middle East peace agreement in the foreseeable future. Part IV analyses the role of external powers in the process – in particular that of the United States. Finally, in Part V of the book general lessons are drawn from the process in the Middle East that could be applied to other areas of conflict such as Northern Ireland.

The central theme of the book is that the argument widely employed by academics and the Arab side that Netanyahu is personally to blame for derailing the peace process is simplistic and not totally accurate. The complexity of the Middle East peace process is such that it was inevitable that the period of euphoria that followed Rabin's handshake with Yasser Arafat would be replaced by a more sombre assessment of the difficult road to peace.

In employing this theme use has been made of secondary sources from both Israeli and Arab sides. In addition, use has been made of interviews conducted by the author, many of which were off the record in order to allow serving personnel an opportunity to more fully express themselves. Moreover, documents and protocols on the various parts of the process discussed in the book are analysed and in some cases reassessed with the hindsight of history.

The major fieldwork stages of the study took place in Israel during March 1998 and the summer of 1998, and involved conducting interviews and visits to the Knesset Records Archive, Labour Party Archives at Beit Berl and the Central Bureau of Statistics. In addition, visits were made to the party headquarters of the major political parties in Israel as well as to the Palestinian Authority (PA) headquarters in Gaza. Moreover, visits were made to academic establishments at Tel Aviv University, the Hebrew University in Jerusalem and Haifa University. By using both interviewed source material (conducted strictly off the record) and documentation along with local press coverage, it is hoped to present as complete a picture as possible of the peace process under Netanyahu and to chronicle the changes that Israel is going through.

The chapters are divided into the following areas which cover the major developments in the peace process towards the end of the twentieth century.

Part I: The Israeli domestic changes

Changes in Israel's political system: internal restraints on Netanyahu

It is argued that the changes in Israel's electoral system which aimed to enhance the power of the prime minister with the holding of direct elections for prime minister in 1996 may actually have had the opposite effect. In addition, it is argued that it is clear that there is a direct relationship between the formation of Israeli policy towards the peace process and these changes in Israel's method of electing its governments. Consequently, this chapter chronicles how Netanyahu has attempted to deal with the peace process from a relatively weak domestic position, and charts his successes and failures as well as examining his limited room for manoeuvre within the Likud party he leads, the Israeli Cabinet and governing coalition.

Netanyahu and the peace process 1996–1998: vision, strategy and restraints

The rise of Netanyahu and his formation of a centre-right government in 1996 have complicated the peace process in that they have led to a perceived hardening of both the Israeli opening and fall-back positions on the Palestinian and Syrian tracks of the peace process. However, in other ways it has meant that any deal that the prime minister signs up to is likely to win support from a far larger segment of Israeli society than occurred during the Oslo process. In essence, Netanyahu may strike a harder bargain but is likely to be able to deliver the Israeli centre-right's support for such a deal. This chapter contains a detailed account of the first set of negotiations between the Netanyahu government and the PA over the Israeli withdrawal of Hebron and troop redeployment. Moreover, it charts the domestic difficulties encountered by Netanyahu during this complex set of negotiations between his government and the PA led by Yasser Arafat.

Part II: The Palestinian track

Security arrangements in the West Bank and the Gaza Strip and the future of Israeli settlements

The issue of future security arrangements in the West Bank and the Gaza Strip is at the centre of the negotiations between the Israeli government and the Palestinian Authority. This chapter includes an examination of how security cooperation has developed between Israel and the PA and how it will work if and when Final Status talks are concluded. In addition, it analyses what would happen if either side tried to impose unilateral security arrangements in these areas if the negotiations were finally to break down. Central to this is the threat by Yasser Arafat to unilaterally declare Palestinian independence (UDI) if the negotiations are deadlocked or have not produced a Palestinian state. Regarding the settlement issue, the present Israeli government is currently considering which of the settlements will remain under Israeli sovereignty. However, it is clear that not all settlements will remain under direct Israeli sovereignty in the long term after the negotiations are completed. Consequently, this chapter explores potential options for the settlements as well as detailing the influence on the Israeli political process of extra-parliamentary settlers groups such as Gush Emunim.

The economic dimension of an Israeli–Palestinian peace: where is the peace dividend?

A study commissioned by the United Nations (UN) in 1997 found that since the Oslo Accords, the average economic wealth of the Palestinians had fallen by 30 per cent. As a result, this chapter analyses the reasons behind the decline of the Palestinian economy and the political ramifications of these problems both for the short term and in the long term for the type of Palestinian entity (state) which eventually emerges at the end of the peace process.

On the Israeli side there has been a clearer economic pay-off from the peace process in terms of increased foreign investment in the stock exchange. Crucially, this improvement in the Israeli economy has not helped the less well-off groups in Israeli society which have not seen a significant improvement in their economic conditions. The chapter explores the relationship between the peace process and economic stability, and the ways in which a secure and lasting peace could benefit the economies of both the Israelis and the Palestinians. Finally, the chapter provides a framework for maximising any peace dividend to both sides. This is seen as vital if support for the process is to overcome the rejectionist groups, particularly on the Palestinian side.

The Palestinian refugees: post-Oslo, continuity and developments

Many of the negotiators from both sides who were responsible for the breakthrough at Oslo have privately stated that they feel the issue of refugees and the right of return of Palestinians to their homes is the major stumbling block that may eventually end the process. Consequently, this chapter explores various options (such as the offering of compensation) which are highly sensitive to both sides. In addition, it addresses the central problems of the negotiations, namely arrival at an agreed definition of who is a refugee and who is not, and the problems of dealing with the seemingly intractable issue of the right of return of the 1948 refugees.

The main argument in this chapter is that the refugee issue has been held hostage to other political issues and that there has been little progress in finding solutions to any of the key problems.

The final status of Jerusalem: Israeli continuity under Netanyahu

The future status of Jerusalem remains one of the most emotive issues in the peace process. The city is claimed by both the Israelis and the Palestinians as their capital. This chapter concentrates on examining the recent proposals from both sides concerning the future of East Jerusalem and the Old City particularly. The argument is put forward that the difference in the position of both sides over Jerusalem is not as unbridgeable as public rhetoric would suggest. In addition, attention will be paid to assessing the extent that Jerusalem could be used as a pay-off by one of the sides as part of an overall settlement between Israel and the Palestinians.

Part III: Israeli relations with the Arab States and the wider Middle East

The developing Israeli–Jordanian peace under the Netanyahu-led government

The peace treaty signed in 1994 between Israel and Jordan officially ended the conflict between the two countries. However, as events in recent years have shown, problematic areas still remain in the post-treaty relations between the two countries. Issues such as the allocation of existing water resources, research into new sources of water, botched assassination attempts by the Israeli security forces in Amman and the lack of progress in other tracks of the peace process have created tensions between the Netanyahu government and King Hussein of Jordan. However, the central argument of this chapter concerns the fact that the relationship between Israel and Jordan would have been increasingly problematic whoever was in power in Israel. In essence, the nature of the problems such as allocations of water resources which were set in the peace treaty were almost certain to lead to future difficulties. Finally, the chapter examines how the peace, which is largely viewed as a moderately warm peace (despite the previously listed difficulties), can be developed into closer ties (particularly economic) and what the consequences of such new relations would be for the Arab world and the Middle East region as a whole.

An Israeli–Syrian peace on the Golan Heights

The key to any Israeli–Syrian peace is the future status of the Golan Heights, which Israel captured from Syria during the Six Day War in 1967. This chapter examines the security, political and economic issues involved in any potential return of part, or all, of the Golan Heights to Syria. In addition, it analyses the internal political dynamics of both Syria and Israel towards securing peace with each other. The main argument put forward in this chapter is that President Asad of Syria has not shown any real interest or commitment to making peace with Israel despite Rabin's offer to return the Golan Heights to Syria (which is documented in detail in the chapter). Furthermore, it is argued that Asad's rejection of Israel's peace overtures is rational in terms of protecting his own regime and his interpretation of Syrian interests. In addition, the chapter chronicles the attempts of the Netanyahu government to restart the negotiations with Syria, which were suspended in spring 1996.

Israeli–Lebanese peace: Netanyahu's no-win options in Lebanon

Israel's northern border is Israel's last active war. This chapter explores the possibility of peace with Lebanon, which is closely related to any potential peace deal with Syria. In addition, it chronicles Israel's conflict with the Iranian-backed and Syrian-controlled Hizbollah guerrilla organisation in the security zone in southern Lebanon, which claims the lives of around two dozen Israeli soldiers every year. In recent years the conflict has entered a highly active phase and this, together with a series of Israeli military disasters such as a helicopter crash which claimed the lives of 80 soldiers, has led many in Israel to question its occupation of the so-called security zone in southern Lebanon. Consequently, this chapter analyses the options Netanyahu has in this area, ranging from a unilateral withdrawal to a gradual withdrawal or a maintenance of the status quo. The central argument of this chapter is that none of these options is particularly attractive for a variety of reasons – all of which are discussed in detail. Finally, it is argued that Israel's best exit out of Lebanon is through securing a peace deal with Syria, the dominant force in Lebanon.

Israel and Turkey: deepening ties and strategic implications
This chapter analyses the developing links between Israel and Turkey which arguably constitute one of the most important developments in the region since the visit of President Sadat to Israel in 1977. Moreover, the chapter analyses the effect of this new alliance on the peace process and the strategic balance in the wider Middle East. It is argued that the alliance between Israel and Turkey, while apparently serving the strategic needs of both countries, is not likely to prove as beneficial in the long term as the political and military planners had suggested. The chapter also examines the highly related development of the recent attempts of Syria to forge closer ties with Iran and the slow re-entry of Iraq into the Arab world via relations with Syria. Finally, it examines the attempted re-entry of Russia into the Middle East and concludes that this development is adding to the already changing strategic relationships in the region.

Part IV: External actors in the peace process: the case of the United States

The development of the role of the United States in the peace process, 1991–1998: is there room at the table for new mediators?
This chapter chronicles the place of the United States in the peace process since Netanyahu's election in 1996 and its three roles: mediator, messenger and guarantor of agreements. Moreover, it analyses the use of pressure by the United States on both the Arab parties (in particular the Palestinians) and the Israelis as a means to maintain the peace process, a policy which has drawn the present US administration, and in particular the Secretary of State, Madeleine Albright, closer than ever into the peace process. The chapter develops the argument that despite the damage done by some of Netanyahu's policies (particularly the expansion of Jewish settlements) to relations between Israel and the US administration, the Clinton administration has not been willing or able to apply sufficient pressure on Netanyahu to effectively change his policies, despite the Wye River Memorandum (see Appendix 8). In addition to this principal aim, the chapter explores the role of other external players in the peace process such as the European Union (EU) and accesses the limitations of

the potential roles that other mediators such as Russia could play in the peace process.

Part V: Applicable lessons of the Middle East peace process for other conflicts

Lessons of the Middle East peace process for other conflicts

The secret Israeli–Palestinian negotiations which led to the Oslo Accords (1993) demonstrated that informal channels can be extremely instrumental in bypassing certain obstacles that conventional diplomacy cannot overcome – particularly the emotionally laden atmosphere of the Arab–Israeli conflict. Furthermore, the Middle East peace process has produced a number of other key lessons, some positive but the majority negative, which can be applied to other conflicts. Consequently, this chapter examines what it considers to be the 11 most important areas of peace making in the Middle East where lessons can be deduced. These lessons include the following areas: interim stages in agreements, rejectionist groups, partners for peace, trust, the role of personalities, the role of external parties, security of agreements when governments change, peace making methodology, peace dividends and reconstruction.

The main argument put forward is that there is a need for both Netanyahu and other Middle East leaders to learn from the positive and negative lessons discussed in this chapter. Moreover, these lessons are of great relevance for leaders in other areas of conflict. The lessons are applied to the Northern Ireland peace process, which culminated in the signing of the Good Friday Agreement, but which is far from secure in the long term.

PART I

THE ISRAELI DOMESTIC CHANGES

1

Changes in Israel's political system: the internal restraints on Netanyahu in Israel

This chapter aims to provide an understanding of the changes in Israel's electoral system and how the new system helped Binyamin Netanyahu win the election in 1996 but has subsequently hindered him in the key area of policy making in the Middle East peace process. In addition, other factors such as Netanyahu's relatively weak intra-party position and the problems of dealing with a Cabinet consisting of eight different parties are discussed.

From the creation of the state in 1948 until 1996, Israel employed the party list electoral system to elect its parliament (the Knesset). The prime minister was the leader of the party that occupied the pivotal role (the largest single party or electoral list) in the complex coalition negotiations which followed each election, and was consequently able to form a winning coalition (61 Members of the Knesset – MKs – out of a total of 120).[1] The single exception to the selection of prime minister occurred between 1984–8, when Israel was governed by a national unity government (NUG) where the position of prime minister was rotated between the leaders of the two major parties (the Israeli Labour Party and the Likud).[2] During the period between 1948 and 1996 Israel was viewed as a classic example of a parliamentary democracy where the Knesset was the centre of political activity and played an important role in policy making both in foreign affairs and domestic issues.[3] However, recent changes to the electoral system have altered Israel's political and

---

1 See A. Diskin, *Elections and Voters in Israel* (New York, Praeger, 1991).
2 For a detailed account of the electoral reasons for the formation of the NUGs see, N. Lochery, *The Israeli Labour Party: In the Shadow of the Likud* (Reading, Ithaca Press, 1997).
3 R. Hazan, 'Presidential parliamentarism: direct popular election of the Prime Minister, Israel's new electoral and political system', *Electoral Studies*, 15–1 (1996), p. 31.

party systems and have played, first, a significant role in determining the composition of the Israeli government, and second, Israeli policy towards the Middle East peace process.[4]

The changes that took place in time for the 1996 election meant that for the first time Israel's prime minister (executive) was directly elected in a separate ballot from the Knesset (legislature).[5] Consequently, the electorate was given the opportunity to vote for a prime minister from one party and support a different party in the Knesset election. In Israel, this separation was of great significance because it allowed voters to cast one vote essentially on the conduct of the peace process (the direct election for prime minister) and one to reflect their ideological perspectives, cultural background or religious beliefs (the Knesset election).[6] Moreover, the changes in the electoral system came on top of the introduction of party primary elections to select and order the party list for the election. Previously, the candidates had been selected in *smoke-filled rooms* by party committees. This system had made it relatively easy for the party élite to maintain party discipline, and thus accordingly the advent of primary election meant that party management in both the major parties had became more difficult. This was most apparent in the growing number of challenges by party members to the policies of the leadership in the area of the peace process within both the major parties during the 13th Knesset (1992–6).

The outcome of Israeli elections in the 1980s (1981, 1984 and 1988) had resulted in near ties between the Labour Party and the Likud, which gave the smaller parties (in particular the religious parties) disproportionate influence in coalition negotiations. Moreover, these parties were quick to exploit their influence and demand financial support and Cabinet portfolios in exchange for supporting one of the major parties.[7]

---

4 For an account of the role of the electoral system in determining the outcome of the 1996 Israeli elections see D. Peretz and G. Doron, 'Israel's 1996 elections: a second political earthquake?', *Middle East Journal*, 50–4, (1996). See also J. Peters 'Israel's new government', The Royal Institute of International Affairs, *Briefing Paper* 33, (July 1996), p. 2.

5 *Israel's Basic Laws: The Elections 1996*, Ministry of Foreign Affairs, Jerusalem.

6 L. Collins, 'One person, two votes, many options', *Jerusalem Post*, 10 May 1996.

7 For the most detailed account of these deals made in the 1980s see D. Korn, 'The National Unity years in Israel 1984–1990', Ph.D. thesis, London School of Economics, London (1991). See also D. Korn, *Time in Grey 1990–1994* (in Hebrew) (Tel Aviv, Zmona Bitan, 1994).

By 1990, the influence of the religious parties especially had reached such a level that the spiritual leaders of these parties (often not even based in Israel) were able to determine which of the major parties would be in a position to form a government. This culminated in what became known in Israel as the *Dirty Exercise* in 1990, where Shimon Peres and the Labour Party resigned from an NUG and attempted, unsuccessfully, to form a new narrow-based coalition government with the aid of one of the religious parties. The extreme demands of the religious parties and the Labour Party's seeming willingness to pay them had a profound effect on accelerating the debate on electoral reform. Consequently, since 1990 Israeli academics and politicians[8] have been involved in examining potential changes to the electoral system to find a system that would reduce the power of the smaller parties and end the political horse trading which followed the outcome of each election.[9]

The eventual decision of the Knesset to endorse the new electoral system for the 1996 elections did not end the academic debate on the merits of the electoral system.[10] On the contrary, it has increased discussions on the merits of the new electoral system, particularly in light of Netanyahu's narrow election victory in 1996 and the fact that the Likud party he leads did not emerge as the single largest party.[11]

---

8 One of the best examples of the discussion was D. Libai, U. Lynn, A. Rubinstein and Y. Tsiddon, *Changing the System of Government in Israel: Proposed Basic Law; The Government, Direct Election of the Prime Minister* (in Hebrew) (Jerusalem, The Jerusalem Centre for Public Affairs and the Public Committee for a Constitution in Israel 1990).

9 Shimon Peres often states that after each election in Israel negotiations are held to see who the victor was.

10 It should be stressed that the Knesset vote in favour of changing the electoral system was passed by only one vote. The Likud leadership at the time opposed the changes. The casting vote was that of the sole Likud rebel, Binyamin Netanyahu. Interestingly, two of the strongest supporters for change were Yitzhak Rabin and Netanyahu who stood to gain most; they were perceived to be more popular in the country as a whole than within their respective parties. For an account of the Knesset debate to change the electoral system and Netanyahu's stand, see: M. Arens, *Broken Covenant: American Foreign Policy and Crisis Between the US and Israel* (New York, Simon and Schuster, 1995).

11 Many in the Likud feel Netanyahu's victory in the direct election for prime minister was achieved at the expense of the Likud in the Knesset elections. For an account of this, see: J. Mendilow, 'The Likud's dilemma in the 1996 elections: between the devil and the deep blue sea', unpublished paper, Rider University.

What has been notable by its almost total absence from this debate has been an examination of the effects of the new electoral system on the central issue of the Middle East peace process. This study therefore intends to draw on the existing work of scholars in examining the electoral system, but to take this a stage further and conduct a detailed examination of its effects on Israeli policy making in the area of the peace process.

The election of Binyamin Netanyahu and his subsequent formation of a coalition government of eight parties from the centre-right have complicated the peace process. This is particularly evident in the government's reluctance to continue the implementation of the Oslo Accords signed by Yitzhak Rabin in 1993 and 1994, which Netanyahu and the Likud strongly vehemently attacked while in opposition. In addition, six of the ruling coalition parties also actively opposed the Oslo Accords and voted against them in the subsequent Knesset ratification votes.

However, during the election campaign in 1996, Netanyahu publicly stated that he accepted the agreement with the PLO as an internationally binding deal which must be honoured and would continue with its implementation, but if possible re-negotiate the parts of the agreements which he believed damaged Israeli security interests. Since assuming power the prime minister has, to some degree, continued the Oslo process as the Hebron Agreement, the release of Palestinian prisoners and the first troop withdrawal from the West Bank have confirmed. What is clear is that the combination of the new electoral system and an ongoing peace process has resulted in a situation where there is no majority with the Cabinet or wider ruling coalition for a peace process which the prime minister is both domestically and internationally committed to implementing.

In addition, the 1996 election further illustrated the linkage of the Israeli electoral system to the peace process, for had the old election system been in place the Labour Party, as the single largest party, would have emerged as the winner. Consequently, it would have occupied the pivotal role in coalition negotiations and its leader, Shimon Peres, would, in all likelihood, have become prime minister. As a result of this, implementation of the Oslo Accords would have proceeded more rapidly with Israel honouring commitments to the interim agreements with a second and third scheduled troops withdrawal from the West Bank and commencing the Final Status talks. (It should be remembered that Peres originally opposed the changes in the electoral system. The process of calling for direct elections was instigated by Yitzhak Rabin as he believed that it offered the best method of getting himself elected.)

Critics of Netanyahu argue that these problems are being cynically manipulated by his government to slow down the implementation of Oslo, which Netanyahu strongly opposed while in opposition. However, it is becoming abundantly clear that Netanyahu's political future is as closely tied to the success of the Oslo process as that of his predecessors as prime minister – that is, Yitzhak Rabin and Shimon Peres. Therefore, this study argues that despite being Israel's first directly elected prime minister, Netanyahu is experiencing great difficulties in his relations with his party and Cabinet as he attempts to exert his authority over them, and it is these factors that are predominantly, but not exclusively, determining the speed and scope of not only the Palestinian track of the peace process, but also to a lesser extent the negotiations with Syria and Lebanon. Put simply, the difficulties facing Netanyahu from his party, Cabinet and wider coalition can be viewed as internal restraints on his conduct of the peace process. Furthermore, in examining these internal restraints on Netanyahu it is first worth analysing what these restraints are, and second, assessing the successes and failures of the prime minister in dealing with them.

Sources of party and coalition conflict

Netanyahu faces both major intra-party and inter-block conflict within his government. (Intra-party conflict is defined as conflict within the Likud and inter-block conflict as being within the parties of the Likud-led block, which, in recent years, have included the parties of the right and the religious parties.) In the Likud party Netanyahu leads is a growing group that feels Netanyahu's election victory was achieved at the expense of the party. This group argues that the deals that Netanyahu made with Rafael Eitan's right-wing Tsomet and ex-Likud member David Levy's Gesher Party to ensure that he was the sole candidate of the right in the direct election for prime minister cost the party dear in terms of its own representation on the Knesset list. In essence, both Eitan and Levy, in securing places on the Likud Knesset list for their respective parties candidates, did so at the expense of leading figures in the Likud.[12]

The Likud–Gesher–Tsomet list won a total of only 32 seats in the 1996 Knesset elections. Out of this 23 came from the Likud (the other places were taken by members of Gesher and Tsomet), which is a drastic reduction for a party that had won on average 45 seats in Knesset elections in the 1980s. Moreover, Figure 1.1 (see page 9) illustrates the extent of the numerical weakness of Netanyahu in the Knesset where he can rely on around only 23 votes and consequently, needs to spend a great deal of time on shoring up his so-called coalition. Furthermore, as a result of his relative lack of strength in the Knesset, Netanyahu's powers of patronage have been greatly reduced, and he is left with a large group of disgruntled Likud national figures who failed to win a seat in the Knesset. Normal patronage tools such as the appointment of new ambassadors could have helped alleviate this problem, but such appointments are normally reserved for disappointed or disillusioned national leaders who have not been included in the Cabinet, and not for larger groups who failed to enter the Knesset.

At the time, Netanyahu was well aware of this problem and tried to solve it by introducing the 'Norwegian principle' where members of the Cabinet resign their Knesset seats and are replaced by the next name on the party's original electoral list. Moreover, crucially for Netanyahu the names from 32 to 40 on the Likud–Gesher–Tsomet list were mainly members of the Likud. However, opposition from Cabinet members who were reluctant to resign their seats proved to be too strong for Netanyahu to force the change through the Knesset. As a result, the eight ministers (not including Netanyahu himself who would have retained his seat) from the Likud–Gesher–Tsomet list kept their seats and the candidates who occupied positions 33 to 41 in the Knesset list were not able to go to the Knesset. In the original Knesset list the Likud members occupied six out of the positions between 33 and 41 and a further three between 42 and 45.

---

12 Netanyahu was well aware of the need to avoid a fragmentation of the Likud-led block's vote in the 1996 election as the Likud had lost power in 1992 partly as a result of internal splits and divisions within the Likud as well as its respective block. The then prime minister Yitzhak Shamir cited the actions of David Levy in dividing the party in 1992 as an important factor in the party's electoral defeat and emphasised the importance of party unity at election time. Interview conducted by the author with Yitzhak Shamir, Tel Aviv, 17 August 1994.

FIGURE 1.1
Netanyahu's limited parliamentary support:
the dynamic Knesset chart, 1996–1998

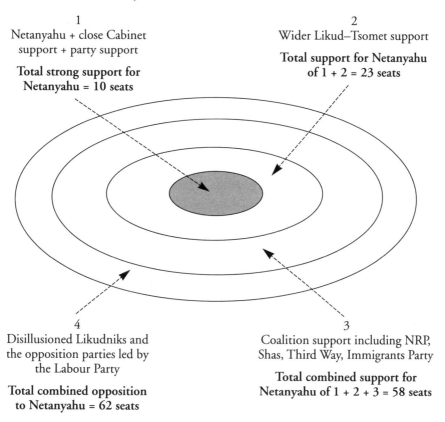

1
Netanyahu + close Cabinet
support + party support

**Total strong support for
Netanyahu = 10 seats**

2
Wider Likud–Tsomet support

**Total support for Netanyahu
of 1 + 2 = 23 seats**

4
Disillusioned Likudniks and
the opposition parties led by
the Labour Party

**Total combined opposition
to Netanyahu = 62 seats**

3
Coalition support including NRP,
Shas, Third Way, Immigrants Party

**Total combined support for
Netanyahu of 1 + 2 + 3 = 58 seats**

Number of seats in Knesset = 120

KEY	
1st band	strongest support for Netanyahu measured in terms of consistent backing of him in Knesset votes.
2nd band	near guaranteed votes for Netanyahu in the Knesset.
3rd band	wider support, though votes cannot be guaranteed.
4th band	non-support from opposition parties and dissident Likud MKs.

An additional problem that faced the new prime minister was the selection of chairpersons and members for the Knesset committees. In the past, this had traditionally been an opportunity for a leader to hand out patronage to loyal clients. Put simply, as head of the largest Knesset party and block the prime minister's choice was almost certain to be confirmed in the subsequent ballot of members of the Knesset (MKs), which selects the chairpersons and composition of the parliamentary committees. However, after the 1996 Knesset election the Likud was not the largest party in the Knesset, and consequently this fact was reflected in its number of committee chairpersons: out of 12 committees the Likud has only two chairpersons, Uzi Landau (Foreign Affairs and Defence) and Naomi Blumenthal (Immigration and Absorption). Conversely, the Labour Party, which remained the single largest party in the Knesset, was able to get five of its members elected as chairpersons. An additional problem for Netanyahu lies in that the number of Likud MKs who sit on these committees also reflects the party's relatively weak parliamentary strength, and therefore its ability to do deals with smaller parties to ensure the election of its members to the committees. Consequently, Netanyahu is not only faced with unhappy Likudniks who feel they were sacrificed on the Knesset list for a deal to enhance his personal election chances, but also many of the Likud members who were elected to the Knesset are disgruntled because they are not occupying positions of prestige or influence within the parliament.

Netanyahu's weakness in the Likud is not only demonstrated by his lack of patronage powers, but also at a more fundamental level in his lack of a clearly identifiable group of constituency support within the party. Both Menahem Begin and Yitzhak Shamir – Netanyahu's predecessors as leader – gained their respective support from the old generation of Herut supporters, many of whom they had fought side by side in the Irgun during Israel's battle for independence. At the time of Shamir's departure after defeat in the 1992 election there were three major internal groupings within the Likud: the Shamir-Arens camp, the Sharon camp and the Levy camp.[13]

Of these Netanyahu was seen as being closest to the Shamir-Arens group (he was, after all, a client of Moshe Arens who had recommended

---

13 For a detailed account of the internal dynamics of the Likud during this period, see Lochery, *The Israeli Labour Party.*

that Netanyahu be appointed as Israel's Ambassador to the UN and had served as deputy foreign minister, not in the Foreign Ministry but rather in the office of Prime Minister Shamir). The surprise decision of Moshe Arens to retire from politics after the 1992 election left the leadership of this grouping wide open. However, Netanyahu was not the heir-apparent of this group: many of its supporters regarded him as too young and inexperienced; others did not like his concentration on the media where he was highly visible both within Israel and in the world via CNN. In short, had the use of primaries to elect a new leader not been adopted by the party it is unlikely that Netanyahu would have been elected as its leader. (As the Likud had been led by only two leaders since its formation it was natural that there was a queue of senior national leaders who were older than Netanyahu and who felt that they had more experience than the man who was regarded as a 'Likud Prince' – a son of a prominent older senior figure in the party.)

In the event, during the primaries Netanyahu was able to portray himself to the 100,000 mass rank and file members of the party as the man most likely to return the party to power. Such an achievement should not be underestimated, for the party was, at the time of the leadership in 1993, still in deep shock following its election defeat in 1992 at the hands of the Labour Party.[14] Following his victory in the primaries Netanyahu moved swiftly to consolidate his power, pushing through a new party constitution which among other things limited the possibility to challenge him for the leadership from within the Likud. However, despite his victory, at no time has Netanyahu enjoyed majority support from within the party institutions. In fact Netanyahu, almost uniquely, in Western-style democracies, has been unable to successfully construct his own sizeable faction within the Likud despite being its leader.

Further complications and restraints on Netanyahu have arisen at inter-block level – in particular in the management of the government coalition. The tensions that have become apparent within the Israeli Cabinet reflect the large number of coalition partners (eight in total) and

---

14 Evidence that the main reason that Likudniks elected Netanyahu was that he offered the best perceived chance of returning the party to power rather than any other motives was put forward by many leading figures in the Likud at the time – for example, in an interview conducted by the author with Dan Meridor, Jerusalem, 17 October 1994.

the relative electoral weakness of the Likud (never in Israel's history has a party been viewed as the major force in a government coalition which has only 32 seats or, as previously mentioned, in real terms only 23 seats).[15]

In the previous Knesset the government of the late Yitzhak Rabin comprised only three parties: the Labour Party, Meretz and the religious party Shas. Even so, Rabin himself complained that much of his time was taken up dealing with coalition squabbles which eventually led to the resignation of Shas in 1993 from the government. Netanyahu, as well as facing a far larger number of partners, also has the key problem that many of the parties in his coalition actively oppose the Oslo Accords which he has committed himself, and therefore his government, to implementing.

Having outlined the problems facing Netanyahu at both intra-party and inter-block level it would be useful to analyse the tools that he has employed to deal with them and to assess how successful these have been, and importantly how these have effected the development of the peace process which Netanyahu is publicly committed to continue.

Netanyahu's management strategy

Netanyahu's major strength in dealing with party, coalition (Cabinet) and parliamentary sources of conflict is that due to a new electoral system adopted for the 1996 elections he is playing by a new set of rules which are developing only as situations arise. Political scientists have debated the significance of the change in the electoral system and its implications for Israel's political system. Put simply, Israel no longer remains a pure example of parliamentary democracy, but nor does it fit the presidential model of government. It is not the purpose of this study to enter the complex debate surrounding Israel's new system of government, but simply to suggest that it has created a high degree of ambiguity in how the government functions.[16] In essence, the relationships between

---

15 The problems of dealing with such a large coalition were emphasised in an interview by the author with David Bar-Ilan, the Director of Communications and Head of Policy Planning in the Prime Minister's Office. Interview with David Bar-Ilan, Jerusalem, 5 March 1998.

16 The most recent detailed account of the changes in the Israeli electoral system and the significance of them (in English) can be found in Hazen, 'Presidential parliamentarism'.

the prime minister, party, coalition and parliament are not as easily identifiable as in the past and are now more open to interpretation and challenge by the prime minister.[17] Paradoxically, this uncertainty is also Netanyahu's major weakness, because with large areas of his power and areas of influence not as clearly defined as those of previous prime ministers, challenges to his authority may prove to be more widespread. In addition, Netanyahu's authority is diminished by the fact that he is the first Israeli prime minister who doesn't enjoy the benefits of leading a party that is the largest force in the Knesset, which makes the prime minister's relationship with the parliament itself a major source of potential conflict. In essence, Netanyahu has to mark out his areas of control, then defend them against, at times, hostile reactions from his own party, coalition and parliament.

A new role for the prime minister's office

One of the first actions of Netanyahu after assuming power was to attempt to develop the Prime Minister's Office along presidential lines. In both pre-election statements and post-election planning, Netanyahu supported the idea of creating an American-style National Security Council which would have been based in the Prime Minister's Office, and consequently taken large powers away from the Defence Ministry. Moreover, control of the privatisation programme, which is viewed as vital to the health of Israel's economy, was taken away from the Finance Ministry and relocated in Netanyahu's office. In addition, the prime minister tried, unsuccessfully, to appoint Cabinet Secretary Danny Naveh to the position of co-ordinator of the various peace talks. The overall level of concentration of power that was envisaged by Netanyahu and his Chief of Staff, Avigdor Liberman, led some Israeli journalists to state that Netanyahu's Prime Minister's Office was to be based not on the White House model but rather on the Kremlin.[18]

Central to Netanyahu's thinking in attempting to maximise the influence of his office was the desire of the prime minister to control all

---

17 Netanyahu and his advisors take the view that it is too early to comment on the effects of the changes in the electoral system but suggest that its results have been far from perfect. Interview with Bar-Ilan, Jerusalem.

18 For a detailed account of the attempt to strengthen the influence of the Prime Minister's Office, see B. Rubin, 'No prime minister: a melodrama in three acts', *Jerusalem Post*, 21 June 1996.

aspects of the peace negotiations. In short, he wanted to minimise the sphere of influence of the Foreign Ministry where he had been forced to appoint his old arch rival, David Levy, as Foreign Minister. In addition, as both Rabin and Peres before him had been aware, control of the Defence Ministry was an important tool in maintaining control over the implementation of the peace process. Netanyahu was not as politically strong or experienced as Rabin and Peres (post Rabin assassination) to be able to hold the portfolio himself in addition to his responsibilities as prime minister. Consequently, he aimed to strip the ministry of its key powers and downgrade the influence of the subsequently appointed defence minister, Yitzhak Mordechai. In a similar fashion the decision to move control of the privatisation programme to his office reflected Netanyahu's attempt again to minimise the influence of a key ministry where he had been forced by the Likud party to appoint perhaps his strongest intra-party rival, Dan Meridor.

Netanyahu and the Cabinet

Netanyahu believed that his victory in Israel's first direct election for prime minister provided him with the authority to alter Israel's traditional parliamentary system of Cabinet government, with the prime minister being *primus inter pares,* to a more presidential system where the real action was kept away from the Cabinet, which was relegated to a discussion and ratification forum. This seemed a natural trend for recent administrations, and in particular the government of Rabin saw an unprecedented move towards the presidential style where the role of the Cabinet had substantially diminished. Privately, Rabin saw Cabinet meetings as little more than press conferences (such was his exasperation at the posturing of ministers and the number of leaks that were traced back to the meetings).

During Netanyahu's first years in office he has achieved some success in the management of the Cabinet, notably on ratification of the Hebron deal and subsequent troop redeployments in the West Bank. However, these achievements should not obscure the fact that the prime minister has failed to alter the balance of power away from the Cabinet and towards his office. On the contrary, many Israeli commentators note that Netanyahu has faced stronger opposition in Cabinet than Rabin did, and that ministers have been far more successful in asserting influence than during the Rabin government. There are two major factors that explain this. First, there is a natural majority within the Cabinet who oppose the Oslo Accords and want nothing to do with them. Therefore, when Netanyahu brings a deal such as the Hebron Agreement to the Cabinet he starts from a position of disadvantage. Second, the fact that there are seven parties in the coalition and Cabinet has further complicated matters. Moreover, Netanyahu's attempts to play the parties off against each other, and in particular to pit the secular parties against the religious parties, has, up to now, been far from successful.

Netanyahu and the Likud

The Likud emerged from the 1996 elections in a state of dazed confusion. It was relieved that Netanyahu had won a narrow victory in the election for prime minister and would be able to form a government coalition, but despondent at the poor performance of the party in the Knesset election. Political analysts and Likud pollsters had indicated that the party's poor performance in 1992, when it won 32 seats, was its bottom point of electoral support. However, in 1996 with Tsomet (which had won eight seats in 1992) joining the Likud they still won only 32 seats. Party leaders were quick to blame the new electoral system, which had led to a greater fragmentation of the vote and a decline in the support for both the major parties in Israel.

It has become evident in the past year (1997–8) that Netanyahu himself probably envisages the party along much the same lines as an American political party – a loosely organised supermarket of ideas that is pulled together at election times. In essence, the days of the party being one of the most important institutions in Israeli society are clearly numbered if Netanyahu has his way. The prime minister's attitude to the party is, to a large extent, a result of his relative intra-party weakness. Party institutions such as the Central Committee are largely controlled by long-time Netanyahu rival Ariel Sharon and to a lesser degree the son of the ex-leader Menahem Begin, Ze'ev (Benni) Begin. The fact that the Likud itself remains deeply divided over the direction of the peace process has inhibited the effectiveness of any inter-party opposition to Netanyahu's blueprint for the future of the party.

In dealing with the party on the key issue of the peace process, Netanyahu has presented himself as far more hard-line than his actions to date as prime minister have indicated he really is. For example, to help neutralise the hard liners in the party Netanyahu has adopted a strategy of saving his more radical statements, notably on Jerusalem, for meetings of the Likud Central Committee that he chooses to address.[19] Clearly, he is well aware of the need to play to his audience who reflect a party where the majority of members are at best sceptical of the Oslo Accords. Currently, there are three camps in the Likud: those who totally reject the Oslo agreements and any contact with Arafat; those who accept the Accords as international agreements that cannot be broken but do not actively endorse the agreement; and those who are in favour of the Accords and view them as the most likely means of securing peace. An additional complication is caused by the fact that those who accept the Oslo agreement in some form do not all accept that this means abandoning the Likud's central ideological point of "Greater Israel". The seeming incompatibility of the view that you can implement the Oslo Accords while maintaining a deep ideological commitment to retaining the West Bank as part of Israel illustrates the problems that many Likudniks still face in dealing with post-Oslo political realities. In addition, it should be stressed that these groups are highly dynamic and between 1996 and 1998 there has been a shift in the party towards acceptance of the Oslo process.

The seeming incompatibility of retaining land and continuing the Oslo process has also been used as a key strategic tactic by Netanyahu in retaining the support of the party for his pursuit of peace. Put simply, he argues that it is possible to retain the land and still work within the framework set out in the Oslo Accords. In effect, Netanyahu is postponing the moment of choice between land and peace by offering the possibility of both. This has meant that the majority of factions within the Likud have, in general, supported his management of the peace process. Even the meeting with Arafat, so long a demon figure in the Likud, passed with only Ze'ev Begin and the old guard attacking Netanyahu. Moreover, the Hebron deal over which Begin resigned from the Cabinet did not create the uproar in the Likud that commentators thought it would, which was in no small part due to Netanyahu's careful preparation of the party

---

19 See, for example, Address of Netanyahu to the Central Committee of the Likud on 3 March 1997. Netanyahu stated: "Jerusalem is ours. Whoever asks Israel to give up the unity of Israel does not understand how this chord plays on our heart. We will build everywhere we decided and no one – no one will prevent us." Likud Party Headquarters, Tel Aviv.

during the months prior to the agreement. However, as Netanyahu has to concede more land as set out in the Interim Agreement then so his position within the party becomes more difficult. Consequently, he needs to give larger pay backs to the party – such as the decision to build a new housing project on Har Homa in East Jerusalem.

In summary, to date Netanyahu has avoided D-day – the day where the Likud is forced to deal with the cold reality of the incompatibility of maintaining its rigid central ideology of "Greater Israel", which has been at the centre of the party's programme since its formation, or continuing with the Oslo process. This is due in no small part to Netanyahu's successful management of the party and the internal divisions within the Likud which show little sign of healing, and may eventually lead to a permanent fragmentation of the party. Consequently, such a split in the Likud would lead to a potential realignment of the political parties in the centre-ground in Israel.

The carrot and stick of a national unity government

The most effective tactic that Netanyahu has employed thus far against the Cabinet, the wider coalition and the Likud has been the threat that he would break up the government and form a National Unity Government with the Labour Party. The prime minister has used a variety of tools to send signals that such a government is imminent – including public statements by himself and controlled leaks from his office. Israeli political commentators have been kept busy by constant rumour, gossip and conspiracy theories that the formation of such a government would take place. Much of the rumour has come from officials in the Prime Minister's Office who have used the possibility of a national unity government (NUG) as a threat against dissenting voices during times of crisis – such as during the round of budget cut negotiations and during ratification of the Hebron Agreement. Netanyahu is not alone in the Likud in contemplating an NUG; senior Likud figures such as Dan Meridor have argued that there are advantages in having such a government in place in order to conduct the Final Status negotiations with the Palestinians. However, the vast majority of Likud leaders and party members strongly oppose the formation of such a government, which they believe would lead to greater concessions being made in the peace process.

Conclusion

The Israeli political system has entered a period of transition, caused to a large extent by the adoption of a new electoral system in 1996, which was designed to reduce the level of political horse trading that had characterised Israeli politics during the 1980s. In reality, the introduction of direct elections for prime minister reflected a shift in Israeli politics away from the central role of ideology and political parties towards a concentration on personality politics where the personality, credibility and policies of the leader become the most significant factor in elections. It is also worth noting that two of the keenest supporters for the electoral reform were the late Yitzhak Rabin and the current prime minister, Binyamin Netanyahu, both of whom occupied relatively weak intra-party positions within the Labour Party and the Likud, respectively. However, crucially both were viewed as having popular appeal within the electorate as a whole and thus stood to benefit in a 'beauty contest' direct election for prime minister. Such was the hunger for power that both Rabin and Netanyahu, as well as the majority of political leaders, failed to see or ignored the drawbacks of the new system for a potential prime minister such as the fragmentation of the Knesset with the decline in support for the two minor parties, and the subsequent difficulty of managing a government coalition that contains a high number of parties. It is Netanyahu himself who has found to his cost just how strong the internal restraints are on a new directly elected prime minister, and how vulnerable the prime minister remains to his own party, the Cabinet and the government coalition.

The internal restraints on Netanyahu have been strengthened by the fact, as this study has attempted to stress, that he is attempting to implement a series of policies that have been pre-determined by the previous Labour-led government (not himself), and which his party and coalition partners oppose to varying degrees. Such a situation is made for presidential government where the executive has the authority to veto policy decisions of the parliament and where the Cabinet is based on the John F. Kennedy style of discussion but not decision making forum. Moreover, a clear set of constitutional rules that spell out the various powers and restraints of each arm of the government and include a constitutional court to rule over disagreements would at least set out the rules for Netanyahu to follow. In the absence of such basic constitutional tools, Netanyahu has been left to try to define the scope of his power through a process or trial and error or, more accurately, attempts to max-imise his authority followed by climb down. This has forced Netanyahu into a series of embarrassing humiliations, not least during his attempts to appoint his Cabinet. Out of 18 ministers, at least three were not the choice of Netanyahu but resulted from pressure from the Likud hierarchy: Dan Meridor at Finance; Ariel Sharon at Infrastructure; and Ze'ev Begin at Science.

Netanyahu's lack of clear authority has been compounded by an additional two factors: his inexperience in government; and his difficult relationship with the party he leads. Yitzhak Rabin, who acted during his second term in office (1992–5) as if he had been directly elected as prime minister, brought with him a higher degree of experience of how government worked, and how he could dominate and control the policy-making process. His centralisation of policy and decision making was almost unique in systems defined as parliamentary democracies. However, Rabin enjoyed advantages that Netanyahu does not. Rabin had a large power base within his party (although not as large as that of Peres), he had been a central figure in the party leadership for 20 years and, importantly, even his opponents accepted his credentials as a security expert.

In lacking all these characteristics, Netanyahu was forced to rely on his popular appeal in Likud primaries rather than in the party institutions and his security credentials were regularly questioned even by members of his own party (such as Ariel Sharon and Rafael Eitan in the Knesset Foreign Affairs and Security Committee between 1992–6). As a result, in making a comparison between Rabin (who *was not* directly elected as prime minister in 1992) and Netanyahu (who *was* in 1996), there is a paradox as Rabin, without a personal mandate, experienced fewer internal restraints than Netanyahu, who has a direct mandate from the electorate. Since coming to power Netanyahu has therefore found it difficult to assert a controlling influence over a party in which many of its national leaders do not accept his leadership credentials. This has been made worse by the decline in patronage powers available to Netanyahu due to the pre-election deal with Gesher and Tsomet and the Likud lists poor performance in the Knesset elections.

2

Netanyahu and the peace process 1996–1998: vision, strategy and restraints

This chapter aims to provide an overview of the Netanyahu administration's policy towards the peace process between 1996 and 1998. In doing so it is important to consider two factors: Netanyahu's own vision and strategy, sometimes obscured by rhetoric but nevertheless ever present; and the effects of the previously discussed internal restraints on the prime minister in the area of peace making. In addition, as always in the Middle East, the chapter will show how events sometimes override and derail the process. The central theme returned to again in this chapter is that the Netanyahu government has made many mistakes in its first years in office but that these have not been the sole determining factor in the increasing problems of the peace process. It should be noted that the chapter concentrates on chronicling Netanyahu's government's actions and responses to the various tracks and events. A more detailed wider study of each area follows in the subsequent chapters.

Netanyahu's third way: pragmatism versus ideology

The first years of the Netanyahu administration have been dominated by a series of crises surrounding the peace process, especially the Palestinian track. However, the complete breakdown of the negotiations, which was so eagerly forecast by many commentators following Netanyahu's victory, has not happened. In fact, the Oslo Accords have proved to be extremely resilient, due in no small degree to the fact that all the actors realise that the Accords are the 'only game in town'. In examining the progress of the various tracks of the peace process there is a need to identify where, together with why, Netanyahu has felt unable to deliver concessions and where he has successfully manipulated, persuaded or coerced his right-wing constituency into accepting compromises in the negotiations.

Before examining the individual restraints on Netanyahu in the various tracks of the peace process it is important to locate just where Netanyahu himself stands on the peace process and specifically the Oslo Accords.

Netanyahu is a politician who, in the past, had prided himself on his rigid ideological beliefs of which "Greater Israel" is the central pillar. In his book *A Place Among Nations*, which is widely viewed as the blueprint of his beliefs, Netanyahu returns time and again to the question of Israel's security and the need for it to maintain the West Bank in order to protect Israel's eastern border.[1] Moreover, taken in conjunction with his hard-line views and actions while in opposition (especially as Likud leader between 1993–6); his non-acceptance of the Oslo Accords, the building of a united national block (including the parties of the radical right) and his leadership of militant and, at times, violent demonstrations against the Accords, led many to presume that Netanyahu was a hard-line Likud ideologue.

However, such conclusions fail to take into account a range of other factors which indicate that Netanyahu's main characteristic is his pragmatism.[2] His education in the United States and the time he subsequently spent living there, both as a businessman and later Israel's Ambassador to the United Nations in New York, helped influence his early years and provided him with a worldly view that is still absent in many of the leaders of the Likud today.[3] Netanyahu has often stressed his admiration for the American political system and, like the majority of American politicians, Netanyahu's guiding light is power.[4] Moreover, he is well aware that in order to gain power there is a need to draw support from a wide spectrum of groups. While he was the opposition leader in Israel he clearly felt a need to unify the nationalist block (or Likud-led block) whose disunity had been one of the main reasons that

---

1   B. Netanyahu, *A Place Among Nations: Israel and the World* (New York, Bantam, 1993).

2   For a highly critical account of Netanyahu's beliefs, see C. Shindler, *Israel, Likud and the Zionist Dream: Power, Politics and Ideology from Begin to Netanyahu* (London, I.B. Tauris, 1995), pp. 284–7.

3   Many Israeli commentators argue that Netanyahu's time as Israeli Ambassador to the United Nations in New York was critical in helping form his views and how his government operates. For a critical examination of this, see Y. Marcus, 'The robber of dreams', *Ha-Aretz*, 22 August 1997.

4   For a reference to his admiration for the United States, see Netanyahu, speech to joint session of Congress, 10 July 1996.

the Likud lost power in the 1992 elections.[5] His robust opposition to the Oslo Accords, which was at the time certainly genuine, served an additional purpose of giving him an opportunity and rallying call to control the development of new ties and strengthen existing links between the Likud and the parties of the right in Israel.

As the election campaign in 1996 started, Netanyahu and his team of advisors moved his positioning strategy to the political centre. In essence, this involved an acceptance of the Oslo Accords and a promise to continue the process of implementing the Interim Agreement.[6] This change, which was made over a period of only a few days, revealed the extent of first, Netanyahu's desire for power far above and beyond any ideological convictions, and second, the new political realities in Israel where acceptance of Oslo was seen as vital to attracting the centre-ground voters.[7] In shifting his strategy Netanyahu risked alienating large parts of his party and the nationalist block, with which he had worked so hard to develop closer ties. However, during the campaign he made it clear that he would be a reluctant participant in the process and would not make the concessions that the Labour Party would offer in final status talks.[8] This strategy was so successful that it not only helped ensure Netanyahu's election victory, but also helped postpone the difficult decisions within the Likud about the future direction of the peace process which were likely to have led to the previously discussed internal party conflict.

Since becoming prime minister, Netanyahu has realised that his future political prospects, and especially his chances of re-election in the

---

5 See, for example, Lochery, *The Israeli Labour Party*.

6 For more detail on the process of changing the positioning strategy, see Mendilow, 'The Likud's dilemma in the 1996 elections'.

7 It should be stressed that although the public shift in Netanyahu's position was remarkably rapid, in private as early as 1994 Netanyahu and many senior figures in the Likud were reconciled to carrying out at least parts of the Oslo process. This was made apparent in interviews conducted by the author with leaders of the Likud at the time – for example, interview with Dan Meridor, Jerusalem, 8 November 1994. However, there remained other senior figures in the party who both publicly and privately rejected all aspects of the Oslo process, notably Ze'ev Begin. This was made clear in an interview conducted by the author with Ze'ev Begin, Jerusalem, 9 November 1994.

8 For an account of the attempts of the Likud to come to terms with the Oslo Accords and the deep internal divisions in the party over the issue see, for example, E. Inbar, 'Netanyahu takes over' in D. Elazar and S. Sandler (eds) *Israel at the Polls 1996* (London and Portland, Frank Cass, 1998), pp. 34–6.

year 2000, largely depend on his management of the peace process. It is also clear to Netanyahu that the Oslo Accords are the only avenue down which the peace process can go, due to the general support for them from the centre-ground Israeli voters (who decide the outcome of Israeli elections), the United States (with whom Netanyahu feels a deep sense of kinship), and the Palestinian refusal to re-negotiate any part of the overall Accords. Put simply, on a personal level Netanyahu feels that the Accords have severe limitations, but politically his pragmatism and deep sense of attachment to power compound him actively to make the Oslo process work.[9] From this it can be deduced that the strongest factor that would change his commitment to Oslo would be if Israeli public opinion shifted significantly against the Oslo process.[10] To date, even after terrorist attacks, there still remains majority support from Israeli society for the Oslo process, and crucially from those members of the public who are identified as centre-ground voters.[11]

---

9 The most detailed account published to date of Netanyahu's views on Oslo and the peace process in general are found in an interview he gave to *Ha-Aretz* entitled 'The Prime Minister would like a few minutes of your time'. (Interview by Avi Shavit, *Ha-Aretz*, 22 November 1996, pp. 18–24.) In addition, see also Netanyahu address to the 1996 General Assembly of the Council of Jewish Federations, Seattle, 15 November 1996 (by satellite). In this address he describes the Oslo Accords as having many failings.

10 A good example of this occurred during what was termed the London Conference on 4 May 1998, where Netanyahu refused to increase his initial offer of a 9 per cent troop withdrawal from the West Bank buoyed by polls at home which showed an increased scepticism among the Israeli electorate about the Oslo process and widespread support for Netanyahu's stand. See poll in *Yediot Aranonot*, 5 May 1998.

11 Evidence of the continued support of the Israeli electorate for the Oslo process can be found in a recent poll conducted for the Tami Steimetz Centre for Peace Studies at Tel Aviv University by Modi'in Ezrachi. The poll was based on a representative sample of 504 Israeli Jews (including those in the territories and kibbutzim) on 29 January 1997. The survey has a 4 per cent margin of error. Questions in the poll include the following. What is your position regarding the Oslo Agreement between Israel and the PLO? 18.1 per cent: support a lot; 26 per cent: considerably support; 29.7 per cent: so-so; 10.3 per cent: considerably oppose; 8.3 per cent: oppose a lot; 7 per cent: don't know. Do you believe or don't you believe that the Oslo Agreement will lead to peace in the coming years between Israel and the Palestinians? 12.4 per cent: believe a lot; 31.1 per cent: considerably believe; 21.8 per cent: so-so; 16.6 per cent: considerably don't believe; 13.3 per cent: completely don't believe; 4.8 per cent: don't know.

In a practical sense what this all amounts to is what can be viewed as the third way. Netanyahu's policies towards the peace process clearly reject the ideological dominated era of Yitzhak Shamir and the visionary new Middle East of his predecessor Shimon Peres.[12] In a keynote speech by Binyamin Netanyahu at the Graduation Ceremony of Cadets of the National Defence College, 14 August 1997, he summarised this vision:

> Between "rose garden" dreams on the one hand, and paranoia and isolation on the other, there is a golden path of realism, of realpolitik. This is the path that Israel chose beginning in the Ben-Gurion era, and this must be our choice today. If we know when to compromise, when to grasp opportunities and when to display determination and decisiveness, we can bring peace with security to our country and to our people.

More specifically, he has set three criteria (or pillars) arguing what a lasting peace must be built on: Israeli security; reciprocity and democracy; and human rights.[13] However, the form that this third way vision takes in the real world remains unclear, and Netanyahu's actions and restraints in each of the major tracks of the peace process need to be examined in order to attempt to provide a clearer picture of his premiership.

The internal restraints on the various tracks of the peace process

The various tracks of the peace process include the Israeli–Palestinian track, and the Israeli–Syrian and Lebanese tracks. Both of these are covered in detail in this chapter.

The Israeli–Palestinian track

The prime minister has needed to employ all his considerable political skills to get the Hebron deal (February 1997) and subsequent troop redeployment deal (February 1997) past the Cabinet and the Likud. However, the decision to proceed with the Har Homa construction project

---

12 For a damning summary of Netanyahu's "third way" see, 'Now for my next trick', *The Economist*, 25 April 1998, p. 71.

13 For a lucid account of these pillars, see Netanyahu, speech to joint session of Congress.

in East Jerusalem, the smaller-than-expected transfer of land to the Palestinian Authority (PA) and the attempt to move the Oslo goal posts with the proposal to conduct Final Status negotiations in six months, indicate what needs to be viewed as the *pay back* to the party and coalition. In addition, the extent of the difficulties that Netanyahu faced over ratification of the Hebron deal was shown with what became known as the Bar-On Affair where he, together with his director of the Prime Minister's Office (Avigdor Liberman) and the Minister of Justice (Tzachi Hanegbi), were all placed under investigation over an alleged plea bargain deal with the leader of the religious party Shas. The deal, as reported in the Israeli media, would have seen Shas ministers in the Cabinet supporting or abstaining in the vote over ratification of the Hebron deal in exchange for a plea bargain for Aryie Deri, the leader of Shas, who is currently on trial on changes of corruption.[14]

Historically, due to its religious significance Hebron has been a sensitive area for both Israeli and Palestinian leaders. On the Israeli side the significance of the proposed hand-over of 80 per cent of the city to Palestinian control was shown by the decision of the then prime minister Shimon Peres to postpone any deal on Hebron until after the Israel election in May 1996. Peres was acutely aware of the need to court the sizeable religious vote in the election, and specifically to receive endorsements from the rabbis who lead the various orthodox and ultra-orthodox groupings in Israel. In the event Peres' strategy failed and Netanyahu won both the endorsement of the rabbis and the subsequent support of 99 per cent of the religious vote in the direct election for prime minister.

As a result of this support, Netanyahu correctly felt that the religious vote was vital in securing his electoral victory and would be so again if he were to seek re-election in the year 2000. This resulted in a natural reluctance to offend this key constituency by handing over Hebron without a fight. Consequently, central to the strategy that Netanyahu employed in the negotiations over Hebron was the need to make any final deal on Hebron with the Palestinians appear due to two factors: first, that the previous Labour-led government had already committed Israel to a withdrawal; and second, due to pressure from the international

---

14 For a detailed account of the Bar-On scandal and the reasons behind it see, N. Lochery, 'Blocking Bibi's bid for power', *The World Today*, vol. 53, no. 6 (June 1996).

community – in particular the United States. An additional integral part of this strategy was to spin out the negotiations with the Palestinians to allow the new Israeli government a period in which to flex its muscles to its largely right-wing constituents before finally accepting a deal. However, Netanyahu failed to foresee two complications to his strategy which almost led to its failure.

The first of these complications concerned the relative lack of experience of the new Israeli negotiators appointed by the prime minister who were in a position of strategic disadvantage with their Palestinian interlocutors who had been present from the very beginning of the Oslo process, and consequently had a detailed knowledge of the issues, protocols and previous agreements. This was compounded by the attempt of Netanyahu to clip the wings of the Israeli Defence Forces (IDF), who he felt had become too politicised under Rabin and Peres with their participation in the peace negotiations. In attempting to reduce the role of the IDF the prime minister preferred instead to introduce his own civilian appointees to the negotiations.[15] The result of such moves was that the new inexperienced Israeli negotiators, many of whom were drawn from the Israeli right and had not changed their view of the PLO as a terrorist organisation, conducted the negotiations in an abrasive and aggressive manner.[16] The atmosphere of the early rounds of talks was so bad there was a real chance the negotiations would have broken down all together if the Americans (in the form of the Special Envoy to the Middle East, Dennis Ross) had not directly intervened to ensure the talks continued. Such an outcome would have damaged Netanyahu's international standing because the previous Israeli government had promised to withdraw from Hebron, which would have made Netanyahu appear the guilty party responsible for the breakdown. In addition, the almost certain Palestinian violence that would have followed in such a scenario would have damaged the prime minister's domestic credibility, especially if persistent terrorist attacks resumed within Israel.

---

15 See S. Rodan, 'Shaky soloist', *Jerusalem Post*, 15 November 1996.

16 Many commentators have noted that the major problem between Israel and the PA in the era of Netanyahu is the almost total lack of trust between the parties. This is in direct contrast to the close working relationships established by the Oslo negotiators. See, for example, D. Margalit, 'Need a giant portion of mutual trust', *Ha-Aretz*, 11 August 1997.

The second complication that arose for Netanyahu was that his strategy was essentially one dimensional; he did not take into account the internal and external pull factors on Arafat not to sign a deal on Hebron. In short, Netanyahu believed that Arafat's desire to increase his control over the West Bank would be stronger than any other factor. In reality, Arafat was in no hurry to agree the Hebron deal for a variety of reasons. While the tense drawn-out negotiations were continuing Arafat was earning valuable good PR from the world's press and diplomatic circles by portraying himself as a moderate leader faced by a new radical Israeli government. Moreover, pressure from Arab states, especially Egypt, on Arafat not to sign an agreement was applied in order for these countries to heap more demands on the Israeli government in this and other areas that served the national interests of the respective Arab regimes. Finally, Arafat was well aware that when Netanyahu eventually signed a deal on Hebron, there would almost certainly be a 'pay back' to Netanyahu's right-wing constituency in the form of new settlements in the West Bank and/or substantial increases to the size of existing settlements.[17]

As a consequence of Arafat's manoeuvrings, Netanyahu was made to look inexperienced to his domestic constituency which therefore increased the pressure on him not to compromise on the question of security guarantees for the Jewish settlers who live in the middle of Hebron. However, as the Hebron negotiations dragged on, the prime minister had pressing domestic policy concerns in the form of persuading the Cabinet to accept substantial budget cuts which were aimed at reducing Israel's growing budget deficit, viewed by economists as the biggest danger to Israel's future economic health. In the event, Netanyahu passed his first real test with the Cabinet by persuading ministers, including the Minister of Defence, to accept the cuts as a requirement for maintaining economic stability. Crucially, the victory strengthened Netanyahu's influence over the Cabinet and in some ways served as a dry run for the difficult task of persuading a majority of a sceptical Cabinet to accept the eventual deal on Hebron.

After eventually signing the Hebron deal Netanyahu brought the agreement before Cabinet for approval. The Labour Party had made it

17 Arafat's motives for not signing a deal are examined in detail by D. Haetzni, 'Netanyahu wants to give: Arafat does not want to take', *Ma'ariv*, 1 November 1996, pp. 6–7.

clear that it would act as a safety net in the subsequent Knesset vote on ratification, thus giving Netanyahu a sizeable majority in parliament. Consequently, the Cabinet became the sole opportunity for the opponents of the deal to secure enough support to reject it. Crucially, had the Cabinet done so, then Netanyahu would have been faced with bringing the deal before the Knesset without Cabinet ratification, and in such circumstances it is difficult to see how the government coalition would have remained intact. However, long before the final deal had been signed Netanyahu had canvassed Cabinet colleagues until he was certain that he at least had a slender majority in favour. When the Cabinet met to ratify the deal the prime minister adopted a strategy of letting every minister speak on the issue in the hope that ministers could let off steam for their various right-wing and religious constituencies that they represented and then reluctantly fall into line for the Cabinet vote. Unfortunately, for Netanyahu his strategy again revealed his inexperience as members of the Cabinet, including some from his own party, were engaged in actively campaigning against the prime minister, such was the strength of feeling against the Hebron deal. Moreover, Netanyahu's lack of authority and a power base in the Likud were embarrassingly exposed. However, much to Netanyahu's credit the deal was ratified by the Cabinet (10 to 7) due largely to the fact that the prime minister was able to convince enough ministers, who were keen to maintain the stability of the government, that the deal would serve the long-term interests of Israel.[18]

Ze'ev Begin, Minister of Science, was the sole minister who felt compelled to resign from the Cabinet over its ratification of the Hebron deal. In the short term, this resignation of one of the Likud ministers was viewed as having little impact on the prime minister; Begin occupied a relatively minor portfolio and had continued publicly to criticise

---

18 Interestingly, the scepticism of the Cabinet did not reflect the majority view of the Israeli electorate about the Hebron deal, which was much more positive. This point was illustrated in the same survey for the Tami Steimetz Centre for Peace Studies at Tel Aviv University, which was used in footnote 11. What is your position regarding the agreement that was signed between Israel and the Palestinians over the redeployment in Hebron and the remainder of the West Bank? 22 per cent: support a lot; 44.7 per cent: considerably support; 17.7 per cent: so-so; 9.1 per cent: considerably oppose; 9.1 per cent: oppose a lot; 6.5 per cent: don't know.

Netanyahu despite being a member of the Cabinet. The long-term significance of it will only become clear as the peace process develops. In essence, what Begin has achieved by his resignation is that he has positioned himself to the right of Netanyahu in the Likud, and with his popularity and large personal following within the party he would present a powerful force should the peace process collapse and Netanyahu's position be undermined.

Having analysed the problems that Netanyahu faced in winning Cabinet ratification for the Hebron deal, the events of February and March 1997 need to be seen within the framework of the internal restraints on Netanyahu which were clearly illustrated in the pay back for the deal that the prime minister made to his party and coalition during this period. The decision to hand over only 9 per cent of West Bank and not the 25 to 30 per cent that the PA had expected was aimed at pacifying the Likud and the coalition by returning the minimum amount of land possible under an Interim Agreement which called for Israeli troop withdrawals from the West Bank.

Again, the prime minister intended to pursue the dual aim of continuing with the Oslo process and Interim Agreements while minimising the land that was handed over to the PA. However, once more Netanyahu had to deal with a hostile Cabinet who objected to the 2 per cent of land which was to be handed over from Area C (under Israeli rule and where almost all the Jewish settlements are located) to Area B (joint Israeli and Palestinian control).

Key members of the Cabinet, including the Likud's Ariel Sharon and Limor Livnat, objected to the agreement stating that no part of Area C should be handed over prior to the Final Status agreements in the year 2000. Eventually, Netanyahu won the Cabinet vote on ratification (10 to 6), but only as a direct result of gaining the support of some of the religious ministers by agreeing, in the week of the Cabinet vote, a package with the religious parties which included the decision to build a new Jewish housing project at Har Homa in East Jerusalem.

The decision to build at Har Homa was, in part, an illustration of Netanyahu's relative intra-party and inter-block weakness. His original strategy of playing to his right-wing constituency by redeploying in only 9 per cent of the West Bank had clearly backfired. Consequently, he turned his attention to Israel's control of Jerusalem, which is a relatively safe domestic issue for any Israeli leader. He correctly calculated that the majority of the opposition Labour Party would support his decision to build homes for 42,000 Jews in East Jerusalem and thus there would be no major domestic political confrontation that could weaken his position. After announcing the decision, which received the expected harsh criticism from the PA and the world, Netanyahu increased his rhetoric notably at meetings of the Likud Central Committee where he declared that Jerusalem is the eternal capital of Israel and that Israel has the right to build where it wants in the city. Moreover, he used the subsequent Palestinian violence in the West Bank and the suicide bombings of a Tel Aviv café and a Jerusalem market to further slow down the pace of the peace process, and allow him to postpone again D-day – where his government has to make the choice between returning large parts of the West Bank or the breakdown of the peace process.

In analysing Netanyahu's management of the Israeli–Palestinian track the presence of high levels of internal restraints on Netanyahu and consequently his lack of room for manoeuvre have been emphasised. The fact that he leads a party and government which, to varying degrees, are reluctant partners with the PLO, and are disinclined to be tied to the Oslo process, cannot be over-estimated. However, it is worth noting once more that intra-party and inter-block needs do not offer a complete explanation of Netanyahu's actions. Clearly, with Final Status talks due to start, Netanyahu is manoeuvring for position (as is Arafat), and consequently any explanation that ignores this fact would be incomplete.

The Israeli–Syrian and Lebanese tracks

In some ways the Syrian and Lebanese tracks are simpler for Netanyahu than the negotiations with the Palestinians. In short, the internal restraints on the prime minister are considerably less than on the Palestinian track, but the external restraints on Netanyahu on both the Syrian and Lebanese tracks remain high. The key question here lies with security and does not contain the complicated additional factor of ideology. Put simply, the Likud, other parties of the right and the religious parties have no ideological claim over the Golan Heights, but rather believe them to be vital to the security of Israel. In addition, the settlements that have been placed on the Golan Heights were done so largely by the Labour Party, and settlers who live there are Labour Party supporters. Moreover, although these settlers groups have expressed their opposition to abandoning their homes in any final deal with the Syrians, it is thought probable that with financial compensation (probably supplied by the United States) the vast majority could be persuaded to relocate to a new location in Israel.[19]

The closely related Lebanese track is also a question of security. In addition, it is in this track that Netanyahu enjoys the lowest level of internal restraints, but conversely the external restraints are complicated by the control that Syria exerts over Lebanon, and to a considerable degree Hizbollah in Southern Lebanon. In short, Netanyahu faces a similar challenge to that of his immediate predecessors as prime minister – that is, to find a way of withdrawing Israeli forces from Southern Lebanon while providing northern Israel with adequate security cover against rocket and terrorist attacks from its border.

The major internal problem for the relatively inexperienced prime minister is that he has within his Cabinet the two men who were responsible for planning and conducting Israel's invasion of Lebanon in 1982: Ariel Sharon (who in 1982 was the Minister of Defence); and Rafael Eitan (who was Chief of Staff of the IDF at the time). The presence of such experienced and strong personalities within the Cabinet makes it difficult, but not impossible, for Netanyahu to mark his authority within both the Likud and the Cabinet on the Lebanese question.

In examining, first, the Syrian track in isolation from Lebanon, it is clear that Netanyahu has adopted the hawkish position that his previous writings and speeches had suggested he would. To some degree, in the short term the prime minister has used the negotiations with Syria as an avenue to prove his hawkish credentials to his party and coalition while making difficult compromises in the Palestinian negotiations. He has refused to resume negotiations with the Syrians via the Americans on the basis of carrying on where the negotiations ended with the previous Labour government, stating clearly that Syria signed no binding inter-national agreement with the previous government, and therefore he is not obligated to continue the policies of the previous government. Labour Party sources have confirmed that Peres was willing to hand back the vast majority of the Golan Heights in return for a full peace with Syria.[20]

---

19 For a detailed examination of the political and security issues relating to the Israeli–Syrian track, see A. Shalev, *Israel and Syria: Peace and Security on the Golan*, JCSS Study no. 24, Tel Aviv University, 1994.

20 For an account of what Rabin and Peres were willing to hand over to Syria in return for peace see, for example, Z. Schiff, 'What did Rabin promise the Syrians?',

The internal restraints that do exist on Netanyahu with regard to Syria come from both the Likud and government coalition. Security experts in the Likud reject the formula of a total return of the Golan Heights for a total peace. In essence, they are searching for a different formula to the one employed with Egypt after Camp David, which saw all of the Sinai returned to Egypt. Suggestions from Netanyahu's close advisors have included confidence-building measures such as the Syrians restraining attacks against Israel from groups based in Southern Lebanon (for example, Hizbollah), discussions about water issues and high-level military contacts to prevent misunderstandings on the Golan Heights. However, the Likud, which is having to address major ideological questions over "Greater Israel", is not ready to radically alter its platform on total opposition to withdrawal from the Golan Heights. Moreover, the coalition contains a party, the Third Way, which was formed by rebel Labour Party Knesset members with the main purpose of opposing any Israeli withdrawal from the Golan Heights. In addition, of the seven parties in the coalition six oppose any withdrawal and only the position of Shas is unclear.

Such negative short-term prospects of the Syrian track should not hide the fact that in the long term Netanyahu may view the option of making peace with Syria by returning a large part of the Golan Heights, as desirable and even necessary to deflect future international pressure which is bound to build on his government as the Palestinian negotiations became more difficult. The mechanism that Netanyahu would have to employ would be complicated as he would, in all probability, have to rely on Labour Party support to ratify any peace agreement. It would also be apparent that a national unity government (NUG) would offer the best possible arena in which to conduct the campaign of selling the agreement to the Israeli public.

However, the problems involved in reaching such an accommodation with the Syrians remain substantial. In essence, on the Syrian track the external restraints (the Syrians themselves) far outweigh the internal restraints on the prime minister. This is confirmed by the fact that there appears from Damascus a feeling that the present time is not the correct

---

Ha-Aretz, 29 August 1997, R. Werter, 'Former ambassador says Assad missed his chance', *Jerusalem Post*, 29 August 1997, and A. Rabinovich, 'Commotion without motion', *The Jerusalem Post*, 29 August 1997.

time to make peace with Israel, and an ailing President Assad seems content to return to the status quo of no war, no peace with Israel.[21] Consequently, many Israeli security analysts suggest that it would be prudent to wait until Assad dies or moves aside and the succession battle in Syria is resolved. Moreover, any agreement would require a strong commitment from the United States – in establishing contacts, during the conduct of negotiations and crucially in monitoring any final agreement which would likely include a sizeable commitment to police the Golan Heights. The new Secretary of State, Madeleine Albright, has not shown the same commitment to the region as her predecessor, Warren Christopher, for a number of reasons: other issues such as the expansion of the North Atlantic Treaty Organization (NATO); and importantly the down-grading of American expectation for peace in the region following Netanyahu's election victory. Moreover, the Americans feel that they were effectively drawn in too deep during the Hebron negotiations where the US acted as a guarantor to both sides, both of whom have subsequently broken commitments made during the talks. Such a precedent has left the second Clinton administration questioning any deep commitment to act as treaty guarantors in the region.

What is not clear at present is the question of secret contacts between Netanyahu and the Syrians. Such a method of negotiating would hold advantages for Netanyahu as it would allow him to present any subsequent peace deal as a *fait accompli* to his party and government, much in the same way as Rabin did with the Oslo Accords.[22] Consequently, this would further enhance Netanyahu's ability to negotiate free from the internal restraints that would otherwise be imposed on him. However, the Syrians are extremely distrustful of such channels as during the years of the previous Labour-led government details of secret meetings, seminars and discussions were leaked to the Israeli press for political profit. The Syrian regime prefers the shuttle diplomacy of the Americans which it feels would maximise the benefits to Syria if Assad were to agree a deal with Israel. Put simply, secret negotiations would suit

---

21 Assad's views are generally kept very close to his chest, but during a visit to Damascus by a group of Israeli Arabs he suggested that Netanyahu kept changing his conditions for peace, and praised Shimon Peres. See L. Collins, 'Assad: Netanyahu and enemy of peace', *Jerusalem Post*, 13 August 1997.

22 David Bar-Ilan confirms this belief stating that secret diplomacy with the Syrians would be better and necessary. Interview with Bar-Ilan, Jerusalem.

Netanyahu, who needs the cover of such talks to prevent a combination of intra-party and coalition opposition that would place severe restrictions on his opening and fall-back negotiating positions. It is also true to say that if the Syrians could overcome their suspicions and dislike of the Netanyahu government, as well as distance themselves from the Palestinian question, then Syria itself would gain from the secret method of negotiation.

The question of Israel's relationship with Lebanon is very closely related to Lebanon's power broker Syria. (The options that Israel now has with regards the security zone are discussed separately.) To summarise, the first years of the Netanyahu government have seen the low intensity war between Israel and Hizbollah continue. Events such as a helicopter crash which killed 73 Israeli soldiers who were on their way into Israel's security zone in Southern Lebanon have moved the Lebanese question up the political agenda.

Netanyahu himself is keen to remove Israeli forces from Lebanon as quickly as possible; he has stated publicly that he wishes to leave "yesterday". However, he is acutely aware of the need to reach some kind of security agreement which would prevent attacks on Israel's northern towns such as Kiryat Shemona. The idea of the "Lebanon first" was muted by Netanyahu in the early days of his term in office. In essence, this plan would have seen Israeli forces withdraw from Lebanon with Syrian agreement to exercise control over Hizbollah, and would have served as a confidence-boosting measure between Israel and Syria. In addition, Netanyahu proposed the plan for a number of other reasons: to see if the Syrians showed any interest in the proposal; to re-establish the link between Lebanon and Syria in the minds of the Israeli electorate; and to remind the Israeli Cabinet that the prime minister would take control of the negotiations over Lebanon. Eventually, after Netanyahu concluded that the Syrians were not interested in "Lebanon first" he considered employing an alternative strategy of targeting Syrian troops in the Beka Valley in Lebanon in the hope that if the Syrians were sustaining casualties then the regime in Damascus would be motivated to help prevent attacks on Israel by Hizbollah. However, this strategy was not used to its maximum potential due to fears that with the increasing political temperature in the region following Netanyahu's election it could have led to direct military confrontation between Israeli and Syrian forces on the Golan Heights.

The major internal restraint on Netanyahu regarding Lebanon is himself and the fact that he promised the enhanced personal security of Israelis. (Netanyahu's campaign slogan had been "Peace with security" and throughout the campaign the security aspect had been highlighted as the biggest failure of the Peres government.) Consequently, despite a growing lobby calling for a unilateral withdrawal from Lebanon, the prime minister fears the results of the anarchy in Southern Lebanon which Israeli security experts argue would follow such a move. It now seems clear that Netanyahu has accepted that the best of the series of bad options is for the IDF to remain in Lebanon for the foreseeable future, and that it is impossible to break the link of any settlement with the Lebanese from a peace agreement with the Syrians. Such a conclusion was also arrived at by the Rabin and Peres governments between 1992 and 1996.

However, despite the low level of internal restraints on Netanyahu on the Lebanon question, his room for manoeuvre is limited by the Syrian control over the country which turns full circle back to restraints on Netanyahu over making peace with Syria, and in particular the question of the future of the Golan Heights.

Conclusion

The prime minister's third way approach to the peace process has been a short-term personal success. Indeed, his reflection of the Israeli national consensus, supporting Oslo but remaining sceptical of Arafat and the Palestinians and reluctant to make the concessions needed to make Oslo work, has helped shore up the prime minister's relatively weak position.

In looking towards the future it is clear that what has been termed as D-day is unavoidable at some given point. Netanyahu's third way has managed thus far to postpone the day, but he has not affected the inevitability of choosing between retaining land and continuing the peace process. Furthermore, large sections of the Likud party and the right in general in Israel have shown worryingly few signs of coming to grips with the new realities caused by the Oslo agreements. Netanyahu cannot therefore rely on any substantial shift in position from the Likud itself which would allow him to make concessions and retain the confidence of a party where he does not have a strong power base.

In examining the strategies available to Netanyahu there are three major options, all of which would bring disadvantages as well as advantages to the prime minister: new elections; an NUG; or a derailment of the peace process in order to preserve the unity of Likud and centre-right in Israel. Netanyahu's decision as to which of the three strategies to adopt will not be made lightly. He has shown himself to be well aware of the internal restraints imposed on him and has attempted, not without some success, to find ways of bypassing them. Consequently, Netanyahu will not want to make the decision until it is absolutely clear to him that his position is so difficult he must decide which direction he will follow. The result of this decision is vital not only to Israel but also to the future of the peace process and, as a result, the Middle East region in general.

Part II

The Palestinian Track

3

Security arrangements in the West Bank and the Gaza Strip and the future of Israeli settlements

The key issue of security arrangements in the West Bank and the Gaza Strip has been the dominant issue in the peace process since the Oslo agreements were signed and have become even more so since Netanyahu assumed office. The security provisions in the Oslo Accords have been heavily criticised by both sides, but in particular by many from the Israeli centre-right and the military establishment. In addition, between 1996 and 1998 political tensions have, at times, led to a total breakdown of even the very basic "on the ground" security arrangements between the two parties. As a consequence, the security issue has become even more politicised with both sides using it as a mechanism to attempt to secure concessions from each other during the interim agreement negotiations.[1]

In charting the deepening problems of this issue it is imperative to examine first how security cooperation has developed between the Palestinian Authority (PA) and the Israeli government, and second, the issue of security in determining what the final status of the negotiations will be. In doing this use is made of the potential likely plans for the Final Status negotiations in the West Bank. Additionally, the related issue of the future status of Israeli settlements is also examined. Finally, conclusions are drawn on the perceived modifications in Israel's position following the change of government in 1996 and the potential for, and the security ramifications of, either side unilaterally trying to impose a settlement in the West Bank.

---

1 On this question, see Z. Schiff, 'A Palestinian–Israeli military confrontation and its ramifications', *Ha-Aretz,* 4 July 1997. For the consequences of a potential long-term breakdown in security cooperation and the probability of violence, see A. Rabinovich, 'A nasty storm fast brewing up', *Jerusalem Post,* 21 September 1997.

This chapter limits itself to a study of the West Bank, which is the major area of contention between the two parties. The vast majority of Israelis appear reconciled to handing over the Gaza Strip and see this area as the centre of the embryonic Palestinian entity. Jewish settlements *do* exist in the Gaza Strip but these are relatively small and are not likely to prove an intractable obstacle to a Final Status agreement in that area. (There are 120 Jewish settlements in the West Bank and only 14 in the Gaza Strip. The settlements in the Gaza Strip and soldiers defending them have come under frequent attack since the Oslo Accords were signed. Israel is reluctant to abandon these settlements as they fear that it sets a dangerous precedent for the settlements in the West Bank.)

Within the Israeli political leadership there is little appetite to re-enter Gaza.[2] Moreover, Israel's main security use of Gaza has receded with the signing of the Camp David Accords in 1978 and the subsequent peace with Egypt which has proved to be stable if not particularly warm. Consequently, Israel has little interest in the area except to prevent terrorist attacks from being launched from Gaza into Israel itself. Providing that Israeli security measures can be strengthened – for example, fences, and monitoring of Palestinian workers entering Israel – then Israel has little security need to enter the area except in hot pursuit of terrorists.

The West Bank is studied here in isolation from issues such as the refugee question and the future status of Jerusalem negotiations although clearly these are inter-related. In other words, compromise by one side on one of the issues is likely to lead to a hardening of its position on the other issues. In addition, the future status of the Jerusalem belt settlements are obviously closely related to the final outcome of negotiations over the future of the city of Jerusalem. The issue of the refugees is discussed in Chapter 5 and the final status of Jerusalem in Chapter 6.

Background

Security cooperation between Israelis and the PA has not developed to produce a satisfactory situation for either side. Israel accuses the PA of major breaches of the Oslo Accords and a general failure to fight terrorism

---

2 This point was made clear to the author in interviews with senior members of the Likud – for example, interview with Dan Meridor, Jerusalem, 8 November 1994.

(for example, Islamic radical groups such as Hamas[3] and Islamic Jihad).[4] More specifically, Israel accuses the PA of failing to dismantle the infrastructure of these groups and on a more limited level of using violence as a way of trying to secure concessions from the Israeli government.[5] Israel holds Yasser Arafat responsible for suicide attacks mounted from PA-controlled territory and for lower-level violence such as rioting in disputed or divided areas such as Hebron.[6] Israeli policy makers accept that there are strong domestic constraints placed on Arafat not to take decisive action but insists that he must make a choice between peace with Israel or developing closer ties with the radicals.[7]

From the Palestinians' perspective the overall security arrangements have been far from successful. Israel still controls most of the West Bank (despite the intention of the Oslo Accords for the Palestinians to be in control of larger parts of it before Final Status talks start) and closures on the territories imposed by Israel have led to increased tensions within these areas. In essence, Palestinian security considerations have been secondary to Israeli concerns in all areas of contention. In addition, there is a clear feeling that the Israelis are using the so-called Palestinian security violations of Oslo as an excuse to slow down and eventually kill the peace process.

On the ground in the West Bank the security situation remains complex with the three designated areas listed below.

1. Area A, land under sole Palestinian control and patrolled by Palestinian police.
2. Area B, land under joint Palestinian and Israeli control and patrolled by joint forces of the PA and IDF.
3. Area C, land under sole Israeli control and patrolled by the IDF.

---

3 On the development of Hamas and its violent reaction to the Oslo Accords, see A. Kurz with N. Tal, 'Hamas: radical Islam in a national struggle', *Jaffee Centre for Strategic Studies Memorandum 47,* Tel Aviv University, 1997.
4 For a comprehensive account of Israel's charges against the PA, see 'Israeli view on Palestinian security commitments', The Prime Minister's Office, Jerusalem, 9 September 1997.
5 Interview with David Bar-Ilan, Director of Policy Planning and Communications in the Prime Minister's Office, Jerusalem, 5 March 1998.
6 On the issue of the links between Hamas and Arafat's Fatah movement, see S. Rodan, 'Where terror lurks', *Jerusalem Post,* 8 August 1997.
7 For more details of an Israeli perspective on Arafat's choice, see Y. Erez, 'Arafat's last chance', *Ma'ariv,* 5 September 1997, pp. 1–2.

The most complex area is clearly Area B with its joint patrols, and it is in this area that relatively close working relationships have been forged between the IDF and PA forces. However, these relationships have shown themselves not to be strong enough to prevent a political crisis such as the opening of a tunnel in Jerusalem (see Chapter 6) leading to violence or armed confrontation between members of the IDF and Palestinian police. Indeed, Palestinian frustrations over the apparent lack of progress in the peace process have placed these operational relationships under intolerable strains. However, even in the darkest hours when security cooperation was suspended by Arafat following the Israeli decision to build at Har Homa (see Chapter 2), some channels of security communication have been kept open, usually by means of a third party (the Central Intelligence Agency – CIA), as both sides retain an interest in controlling or limiting the levels of violence in their respective areas.

Security issues and Final Status talks

Clearly, long-term security prospects in the area depend on an acceptable agreement being reached between the sides on a final and permanent status of the West Bank. In arriving at such a deal there are a number of factors that each side needs to take into account and it is argued here that Israel's map of interests under Netanyahu bears a remarkable resemblance to that of Rabin's.[8] In essence, once Netanyahu embraced the Oslo Accords over any Israeli ideological claim to the whole West Bank he moved to dealing with the issue of the Territories using primarily a pragmatic security framework rather than an ideological perspective.

The definition of Israel's security needs are to some degree open to interruption – for example, the left may insist on a slightly lower security level assuming that a permanent and stable peace can be reached; the

---

8 An examination of the 1996 Likud Party platform and *The Israel Labour Party's Peace and Security Platform for Elections to the 14th Knesset* reveals striking similarities in their perception of Israel's security interests. Both see the River Jordan as the eastern border of Israel. The major differences are that the Likud platform rules out a Palestinian state and the Labour Party platform rules out the building of any new settlements. See Chapter 1: Peace and Security, *The Likud Party Platform 1996*, Likud Party Headquarters, Tel Aviv, 1996, p. 2 and 'The Peace Negotiations', *The Israel Labour Party's Peace and Security Platform for Elections to the 14th Knesset*, Labour Party Headquarters, Tel Aviv, May 1996, p. 2.

right generally insists on a higher level of security due to a stronger feeling of scepticism that such a peace can be reached. However, there is a general consensus among Israeli policy makers as to what Israel's basic security needs are perceived to be in the West Bank.[9] Such thinking is based on two assumptions: first, that any proposed Palestinian entity is a de-militarised zone; and second, that the peace deal with Jordan remains stable thus ensuring strategic depth between Israel and Saddam Hussein's Iraq. If these two variables can be controlled then Israel will seek to maintain its security needs in the following five ways.

1. Israel to annex the Jordan valley as in the Allon Plan and the Israeli settlements in the Jordan Valley would remain intact.
2. Permanent station of IDF in the Jordan Valley. In essence, this to be Israel's eastern border (the major Palestinian argument against this is that it would physically disengage any potential Palestinian entity in the West Bank from the Arab world).
3. Settlements encircling Jerusalem to be annexed including to the eastern approaches in Ma'aleh Edumim and the surrounding areas (such a potential annexation would harden Palestinian demands on East Jerusalem).
4. The Gush Etzion area south of Jerusalem and surrounding areas to be annexed (this may prove to be the least contentious of annexations).
5. Increasing the thickness of the Jerusalem corridor from the coast and the area near Ben-Gurion Airport by annexing land around the airport and on the approaches to Jerusalem.

These requirements are only Israel's basic security requirements and are not based on other factors such as maintaining control over water resources, economic factors, or any historic or ideological claim on particular areas or cities such as Hebron. Moreover, these demands have not altered from the late Yitzhak Rabin to Binyamin Netanyahu. Although Rabin took his plans for a Final Status solution with him to the grave, indications from his speeches were that his criteria for protecting Israeli security interests were based on the above framework.[10] In addition, the

---

9   A lucid account of Israel's security needs is provided in J. Alpher, 'Israel's security concerns in the peace process', *Journal of International Affairs*, vol. 70, no. 2, (1994), pp. 229–41.

10   One of Rabin's more detailed accounts of his vision of Israeli security interests was made in a speech at Haifa University where he mapped out plans for deployment

vast majority of this framework was devised by the planning division of the Israeli army, a unit which in the past closely reflected Rabin's thinking.

From a Palestinian perspective their security requirements are largely territorial in the West Bank and include the following three basics.

1. Connection through a secure road link between Gaza and the West Bank.
2. Access to air and seaports.
3. Security provisions for Palestinians against Israeli settlers who may reject any agreement and seek to derail its implementation through violent actions, or perpetrate acts of revenge against suspected Palestinian attacks on remaining outlying Israel settlements.[11]

In addition to these basic security provisions there remains the territorial issue that the Palestinians believe they require enough land to make the Palestinian entity into a viable state. This would include control over the entire Arab population for the West Bank, and room for growth to absorb refugees and general development. It is worth stressing that with all the concentration on Israeli security needs via the drawn-out negotiations over the interim troop redeployments, this framework of Palestinian security needs equally has the potential to derail the Final Status talks.

Final Status options: compromise or stalemate in the West Bank?

In assessing the options for bridging the gaps in the security needs frameworks discussed earlier there is a range of plans available that deals with the specific aims of each party. As this chapter is restricted to discussing security issues it will largely ignore plans that cover other areas such as water resources and focus solely on the options for providing acceptable security provisions for both sides. It should be pointed out that these plans encompass a strong political dimension – for example, the

---

in the West Bank, Israel's unwillingness for tactical reasons to abandon a single settlement at this stage of negotiations and the difficulties over the redeployment in Hebron. Speech by Yitzhak Rabin on the occasion of his receiving an honorary doctorate, Haifa University, 5 June 1994.

11 See J. Alpher, 'Settlements and borders', *Final Status Issues: Israel–Palestinians, Study 3*, Jaffee Centre for Strategic Studies, Tel Aviv University, 1994, p. 34.

willingness to give ground in one area in order to secure a comprehensive agreement on the whole of the West Bank.

Israeli withdrawal from the vast majority of the West Bank

This would involve Israel withdrawing from all the territories and a return to the 1967 lines with the exception of Jerusalem. Minor modifications to the border would be negotiated, which could lead to Israel annexing more areas of land in the Latrun area and the settlements at Gush Etzion. This plan would suit the security needs of the Palestinians; it would provide them with links to the Arab world and proponents of this plan claim that security problems would be easier to deal with as the two populations would be clearly separated (that is, no Jewish settlements remaining on Palestinian lands). In terms of protecting Israel's eastern border this plan calls for the permanent stationing of Israeli forces on Palestinian territory.

Obviously there are many problems for Israel with such a plan. First, it would mean the removal of the 120,000 settlers in the West Bank and the dismantling of the settlements. The settlers in groups such as Gush Emunim represent a strong and powerful pressure group in Israel with close connections to political parties.[12] Although some of the 120,000 would no doubt accept financial compensation and leave, many would not. Consequently, it would be difficult to see any Israeli government surviving such a situation unless perhaps a national unity government (NUG) was formed. Moreover, many of these settlements have been developed for security reasons and it would be difficult to sell the idea that Israel's security had not been badly eroded by such an evacuation.

Territorial compromise on varying degrees

These plans vary from the Sharon Plan, which calls for some 50 per cent of the West Bank to be annexed by Israel, to the Allon Plan, which calls for areas vital to Israel's security needs to be annexed to a more moderate plan in which Israel would annex only around 11 per cent, and the Netanyahu Plan (Allon Plus), which bears resemblance to the Allon Plan,

---

12 For an account of the role of the largest settlers movement in the peace process, see L. Weissbrod, 'Gush Emunim and the Israeli–Palestinian peace process: moderate religious fundamentalism in crisis', *Israel Affairs*, vol. 3, no. 1 (1996), pp. 86–103.

the first Israeli plan to deal with the status of the West Bank. Indeed, the relevance of the Allon Plan should not be under-estimated as it still has many supporters among key personalities in the Israeli centre-ground. In reality, the Netanyahu Plan is an updated version of the Allon Plan taking into account the development of Israeli settlements in the West Bank which took place after Allon drew up his plan in the late 1960s.

The Sharon Plan calls for Israel to annex 50 per cent plus of the West Bank, and for the Palestinians to control only municipal enclaves in surrounding Hebron, Tulkarm, Jenin, Nablus, Qalqilya and Ramallah. Israel would annex the Jordan Valley, the Etzion block and move the Green Line further eastwards towards the border with Jordan. Consequently, the Palestinians in the West Bank would be cut off from the Arab world (and indeed their fellow Palestinians in Gaza) and the Palestinians would not have control over the majority of territory in the West Bank. Consequently, such a proposal would be totally unacceptable to Arafat and the PA. The principal aim of the Sharon Plan is to maximise the area Israel controls in the West Bank and to minimise the number of Palestinians over which it has to rule. It also aims to prevent the possibility of a viable Palestinian state being formed in the West Bank, and is regularly updated by Sharon to take into account demographic and political changes.[13]

The moderate plan for Israel to annex some 11 per cent of the West Bank following agreement in Final Status would appear to be the most acceptable to the Palestinians and holds limited advantages for an Israeli government as well. This plan would involve the annexation by Israel of parts of Western Samaria, which are heavily populated with Jewish settlements. In addition, Israel would annex the Latrun salient, Givat Ze'ev area north of the Jerusalem corridor and Gush Etzion south of the corridor as well as Ma'aleh Edumim to the east of Jerusalem. The Jordan Valley would be turned over to Palestinian control but with Israeli forces present for a limited period (something like 15 years) on the eastern slopes of the mountain ridge in order to repel any attack from the east. After this period, and providing that a secure and stable peace had endured, Israel would withdraw these forces. Moreover, Israel

---

13 Interestingly, Sharon was one of the first senior figures in the Likud to accept the Oslo Accords as a *fait accompli* and put forward his plan as a way of ensuring that a Palestinian state could not be formed at the end of the Oslo process.

would be allowed to install early warning stations in this area. All the rest of the West Bank would be handed over to the Palestinians with any settlers who remained in these areas being subject to Palestinian rule.

The major security advantages for Israel in this plan are that it ensures that its eastern border is well protected and that it has a force on site to repel any hostile attack from the east. In addition, the defences and approaches to Jerusalem are strengthened and Israel will control the historically sensitive area of Gush Etzion and maintain partial control of a small enclave in the centre of Hebron. Crucially the annexations would mean that some 70 per cent of the settlers would remain within Israel's sovereign borders and only some 10,000 to 20,000 Palestinian Arab villages would be included in Israel's limited annexations.

For the Palestinians the limited advantages include the following: a retention of nearly all the territory of the West Bank (89 per cent); common borders with Jordan and Egypt; and access to a corridor linking the Gaza Strip and the West Bank. In terms of security the size of the territory would help make a Palestinian state a viable and likely possibility. Although the loss of the annexed land to Israel would be difficult to accept for some Palestinians who see the 1967 borders as the minimal borders for a Palestinian state, it is not inconceivable that the leadership would accept such a plan as part of an overall agreement.

The Allon Plus Plan, which became public on 29 May 1997, was put forward by the planning division of the Israeli army and was endorsed by the Israeli prime minister, Binyamin Netanyahu, as defining the map of Israeli interests.[14] The plan, which had nine points, outlined below, called for Israel to annex around 60 per cent of the West Bank, including the Jordan Valley and a wide area around Jerusalem. Furthermore, the Palestinian area of control was to be divided into four separate enclaves and there would be no link between the enclaves in the south and north. The lack of links clearly reflected an attempt by the Israelis to prevent a Palestinian state being formed.

The nine-point plan was as follows.

1.   Israel would control the areas of the West Bank east of the 1967 Green Line to the first ridge line.

---

14   Details of the plan were disclosed by *Ha-Aretz*'s military correspondent; see Z. Schiff, *Ha-Aretz*, 29 May 1997, p. 1.

2. The Jordan Rift Valley and the hill slopes would remain in Israeli hands to a depth of 15 kilometres from the River Jordan and the Dead Sea shore into the Judean Desert.

3. The Palestinians would get the north-eastern shore of the Dead Sea, with a corridor from the Ramallah area to Jericho.

4. Greater Jerusalem would be expanded in the direction of the settlements of Ma'aleh Edumim and Kfar Edumim in the east, Gush Etzion in the south and Beit El in the west.

5. The corridor from the coastal plain to Jerusalem would be expanded on both sides, from Gush Etzion in the south to the Beit Horon area in the north.

6. The settlements near Nablus and Jenin would have to remain in Palestinian territory or be evacuated.

7. The Palestinians would have a safe passage from the West Bank to the Gaza Strip, in accordance with the Oslo agreement, and another three transit corridors from their area in the West Bank to the towns of Tulkarm, Qalqilya and Jericho.

8. Israel would have four safe passage roads, crossing the West Bank from east to west to the Jordan Rift Valley.

9. In Jerusalem there would be a "functional solution" for the Islamic and Christian holy places. This had not been finally worked out and was not included in this territorial chapter of the proposal.

This was to be Israel's opening position or "maximum plan" in Final Status talks with the government's fall-back positions or "minimum plan" that the Palestinians would gain control of 60 per cent of the West Bank.[15] In order to attempt to soften the blow to the Palestinians it was made clear that more land could be on offer in the long term if the peace proved secure and durable.[16] This provided an early indication of the possibility that Final Status talks would not be the last set of negotiations between the Israelis and PA.[17] Unsurprisingly, given the fact that the

---

15 In addition to the territory question, Netanyahu wanted to allow the PA no more than the status of a semi-state (with no army) along the Puerto Rico or Andorra model. See U. Benziman, 'The gap between the final settlement and reality', *Ha-Aretz*, 21 September 1997.

16 On the issue of the potential for more land to be handed over to the Palestinians, see A. Fischmann, *Yediot Aharonot*, 29 May 1997, p. 1.

17 There were indications that Netanyahu preferred to leave some difficult issues to a post-Final Status period on this – see, for example, N. Lochery, 'Israel's political

Allon Plus Plan reflected solely Israeli security needs, the PA was quick to reject the plan as a non-starter.[18] However, these security needs as endorsed by Netanyahu were almost identical to Israel's basic security needs outlined earlier in this chapter. From this the conclusion can be drawn that Israel's basic positions had remained intact despite the change of government and the Likud's so-called hawkishness on the question of the West Bank. Finally, although there was a certain degree of PR in the timing of the plan (it was designed to take attention away from the election of the new Labour Party leader, Ehud Barak, at the start of June), the plan provided a clear definition of what the IDF felt that Israel's security interests were in the West Bank and, importantly, the first clear sign of Netanyahu's line of thinking.

The future of Israeli settlements in the West Bank

Central to any agreement between the Israelis and the Palestinians is the issue of the future status of the Israeli settlements. This chapter with its concentration on security issues does not examine the settlements in terms of the question of historic rights, legitimacy or religious value but solely within a pragmatic security framework.[19] In essence, there is a division between settlements that were constructed for security reasons and settlements that are developed for other reasons. The definition of what constitutes a security settlement and what does not is somewhat contentious. One of the architects of the distinction, Yitzhak Rabin, was deliberately vague about the definition for domestic and international political purposes, but settlements such as the Jewish enclave in Hebron are clearly not examples of security settlements.

There are two security considerations for any Israeli government to consider regarding the future of the settlements. The first of these, Israel's security on the eastern border and in the West Bank, has already

---

Houdini', *The World Today*, Royal Institute of International Affairs, vol. 54, no. 5 (May 1998), pp. 125–7.

18 Ahmed Tibi, Arafat's adviser on Israeli Affairs, described the Plan as shooting with automatic fire at the dying body of the Oslo Accord. Interview with Ahmed Tibi, Israeli Army Radio, 29 May 1997.

19 For an account of the physical and geographic development of the Jewish settlement movement in the West Bank, see D. Newman, 'The territorial politics of ex-urbanisation', *Israel Affairs,* vol. 3, no. 1 (1996), pp. 61–85.

been discussed; the second is the effect that any abandonment of Israeli control over settlements or evacuation would have on Israeli domestic security.[20] In the event of Israel leaving the majority of the settlements there would be a large potential for violent resistance from the settlers and their supporters. This could take the form of attacks on Palestinian targets in an attempt to disrupt the peace process or organised violence against Israeli leaders. Although there has been a marked reluctance among settlers groups, both moderate and extreme, to take to the street following the murder of Rabin, this would, in all likelihood, alter if the majority of settlements were to be placed under Palestinian control and/or evacuated.[21] Consequently, from an Israeli domestic perspective such a scenario is to be avoided at all costs.

Accepting that it probable that in any final agreement the Israelis do abandon control of some settlements, there are three options for the future status of these areas. First, the settlers could continue to exist under Palestinian sovereignty; second, they could evacuate the settlers and resettle them in areas under Israeli control or back within the Green Line; and third, the settlements could remain in areas which were designated special status areas (which although officially under Palestinian control would still be under Israeli sovereignty or some form of special status regions). The latter would not be attractive to the Palestinians whose opening negotiating position calls for the dismantling of all Jewish settlements in the West Bank. The first and second options could still contain many problems and may be difficult to make work. To a large degree the negative factors depend on how many settlements Israel will relinquish in Final Status talks.

It is becoming more apparent that Israeli plans are based on the majority of the settlements remaining under Israeli control. In such a case it may prove possible to use the offer of generous financial compensation to the populations of settlements over which Israel cannot maintain control to induce the settlers to relocate of their own free will. (The

---

20 For a detailed account of the role of Gush Emunim in Israeli domestic politics see, for example, Z. Flamhaft, *Israel on the Road to Peace: Accepting the Unacceptable* (Boulder, Colorado, Oxford, Westview, 1996), pp. 140–9. For a concise history of the development of Gush Emunim, see D. Peretz and G. Doron, *The Government and Politics of Israel* (Boulder, Colorado, Oxford, Westview, 1997), pp. 254–7.

21 See, for example, N. Shragai, 'Meanwhile in the Jewish settlements', *Ha-Aretz*, 14 September 1997.

United States is the most likely source of any financial compensation deal, which could be in the region of $6 billion.) Previous studies have concluded that of the 120,000 settlers some 60 per cent are defined as economic settlers; they moved across the Green Line primarily because of the generous economic inducements provided by previous mainly Likud-led governments to do so. However, the majority of this group lives within range of the Green Line and not in the smaller more isolated settlements that Israel would probably be obliged to cede control of. Moreover, of the other 40 per cent their motivations are mainly ideological and consequently would prove more problematic to resettle. Indeed, a minority of this group (but still numbering several thousand) would potentially use violence to oppose any Israeli withdrawal. (Netanyahu is well aware of the need to deal with the radical settlers. Prior to his agreement with Arafat on Hebron, the IDF arrested several leading settlers from radical groups – including a former spokesman for the outlawed Kach movement.) In addition, the majority of the non-violent ideological settlers belong to Gush Emunim which, with its close ties to the Israeli right, would make it politically difficult, but not impossible, for any right-wing leader to compromise on the settlement issue.[22]

Finally, the issue of the feelings towards the settlements of the 93 per cent of Israelis who live within the Green Line needs to be considered. It is clear that, providing Israeli security needs can be met in the east, the majority of Israelis would be willing to cede control of at least some of the smaller outlying settlements. However, such feelings could conceivably change if, for example, Hamas or Islamic Jihad were to continue to launch suicide attacks in Israeli cities from bases in parts of the West Bank under Palestinian rule. It is not clear what the effects of a prolonged bombing campaign, as happened in February and March 1996, would have on Israeli domestic public opinion. Consequently, although there would appear to be a strong consensus within the vast majority of Israeli society for the need to leave some settlements in the West Bank as part of an overall territorial compromise, such feelings cannot be taken for granted – especially for governments who rely on the Israeli centre-ground voters.

---

22 See Flamhaft, *Israel on the Road to Peace,* pp. 144–9.

Netanyahu and Rabin: change and continuity on Israeli security interests

In analysing the changes in Israel's position on the final status of the West Bank, two points have become increasingly important. First, the changes in Israel's positions are more in strategy than on substantive issues. The most apparent change in strategy has been the attempt by Netanyahu to weaken, but not destroy, Arafat before the commencement of Final Status talks. This is in direct contrast to Rabin who tried to strengthen Arafat's position in order to help secure Palestinian support for the Oslo Accords. Second, Netanyahu has sought to lower Palestinian aspirations that they were to gain between 90 to 100 per cent of the West Bank, which they were encouraged to think during the original Oslo negotiations would be Israel's position. In essence, Netanyahu argued that the Palestinians had been promised too much by the previous administration and this did not reflect the realities of Israeli and Palestinian positions of strength and weakness.

This battle over strategy and positioning largely obscured the more important fact that Netanyahu has a clear map of Israeli security interests, and that under all the bluster and posturing of the Israeli prime minister these interests mean that he is willing to cede around 50 per cent of the West Bank as his opening position. Had Rabin lived and been re-elected this would likely also have been his opening position in Final Status talks. Consequently, the problems that arose between the Netanyahu government and the PA are more to do with trust between the parties rather than more substantive issues. In other words, Rabin's opening position would have been considered a starting point for Final Status (along with Arafat's opening position), but Netanyahu's opening positions were considered nothing more than an excuse, on his part, to stall or end the peace process.

In reality, the Netanyahu government has more in common with the cautious characteristics of Rabin than the latter had with the brief post-assassination government led by Shimon Peres. In other words, the difficulties such as Arafat's reluctance to dismantle the terrorist infrastructure and disputes over the extent of interim stage troop redeployments that have dogged the process from 1996 onwards would have arisen under a Rabin government as well. After all, it was Rabin himself who coined the famous phrase that the Oslo timetable wasn't set in stone and every stage of the interim agreement up to his death had been late or had been postponed to a later date.

In charting the developments in the security arena in the Netanyahu era it is important to remember the above points and accept that the prime minister has been attempting to implement a clearly defined long-term strategy. Moreover, it is also apparent that the prime minister, like Rabin, has regarded this strategy as his own domain and did not consult widely with his Cabinet colleagues between 1996–8. Indeed, the relationship between the prime minister and David Levy, his foreign minister, was so bad at times prior to Levy's eventual resignation that they appeared to contradict each other in key areas of security policy making.

In terms of specific plans for the West Bank Netanyahu has suggested, as previously described, his opening position will give the Palestinians no more than 50 per cent of the land. Consequently, the protracted negotiations over the interim stage troop withdrawals from the West Bank have reflected this position. It is clear to Israeli policy makers that once land is handed over to sole PA control in Area A, the Palestinians are unlikely to return any of it in any final agreement. Consequently, every withdrawal is strengthening the Palestinians' and weakening Israel's position. In simple terms, although the area map of the West Bank is only for the interim period, in reality both sides have taken it to be the framework for final borders. This is largely confirmed by the stand of Netanyahu holding out against returning land (for example, near Ben-Gurion Airport) to Palestinian control and the insistence of Arafat between 1996–8 that the interim stages are carried out before moving towards Final Status.

Consequences of an attempt to impose a unilateral settlement in the West Bank

In the event of a breakdown in negotiations Arafat has made it clear that he will unilaterally declare a Palestinian state in the West Bank and the Gaza Strip.[23] In order to prepare for such an eventuality he has between

---

23 Arafat has stated this in public on many occasions. See, for example, an interview on French radio in which he stated that at the end of Final Status talks he would declare a state whatever the outcome of the talks. Reported by J.

1996 and 1998 been courting international support for such a declaration. Netanyahu has responded forcibly to such statements by Arafat and insists that if such a state is unilaterally declared then he will similarly unilaterally annex parts of the West Bank that he feels are necessary for Israeli security.[24] It is not within the scope of this study to examine the, at this time, hypothetical nature of these moves but rather to chart the effect that these threats have had on the negotiations and what the consequences would be for a long-term stable peace in the West Bank.

There are two interpretations of the effects of a unilateral declaration supported by Arab and many Third World countries. First, the potential for such a declaration is allowing both Arafat and Netanyahu to adopt more rigid positions than would otherwise be the case. Second, it is pushing them towards compromise as neither wants to take the massive risks that any unilateral acts would require.

The advantages of a unilateral declaration to both sides are extremely limited. Such a declaration merely reflects that the negotiations have failed and limits the chance of a stable and comprehensive peace. Consequently, it is only in the arena of domestic politics that there are possible potential advantages for both sides. For Netanyahu this would mean that he was not the leader who sanctioned a Palestinian state and possibly American support (or informal understandings) in recognising the parts of the West Bank he subsequently attempted to annex as Israeli territory.[25] However, greatly outweighing this would be the fact that Netanyahu knows that he was elected in order to continue the peace process and it would be

---

Immanuel, 'Netanyahu warns Arafat: don't declare a state', *Jerusalem Post*, 24 November 1996.

24 A typical response from Netanyahu to Arafat's statements about a unilateral declaration of a state came in an interview on US television in May 1998. In answering a question about such a scenario the prime minister replied with the following: "That's going to be an egregious violation of the Oslo Accords. It would effectively dissolve them, and any unilateral action on the Palestinian part would be met with unilateral action on the Israeli part. I think that would be unfortunate. We want a negotiated peace. We want a commitment, in fact, a precise commitment, to the Oslo Accords. We're prepared to fulfil our part and the Palestinians have to do theirs. A negotiated solution is the only way to go and the unilateral declaration of a Palestinian state that could very well turn into another Iran or another Iraq at our doorstep and jeopardise our security; those unilateral actions are not the way to go. They should be avoided at all costs."

25 Interview with Netanyahu on ABC, 17 May 1998.

difficult to see him winning a second term in such circumstances. For Arafat, the major advantages would be twofold: first, a show of strength to an increasingly sceptical Palestinian public that he is able to withstand Israeli pressure; and second, the deliverance of a Palestinian state.

The disadvantages of any unilateral action are all too predictable. It is difficult to see any move towards statehood not ending in violence, either direct between the IDF and armed Palestinian police or through battles involving Israeli settlers and Palestinians. The US Secretary of State, Madeleine Albright, has used such a nightmare scenario as an impetus to try to move the negotiations along towards an agreement. In addition, should Israel decide to re-occupy areas that are presently in Area A (such as any of the major Palestinian cities or their municipal areas) then casualties on both sides are likely to be very high. The reaction of Arab states to such a war would be unclear. It is thought highly probable by Israeli military planners that no Arab army would directly intervene but that Egypt would move its army into the demilitarised zone in the Sinai Desert, thus forcing the Israelis to mobilise large-scale forces in the south and away from the Palestinian areas.

This worst case scenario could be avoided with private agreements between Israeli and Palestinian leaders in the event of a failure to agree on a Final Status settlement to postpone decision on sovereignty and maintain the status quo. However, such a situation would be heavily in favour of the Israelis who would maintain control over the majority of the West Bank and therefore be unacceptable to the Palestinian side. A second option of placing parts of the West Bank under international supervision would be unacceptable to Israel. Unfortunately, despite the no-win situation it remains a distinct possibility that if there is no agreement on Final Status then at least one of the sides will try to impose a unilateral settlement.

Conclusion

Since coming to office in 1996, Netanyahu has attempted to maximise Israel's position for the Final Status talks. While in opposition his major charge against the Oslo Accords was that the end result of the interim stages would be a fully independent Palestinian state in the Gaza Strip and the West Bank. Netanyahu's strategy in office towards the territories has been abundantly clear with three identifiable central strands present:

first, Israel limiting the percentage of territory it offered to return during the interim stages to prevent the formation of a viable fully sovereign Palestinian state; second, he has attempted to reduce Palestinian aspirations to reflect what he considers to be the realistic balance of power between the two sides; and third, he has continued to allow Jewish settlements to develop both for internal domestic reasons (see Chapter 1) and to strengthen further Israel's position in the West Bank.

In terms of Netanyahu's vision of the future of the West Bank, two important points have become clear. The prime minister's opening position is based on a modified version of the Allon Plan and therefore largely on the moderate territorial option. Furthermore, he is willing to cede control of some of the outlying Jewish settlements in return for maximising Israel's position within the major settlement blocks and strategic areas around Jerusalem. Moreover, these positions reflect the thinking of the late Rabin as an opening position in the negotiations. In terms of a fall-back position Netanyahu has hinted that there is more territory on offer in the West Bank, but that this may depend on a successful period of stable peace. In other words, the transfer of territories to the Palestinians could continue well beyond the turn of the century.

On the Palestinian side it is clear that it will not get the 100 per cent of territory that its opening negotiating position demands, nor will all Israeli settlements in the West Bank be dismantled. In addition, it is possible that the Jordan Valley will remain in Israeli hands, thus preventing the Palestinians having a common border with the Jordanians. Consequently, the Palestinian leadership is likely to be faced with difficult choices in the West Bank. In addition, it should be noted that a failure by the Palestinians to obtain the majority of their goals here is likely to lead to a hardening of their position on other issues such as Jerusalem and the refugees.

The issue of the future of West Bank territory has been partially overshadowed by the near continuous security problems during the interim agreements. The problems of the violence that followed the opening of a tunnel in Jerusalem between the Palestinian police and IDF, together with the frequent outbreaks of serious rioting in the West Bank towns such as Hebron, illustrate the problems that remain. In addition, the Islamic fundamentalist groups of Hamas and Islamic Jihad continue to be a major de-stabilising factor in the peace process. Linking progress on the peace process to the PA's effort to combat terrorism illustrates that

Israel clearly holds Arafat responsible for attacks launched from territory under his control. Moreover, the security issue has been used by the rejectionist forces on both sides to illustrate the point that in their view the Oslo process and its security framework are simply not working.

Finally, although the potential security arrangements in the West Bank and Gaza are far from settled, there is a strong basis for negotiation. Netanyahu, in rejecting the ideological approach of his Likud predecessor, Yitzhak Shamir, and the more hawkish plans of Ariel Sharon, has shown a more pragmatic approach to dealing with the issue. Indeed, as has been argued in this chapter Netanyahu, with his similar map of security interests to Rabin's, has a lot more in common with the positions taken by the late prime minister and architect of the Oslo security agreements than would appear obvious at first. The risks of not reaching an agreement for either side far outweigh the potential gains. Consequently, from this it can be deduced that underneath all the rhetoric it is in the interests of both Arafat and Netanyahu to devise a workable agreement on the West Bank and the Gaza Strip with all the necessary security arrangements.

4

The economic dimension of an Israeli–Palestinian peace: where is the peace dividend?

Any successful permanent peace agreement between the Israelis and Palestinians needs to be underpinned by a clear improvement in the living standards of first, the Palestinians and second, the Israelis (especially in the development towns on the periphery).[1] The then Israeli prime minister, Yitzhak Rabin, in a policy statement to the Knesset expressed an understanding of this:

> Many countries have mobilised to render economic assistance to the Palestinians, and we are encouraging this in every way because it is also our interest, security and otherwise, that the residents of Gaza and Jericho achieve prosperity and a better life.[2]

In short, this chapter asserts that the economic well-being of both sides represents one of the three most important ingredients required for establishing a stable peace between the two sides. The other two (territory and security) were discussed in the previous chapter. However, since the Oslo Accords were signed in 1993 there has been an understandable over-concentration on the issue of land and security at the expense of the economic question. In addition, there has also been a marked failure by some senior figures on both sides initially to fully grasp the inter-related

---

1 See M. Yakan, 'From war to peace, prospects and implications of the Middle East peace process' in Efraim Karsh (ed.), *From Rabin to Netanyahu: Israel's Troubled Agenda* (London and Portland, Frank Cass, 1997) pp. 133–69 (see particularly pp. 148–50).
2 Policy statement by Yitzhak Rabin to the Knesset, 3 October 1994, Knesset Records, Jerusalem.

nature of the economic and political development in both the Palestinian areas and in Israel itself.[3]

Unfortunately, due to a number of reasons – some structural, others political (both external and internal), many through wastage and corruption – to date a peace dividend for the Palestinians has not materialised. Indeed, the average living standards of Palestinians living in the West Bank and the Gaza Strip have actually declined markedly since the signing of the Oslo Accords.[4] Consequently, such economic hardships have led to a naturally increased feeling of scepticism towards the peace process from Palestinians and, to a certain degree, a drop in support for Arafat's Palestinian Authority (PA) and a corresponding increase in support for the radical Islamic groups such as Hamas. Crucially, the lack of development of the Palestinian economy will have a direct impact on the type of Palestinian entity (state) that is likely to emerge at the end of the political negotiations.

In chronicling the increasing economic problems for the Palestinians, this chapter will, first, provide an understanding of the reasons behind the economic difficulties and, second, address the question of the likely political scenarios if this economic decline is not reversed. Finally, it will attempt to suggest means to alleviate the situation both in the short and medium term.

Although it should be stressed that the Israeli economy has not experienced the type of marked decline that has occurred in the Palestinian sector it is none the less clear that the peace dividend which Israel would appear to have received from the peace process is smaller than expected.[5] Moreover, some economists suggest that limited economic

---

3 Furthermore, this has been particularly true of Arafat, who has concentrated on gaining as many territorial and political concessions from the Israelis rather than economic ones. This was largely confirmed by comments by Arafat's economic adviser, Khaled Islam and reported in S. Rodan, 'Crisis of confidence', *Jerusalem Post*, 17 July 1997.

4 For a full statistical account of this economic decline, see *Recent Economic Developments, Prospects and Progress in Institution Building in the West Bank and Gaza Strip*, Middle Eastern Department, International Monetary Fund, Washington, DC, 6 March 1997.

5 A summary of the positive developments for the Israeli economy from the peace process can be found in Rafi Bar El, 'Growth from peace', *Israel Business Arena*, 29 March 1996. For a more detailed appraisal of the arguments, see B. Zilberfarb, 'The effect of the peace process on the Israeli economy', *Israel Affairs*, vol. 1, no. 1 (1994), pp. 84–95.

gains that the peace process has brought Israel are under threat from the Netanyahu government with its political agenda of slowing down the peace process. Consequently, this chapter also charts the potential for the Israeli economy to utilise any potential peace dividend and examines how closely related the health of the Israeli economy and the peace process are in reality.[6] In returning to the theme of the book the chapter also analyses the changes that have taken place under Netanyahu in Israel both in terms of the continuing Palestinian economic problems and the development of the Israeli economy.

In organisational terms this chapter is divided into three sections: the first deals with the problems of securing Palestinian economic development and its subsequent effect on the Palestinian political entity that is set to emerge; the second examines the linkage of the Israeli economy to the peace process and assesses the latter's vulnerability to a collapse in the political negotiations; and the third gives recommendations for improved development of the Palestinian economy and for maximising the Israeli peace dividend over the coming years.

The Palestinian economy: post-Oslo, pre-Final Status

There are a number of reasons for the lack of development of the Palestinian economy in the West Bank and the Gaza Strip since the Oslo Accords were signed – not least the political instability in the area, making both Palestinian and foreign investors wary of financial investment in the West Bank and the Gaza Strip. As a consequence, levels of investment have been falling dramatically since 1993.[7] Interestingly, this has been very apparent in Palestinian investment: in 1992 it was $1.2 billion and in the first full year of the PA it dropped to $500 million; in 1996 it fell

---

6 On the relationship between the peace process and the economy (especially the level of foreign investment) in Israel, see B. Zilberfarb, 'The Israeli economy in the 1990s: immigration, the peace process, and the medium term prospects for growth', *Israel Affairs*, vol. 3, no. 1 (1996), pp. 10–11.

7 Overall, investment fell from 28 per cent of gross national product in 1992 to just over 18 per cent in early 1997. In addition, the IMF report estimates that private investment over the same period fell from 25 per cent to just 10 per cent of GDP. Source: *Recent Economic Developments, Prospects and Progress in Institution Building in the West Bank and Gaza Strip*.

further to $250 million.[8] In short, the major source of the instability in the PA territories is that the investors do not know what the political status of the West Bank and the Gaza Strip will be at the conclusion of Final Status talks. Moreover, other factors have included the lack of a legal framework, fully functional court system, and a tax and trade policy. In short, the absence of a fully modern government has made it difficult for investors to secure their investments within the framework of workable and enforceable laws.

Publicly, Palestinian investors cite the problems caused by the security closures by Israel on the territories, but in Palestinian forums they state that they are not investing because in essence they do not trust the PA and Arafat.[9] In reality, it is the combination of all these factors that has led to a crisis of investment in the areas controlled by the PA. Among those who have proved reluctant to invest in PA areas are the Palestinian banks themselves. By the end of 1996 they had invested $301.7 million or 23.5 per cent of their deposits. This ratio was remarkably low as, for instance, Israeli banks invested 78 per cent of their deposits and Jordanian banks 64 per cent during the same period.[10]

Similarly, foreign investors share the above concerns, and the majority of aid from donor countries has been used to help finance the PA (and its large bureaucracy) and oversized security forces – with almost nothing going to the private sector. In addition, the international aid donors have been unable to fill the public investment gap in PA areas because of the lack of coordination with the Palestinians, and subsequently due to the physical closures imposed by Israel after terrorist attacks.[11]

The closure of the borders imposed by Israel on PA areas is estimated to cost $1.35 million per day of the closure in lost earnings of the estimated

---

8 Figures quoted by Mohammed Zuhdi Nashashibi, Palestinian Authority, Minister of Finance (1997).

9 On the reasons for a lack of Palestinian investment, see S. Rodan, 'Crisis of confidence'.

10 On the question of investments by Palestinian banks, see S. Abadi, 'Investment by Palestinian banks', paper presented at conference on investment in the northern West Bank, Centre for Palestine Research and Studies, Nablus, July 1997.

11 An IMF report found that of the $2.49 billion pledged in 1994–6, only $1.35 billion had been distributed by March 1997. See *Recent Economic Developments, Prospects and Progress in Institution Building in the West Bank and Gaza Strip*.

35,000 Palestinians who enter Israel to work each day.[12] In a typical period when the closures were imposed (31 July to 28 August 1997) the losses amounted to some $31.1 million. In addition, the closures damage Palestinian exporters who cannot get their products out of the West Bank and Gaza.[13] Moreover, the internal closures[14] imposed by Israel in the summer of 1997 meant that many farmers could not even gain access to their lands in order to harvest the fields, and consequently many crops remained unharvested and were left to rot.[15]

The issue of corruption has played a significant role in deterring investors in the areas controlled by the PA, but the real extent of the corruption is more difficult to measure. However, two points remain clear: first, initially the accounting procedures of the PA were simply insufficient for controlling and reporting where and to whom funds were going; and second, in late 1996 there were damning reports in the Israel media of a special slush fund of $200 million, which had been transferred to Arafat into a Tel Aviv bank account.[16] Although the true use of the money was never fully discovered it attracted a great deal of unwelcome publicity for Arafat and the PA. In addition, there were a number of highly publicised cases of reported corruption among some of Arafat's Cabinet, varying from running up excessive mobile phone and restaurant bills to more serious cases of financial impropriety.

Unsurprisingly, economists with close links to the PA played down the corruption question. For example, Mohammed Shtayyey, head of the Palestinian Economic Council for Development and Reconstruction (PECDAR) and leader of the Palestinian delegation to the Multilateral

---

12 Source for statistics is the World Bank, summarised in J. Dempsey, 'Israel eases bar on Palestinian workers', *Financial Times*, 2 September 1997.

13 Export revenue lost during the closures in the summer of 1997 totalled some $29.9 million out of an IMF estimated total exports of $366 million for whole of 1997.

14 On internal closures, see D. Rubinstein, 'A renewed occupation or security measures?', *Ha-Aretz*, 4 August 1997.

15 Israel imposes two types of closures: first, a sealing of the borders between PA areas and Israel, and second, what is termed as internal closures where Palestinians' movements are restricted to their own area and they cannot travel between the various PA-controlled areas through Israeli check points.

16 The money was supposed to be part of the PA's operating budget. The money came from gasoline tax rebates promised to Arafat under the terms of the Oslo Accords, but no Israeli knew where it went. On this issue, see the Editorial, 'The PA slush fund', *Jerusalem Post*, 10 September 1996.

Economic Cooperation Working Group (REDWEG), appeared to imply that the issue of corruption had been resolved. As he put it: "I am not aware of any corruption. I know all these types of things were settled long ago. In the past a percentage of these revenues was going to accounts not under the direct control of the Ministry of Finance."[17]

However, in interviews conducted by the author of London-based companies which have made, or were considering making, investments in areas controlled by the PA, the issue of corruption was cited as one of the negative factors against making investments. Moreover, in some instances the case of corruption had led to the company withdrawing its original investment or minimising its longer-term commitment. In addition, in some instances it was clear that companies were put off by a perception of the general presence of corruption in the PA, and not by specific reported cases which had damaged their investments. It should be stressed that the issue of corruption was only one of the many reasons suggested for the limited investment, but was mentioned by nearly all the interviewees.[18]

In summary, when taken together, the issues of, first, the lack of a fully functioning modern government, second, strict security closures imposed by Israel, third, the corruption in the PA, and finally the political instability of a stalled peace process, have led to a lack of investment in PA areas. As a result, this lack of investment has, in turn, led to a state of near-permanent economic crisis in the West Bank and the Gaza Strip since 1993. This is borne out in statistics such as a near-doubling in the unemployment rate between 1993 and 1997 and a reduction in per capita income of around 20 per cent.[19] Consequently, the attempt by the Palestinians to develop a strong economic infrastructure and financial

---

17 Interview with Mohammed Shtayyey in D. Harris, 'A closed economy', *Jerusalem Post*, 9 October 1997.

18 The interviews were conducted in London during the summer and autumn of 1997. The interviews were not conducted in a regimented scientific manner, but rather were informal discussions and were conducted for business reasons strictly off the record. The question of corruption was not pre-empted by the author's questions during the interviews and was introduced only by the interviewees.

19 Source: *Recent Economic Developments, Prospects and Progress in Institution Building in the West Bank and Gaza Strip*. The unemployment rate in the West Bank in 1996 was 38 per cent of the workforce; in the Gaza Strip for the same period it was 51 per cent.

stability during the interim stages of the Oslo Accords has clearly failed.[20] The extent of this failure has important ramifications for helping determine what type of Palestinian economic entity (state) emerges from the Final Status talks. Consequently, to help illustrate this linkage four potential types of Palestinian entities are discussed below.

1. A highly dependent state, shackled to Israel with an economy in recession and where the authorities rely mainly on coercion to suppress any opposition. Aaron Segal suggests that this scenario is the most probable because the Palestinian leadership does not have the ability to respond to those (mainly young) people who call for radical change.[21]

2. The Palestinian entity (state) would achieve modest growth with the presence of a vocal civic society, which provides some checks on the government. There would be some limited progress on issues such as improving the status of women and human rights. However, this scenario is less likely than the first because the poor economic prospects would appear to make such growth highly limited.

3. Less likely is the scenario that the entity (state) would achieve transition to full democracy with rapid economic growth and much improved human rights. Once more, the economic prospects show no signs that such rapid growth could be achieved in the first years of independence.

4. With deep economic hardship and a near breakdown in civil society, the entity would become a base for terrorism ruled by a radical regime. This scenario would appear unlikely because Israel and probably Jordan would intervene. In addition, with the dependence of any Palestinian economy on Israel it is difficult to foresee a Palestinian regime totally cutting economic relations with Israel.

This chapter does not assert that economic factors will be the only ones in determining the nature and development of the entity, but rather argues that they will play an important role among other political factors. In addition, it is clear that any independent Palestinian entity

---

20 See P. Inbari, 'Economics and the Palestinian question', *Jerusalem Post*, 12 June 1996.
21 See A. Segal, 'What a Palestinian state would look like', *Wall Street Journal*, 31 January 1997.

(state) would have to compete to develop stable economic and political relations not only with Israel but also with Jordan. The relationship with the latter could prove to be more complex in the economic field as in any areas they are likely to compete against each other.

In summary, it is clear that since the signing of the Oslo Accords in 1993 the Palestinian economy has not developed as intended. To a large extent this has been caused by the nature of the interim stages that were designed to allow the PA-controlled areas to expand both in terms of territory and economic growth. Subsequently, at Final Status talks the PA was meant to be holding areas of land which were to make a Palestinian entity (state) at the end of 1999. In reality inter-related factors, the lack of investment, slow development of modern government, corruption, failure of international donors to commit funds that were initially promised and the impasse in the peace process have meant that this economic development has not taken place. In addition, attacks by radical Islamic groups opposed to the peace accords have brought swift economic retribution from Israel in terms of punishing the PA with costly internal closures. Unfortunately, the economic crisis in the West Bank and the Gaza Strip has tended to see an increase in support for these radical groups who themselves receive generous financial support from abroad. The more attacks these groups mount on Israel the stronger the economic measures Israel takes against the PA, and correspondingly this further weakens the Palestinian economy and leads to greater tensions in PA-controlled areas.[22] Later in the chapter suggestions are made in order to attempt to break this vicious circle.

The Israeli economy: limited economic gains and losses from the peace process

There are a number of factors that make it more difficult to measure the extent of the effect of the peace process on Israel. These include the arrival of some 750,000 new immigrants from the former Soviet Union

---

22 Following a suicide attack in July 1997, Israel, for the first time, imposed economic sanctions on the PA which included withholding around NIS 100 million in tax returns from the PA. For more details on the sanctions, see O. Koren, 'Israel imposes economic sanctions for the first time', *Israel Business Arena*, 31 July 1997.

in the 1990s, and an ability to identify the factors that have encouraged increased investment in the economy. Moreover, senior Israeli economists are themselves split on the question. The Governor of the Bank of Israel, Jacob Frenkel, takes a middle ground line and as he put it in response to a question on the link between the economic slowdown in Israel (1997) and the peace process:

> There is a link between the geopolitics and the atmosphere of uncertainty, which in turn impact the economy. Some sectors are highly responsive to the atmosphere such as tourism. Meanwhile, we see a very significant increase in high-tech investments. Where was the peace process there? There is a link, but we need to be more subtle about analysing it.[23]

However, two points are clear: first, that the Israeli economy has not been harmed by the peace process (and in particular since the 1993 signing of the Oslo Accords the economy has, in certain areas, benefited from the increased access to markets such as Turkey and to a lesser degree Jordan); and second, that the Israeli economy is not as vulnerable as the Palestinian economy to an impasse in the peace process or to previously outlined economic difficulties caused by the interim stages of the Oslo Accords. Indeed, many economists insist that the Israel economy could withstand a partial breakdown in the peace process.

Regarding the first point, at a national level the Israeli economy would appear to have made some limited gains from the peace process. Furthermore, it is clear that any Israeli economic benefit has come in the form of increased foreign investment (mainly from the US) and not in terms of any major change in its trading relationship with Middle Eastern countries. To date this level of foreign investment has continued to increase rapidly (both under the Rabin–Peres and Netanyahu governments) – for example, in 1990 it totalled only $81 million, by 1994 it was $750 million and by 1995 it rose to more than $2 billion.[24]

Consequently, the Israeli economy has not developed as Shimon Peres's vision of the new Middle East originally intended. This vision

---

23 Interview with Jacob Frenkel in A. Asa-El, D. Gerstenfeld and D. Harris, 'Frenkel to the defence', *Jerusalem Post*, 5 October 1997.

24 Figures from *Statistical Abstract of Israel*, editions from 1990–6, Central Bureau of Statistics, Jerusalem.

foresaw Israel providing the technological expertise helping to harness the financial resources of the Gulf States and the labour of Arab and North African countries to develop a Middle Eastern version of the Common Market.[25] There are a number of reasons outlined below why, even during the period of accelerated peace making under the Rabin and Peres governments, such visions did not reflect the political and economic realities of the region.[26]

First, Arab suspicion that Israel's efforts to integrate itself into Middle East and to develop regional financial infrastructures similar to the European Union (EU) model marked an attempt at a form of economic colonisation.[27] These suspicions were partly based on the size of the Israeli economy whose GDP is greater than that of all its Arabs neighbours put together. Second, the majority of trade does not presently take place between counties in the region (Israel–Arab or between Arab countries), but rather between individual countries and external powers, for example the US. Third, the problems of attracting foreign investment in the PA is a problem that is still mirrored in many of the Arab regimes in the region. In addition, there would appear to be little prospect for official investments in the form of a regional development bank due, once more, to Arab fears of potential Israeli domination of such a bank. Fourth, the Arab boycott of Israel has not been lifted despite a partial removal of the secondary boycott in the mid-1990s.

As a result of these factors Israel has still not been fully integrated into the Middle East economic systems and since the election of the Netanyahu government in 1996 the government's concentration has shifted away from attempts at regional integration and trade within the region towards new trading partners in areas such as the new Central Asian Republics to add to the US and EU countries that have been Israel's traditional trading partners. (One further development in regional economic cooperation took place with the Middle East and North Africa Economic Summit in Cairo in November 1996, though Israel's

---

25 Peres outlined this vision in detail in S. Peres, *The New Middle East* (New York, Holt, 1993).

26 For more details on this, see D. Zakheim, 'Economic security after a settlement: the prospects for Israel', *Israel Affairs*, vol. 2, no. 1 (1995), pp. 13–31.

27 On the extremely limited prospects for institutionalising any increased trade links between Israel and the Arabs, see E. Kanovsky, 'Middle East economies and Arab–Israeli peace agreements', *Israel Affairs*, vol. 1, no. 4 (1995), pp. 22–39.

foreign minister, David Levy, concluded his message to the conference by accepting that many obstacles to regional economic integration and development still existed.) In essence, Israel's trade with Turkey (see Chapter 10) and to a lesser degree Jordan (see Chapter 7) has been the exception rather than the rule in the wider Middle East region.

In relation to the second point of Israel's economic ability to withstand an impasse in the peace process, it is clear that foreign investment continued to increase despite the election of Netanyahu and the slowing down of the peace process.[28] For example, the level of foreign investment during the first half of 1997 was $1.4 billion, which was up from $1.3 billion for the corresponding period in 1996.[29] Consequently, from this it can be deduced that the overall Israeli economy is not as vulnerable to the uncertainties and problems in the peace process as the Palestinians'.[30] This view is largely supported by investment banks such as Alex Brown and Sons whose chairman of its Israeli affiliate CEO of Giza, Ze'ev Holtzman, stated that he didn't expect the political situation to affect foreigners' plans to invest in local high-tech industries, even in the short term, as the majority of these high-tech firms' activities are in the international market.[31] Moreover, Stanley Fisher, a leading economist at the International Monetary Fund (IMF) drew similar conclusions in 1997, arguing that Israel's economy was in no danger of crisis unless the Middle East was drawn into political madness.[32] However, some areas of the Israel economy suffer from short-term declines as a result of violence such as suicide bomb attacks. For instance, the tourist industry has experienced a number of problems following upsurges in violence – for

28 A risk analysis of Israel conduct by *Israel Business Arena* in 1997 found that Israel received an overall risk rating of 4.5 (on a sliding scale of 1–10). This score was similar to that of the corresponding period of the previous year. See 'Quarterly risk report', *Israel Business Arena*, 27 July 1997.

29 See *Half Yearly Economic Survey*, Central Bureau of Statistics, Jerusalem, September 1997.

30 Initially, there was a slight fall in the levels of direct foreign investment with daily volumes down by between $5 to $7 million in November 1996. On this, see J. Dempsey, 'Israel waits for Netanyahu to deliver', *Financial Times*, 22 November 1996.

31 Comments reported in E. Winter, 'Business in the Bibi era', *Jerusalem Post*, 25 June 1996.

32 Reported in S. Plotzker, 'Economists around the world say we're doing fine', *Yediot Aharonot*, 26 September 1997.

example, a 15 per cent decline following the wave of bombings in early 1996.[33]

A final factor in the Israel economy which may have limited the peace dividend has been the slow process of economic liberalisation of which the privatisation programme is the centre-piece.[34] Despite the well-documented problems of this process it is clear that the peace process is one of the factors that has made it possible for Israel to sell off state companies and in general terms encourage a reduction in centralised control over the economy.[35] Furthermore, if this process is accelerated, then Israel is likely to attract more foreign investors, providing the political situation has not markedly deteriorated.

Overall, it needs to be stressed that Israeli economic growth during the first part of the 1990s was initially fuelled by the arrival of the Soviet Aliyah which brought some 750,000 new immigrants to Israel.[36] At the same time, Israel's high-tech industries started to expand and it was largely these two factors that led to the Israeli economic growth of on average six per cent a year since 1992. The peace process has helped create a feel good factor for investors in the economy which, in turn, has helped to continue the pattern of sizeable economic growth just as the number of new immigrants arriving from the former Soviet Union has dropped dramatically. However, the economy has shown signs of slowing down towards the end of the decade, but in the context of this study it is important to emphasise that this slow-down has not been primarily caused by any change in the state of the peace process with the change of government in Israel in 1996.

These factors indicate that the Israeli economy has, to a certain degree, benefited from the peace process, but within Israel society these improvements have not been passed on to the poor, mainly the Sephardim population in the development towns. In political terms this group has proven to be the most sceptical about the peace process, and in particular

---

33 Figures published by Central Bureau of Statistics, Jerusalem, 1997.

34 For a detailed analysis of the programme of privatisation in Israel, see 'Privatisation in Israel', prepared by Giza Group, *Israel Business Arena*, October 1996.

35 For more details on the problems of economic liberalisation in Israel, see E. Murphy, 'Structural inhibitions to economic liberalisation in Israel', *Middle East Journal*, vol. 48, no. 1 (1994).

36 On this, see Zilberfarb, 'The Israeli economy in the 1990s: immigration, the peace process, and the medium term prospects for growth', p. 10.

the negotiations with the Palestinians.[37] As early as 1994, Israelis such as the director of the Tel Aviv-based International Centre for Peace in the Middle East, Offer Bronstein, were stressing the necessity for the economic needs of this group to be addressed if the peace process was to succeed in the long run.[38] In addition, though the average living standards of this group did increase during the early 1990s the Rabin-led government did not do enough to explain and illustrate any perceived linkage between the peace process and the improved economic climate. In short, the development of better infrastructure in the development towns with improved roads and services did not persuade the majority of this group as was shown by its support of Netanyahu in the 1996 elections.

As outlined in the opening section of this book, Netanyahu is extremely sensitive to the views of this typical Likud constituency and if he were to make significant political compromises with the Palestinians he would require some economic inducements to help maintain the support of this key group.

Improved economic performance: maximising any peace dividend

One of the major economic problems for the Palestinians that this chapter has attempted to highlight is the continued uncertainty caused by the structure of the Oslo Accords and, in particular, the presence of the interim periods. It is clear that the original reasons for building these stages into the process are no longer as relevant as in 1993.

First, on the issue of territory the PA has not secured the hoped-for percentage of the West Bank before entering Final Status talks. Second, on economic issues the PA has failed to build a strong economy which it hopes can be transformed into a viable independent state. In addition, the interim stages have helped to create a feeling of political uncertainty, which has damaged the prospects for attracting investment. Moreover, the closures imposed by Israel following terrorist attacks have added to the economic difficulties and illustrated to the Palestinians the extent of their economy's dependence on Israel and Israeli markets.

---

37 On this see Lochery, *Israeli Labour Party*.
38 Interview conducted by the author with Offer Bronstein, Tel Aviv, 9 August 1994.

Consequently, there is a need to move towards a rapid Final Status agreement with Israel. This would reduce the period of uncertainty and offer an end to the cycle of closures. In essence, the rationale for the interim stages of gaining more negotiating for the Palestinians in these talks no longer exists. A central element in Netanyahu's strategy has been to lower Palestinian aspirations for the Final Status talks by severely limiting the amount of land that he is willing to hand back in the interim stages agreements.[39] Consequently, the price of economic damage to the PA's economy is not worth paying in order to make potentially minimal political gains.

Second, the PA and Arafat have taken steps to develop their accounting methods after initially failing to satisfy many of the donor nations' demands in this area. However, much more needs to be done if the widely held feeling of major corruption (real or simply perceived) is to be successfully addressed. As previously argued the issue of corruption was cited by many investors as a major reason for the lack of investment in PA areas.

Third, there is a clear and urgent need for the development of modern government in PA areas. Furthermore, this is very apparent in economic laws where rights and ownership need to be more fully protected and enforced by an impartial police force. In short, the Palestinian entity (state) that is formed at the end of Final Status talks will need a programme of radical and rapid transformation of its legal system.

Fourth, the PA needs to develop close economic relationships with its neighbours. Presently, it remains unclear what type of relationship it will develop with Jordan and if such a relationship will become institutionalised in economic areas. However, given the somewhat strained relations between King Hussein and Yasser Arafat, the relationship is likely to encounter political difficulties. However, the King has made it clear that he is ready to help the Palestinians and has no intention of trying to replace the PLO as the representative of the Palestinians.[40]

Fifth, there is a need to develop infrastructure such as a seaport and an airport which will help to lessen the dependency on using Israeli infrastructure. However, Arafat has shown himself willing to sacrifice the development of such vital infrastructure in order to attempt political

---

39 On Netanyahu's strategy, see Lochery, 'Israel's political Houdini'.
40 See Inbari, 'Economics and the Palestinian question'.

advantage. (For example, prior to the so-called London Conference hosted by Tony Blair in May 1998 officials in the Netanyahu office confirmed that agreements were reached about an airport, a seaport and the development of a major industrial park on the Gaza Border, but Arafat blocked them in order to attempt to apply maximum political pressure on Israel.) This strategy is misplaced, though to a degree understandable, and is highly damaging for Palestinian economic prospects.

Overall, there is a fundamental need to redress the balance between political (nationalist) aspirations and economic realities. Arafat's strategy is simple and clear – attempt to maximise political concessions from Israel (through negotiations and international pressure). However, in pursuing this strategy the question of economic development has appeared, at times, to be of secondary importance. Moreover, as outlined earlier in this chapter the economic development of the West Bank and the Gaza Strip will have a direct effect on the type of Palestinian entity (state) that finally emerges.

Israel needs to contribute much more to the economic development of the Palestinian entity. Moreover, it is clearly in Israel's interests that the Palestinians' economy improves and that the Oslo Accords are seen to be delivering improved economic prospects rather than the decline that has been apparent during the interim stage. However, it is difficult to foresee any Israeli government not imposing closures on PA areas following terrorist attacks launched from PA-controlled areas against Israel. Within Israel such security measures are not only popular, but also considered to be the minimum action required by its government. Consequently, it is unlikely that Israel will abandon these security measures despite the economic damage they inflict on the Palestinian economy and their questionable security value to Israel.[41]

---

41 Netanyahu affirmed that the Palestinian economy made a marked improvement in early 1998, and accepted the argument that the Israeli closures have had a strong negative impact on the Palestinian economy. However, he gave no indication that the closures would not be re-imposed if there were further terrorist attacks. In a meeting with the US Under-Secretary of State for Economic Affairs, Stuart Eizenstat on 14 June 1998 the prime minister stated the following: 'We see the improvement in the economic situation of the Palestinians. I can report that 1998 will be the first year since the Oslo agreement was signed in which there has been a rise in the Palestinian GNP. This contrasts with previous years, when terrorism had an adverse affect on the Palestinian economy. In the past two years, as a result of the decline in acts of terrorism and the liberal policy

However, economic cooperation needs to be more fully developed and not totally held hostage to the political negotiations.[42] On the positive side, there is an increasing awareness of this need by the Netanyahu government and this was summarised by the finance minister, Dan Meridor:

> The Palestinian economy must be brought back on track. For this to be achieved there has to be openness, coordination and willingness to take part in the process. Each side has to do what is demanded of it by the agreements.[43]

we have adopted, the Palestinian economy has returned to growth, and the numbers show this.' Meeting of Netanyahu with Eizenstat, 14 June 1998, the Prime Minister's Office, Jerusalem.

42 One major instance of economic progress being held hostage to problems was Arafat's stalling of a joint industrial park on the Gaza border in early 1998 in order to attempt to exert maximum international pressure on Israel in negotiations over the size of an Israeli troop redeployment in the West Bank. An official Israeli report outlined the advantages of the scheme as follows.

E. Industrial areas and investments
1. As part of its efforts to improve the economic situation of the Palestinians, Israel is acting, together with the Palestinian Authority, to build additional industrial parks in Gaza and the West Bank.
2. The concept of joint industrial parks along the dividing line, elaborated several years ago, has several advantages:
    (a) Economic development (Palestinian and Israeli); (b) Reinforcement of Israel–Palestinian economic cooperation; (c) Convenient access for workers and employers; (d) Preventing friction between Palestinian workers and Israelis.
3. One industrial park is in operation today, at Erez. More than 80 enterprises are located there, providing jobs for 3,000 workers from Gaza. Almost half of the enterprises are owned by Palestinian entrepreneurs.
4. The plan to establish an industrial park at the Karni checkpoint (GIE–Gaza Industrial Estate) is in its advanced stages of implementation. Israel has contributed $7.5 million to the project, which is expected to become operative in the middle of 1998. The Karni industrial park, located in territory controlled by the Palestinian Authority, is to serve as the central industrial area of the Gaza Strip and to provide tens of thousands of jobs.
5. Additionally, staff work is being done by the relevant agencies (Ministry of Industry and Trade, Ministry of Defence, Co-ordinator of Government Operations in the Territories) to designate a site for the first joint industrial park in Judea–Samaria.

43 Joint press conference with Dan Meridor and the PA economy, trade and industry minister, Maher Masri, 28 August 1996. Source: Background paper: 'Economic relations between Israel and the Palestinian Authority', Israeli Ministry of Foreign Affairs, Jerusalem, February 1998, p. 1.

On the negative side, such awareness has not yet been fully transformed into more radically needed support to help develop the Palestinian economy.[44] In addition, what attempts there have been were hampered by Arafat's political priorities.

In the Israeli economy there is a need to help improve the economic condition of the poor, and in particular the development towns, where support for the peace process is limited. The electoral strength of this constituency makes it essential to address these problems and to invest in these areas. Possibilities include projects, funded by international organisations and agencies, with the intention of helping underpin support for the peace process such as improved medical care, education, infrastructure and recreational facilities. In addition, the government needs to illustrate the economic advantages of any peace settlement for the Israeli economy. In conducting interviews with senior business figures in leading corporations it was discovered that many were adopting a "wait and see" approach about investing in Israel.[45] Consequently, any final peace deal is likely to lead to an investment boom in Israel, which in turn will help secure the Israeli economy.

Conclusions

The inability to date to deliver an economic peace dividend to the majority of Palestinians in the West Bank and the Gaza Strip represents one of the biggest failures of the Oslo Accords. Moreover, this failure has the potential to severely undermine Palestinian support for the Accords, especially given that the likely outcome of Final Status negotiations will fall short of satisfying Palestinian political aspirations.

In public many Palestinians blame Israel for their economic plight, but in private many more cite the failings of the PA, and in particular

---

44 On Israeli–PA economic cooperation and the help Israel provides to the PA, see Israeli–Palestinian Economic relations update, Israeli Ministry of Foreign Affairs, 25 May 1998.

45 Interviews conducted in London, summer 1997. It should be stressed that many businesses had made initial investments in Israel but were awaiting the outcome of the peace process before making more substantial investments. However, the leader of the British Overseas Trade Group for Israel (BOTGI) argued that providing there was some form of a peace process, investment levels would not drop.

Arafat, to build the necessary modern system of government, and the failure to root out corruption both from within the PA and wider Palestinian economic society. In addition, Arafat's insistence on personal control over much of the economic decision-making process has not helped the situation.

In reality, the seemingly worsening problems of the Palestinian economy have been caused by a number of factors which have previously been outlined in this chapter: the structure of the Oslo Accords themselves with the interim stages; the failure of the PA to develop a modern system of government; and the Israeli-imposed closures of the West Bank and Gaza. Consequently, in returning to the central theme of the book it is argued that the election of Netanyahu is not one of the primary reasons behind these Palestinian economic difficulties although his government has actively subscribed to use of closures as a means of collective punishment against the Palestinians. In addition, the only major new development under the Netanyahu government of imposing economic sanctions on the PA following a suicide bomb attack in Jerusalem was of limited effect. Pressure from the US and the EU ensured that these sanctions were short term in nature. In addition, the main reason for imposing them was simply to illustrate a new tougher approach by Netanyahu to his domestic audience rather than any belief that the sanctions would achieve their aim of persuading Arafat to dismantle the terrorist infrastructure in PA areas.

In essence, the Netanyahu government's policy towards the PA economy has been twofold. First, it ensures that the Palestinian economy remains deeply dependent on Israel. Moreover, this functionalist approach of Netanyahu to the future status of the West Bank draws a great deal from Moshe Dayan's vision of the economic tying together of the Palestinian economy to that of Israel in order to ensure a high degree of Israeli economic control over the Palestinians. In this respect the Netanyahu government has been keen to promote joint infrastructure projects with the PA such as the building of a new industrial park on the Gaza–Israel border, but less enthusiastic in allowing the development of independent Palestinian economic infrastructure such as the creation of a seaport and new international airport in Gaza.

Second, it helps to ensure that the PA economy did not develop at a rate that would open the possibility for a strong and genuinely independent Palestinian entity (state) to emerge from Final Status talks.

At the same time, the Israelis did not want a breakdown in social order in PA areas caused by economic deprivation with the resultant outbreak of violence (in all probability directed against Israeli targets) and the potential overthrow of Arafat and his replacement by more radical elements. In simple terms, the Israeli government has, for example, sought to encourage investment in the PA but not helped to create the types of condition that would help to attract this investment (through, say, a quicker lifting of the closures).

Within Israel the failure of a major economic peace dividend, although less serious than within Palestinian society, has none the less damaged support for the peace process from the poor mainly Sephardim constituency. Moreover, the plight of this group is often overlooked both in Israel and by Arab decision makers. However, this group remains a demographically increasingly important constituency whose votes largely determine the outcome of Israel elections, and consequently their economic problems must be successfully addressed if any Israeli government is to make difficult, and perhaps unpopular, political compromises in Final Status talks.

Finally, having outlined the economic problems and their linkage to the political process there is a clear case for the political process to be accelerated in order to end the period of uncertainty that is damaging the economy of the PA and, to a lesser degree, that of Israel as well. Furthermore, it has been strongly argued that the initial rationale behind the insertion of the interim stages into the Oslo Accords, namely to allow the development of economic infrastructure in PA-controlled areas, has not been successful. Consequently, it is vital that a Final Status agreement is arrived at quickly so that the Palestinian entity's status and borders are known. As a result, it is hoped that investment levels will rise as investors gain more confidence as one of the major sources of uncertainty is removed.

5

The Palestinian refugees: post-Oslo, continuity and developments

The issue of the Palestinian refugees remains one of the most emotive, complex and important issues of the Israeli–Palestinian negotiations which needs to be resolved in the Final Status negotiations. As an Israeli daily newspaper, the *Jerusalem Post*, put it during the negotiations following the Madrid Conference which marked the start of the current peace process:

> Resolving the problem [refugees] is arguably the most crucial prerequisite for progress towards peace. Without resettlement of refugees – both those living in Israel and the administered territories and those in surrounding countries – all talk of ending terrorism and bringing stability to the region is futile.[1]

The issue would appear to be similarly recognised by the Palestinian leadership as Yasser Arafat argued:

> On the political level, the refugee issue will continue to be a hot and vital issue until the rights of Palestinian refugees are fulfilled. A just and lasting peace cannot be achieved without resolving the problem of the refugees by enabling them to return to their lands.[2]

Furthermore, there are two additional factors that complicate the difficult negotiations on refugees: first, making a distinction between 1948 refugees (displaced during or as a result of Israel's War of Independence in 1948) and the 1967 refugees (displaced during or as a result of the Six Day War in June 1997); and second, the problem in agreeing on the actual number of displaced persons for both the 1948 and 1967 refugees.

---

1 Editorial, 'The PLO and the refugees', *Jerusalem Post*, 11 October 1992.
2 Y. Arafat, *Al-Ayyam* newspaper, 29 December 1997.

Unsurprisingly, the Palestinian figure is much higher than the corresponding Israeli estimate, which does not include any offspring of the refugees.

In essence, one of the central features of the negotiations has been attempts at devising a criterion for agreeing who is a refugee and who is not. Central to this debate is the issue of the right of return of the 1948 refugees. The majority of these people were displaced from homes that today lie within the legally recognised international borders of Israel itself. As a result, this issue continues to prove a highly emotional matter for both Israel – which categorically refuses to accept the principle of the right of return – and for the Palestinians – many of whom are today living in squalid conditions in refugee camps in Lebanon and other Arab countries. Within Israel, the principle of denying the right of return is solidly agreed by all the main Zionist parties across the political spectrum and this reflects the feelings of the vast majority of Israeli society.[3] For instance, article 3.1.7 of the Labour Party's platform for elections to the 14th Knesset states:

> Settlement of the Palestinian refugees problem outside the borders of Israel, rejecting the right of return.[4]

Moreover, any possibility of compromise on this issue by Israel has been rejected by leading figures in the peace process such as Yossi Beilin who argued categorically that the 1948 refugees would not be allowed to return as part of any Final Status agreement and that the old UN Resolution 194[5] on the issue is now redundant because so much has changed on the ground since it was framed.[6] In practical terms, there would appear to be little prospect of this group being able to return to their original homes in communities in Israel (many of which do not exist today) and Israeli governments are fearful of this group relocating to Palestinian Authority controlled areas in the West Bank and Gaza.[7]

3 For more details on this consensus and the call for a debate in Israel on the right of return, see G. Levi, 'The time has come to face up to the fearsome right of return for refugees', *Shaml Newsletter*, no. 8 (October 1997).
4 Quoted from article 3.1.7, *The Israel Labour Party's Peace and Security Platform for Elections to the 14th Knesset*, Labour Party Headquarters Tel Aviv, 1996, p. 2.
5 For a Palestinian perspective on UN Resolution 194, see the editorial, 'Israeli myths on refugees', *Shaml Newsletter*, no. 9 (December 1997).
6 See Y. Beilin, 'Principles for negotiations', *Ha-Aretz*, 10 August 1994.
7 The successive Israeli governments' refusal to accept the right of return has been based on first, the previously discussed problems of defining who is a refugee;

From a Palestinian perspective, Yasser Arafat and the Palestinian Liberation Organization (PLO) argue that the right of return for the 1948 refugees is holy, but Palestinian moderates state that although the right of return remains a principle, they accept that some form of compensation may be the only way to recognise the principle.[8] Consequently, in light of the fact that there is little chance that Israel will radically shift its position on the 1948 refugees, the reality for Arafat is that he has two options: first, to pursue this issue and risk derailing any peace process with Israel; or second, in stark terms to sacrifice this group in order to advance the standards and prospects of those Palestinians living under PA control and potentially also those of the 1967 refugees.[9]

From an Israeli perspective, its position is defined by two central fears about a potential mass relocation of the 1948 refugees to Palestinian-controlled areas in the West Bank and the Gaza Strip. The first is what is termed as a Lebanonisation of the PA entity (state), where central authority collapses due to the weight of internal conflicts and struggles.[10]

---

second, the legal status of this group; and third, the security issue. On the latter an official government publication argues: "Until quite recently, the overwhelming majority of Arab states and Palestinian organisations actively sought to undermine the very existence of Israel as a state. Even now, as the peace process is evolving, there are Palestinians – including elements within the PLO – who remain opposed to peace, and who will use violent means to express their opposition. The entry into Israel of masses of refugees would pose a very real threat to security, law and order, and the viability of Israel's social fabric, as well as to the demographic viability of Israel as the world's only Jewish state." From 'The refugee issue: a background paper', Government of the State of Israel, Jerusalem, October 1994.

8 For more details on the internal Palestinian debate over the issue of the right of return and potential compensation for the refugees, see J. Immanuel, 'Palestinian conference rejects compensation for refugees', *Jerusalem Post*, 22 September 1996.

9 Many Palestinians always suspected that Arafat made this choice by signing the Oslo agreements and consequently this has been reflected in opinion polls in the camps in Lebanon where the majority of respondents reject the Oslo Accords believing that they will not bring them back to their homes. On Arafat's choice and Palestinian opinion in Lebanon, see E. Ya'ari, 'Neighbourhood watch: the formula', *Jerusalem Report*, 4 June 1995.

10 On this, see the work of Shai Feldman – for example, S. Feldman and A. Toukan, *Bridging the Gap: A Future Security Architecture for the Middle East* (Lanham, Maryland and Oxford, Rowan and Littlefield, 1997), p. 12.

In this scenario, Palestinian groups and factions would continue their opposition to the Jewish state through acts of terrorism launched from within the PA entity. As a result, Israel would be faced with the nightmare situation of not only having to deal with radical Islamic groups on its doorstep, but also all the old rejectionist Palestinian groups (largely based in Lebanon and Damascus) who do not accept the concept of Israel's right to exist. If such a situation were to occur it is difficult not to foresee Israel re-deploying the IDF in the Palestinian areas and after a bloody battle once more assuming direct control over the Palestinian population.

Israel's second fear concerns the argument that if a fully independent Palestinian state were able to absorb the refugees in large numbers, and particularly those from 1948, then this could be seen as a threat to Israel's existence. The principle of the right of return for Palestinians to their communities that were left in the 1948 war still remains the official policy of the PLO and consequently this Palestinian entity (state) could attempt to regain control over the land lost in the 1948 war. Moreover, Arafat does not help to alleviate this fear in his speeches which talk of the Oslo agreements marking only the next stage of the battle to reunite all of Palestine (that is, the destruction of Israel).[11]

Consequently, as it appears almost certain that Israel will block the right of return to the 1948 refugees this chapter will examine the question of the 1948 refugees within the framework of the potential for a compensation package in the form of international aid distributed collectively or individually. Moreover, despite the seemingly physical impossibility of these refugees returning, this does not mean that the

---

11 Arafat has referred to the Oslo agreements as a temporary truce in the battle – for example: "**Question**: Do you feel sometimes that you made a mistake in agreeing to Oslo? **Arafat**: No . . . no. Allah's messenger Mohammed accepted the al-Khudaibiya peace treaty and Salah a-Din accepted the peace agreement with Richard the Lion-Hearted." (Note: Arafat is referring to the Khudaibiya agreement made by Muhammad with the Arabian tribe of Koreish. The pact, slated to last for ten years, was broken within two years, when the Islamic forces – having used the peace pact to become stronger – conquered the Koreish tribe. His reference to Salah a-Din is to the Muslim leader who, after a cease-fire, declared a jihad against the Crusaders and captured Jerusalem. This marked the second time in a month that Arafat compared the Oslo Accords with the temporary truces signed by Muhammad and Salah a-Din. Previously, he made the comparison in an interview with Egyptian Orbit TV on 18 April 1998.) Interview with Yasser Arafat in *Al-Quds*, 10 May 1998.

issue is not significant in the overall context of the negotiations. In short, it has been used by the PA in the negotiations as, at the very minimum, a trade-off card and consequently this chapter also examines how this has worked to date.

The issue of the 1967 refugees refers to those Palestinians who were displaced by the fighting in 1967 and Israel's conquest of East Jerusalem, the West Bank and the Gaza Strip. This issue, though extremely complex, does not entail the refugees returning to within Israel itself, but rather to areas such as the West Bank which are likely to come under the control of the PA entity (state) that emerges as a result of Final Status negotiations. On this issue, there would appear more potential for compromise between the two sides, but to date the negotiations have not moved forward a great deal since the signing of the Oslo Accords. However, since the setting up of committees under the original remit of the Madrid Conference in 1991 there has been little progress to date on the issue regardless.

The numbers game: problems on agreeing the definition of a refugee

In terms of the 1948 refugees, Israel recognises 590,000 refugees from that war while Palestinian sources suggest a figure of 2.5 million including offspring. Regarding the 1967 refugees, the negotiations have revolved around defining who is a refugee. International and Palestinian estimates have traditionally been some four times higher than Israeli figures.[12] The Israeli government estimates that the number of displaced persons from the 1967 war is between 200,000 and 220,000, which does not include the offspring of this group.[13] Moreover, during the negotiations Israel has consistently stated that it does not recognise the right of return for these offspring. However, the Palestinians do include offspring in their displaced persons definition and their total is over 800,000, which is based on those who are registered in Jordan – the country where most of them currently live.[14] The United Nations Relief and Works Agencies

---

12 See, for example, J. Immanuel, 'Abu Mazen call for state at final status talks', *Jerusalem Post*, 6 May 1996.
13 Israeli figures from Israeli Ministry of Foreign Affairs, Jerusalem, 1995.
14 Palestinian figures from Palestinian Authority, Gaza, 1995.

(UNRWA) suggests a figure of a total of over 3.3 million refugees who are registered with the organisation (see Table 5.1 for complete figures).

TABLE 5.1
Palestinian refugees registered with UNRWA, 1996

Field	In camps	Not in camps	Total
Jordan	242,922	1,115,784	1,358,706
West Bank	147,302	385,136	532,438
Gaza	378,279	338,651	716,930
Lebanon	182,731	169,937	352,668
Syria (SAR)	89,472	257,919	347,391
Total all fields	1,040,706	2,267,427	3,308,133[a]

Source: UNWRA, 1996
Note: (a) Figure includes 604,220 refugees displaced from the West Bank and Gaza (8,379 from Gaza).

Unofficial Palestinian sources place the figure higher claiming that there is a total of nearly 5 million Palestinian refugees in the world in 1998 (see Table 5.2). The difference in the figures between the Israelis, official organisations and various Palestinian groups is significant. In the event of any Final Status agreement between Israel and the Palestinians it is highly probable that a compensation package for Palestinian refugees will be included in the deal. Consequently, the number of refugees, and the rationale employed for defining the term, will in part determine the amount of compensation that the international community will pay the Palestinians.

Currently, under the provisions of the Oslo Accords some 10,000 people (2,000 families) have been allowed to return each year under the framework of family reunification. (By 1998 some 100,000 Palestinians had returned under this framework.) In addition, many people who had previously been expelled by Israel have returned with their families to serve as policemen and PA officials.[15] However, in the long term there are

---

15 On this, see J. Immanuel, 'Refugee talks could set precedent', *Jerusalem Post*, 7 March 1995.

TABLE 5.2
Unofficial estimated number of Palestinian refugees

Place of refugees	(1998) All population	Of which: refugees
Israel	953,497	(200,000 internal)
Gaza Strip	1,004,498	766,124
West Bank	1,596,554	652,855
Jordan	2,328,308	1,741,796
Lebanon	430,183	408,008
Syria	465,662	444,921
Egypt	48,784	40,468
Saudi Arabia	274,762	274,762
Kuwait	37,696	34,370
Other Gulf States	105,578	105,578
Iraq, Libya	74,284	74,284
Other Arab countries	5,544	5,544
The Americas	203, 588	173,050
Other countries	259,248	220,361
Total	7,788,186	4,942,121

Source: Palestinian Diaspora and Refugee Centre, Shaml, 1996

a number of factors that are likely to restrict the levels of the return of the 1967 refugees to PA entity (state). The question of the return of the 1967 displaced persons was included in the 1979 Camp David agreement between Egypt and Israel which stated:

> During the transitional period, representatives of Egypt, Israel, Jordan and the self-governing authority will constitute a continuing committee to decide by agreement on the modalities of admission of persons displaced from the West Bank and Gaza in 1967, together with the necessary measures to prevent disruption and disorder.

The wording of Article 12 of the Oslo Accords is almost exactly the same. In essence, both the Rabin–Peres and Netanyahu governments in Israel argue that the number of returnees should be limited by the capacity of the PA to absorb them. Without such limitations the Israeli government argues that their return could lead to economic and security problems.

In addition, at some later stage Israel may offer financial compensation to those Palestinians who decide not to return. From a Palestinian perspective there are two key points: first, the PA claims that most of the

1967 refugees have families who live in PA-controlled areas with whom they can stay and therefore the absorption will not present any major economic or security problems.[16] Second, the PA accepts the principle for a timetabled return of this group over a period of years. The PA's acceptance of some form of timetable suits both itself through not imposing impossible strains on its ability to provide work and housing for the returnees, and helps to alleviate Israeli concerns about a rapid mass return and the previously mentioned problems which Israel fears will arise as a result of this.

The question of Jewish refugees in the context of a settlement for the Palestinians

Although it goes beyond the scope of this study to present the detailed arguments surrounding the responsibility of Arab states for creating a Jewish refugee problem from Arab states following the 1948 war, it is none the less important to stress the fact that the refugee problem was not from the outset a one-way affair. The figures in Table 5.3 illustrate the level of Jewish emigration from specific Arab countries between Israel's Declaration of Independence and 1972.

TABLE 5.3
Number of Jewish immigrants to Israel from the Middle East and North Africa, 1948–1972

Morocco	260,000
Iraq	127,000
Tunisia	56,000
Yemen	51,000
Libya	35,600
Egypt	29,000
Algeria	14,500
Lebanon	6,000
Syria	4,500
Afghanistan	4,500
Total	**588,100**

Source: Israeli Ministry of Foreign Affairs, Jerusalem, October 1994

16 For a detailed analysis on the restraints and possibilities for integration of the this group of refugees, see N. Van-Hear, 'Reintegration of the Palestinian returnees', *Shaml Monographs*, no. 6 (February 1997).

Although there were a number of push and pull factors that affected individual decisions to emigrate to Israel, ranging from economic to ideological, it is argued that there was a clear pattern of persecution and enforced expulsions of Jews in many of the above countries. As a result, though the total number remains considerably less than international estimates of the number of Palestinian refugees, the figures still represent a large number of people that Israel had to absorb. From an Israeli perspective the linkage between the Jewish and Arab refugees has been made by Israeli governments which was summarised in an official paper in 1994 stating:

> Clearly it is unjustified, both morally and historically, to expect Israel to carry the burden of rehabilitating both Jews and Arabs who became refugees in the wake of the Arab refusal to accept the right of Israel's existence.[17]

In addition, the cost of absorbing Jewish emigrants from Arab countries was put at around $10.88 billion by organisations such as the World Organisation of Jews from Arab Countries (WOJAC) and the American Jewish Committee.[18] Though Israel has ideologically welcomed, and indeed encouraged, such immigration, two points need to be stressed: first, the Arab countries made no contribution to the cost of absorbing those Jews who were forced to leave their countries of origin; and second, the vast majority of these Jews cannot return to their countries of origin if they so wished.

The refugee issue under the Netanyahu government in Israel

The negotiations over the question of refugees has been a victim of the impasse in the Israeli–Palestinian track of the peace process. The absence of the Final Status talks, which were scheduled to begin in May 1996, meant that the status of the 1948 refugees was not discussed (the 1948 refugees are due to be discussed only in the Final Status talks). In addition, the atmosphere of mutual suspicion and mistrust which has characterised the entire Israeli–Palestinian track since 1996 meant that

---

17 .'The Refugee Issue: a background paper', p. 18.
18 Figures available from the organisations and are for the period 1948–86.

there was little progress in dealing with the question of the 1967 refugees.[19] In addition, from an Israeli perspective, the refugee question has been at the centre of attempts by the Netanyahu government to lower the expectations of the Palestinians which the current Israeli government believes were too high, encouraged by the previous Labour-led governments in Israeli. In essence, the Netanyahu government has made it clear that there is no prospect of a return for the 1948 refugees and it will insist on strong controls over any re-settlement of the Palestinians who were displaced in 1967.

From a Palestinian perspective there has been a growing awareness of two factors: first, the need to exploit the refugee issue to the maximum effect for domestic political consumption; and second, a feeling that Palestinian aspirations on this issue are unlikely to be fulfilled, and consequently, the PA leadership is likely to be faced by the brutal choice, outlined earlier in this chapter, of choosing between accepting a semi-imposed agreement on this issue by the Netanyahu government with the probable support of the US or rejecting such a deal with all the ramifications that that would have for the Palestinian nationalist agenda.

In the absence of substantive negotiations between the PA and the Israeli government during the first years of the Netanyahu era in Israel, a number of private peace proposals for Final Status (including details on

---

19 This situation was largely confirmed in the Report of the Commissioner-General of the United Nations Relief and Works Agency for Palestine Refugees in the Near East, 1 July 1996 – 30 June 1997, General Assembly Official Records – Fifty-second Session, Supplement no. 13 (A/52/13), which stated: "The regional environment in which the Agency worked was characterised by a deterioration in the peace process and a marked increase in violence affecting Israel and the occupied territory. In that context, Agency operations in the West Bank and Gaza Strip continued to face constraints arising from measures imposed by the Israeli authorities invoking security-related considerations . . . By mid-1997, the peace process was widely acknowledged to be in deep crisis, and despite signs of cooperation the prevailing atmosphere was one of tension and mistrust. Further redeployments of Israeli forces in the West Bank, as called for in the Interim Agreement, had not taken place. Moreover, after having been formally opened on 5 May 1996, the permanent status negotiations, which were to include the issue of refugees, were repeatedly postponed and still had not commenced in substance by the end of June 1997. In that context, the prospect of a solution to the Palestine refugee problem as foreseen in previous agreements between the parties, and with that the eventual completion of the Agency's mission, appeared increasingly remote."

proposals for the refugees) have been put forward in Israel. The first of these was the Beilin–Eitan plan for a final agreement with the Palestinians in 1996, which is noteworthy for two reasons: first, it reflected the first cross-party attempt in Israel at framing an Israeli position for the Final Status talks; and second, because of the presence of one of the major architects of the original Oslo process, Yossi Beilin in the group. Members of the group included members of the Knesset (MKs) from both the Labour Party and Likud (led by the Likud chairman of the Knesset faction and subsequently Minister of Science, Michael Eitan), academics and senior retired members of Israel's security forces. The forum that was put together following the murder of Yitzhak Rabin defined its purpose as the following:

> Members of Knesset from the Likud–Gesher–Tsomet faction and from the Labour faction came together with the common objective of clarifying the areas of agreement and disagreement between them regarding the future negotiations with the Palestinians on a permanent settlement. Following a series of discussions and clarifications they have arrived at the conclusion that it is necessary to reach a national consensus on the basis of the following three principles.
>
> 1. It is necessary to continue the dialogue with the Palestinian representatives and to pursue exhaustively every opportunity to achieve a permanent agreement with them. In the framework of such an agreement it is necessary to permit the establishment of a Palestinian entity whose status will be determined in negotiations between the parties and the limits on the sovereignty of which will be discussed in the following sections.
> 2. Under conditions of peace and following the achievement of an agreement on the issue of the permanent settlement, the State of Israel must preserve its ability to prevent every attack or risk of an attack on its territorial integrity, the safety of its citizens and their property, and in its vital interests in Israel and in the world.
> 3. No agreement signed by the Israeli government can include a commitment to uproot Jewish settlements in the Western Land of Israel, nor will any agreement compromise the rights of the residents to keep their Israeli citizenship and their ties as individuals and as a community with the State of Israel.

The Beilin–Eitan agreement on Final Status negotiations contained the following section, which dealt with the refugee question.

E. Refugees

1. The right of the State of Israel to prevent the entry of Palestinian refugees into its sovereign territory will be recognised.
2. The administration of the entrance of refugees into the Palestinian entity and the limits to that entry will be decided upon during the negotiations of the permanent settlement, within the larger discussion of Israel's security issues.
3. An international organization will be founded, in which Israel will play an important role, with the goal of financing any carrying out of projects for compensation and rehabilitation of the refugees in their places. The organization will also address Israeli claims for reparations for Jewish refugees from Arab countries.
4. Israel and the Palestinian entity, each within its own boundaries, will rehabilitate the refugees on the basis of the disengagement of the UNRWA, the repealing of the refugee status, and the arrangement of housing and employment and housing with international aid. (For Israel this refers to the Shoafat and Kalandia refugee camps in Jerusalem.)
5. Israel will continue its policy of family reunification on the basis of existing criteria.[20]

The five points reflected the likely final position of a centre-ground Israeli government and despite Netanyahu's public criticism of the overall document the section on refugees did not contain any major points that would have alarmed the prime minister. Indeed, it illustrated the common ground between the two major parties in Israel (Likud and Labour) on the issue of blocking any return of 1948 refugees and the previously discussed linking of any entrance of refugees into the Palestinian entity to discussions on Israeli security. Moreover, from an Israeli perspective the Beilin-Eitan plan goes as far as any Israeli government is likely to move on the refugee issue during Final Status negotiations. In fact, Netanyahu criticised the agreement for two reasons:

---

20 Quoted from Beilin–Eitan Agreement: National Agreement Regarding the Negotiations on the Permanent Settlement with the Palestinians.

first, the presence of the leading dove, Yossi Beilin; and second, to help placate criticism from the right in Israel and in particular right-wing parliamentary and extra-parliamentary pressure groups who were alarmed that the forum would hijack the debate on Final Status positions within Israel.[21]

A similar exercise conducted by the Israeli pressure group Peace Now and the Egyptian Peace Movement in June 1998 arrived at more radical conclusions. The seven-point plan, which came out of a series of meetings in Cairo in June 1998, called for the formation of a Palestinian state and an abandonment of Israeli settlements that fell within the boundaries of the new state. In addition, it included a section on refugees which argued that the Palestinian state should be allowed to absorb the 1948 refugees and displaced Palestinians from the 1967 war. Moreover, the refugees should also receive compensation from the international community.[22]

Although the plan was not devised or endorsed by any Israeli political party its importance should not be under-estimated. However, the plan's seven points fail to discuss any detailed provisions for how the settlement of the refugees would be undertaken. Consequently, the plan reflected more of an attempt to initiate a debate rather than offering any new ideas of the issue. At the centre of the plan was the concept that the Palestinian state should have the right to absorb the 1948 refugees, even if in reality the economic and social constraints would prevent the majority of this group being able to relocate to the Palestinian state. The logic behind this argument is twofold: first, the need to hold out some hope to the refugees in the camps in places such as Lebanon that there is a prospect that they will be able to live under a sovereign Palestinian state; and second, to help prevent a irretrievable split in the Palestinian movement between those who stand to benefit from the Oslo Accords and those who perceive themselves as being sacrificed in the pursuit of the peace process.

---

21 The major source of alarm was not over any issue of substance but the suspicion on the right of such personalities as Yossi Beilin, who the right always accuse of having hidden agendas on the peace process.

22 On this, see AP report, 'Egyptian and Israeli activists propose seven point plan', *Ha-Aretz*, 9 June 1998.

A framework for negotiations over refugee issues

The various committees set up within the framework of the Madrid Peace Conference have made a valuable contribution by creating a limited degree of progress on the complex issues involving refugees. However, progress has been impeded by the structure and public domain of many of these committees which tended to encourage posturing and a playing to domestic audiences. Consequently, these lengthy negotiations need to be continued but there is a clear need for a higher, more centralised level of negotiation to reach agreement on the substantive issues. In essence, the negotiations over refugees would likely benefit from secret discussions with a third party (US and EU) in which an overall framework could be agreed upon for the potential return of the 1967 refugees and/or compensation.[23] Regarding the 1948 refugees, as outlined earlier in this chapter, Israel's position is likely to preclude any return of this group to Israel and in the short term will block a mass return to the Palestinian entity. In addition, regardless of any internationally financed compensation package to which Israel agrees for this group there would still remain difficulties with the question of the right of return which Israel will not accept and which the PA leadership is not (publicly) able to abandon. The Final Status agreement on 1948 refugees would have probably resembled the three points below if an agreement on refugees had been reached.

Three point negotiated framework to the 1948 refugee issue at Final Status talks

1. Israel agrees to a compensation package for the 1948 refugees to be funded by international community.
2. Israel insists that this package does not mean that it recognises the right of return of the 1948 refugees.
3. The PA accepts the package but insists that it will not revoke the right of return which will remain (in theory) a principle and an aspiration.

There are two conditions that are required for such an agreement. The first is a high level of trust between the two parties, for point three will entail a certain degree of constructive ambiguity if it is to work. In essence,

---

23 The US and EU are put forward as the most probable two third parties as they are likely to be two of the major contributors to funding the compensation package.

Israel will have to trust Arafat and the PA that the issue of right of return will not be used by the Palestinians in an attempt to extract further concessions from Israel in the post-settlement period. The second is that Israel would have to accept a degree of public rhetoric from Palestinian leaders (and Arafat in particular) that the right of return will be pursued and that it remained an important issue in the Palestinian struggle. In short, Arafat would need to continue the balancing act that he has to date been forced to do throughout the Oslo process between presenting assurances to the Israelis and not totally alienating the 1948 refugees, the majority of whom reject the Oslo Accords as a sell out. Moreover, some hope would have to be given to the Arab states where the majority of these refugees are located that there would be some possibility of long-term hope of these refugees leaving the host country. In essence, countries such as Lebanon wish to avoid any moves that would lead to a permanent settlement of the refugees in their respective countries, which could lead to political de-stabilisation and unwelcome changes in the demographic balances of power in these states.[24]

Returning to the central theme of the book the major differences between the Rabin–Peres government and the Netanyahu-led adminis-tration are not in the substance of an agreement on the question of refugees, but rather in the use of ambiguity and a lack of faith in Arafat. In short, Peres and, to a lesser degree Rabin, maintained that Arafat was a real partner for peace and that he would keep his side of the bargain on issues such as potential agreements on the refugees. In addition, the Labour-led government appeared more inclined to offer Arafat more freedom of manoeuvre in order for him to address his domestic audience with statements that were not in the spirit of the Oslo agreements. As a result, the basic three-point plan, despite all its deficiencies, could have been successfully implemented within the wider framework of an overall agreement on all the outstanding issues to be discussed during Final Status talks.

However, one of the pillars of the Netanyahu-led government policy is the attempted removal of much of the ambiguity that is enshrined within the Oslo Accords. In short, this means that there are limited prospects for an agreement of point three under the Netanyahu government. In

---

24 For more on this, see Yakan, 'From war to peace, prospects and implications of the Middle East peace process'.

essence, the lack of trust and bad faith between the Netanyahu government and PA between 1996 and 1998 have further heightened the difficulties in reaching accommodation on such complex issues as the refugees, and in particular the thorny question of the return of the 1948 refugees.

Within the wider Final Status negotiations the Israeli government fears that if the refugee issue remains the only issue that has not been resolved then the Palestinians, at some later date, will attempt to re-introduce the issues of the right of return at a time when Israel has already made all the concessions on other issues. At this time, Israel would have no additional cards at the table to play and the PA could once more attempt to mobilise international pressure to apply on Israel to make further compromises on the issue of refugees, despite that fact that Final Status agreement was already being implemented.[25] Hence, it is on the question of constructive ambiguity of the refugee issue that the major difference lies between the past Labour-led Israeli governments and the present Netanyahu administration.

However, in once more highlighting the increasing complications in the peace process, regardless of government, it would have been highly probable that the relationship between any Labour-led government and the PA would have placed an enormous strain during Final Status talks. As a result, it is not inconceivable that there would have been a similar reluctance from Peres, or particularly Rabin, to reduce the potential for ambiguity on the refugee issue.

In summary, despite the presence of numerous committees on the issue of refugees the overall framework of a settlement is best worked out in secret negotiations where the two parties can work on practical solutions to the existing problems that have been outlined above. In addition, such a setting would help to minimise the potential for political showboating and help to reduce the prospect of violent attacks by rejectionist groups during the sensitive negotiations. Moreover, such reasoning provided the impetus for Netanyahu to call for the accelerated Final Status talks to discuss the refugee issue along with that of borders, settlements and the status of Jerusalem.[26] However, Arafat and the PA have

---

25 This fear was conveyed to the author by senior past and present Israeli negotiators in interviews conducted in June 1998.

26 Netanyahu's call for fast-track negotiations was backed by many in the opposition Labour Party including the senior figure of Yossi Beilin. On this, see Lochery, 'Israel's political Houdini'.

proved reluctant to enter into such talks for a number of reasons not related to the refugee issue, but which concern the other elements of Final Status negotiations.

Conclusions

Under the Netanyahu government in Israel there remain a number of difficulties in the negotiations on refugees such as defining who actually is a refugee and how many Palestinian refugees there are in the world. In addition, the negotiations that have taken place to date have been characterised by the refugee issue becoming further intertwined with other Final Status issues such as settlements and border questions. In short, the talks have suffered from the general lack of progress on the Israeli–Palestinian track of the peace process due in part to the increasing bad faith and lack of trust between the Netanyahu-led government and Arafat. This has largely been caused by disagreements over the expansion of the Jewish settlement programme and delays in agreeing Israeli withdrawals from the West Bank and not by issues directly related to the refugee issue.

This chapter, in suggesting ways of dealing with, and reaching agreement on, the refugee issue, has drawn two major conclusions: first, on the type of negotiations required to maximise the potential for progress on the issue; and second, the need for mechanisms for dealing with the question of the theoretical right of return of the 1948 refugees in order to prevent it from wrecking an overall agreement on refugees.

Secret negotiations, it is argued, provide the best opportunity for conducting negotiations away from the spotlight of an ever-increasingly demanding media keen to exploit points of division between the parties and, at times, push their own political agendas. In addition, as discussed in the first part of this book, Netanyahu's relatively weak domestic position makes it essential that elements from within his own ruling coalition and Cabinet should not be allowed to wreck the prospects for an agreement on this highly emotive issue. Moreover, this is just as important for Arafat who is faced with strong internal opposition to what many Palestinians call the sell out to Israel. Furthermore, it is difficult to imagine the rejectionist Palestinian groups refraining from damaging attacks during public negotiations which are likely to seal the fate of these groups' supporters in the camps in Lebanon and elsewhere in the region.

The right of return would appear to be the largest obstacle to an overall agreement and this chapter has charted a highly pragmatic way of not allowing this issue to damage the prospects of an overall agreement on the issue. However, as discussed, such a use of constructive ambiguity requires a high degree of trust and good faith from the two parties which, during the first years of the Netanyahu administration, has not been apparent from either side.

In reality, the final outcome of the refugee issue is directly linked to what type of Palestinian entity (state) emerges from either a Final Status agreement with Israel (or from a unilateral declaration of independence). In essence, the ability of the new entity (state) to absorb the refugees will depend on both economic and political factors. Regarding the former, the economic state of the Palestinian economy is central to the PA's ability to have the financial resources to make such a relocation of vast numbers of refugees viable (see Chapter 4). Regarding the latter, political factors include the degree of independence the entity (state) has secured and the amount of territory it commands in the West Bank and the Gaza Strip (see Chapter 3).

In addition, the extent that the PA has to compromise on other issues such as refugees to maximise the prospect of a viable state in Final Status talks will also help to determine the fate of the refugees. In this respect, this chapter has attempted to highlight the increasing set of difficult choices for Arafat surrounding the key problems of whether the issue of refugees should be allowed to prevent the attainment of the basic Palestinian nationalist aspiration of a homeland.

From an Israeli perspective, it is abundantly clear that the Netanyahu government has every intention of blocking the return of the vast majority of both 1948 and 1967 refugees to the Palestinian entity (state) for a number of reasons, which have been outlined in this chapter. Moreover, such a position is not new, and indeed is remarkably similar to that of previous Israeli governments. Furthermore, the nature of the Oslo agreements and, more specifically, the interim agreements contained within the Accords, mean that the Netanyahu government has attempted to use mechanisms such as making a strong stand on refugees in order to reduce the potential for a strong Palestinian state emerging at the conclusion of Final Status talks. Returning to the theme of the book such tactics are not unique to the Netanyahu government, but rather reflect a continuity in policy from previous Labour-led governments towards the refugee question.

As a result of the complexities and difficulties discussed in this chapter there is a possibility that the refugee issue, notably the right of return, may not be agreed upon within the framework of the Final Status talks but rather left to a post-Final Status period taking the talks well into the next century. Finally, the international community still has a major short- and long-term role to play in helping to resolve the refugee problem. The United States and the European Union as the probable major sources of the potential compensation that will be offered to the refugees under any final agreement have a major role in helping to secure the deal that they will eventually underwrite.

6

The final status of Jerusalem: Israeli continuity under Netanyahu

The question of the future status of Jerusalem is one of the most complex and seemingly intractable problems of the peace process. Since Netanyahu's election victory the question of Jerusalem has remained prominent with events such as the riots, which followed the decision to open a tunnel in the old city in September 1996, and the announcement of plans to build a new housing project at Har Homa in East Jerusalem in March 1997. This chapter therefore covers, first, the detailed public positions of the various Israeli parties towards Jerusalem as outlined in the 1996 elections, and second, an analysis of how the issue of Jerusalem fits into the framework of current Israeli domestic politics – with particular reference to the actions of the present Likud-led government of Binyamin Netanyahu. In addition, it provides a further analysis – that of the negotiations conducted under Shimon Peres about Jerusalem and the reaction of the Israeli right (and Netanyahu in particular) to these secret talks. Moreover, the use that the Likud made of the Jerusalem issue in attacking Peres during the 1996 election campaign is chronicled, as are the effects that this has had on Netanyahu's potential room for manoeuvre. Two Arab perspectives are considered: first, the Palestinians' claim to East Jerusalem and the possibility for compromise on this; and second, the consequences of growing Jordanian unease at potential Palestinian control over the old city and the holy sites.

The issue of Jerusalem is considered to be one of the most emotive, but non-divisive, questions within Israeli society where all the Zionist political parties agree that the city is the eternal capital of the Jewish state and that it will never again be divided. Moreover, such is the strength of feeling towards Jerusalem that parties go to great lengths to establish their commitment to Jerusalem in party programmes and speeches by respective leaders. However, the future status of Jerusalem is scheduled to be discussed in the Final Status talks between the Israeli and Palestinians, which were due to have started in March 1997. In essence, if the Oslo peace process, started by the late Yitzhak Rabin, is to prove successful then clearly some compromise on Jerusalem will have to be reached between the Netanyahu-led government and the Palestinian Authority (PA).[1]

Israeli political parties and Jerusalem

The 1996 Israeli election manifestos illustrate the public positions of the various Zionist parties. The current governing Likud party's manifesto simply stated:

> United and undivided Jerusalem is the capital of the State of Israel. Activities which undermine the status of Jerusalem will be banned, and therefore PLO and Palestinian Authority institutions in the city, including the Orient House, will be closed.[2]

The reference in the second sentence to the closing down of PLO and PA institutions in Jerusalem highlighted what the Likud felt to be a breaking of the spirit of Oslo by the Palestinians in opening offices, and in particular Orient House, which the Likud charged was being used as the Foreign Ministry of the PA. The Israeli Labour Party clearly stated that:

> Jerusalem, capital of the state of Israel and the focal point of the Jewish people, will remain undivided, under Israeli sovereignty.[3]

In addition, the Labour Party went on to argue that during the course of the peace negotiations the government would maintain its position that the areas surrounding Jerusalem – including Ma'ale Adumim, Givat Ze'ev, the Etzion Bloc and the area to the north-west of the Dead Sea

---

1 One of the most comprehensive accounts of the process that led to the Oslo agreements and the centrality of a deal on Jerusalem to the long-term success of the process can be found in D. Makovsky, *Making Peace with the PLO: The Rabin Government's Road to Oslo* (Boulder, Colorado and Oxford, Westview Press, 1996).

2 Quoted from Chapter 1: 'Peace and security', *Likud Party Platform 1996*, Likud Party Headquarters, Tel Aviv.

3 Quoted from 'Peace and security', *The Israel Labour Party Platform for the Elections to the 14th Knesset*.

– would remain under Israeli sovereignty. In essence, both the major parties agreed that Jerusalem would remain undivided and that both would attempt to secure and maintain Israeli control over surrounding areas of the city.

The smaller Zionist parties all made similar references to Jerusalem; even Meretz, the left-wing coalition partner of the Labour Party in government between 1992 and 1996, outlines its position of Jerusalem in the following way:

> Jerusalem, the capital of Israel, will not be divided again. The permanent status of the city, as determined by the peace accords, will take into consideration all of Jerusalem's unique religious, national and ethnic populations.[4]

Moreover, the religious parties, and in particular the more militant National Religious Party (NRP), adopt a hawkish line on Jerusalem. The NRP platform, as well as stating that the status of Jerusalem is non-negotiable and including the additional parts of both the Likud and Labour Party's platforms relating to Jerusalem, deals with the question of east Jerusalem where, as the platform puts it:

> Jewish settlements in East Jerusalem must be broadened and strengthened.[5]

In short, the public positions of the parties towards Jerusalem are, in reality, very similar and reflect what the parties believe to be a common consensus within the wide spectrum of Jewish Israeli society over the status of Jerusalem.

Netanyahu and Jerusalem: an inseparable love affair?

A central theme of Netanyahu's successful election campaign in 1996 was that the Labour Party and its leader, Shimon Peres, were planning to divide Jerusalem as part of the Final Status talks with the PA if it was returned to office. The initial phase of the campaign was full of Likud accusations, some based on fact, others on rumour and gossip among Israel's political "chattering classes", that what was termed as second-strand

---

4 Quoted from *Principles of the Meretz Platform 1996*, Tel Aviv, Meretz Headquarters.
5 Quoted from *National Religious Party Platform 1996*, NRP Headquarters, Jerusalem.

talks had taken place in secret between Israel and the PA, and that agreement had been reached on Final Status issues, including Jerusalem.[6] Moreover, despite continued denials from Peres and the chief Israeli negotiator, Yossi Beilin, to the contrary, the Likud persisted with this line from the very outset of the campaign on 18 February 1996 up to its conclusion at the end of May 1996 in television adverts, speeches and posters. In short, the question of the future status of Jerusalem was used by Netanyahu and the Likud to question the personal credibility of Peres and Labour, and portray Netanyahu as the safe keeper of Jerusalem's future.

To some degree, the Labour Party was well aware of the damage of such attacks against it during the campaign and, consequently, the manifesto dealt with the question of Jerusalem and the surrounding area in greater detail than any of the other major political parties. Moreover, Labour Party leaders constantly reminded the public that it was a Labour-led government, which had given the order to take the old city in the 1967 war, thus reuniting the city. Interestingly, a decision was taken by the leadership to respond to the Likud's attacks by leaking details of the so-called Beilin–Abu Mazen plan at the start of the campaign to bring the issue to a head at an early stage of the campaign. However, the importance of Jerusalem in Israeli domestic politics was illustrated by the Likud's decision to use it as its major weapon to try to inflict damage on Peres and the Labour Party. In the event, the Labour Party was able, to some degree, to combat the attacks on it about Jerusalem, but at a price. Put simply, had Peres and the Labour Party been returned to power in 1996, their room for manoeuvre on Jerusalem would have been greatly reduced due to the more hawkish manifesto commitments it had made about the city in order to deflect the attacks of the Likud.[7] Consequently,

6 For a detailed account of these accusations and the effect on the campaign, see G. Steinberg, 'The impact of the peace process and terror' in D. Elazar and S. Sandler (eds) *Israel at the Polls 1996* (London and Portland, Frank Cass, 1998), pp. 219–20.

7 To some degree the Labour Party position on Jerusalem was undercut by leaders of its left-wing coalition party, Meretz, which appeared at times to present a more flexible position of the future status of the city. Many in the Likud claimed that Meretz was saying what the Labour Party was too afraid to say and that once elected, the Labour Party's position would become more dovish in line with that of Meretz. On this argument, see comments by D. Meridor, *Ha-Aretz*, 8 April 1996, p. 4.

there is little to choose between the two major parties on the Jerusalem issue. Neither wants to, or can make a move towards, compromise without risking alienating the much sought-after centre-ground voters who are against compromise on Jerusalem.

Consequently, Netanyahu's room for manoeuvre on Jerusalem is also extremely limited to some degree as a result of the prominence that he himself and the Likud awarded the issue, and in particular his portrayal as the saviour of Jerusalem during the election campaign. In short, ignoring Netanyahu's personal commitment to Jerusalem, the prime minister is experiencing internal restraints on his ability to act on Jerusalem from all directions in mainstream Israeli political society.[8] Within the Likud there are currently three major factions that can largely be defined by their attitude towards the Oslo process. These are: a faction that supports the peace accords; a second faction that opposes them as well as any contact with the PLO; and a final grouping that is sceptical about the accords, but views them as international agreements that have to be implemented.[9] However, the issue of the non-negotiability of Jerusalem is perhaps the one unifying issue within a party that is still currently attempting to come to terms with the new set of realities that the Oslo process created. Consequently, Netanyahu, who himself is experiencing difficulties with his own party, has been reluctant to publicly diverge from his hard-line electoral statements on the future of Jerusalem.

Indeed, Netanyahu has used meetings of the Likud party organs to make some of his most hawkish statements – for example, in response to Palestinian and world condemnation of the decision to build Jewish housing at Har Homa in Arab Jerusalem he put it to the Central Committee in Tel Aviv on 3 March 1997 that:

> Jerusalem is ours. Whoever asks Israel to give up the unity of Jerusalem does not understand how that chord plays on our hearts . . . We will build everywhere we decide and no one – no one will prevent us.

---

8 See N. Lochery, "The internal restraints on Netanyahu in Israel: The Middle East peace process, 1996–1997", unpublished working paper, University of Exeter.

9 For a detailed account of the internal dynamics of the Likud during this period, see Lochery, *The Israeli Labour Party*.

In addition, in the prime minister's keynote speech to a special joint session of the United States Congress he devoted a whole portion of it to Israel's emotional, historical and political claim on Jerusalem:

> Countless words have been written about the city on the hill [Jerusalem], which represents the universal hope for justice and peace. I live in that city on the hill. And in my boyhood, I knew that city, when it was divided into enemy camps, with coils of barbed wire stretched through its heart. Since 1967, under Israeli sovereignty, united Jerusalem, for the first time in 2,000 years, became the city of peace . . . There have been efforts to re-divide this city by those who claim that peace can come through division – that it can be secured through multiple sovereignties, multiple laws and multiple police forces. This is a groundless and dangerous assumption, which impels me to declare today: there will never be a re-division of Jerusalem. Never. We shall not allow a Berlin Wall to be erected inside Jerusalem. We will not drive out anyone, but neither shall be driven out of any quarter, any neighbourhood, any street of our eternal capital.[10]

This speech set the tone for Netanyahu's government towards Jerusalem during the first two years of his term. Reducing the Palestinian leadership's expectations over Jerusalem became a central plank of Netanyahu's strategy. The prime minister clearly felt that he had inherited a situation where the previous government had first allowed the question of the future status of Jerusalem to be placed on the agenda and second, had stoked Palestinians' aspirations that they stood to gain at least a foothold in East Jerusalem and the old city. As a result, events between 1996 and 1998 need to be viewed in the context of the prime minister attempting to redress the balance back towards a position that he and his government considered more realistic for Israel. The Palestinian side was equally wise to what was happening, and waged a political and public relations war[11] to ensure that Jerusalem remained firmly on the agenda and at the centre of world attention.[12]

---

10 Address by Binyamin Netanyahu to a joint session of Congress, Washington, DC, 10 July 1996.

11 On the question of the PR war, see D. Makovsky and E. Rabin, 'PM's office: we are facing a propaganda war with the Palestinians', *Ha-Aretz*, 14 July 1997.

12 The Palestinian strategy was relayed to the author in closed seminars which took place in Exeter, England, in May 1997 and involved senior figures in the PA and

Within the Israeli Cabinet the six other parties, in addition to the Likud, would all bitterly oppose any deal that involved significant compromises on Jerusalem. Indeed, it is difficult to see the coalition being able to function in such circumstances, and Netanyahu would therefore be forced to rely on the Labour Party for support and as previously described, this, depending on the extent of the compromise, would be far from guaranteed. Moreover, the six other parties would find any deal on Jerusalem difficult to sell to their respective right-wing or religious constituencies and would probably rather leave the government than be party to such a deal with the Palestinians.

The internal restraints on Netanyahu placed the prime minister in a difficult position for, as previously mentioned, without some form of negotiation over Jerusalem the Palestinians would not have signed the Oslo agreement in 1993, and clearly the PA will demand concessions from Israel on the issue during the Final Status talks. Importantly, during the 1996 election campaign Netanyahu committed himself, and therefore the government, to implementing and continuing the Oslo process. (One of the Likud's central charges against the Oslo Accords has always been that Rabin and Peres allowed Jerusalem to be put on the agenda. The Likud charges that by so doing implied that at the very least Israel would have to use its continued control over the city as a trade-off card with another area of the process or, at worst, make large concessions on the control of the city.) Moreover, such a commitment was vital in helping him secure his narrow victory over Peres.[13] Consequently, Netanyahu's future political prospects will, to a large degree, be determined by the success of the Oslo process in creating peace with the Palestinians so long as Israeli public opinion continues to support the accords.[14]

Orient House. It was very apparent that these Palestinians were acutely aware of Netanyahu's strategy and also provided some enlightening comments on the methods employed in the Palestinian struggle for Jerusalem.

13 For an extensive analysis of the election campaign, issues and results, see Peretz and Doron, 'Israel's 1996 elections: a second political earthquake?'.

14 For evidence of the support of the Israeli electorate for the Oslo process, see the poll conducted for the Tami Steimetz Centre for Peace Studies at Tel Aviv University by Modi'in Ezrachi in Chapter 2. Moreover, a similar poll conducted by the same organisation in May 1998 for the Tami Steimetz Centre found that 77 per cent of the respondents were greatly or somewhat supportive of the peace process with 13 per cent uncertain. Asked more specifically about the Oslo Accords, 39 per cent of respondents believed that they would bring peace between

However, the support of Israelis for the Oslo process is not matched by support for the painful concession that Israel will have to make in the Final Status talks, and in particular over the future of Jerusalem. A recent survey suggested that some 85 per cent of the Israeli electorate rejected concessions on Jerusalem under any condition.[15] Put simply, there is majority support for the Oslo process, but crucially not for the concessions that would make a deal acceptable to the Palestinian side. Such a problem would have been difficult enough for Peres and the Labour Party to deal with, but is made more difficult for Netanyahu by his right-wing constituency and some senior personalities within his own Likud party who remain at best sceptical about the Oslo process itself, and are certainly not willing to accept any concessions on Jerusalem.

The Jerusalem issue under the Likud-led government 1996–1998

Tension and the threat of violence never have been far away from Jerusalem as the peace process has failed to move forward. This feeling of high tension has transferred itself into the actions of the political leadership of both sides, while the events and strength of feeling on the ground are making it increasingly difficult for leaders on both sides to maintain control. In essence, events have, at times, intervened to hi-jack what little progress has been made behind the scenes. Between 1996 and 1998 there were three major events in Jerusalem which, to a large extent, shaped the whole peace process between the Israelis and the Palestinians: the violence sparked by the opening of a new entrance to the Hasmonean Tunnel in the old city (September 1996); the decision to build at Har Homa (March 1997); and suicide bomb attacks by Islamic extremists at Mahane Yehuda market and Ben-Yehuda Street. Added to this was the continued Israeli attempt to complete the chain of Jewish housing projects (settlements) around greater Jerusalem.

The decision to open a new entrance to the Hasmonean Tunnel under the old city was taken by Netanyahu after Israel's three most recent prime ministers – Shamir, Rabin and Peres – had all refused to undertake it during their respective periods of office. They feared a

---

Israel and the Palestinians in the coming years, while 20 per cent were uncertain and 36 per cent thought they would not.

15 Poll quoted from Mendilow, "The Likud's Dilemma in the 1996 Elections".

violent backlash from Palestinians who claimed that the tunnel was a threat to their holy sites as it passed close to Islam's third holiest site, the Al-Aqsa mosque. The resultant violence that took place throughout the West Bank involved for the first time direct clashes between the IDF and Palestinian Police, and claimed the lives of over 44 Palestinians and 11 Israelis. Moreover, it was used by the Oslo rejectionists on both sides as evidence as to why the peace process was not working.[16]

The Israeli right attacked an Oslo deal that had allowed the creation of an armed Palestinian police force who had turned their guns on the Israelis. The leader of the radical right-wing party Moledet, Rehav'am Ze'evi, summarised the key argument of the right in Israel:

> We're acting like idiots, Palestinian policemen are shooting at us with weapons we gave them, and to calm them we don't let Jews go to Rachel's Tomb or Joseph's Tomb, which is like a reward.[17]

In addition, the right cited the oversized Palestinian police force (a ratio of one Palestinian policeman to 60 civilians) as a major violation of the Oslo Accords. Palestinian Oslo sceptics such as Hanan Ashwari stated that the peace process was going nowhere and that all the Palestinians heard from the Israelis were empty words. In the longer term, the events at the tunnel had two major effects: one specifically for Netanyahu's *modus operandi*, and the other on putting Jerusalem back on the agenda. Neither of these was welcomed by Netanyahu but nevertheless he showed signs of learning clear lessons from both which helped refine his strategy for dealing with Jerusalem.

Regarding the first, Netanyahu's failure to consult with the army over the opening of the tunnel was exposed as a tragic mistake. The IDF Chief of Staff, Amnon Shahak, knew of the prime minister's decision only hours before the tunnel entrance was opened.[18] Consequently, the army

---

16 For a balanced account of the events surrounding the opening of the tunnel and an analysis of the effects on the peace process, see J. Dempsey and A. Machlis, 'Opening of a tunnel blocks the road to peace', and J. Dempsey, 'Israeli tanks enter West Bank', both *Financial Times*, 27 September 1996.

17 Quoted from L. Collins, 'Riots are an eye opener', *Jerusalem Post*, 27 September 1996.

18 Netanyahu's failure to inform Shahak any sooner reflected the difficulties and complexity of their relationship. For more background on this crucial relationship, see Y. Marcus, 'A Chief of Staff of their own too?', *Ha-Aretz*, 8 July 1997.

was under-prepared for the wave of Palestinian violence that followed in the West Bank. In a television interview at the time, Netanyahu claimed that he had consulted widely and had been given the green light by the security establishment. As he put it:

> It's not what my experts told me; I can tell you that. And they admitted as much, I must say, very courageously and openly.[19]

Despite the claims of the prime minister, this marked the lowest point in the relationship between Netanyahu and the Israeli security forces – including intelligence agencies. As previously described, the prime minister had been deeply distrustful of senior officers in the IDF claiming that they had become too politicised and powerful under the Oslo process and favoured the Labour Party. However, reports in the media that the Chief of Staff was preparing to resign over the lack of consultation proved to be exaggerated. As for Netanyahu, who was humbled by the experience, he started to consult more widely with the mainstream of the security establishment and not merely with personnel who provided him with the answers he wanted to hear. This coincided with a general feeling within the IDF of increasing scepticism towards the Oslo agreements caused in no small part by the violence instigated after the opening of the tunnel. In particular the army was concerned about how much of it was orchestrated by Arafat or, conversely, if he was not responsible, by how little he managed to control or limit it.

Netanyahu's second lesson was that by opening the tunnel he had inadvertently placed Jerusalem on the political agenda with all the publicity and international reaction. The prime minister, already unhappy with the Oslo provision which included Jerusalem in the Final Status talks, had no desire to increase the debate on the city's future in the interim stages. Arafat was encouraged by the international reaction, which at best indirectly blamed the prime minister for the violence and at worst apportioned direct blame on the Israeli government.[20] Following

---

19 Interview with Ted Koppel of Nightline, 2 October 1996.

20 An example of the indirect blame came from the United States. In a press conference in the White House on 26 September 1996 President Clinton used the tone of American language normally employed for responding to the announcement of new Israeli settlements. As he put it: 'I'd like to just repeat what I have said consistently: I think that all the parties should avoid any actions which are likely

these events the prime minister was careful not to undertake actions where the potential gain factor to Israel was so low and the risk factor so high.

The decision in March 1997 to build at Har Homa was altogether different. As outlined in Chapter 2 this was intended to be the pay back to Netanyahu's right-wing constituency for his signing of the Hebron Accords and the subsequent troop redeployment from the West Bank. The difference between Har Homa and the Hasmonean tunnel opening was that the potential gain to Israel was large – the development of housing units for 35,000 and a further stage in Israel's attempt to encircle Jerusalem. In addition, this time Netanyahu consulted widely with his security chiefs and the army was ready to quell any resultant Palestinian violence. Once more the Jerusalem question was used to derail the peace process. The subsequent suspension of the Oslo peace process when the Palestinians refused to return to talks until Har Homa was cancelled again revealed the centrality of the Jerusalem issue to the whole peace process.

The suicide bomb attacks in Jerusalem at Mahane Yehuda central market-place (30 July 1997) and the Ben-Yehuda shopping mall (4 September 1997) by radical Islamic groups in the summer of 1997 were clearly designed to derail a peace process which was showing signs of getting back on track following the suspension of talks over Har Homa.[21] The explosions, which killed 20 people and wounded hundreds more, were particularly hard for Netanyahu to deal with. The prime minister, elected on the slogan of "peace with security", faced his first major challenge to his self-proclaimed security credentials. Two interesting conclusions emerged from the terrorist outrages.

---

to undermine the progress of the peace. Now the important thing is to end the violence and to get back to implementing those peace agreements. All I can tell you today is I hope that everyone will heed our position, which is to do nothing that will provoke a disruption and instead to get back to the talks and to the business of resolving their differences. I deeply regret the injuries and the loss of life we've seen on the West Bank and Gaza in the last few days. It [the violence] points to the urgency for both sides not only to end the violence but to take positive steps to resolve the issues that divide them.'

21 The US Special Envoy, Dennis Ross, was due in the region with proposals to restart the peace talks. For a detailed analysis of the positive signs in the peace process at this time, see C. Shalev, 'Beneficial to peace opponents', *Ma'ariv*, 31 July 1997. In addition, see also Erez, 'Arafat's last chance'.

First, the prime minister's security response was almost identical to that of Rabin and Peres – sealing off the West Bank, restricting Palestinian workers from entering Israel and charging that Arafat was to blame for failing to dismantle the terrorists' infrastructure. The only major difference was that Netanyahu imposed economic sanctions against the PA which, he claimed, were guilty of failing to prevent the attack.[22] Second, unlike Rabin and Peres whose popular support decreased with each bomb, Netanyahu's level of support remained constant and even rose a little in the immediate aftermath of the attacks.[23] Israelis clearly felt more at home with the prime minister's more robust vocal response than with Peres's calls after each attack for the peace process to continue. Moreover, there were no ugly scenes at the sites of the attacks claiming that Netanyahu was a traitor nor any mass protests about the peace process.

Since coming to power the prime minister has waged what he has termed a propaganda war over Jerusalem and its future in the Final Status maps. In many ways, the Jerusalem issue can be said to have reflected the first years of his premiership. Initial mistakes have been replaced by more carefully formulated long-term strategy to ensure that the status quo remains intact without adversely damaging Israel's international relations. Consequently, it is clear that the prime minister has made the retention and development of Jerusalem the major red line that he will not cross.

Palestinian claims and Jordanian anxieties

One of the less frequently charted developments during Netanyahu's period as opposition leader was the deepening ties between King Hussein and the Likud. In the last months of the Peres government there was growing unease with revelations of secret negotiations between the Palestinians and Israelis on Final Status issues – which included Jerusalem. Jordan also wanted a major role in East Jerusalem and in particular the holy sites. Consequently, during the Israeli election campaign in 1996 King Hussein did not join the long list of international

---

22 On Netanyahu's response to the bombs, see M. Heller, 'A policy of his own', *Jerusalem Post*, 22 August 1996.

23 For an explanation of this, see G. Samit, 'The bomb and the marvel', *Ha-Aretz*, 1 August 1997.

statesmen intervening on behalf of Peres. Indeed, King Hussein gave the Likud and Netanyahu (with its very public hawkish stance on Jerusalem) heightened credibility by inviting Netanyahu to Amman for a meeting as well as arranging several lower-level meetings involving officials from the Likud and Jordanian ministers.[24]

From a Palestinian perspective the question of Jerusalem is as difficult and complex as on the Israeli side. However, despite endless public pronouncements from Palestinians leaders about East Jerusalem being the capital of a proposed Palestinian state, there remains in private a degree of understanding that they will not get all they want from negotiations over Jerusalem.[25] For Palestinians the change of government in 1996 has meant much of the same. Even under Rabin and Peres the Israeli drive to tighten physical control over Jerusalem continued.[26]

Returning to our central theme of Netanyahu's government's handling of the peace process it is clear that under Netanyahu essentially nothing has changed on the Jerusalem issue. The most important change has taken place not on issues of substance but in the increased bad faith between the parties. Consequently, issues such as Har Homa have attracted greater attention and have been used by the Palestinian side in its international public relations war with Israel. In essence, had Rabin lived and been subsequently re-elected in 1996 we would likely be at a similar point over Jerusalem as we are under Netanyahu. With Rabin ceding land in the West Bank, Gaza Strip and potentially on the Golan Heights, it would have been difficult to imagine his making a territorial compromise on Jerusalem.[27] In addition, though Shimon Peres was publicly critical of Netanyahu's decision to proceed at Har Homa these are the comments of an opposition spokesman. In simple terms, had Peres been prime minister with all the difficulties of maintaining a

---

24 See, for example, Steinberg, 'The impact of the peace process and terror', p. 220.
25 For a Palestinian perspective on Jerusalem, see M. Abdul Hadi, 'The ownership of Jerusalem: a Palestinian view' in G. Karmi (ed.), *Jerusalem Today* (Reading, Ithaca Press, 1996).
26 For an account of the leadership of the post-Oslo agreement Labour Party policies towards Jerusalem see, for example, I. Sharkansky, 'The potential for ambiguity: the case of Jerusalem' in E. Karsh (ed.), *From Rabin to Netanyahu: Israel's Troubled National Agenda* (London and Portland, Frank Cass, 1997), p. 197.
27 See M. Dumper, 'Demographic and border issues affecting the future of Jerusalem' in G. Karmi (ed.), *Jerusalem Today*, p. 93.

centrist coalition, then his room for manoeuvre on this issue would also have been highly limited.

Proposals for Jerusalem in the Final Status talks

Having examined the internal restraints on Netanyahu and the actions of the government during 1996–8 it is worth analysing potential solutions to the Jerusalem question, and the ability and motivation of the prime minister to implement them. In recent years Israeli academics, think tanks and officially commissioned papers have put forward some 90 sets of proposals about the future status of Jerusalem.[28] This study aims to analyse only one of the them (although this plan contains elements of many of the previous Israeli studies about Jerusalem) – the Beilin–Abu Mazen non-paper, the majority of which has been subsequently revealed by Beilin. (A non-paper is defined as a paper that was produced for non-public consumption and is not officially endorsed by either side in the formal negotiations. In short, this allows both sides the possibility of denial if part of the paper is leaked to the media. The contents of the non-paper were revealed to the author in a closed address by Beilin at the Royal Institute of International Affairs, London, July 1997.) The significance of what has since been termed the Beilin–Abu Mazen plan was twofold: first, the participants were the same as the original Oslo process; and second, it marked the first semi-official discussion between the Israeli government and the PA on Final Status issues such as Jerusalem and Palestinian statehood. In addition, the plan could have served as the centre-piece of Final Status negotiations between a Labour-led government and the PA. Moreover, although the Labour Party is no longer in power, the plan still serves as a useful measurement for the price any Israeli government can expect to pay in reaching a final agreement with the Palestinians.

The centre-piece of the plan was the linkage of the status of Jerusalem to an Israeli acceptance of a Palestinian state in the West Bank

---

28 The figure of 90 is quoted from an Israeli diplomatic source and appeared in S. Rodan and B. Hutman, 'Of talks and traps', *Jerusalem Post*, 3 May 1996. In addition, this article contains some of the most informed and clear analysis of the pre-Final Status rounds of unofficial talks between the Israelis and Palestinians with special reference to the discussions on Jerusalem.

and the Gaza Strip. Moreover, although the contents of the paper are not officially acknowledged, its co-author, Yossi Beilin, presented the general points to a meeting of a Labour Party faction in September 1996. The following represent the key understandings that were reached.

1. A Palestinian state would be created in Judea, Samaria and the Gaza Strip.
2. The capital of this state would be called Al-Quds, namely those parts of Jerusalem that are located outside the municipal borders of Israeli Jerusalem, but which are considered by the Palestinians to be part of the city.
3. The PA would recognise Israeli sovereignty over West Jerusalem, while sovereignty over East Jerusalem would remain open for discussion.
4. The Palestinians would respect the principle of the open city of Jerusalem.
5. The Temple Mount would come under Palestinian control and a Palestinian flag would be raised on the site.
6. The Old City would be without official sovereignty, but Israel would retain control over it.[29]

Clearly, on the surface all these proposals are unacceptable to Netanyahu and would appear to be a total non-starter. In addition, even if Netanyahu accepted the parts about Jerusalem, there would be little chance of his getting it through the Likud and coalition partners. However, the Beilin–Eitan Forum, which consisted of Yossi Beilin, Michael Eitan (Likud MK), other members of the Knesset (including Likud MKs), academics and ex-senior military personnel, attempted to find a common consensus for Israeli positions for the Final Status talks including Jerusalem. In doing so it was accepted that Israel would have to make some concessions on Jerusalem, but that these could be minimised by the acceptance of the Palestinian state much in the same way that the Beilin–Abu Mazen plan had previously suggested. Moreover, it is difficult simply to dispose of the Beilin–Abu Mazen plan because it provides the

---

29 For more detailed accounts of the outline of the Beilin–Abu Mazen non-paper, see the following: P. Inbari, 'Labour's Mashov Circle backs recognition of Palestinian state', *Jerusalem Post*, 11 September 1996; and J. Dallal, 'Colour blind', *Jerusalem Post*, 28 August 1996.

first direct evidence of what the Palestinians may be willing to accept as a final status. In essence, although the PA has made no formal comment on the plan, it would appear that it could serve as a potential basic framework for solving the Jerusalem problem, and in particular the difficult task of finding a solution, albeit perhaps temporary, to the key issue of sovereignty.

In private, Netanyahu is resigned to having to make some painful concessions. Moreover, much of Netanyahu's hawkish rhetoric needs to viewed as a smoke screen as he attempts to keep secret his negotiating fall-back positions for the Palestinian track. What is clear is that the prime minister's very public opposition to any form of Palestinian state is not as rigid in private.[30] Consequently, it is not inconceivable that Netanyahu will attempt to maintain control over Jerusalem by (like, the Beilin–Abu Mazen plan) trading this for acceptance of a Palestinian state. However, such a scenario would almost certainly require the formation of a government of national unity in Israel to negotiate and ratify the deal. In essence, the right would bring down his government before he had been given the chance to finalise any deal. Consequently, just as negotiations about Jerusalem's future are due to start Netanyahu has became ever-more dependent on his right-wing and religious party coalition members, which makes a final deal all the more difficult for Netanyahu to achieve.[31]

Conclusions

The negotiations over the future of Jerusalem remain one of the most complex and difficult for any Israeli prime minister to have to conduct.

---

30 It needs to be stressed that Netanyahu is opposed to a Palestinian state without any (Israeli) restrictions imposed upon it. In speeches he has made between 1996 and 1998, he has clearly articulated the rationale behind such a position. Consequently, this so-called state would resemble more an elaborate form of Palestinian autonomy rather than a fully independent sovereign state. See, for example, his argument against a sovereign Palestinian state in an interview with J. Bushinsky, 'Arafat must make a choice', *Jerusalem Post*, 5 September 1997.

31 There is evidence that informal negotiations on issues such as the final status of Jerusalem have been taking place between the Likud Mayor of Jerusalem, Ehud Olmert and the Orient House's Faisal Huseini. See M. Benvenisti, 'Recycling injustices', *Ha-Aretz*, 24 July 1997.

Moreover, this has been compounded in Netanyahu's case by his use of the issue during his election campaign, which makes it difficult for him personally to compromise on Jerusalem and retain his domestic political credibility with the Israeli electorate. However, Netanyahu's acceptance of the Oslo agreements during the same campaign has meant that he is forced to discuss Jerusalem in Final Status talks. In essence, two of the key issues that won the election for Netanyahu are pulling him in opposite directions, and at some given point he will have to choose between either a breakdown of the Oslo process or an acceptance of some form of limited compromise on Jerusalem. Importantly, Netanyahu, in attempting to broaden his coalition into a national unity government (NUG) at various times between 1996 and 1998, has shown that he is well aware of the need to conduct the negotiations with the broadest spectrum of support possible to reduce the influence of his hawkish coalition partners. In addition, Netanyahu is also aware that he needs the Labour Party to deflect the criticism of any concession he is forced to make on Jerusalem. Unfortunately, in the wake of the Bar-On scandal and other internal problems, such a government no longer appears to be a realistic prospect.

The Israeli Internal Security Minster, Avigdor Kahalani, summed up the government's strategy on Jerusalem stating that the battle for Jerusalem had begun. In reality, this battle has been underway for considerably longer. Indeed, the policies of Netanyahu on Jerusalem reflect those of the Rabin and Peres governments who both consistently refused to impose a freeze on the building of new Jewish homes in disputed areas of Jerusalem. The Israeli battle to maintain control over Jerusalem started with the signing of the Oslo Accords. As previously described, both Rabin and Peres were acutely aware that the agreements had placed Jerusalem on the agenda and acted accordingly.

Finally, the outlined restraints on the current prime minister limit the potential for any deal on Jerusalem to come out of the Final Status talks – whenever they take place – and remain high as does his personal commitment. However, the increasing awareness of a limited form of compromise on parts of Jerusalem that fall outside the new municipal borders of the city by the Palestinian leadership may prove to be the way forward. If Netanyahu can accept the thought of a Palestinian state with limited powers then there is potential for agreement on the issue of Jerusalem and consequently an overall solution to the Israeli–Palestinian

PART III

ISRAELI RELATIONS WITH THE ARAB STATES AND THE WIDER MIDDLE EAST

7

The developing Israeli–Jordanian peace under the Netanyahu-led government

Although a formal peace treaty was signed between Israel and Jordan on 26 October 1994 it has still not become totally apparent what type of peace will transpire in the long term between the two countries. Consequently, this chapter examines the dynamic development of Israeli–Jordanian relations under the Netanyahu-led government in Israel and its potential impact on the Middle East region. In returning to the central theme of the book it is argued that many of the problems that have arisen in the post-treaty relationship – particularly over water resources and the failure of a substantial economic peace dividend for Jordan to emerge – would have been encountered even if the Labour Party in Israel had been returned to power in 1996. Moreover, it is shown that the shared mutual interests of Netanyahu and King Hussein are similar (or actually greater) than those present when the previous Labour government was in power in Israel. In illustrating these points the chapter examines the relationship on two separate, but closely related, levels: first, the events and decisions that would appear in the short term to have damaged the prospects of a warm peace; and second, a more in-depth evaluation of the long-term potential of maintaining, or even deepening, the strategic relationship between Israel and Jordan which it is argued has not been irreparably damaged by the short-term difficulties.

Background

Before examining the growing complications in the Israeli–Jordanian relationship it is important to analyse the development of the relationship and the expectations that both sides had of it during the period of the previous Labour-led governments of Rabin and Peres in Israel. In the euphoria that followed the signing of the peace treaty by Yitzhak Rabin and King Hussein in 1994 and the expectations of the new relationship that was to emerge from the agreement were extremely high. There were a number of reasons for this hope, many of which were related to the contrast that was apparent in the style and outcome of the negotiations between Israel and Jordan from those involving the Israelis and Palestinians and earlier with the Egyptians.

First, King Hussein was perceived by many Israelis as the one Arab leader who had crossed over the great divide and who personally sought a warm peace with the Jewish state. Moreover, it was apparent that the King and Prime Minister Rabin enjoyed a strong personal chemistry which was highly visible in the joint public appearance that the two leaders made.[1] This was in direct contrast to the tense, often hostile, public images of Rabin and Arafat together emerging from negotiations.

Second, the potential for joint projects such as the development of parts of the desert, joint water projects and economic investments, was highlighted by both sides in contrast to, for example, the failure of any real joint projects with Egypt in over 15 years of peace. Moreover, it was hoped that both sides would work together to develop the Jordan Valley area and tourist areas in the Red Sea resorts.

Third, the development of strategic cooperation, which had secretly occurred for many years, and which was to be organised into more formal structures and related to Israel's deepening ties with Turkey (see Chapter 10). In short, the Israeli–Jordanian peace was to be in direct contrast to the increasingly cold peace that Israel had maintained with Egypt since the signing of the Camp David Accords in 1979 and the increasing difficulties and complications that the negotiations with the Palestinians were facing.

As a result of these factors, the then Israeli foreign minister, Shimon Peres, saw the developing relationship with Jordan as an integral part of his vision of a new Middle East. He summed this up in a speech in Jordan three months before the formal peace treaty was signed:

> The peace process will not end with the signatures of our political leaders. Indeed, only then will it begin. And our target should be that, before the end of the 20th century, we will face a new political

---

1 On the issue of the personal friendship between the King and Rabin and its effect on the negotiations which led to the peace treaty see, for example, M. Zak, 'A friendship that conquered all', *Jerusalem Post*, 18 October 1996.

and economic landscape. A landscape where borders will be open, where Jordanians will not be stopped at Eilat or Israelis in Aqaba. Where new, sophisticated industries will offer job opportunities to the young generation. Where waterways will cover the brown deserts, and where sea ports and airports will be combined to serve all tourists to visit holy places, to be cured in the hot springs or to view the beautiful antiquities. Where the skies will be open to competitive aviation and land distances will be shortened by new railways and highways. Where water and oil will be carried in pipelines laid to answer economic needs rather than strategic worries. And where electricity systems will be connected to save billions of dollars. Even before the sunset of this new century we can, together, reclaim land lost to the desert. We can reclaim sea water to irrigate new fields, new gardens, new cities. We can change the face of the map, and create in the broken rift a new structure of life. We have prepared our view how the future will look in a rather detailed manner. We can transform a boundary of gloom into a valley of hope. Farmers will replace soldiers, greenhouses will come instead of barracks, dunes will submit to plantations.[2]

Within the framework of Peres's vision of the Middle East the peace agreement between Israel and Jordan was viewed as having the greatest potential of all the various tracks of the peace process for delivering something similar to the new Middle East that Peres outlined in the above extract.[3] This belief was shared by many Israelis whose expectations were fuelled by very public shows of movement towards rapid normalisation such as King Hussein piloting his jet over the skies of Jerusalem and the rapid opening of the border for Israelis tourists to visit Jordan for the first time.[4]

Expectations of the peace between Israel and Jordan need to be carefully viewed in the context of the wider Middle East process in 1994. Rabin had made substantial concessions to the Palestinians (recognition of the Palestinian Liberation Organization (PLO) as negotiating partners for peace at this time perhaps being the most difficult for Israelis to absorb after years of it being perceived as terrorist organisation). The

---

2 Address by Shimon Peres at the opening of the fifth session of the trilateral talks in Jordan between Israel, Jordan and the United States, 20 July 1994.
3 See a detailed account of Peres's viewpoint on the potential of the Israeli–Jordanian peace in S. Peres, *The Valley of Peace* (Jerusalem, Minister of Foreign Affairs, 1994).
4 On expectations of Israelis, see the editorial in the *Jerusalem Post*, 'The Jordanian option', 10 October 1996.

bitter internal debate in Israel over the future of the West Bank which was to lead to the murder of Yitzhak Rabin in November 1995 was already underway. Consequently, expectations on the Jordanian track where there was widespread national support for the peace accords tended to gloss over any difficulties that would have to be dealt with in the medium to long term. In essence, the price that Israel paid for peace with Jordan in terms of short-term concessions appeared to be very small. From the peace agreement these could be summarised as the following.

Israeli concessions to Jordan in the peace treaty signed in October 1994

1. The return of an area of farming land to Jordanian sovereignty. This land was subsequently leased back to Israel.
2. Slight adjustments to parts of Israel's eastern border with Jordan.
3. Agreements over water resources and the commitment for future joint water projects aimed at providing water for both Israel and Jordan.
4. A special role for Jordan in the religious institutions in Jerusalem.

The seemingly small price that Israel paid was illustrated by the fact that even the Likud with its Revisionist ideological claim on the land on the eastern bank of the River Jordan accepted the peace accord.[5]

---

5 Some members of the Likud were somewhat critical of certain parts of the accord though accepted the deal as a complete package. In the Knesset ratification debate the main speaker for the Likud, Moshe Katsav, said that the Likud welcomed the agreement despite its flaws. However, much of his speech was devoted to attacking the parts of the accord that were difficult for some Likud supporters to embrace – namely, Jerusalem's and Israel's eastern borders. As he put it: "Do the Jews, the Jewish people . . . have no rights, no standing on the Temple Mount, now or at any time in the future?" Katsav also criticised the agreement for stating that the River Jordan represented the border between Jordan and the administered territories, with no statement as to the meaning of the border of Israel. However, Netanyahu in his short ten-minute speech chose to emphasise the positive aspects of the deal. He said: "This is fundamentally a good agreement, an agreement that will bring peace. It does not entail territorial concessions . . . it doesn't entail bringing in foreign soldiers. The advantages of the agreement clearly outweigh its disadvantages." Details of speeches from the Protocols of the Knesset, 25 October 1994. Note: each member of the Knesset was granted ten minutes to speak in the debate in addition to Rabin's opening remarks for the government and the formal reply of Katsav for the opposition. During the debate the extreme right-wing party Moledet was the only party to come out explicitly against the deal.

The strategic part of the agreement was very clear with Jordan in effect acting as a buffer state between Israel and Iraq. This was a direct development from the agreement reached by the former Likud prime minister, Yitzhak Shamir, and the King on the eve of the Persian Gulf War in 1991. The agreement was reached in secret meetings in London between Shamir (and his advisers – the then Israeli Deputy Chief of Staff, General Ehud Barak, Elyakin Rubinstein and Yossi Ben-Aharon), the King and his military adviser, General Zeid bin Shakir on 4 and 5 January 1991. At the meeting, Hussein pledged to prevent Iraqi troops from entering Jordan (including so-called training flights by the Iraqi air force, which had taken place on Israel's border). In return Shamir agreed that Israel would not violate Jordanian sovereignty although if Iraq took over control of Jordan, Israel would respond.[6] Subsequently, these understandings were confirmed in a letter from Shamir to US President George Bush, which was sent after hostilities broke out and stated that Israel had no intention of attacking Jordan but that an entrance of Iraqi forces into Jordan would be considered to be a crossing of "the red line".

In summing up the Israeli–Jordanian peace under the Rabin government (and in the brief period of office of Peres, which followed Rabin's murder) it would seem that on one level the relationship had the necessary ingredients for a successful and warm peace. These can be defined as good personal relations between the leadership, a peace treaty that contained imaginative solutions to the question of sovereignty of lands, the potential for joint projects and rapid moves towards normalisation (including tourism and shared natural resources and infrastructure). In addition, there was a strong potential for deepening strategic ties based on a set of mutual interests and strategic needs.

However, on a deeper level there remained a number of problems in the relationship. First was the widespread opposition in Jordan towards the peace treaty, particularly among East Bankers and Palestinians. This opposition has grown as the economic peace dividend has not materialised to the extent hoped for. Paradoxically, one of the main reasons for this lack of this economic dividend has been due to Jordanian domestic opposition against closer economic links with Israel. In addition,

---

6 On the issue of the secret meetings and agreements, see a comprehensive account in M. Zak, 'Israel and Jordan: strategically bound', *Israel Affairs*, vol. 3, no. 1 (1996), pp. 39–60.

many commentators have cited the lack of an increase in aid for Jordan in comparison with the massive programme given to Egypt following Camp David.[7] In statistical terms Egypt has received some $40 billion in aid mainly from the US since the Camp David Treaty while Jordan has received only $1 billion in a write-off against its foreign debts.[8] Second was the death of Rabin, which robbed the relationship of its biggest asset, the personal chemistry between Rabin and the King. Moreover, as outlined in Chapter 6, there was a suspicion in Jordan that Rabin's successor, Shimon Peres, would concede too much to the PLO on the future status of Jerusalem and failed to take account of Jordan's special role in the city.[9]

Third was the Arab pressure exerted on Jordan (particularly from Syria and Egypt) not to develop closer strategic ties with Israel which Arab countries argued were both premature and would lead to negative changes for the wider Arab world in the strategic balance of the Middle East.

As a consequence when Netanyahu came to power in 1996 there were already signs that the relationship, although not in a state of crisis, was entering a transition (or a maturing phase). During this phase the realities of Middle East politics and economics were starting to become more apparent over the initial euphoric visions of the relationship being the centre-piece of a new Middle East vision. Moreover, it was apparent that the pressure on King Hussein to slow down normalisation with Israeli was likely to grow whatever the outcome of the Israeli election in 1996 as pressure from both Arab states and internal opposition in Jordan increased as the peace process entered a more complex phase in which difficult choices and compromises would have to be made.

---

7 On the lack of aid to Jordan following its signing of a peace treaty with Israel, see B. Rubin, 'Jordan's economic woes could threaten warm peace with Israel', *Jerusalem Post*, 18 August 1996.

8 See D. Gardner, 'Peace crisis crushes hopes: survey of Jordan', *Financial Times*, 1 November 1996.

9 Article 9 – Places of Historical and Religious Significance, in the peace treaty between Israel and Jordan stated: 'Each party will provide freedom of access to places of religious and historical significance. In this regard, in accordance with the Washington Declaration, Israel respects the present special role of the Hashemite Kingdom of Jordan in Moslem holy shrines in Jerusalem. When negotiations on Permanent Status will take place, Israel will give priority to the Jordanian historic role in these shrines.'

Developing Israeli–Jordanian ties under Netanyahu: crisis and consolidation

Upon Netanyahu's election, King Hussein was the only Arab leader to suggest that he be given a chance to prove himself.[10] Indeed, between 1994 and 1996 Netanyahu had met with Jordanian leaders on several occasions to discuss Israeli-Jordanian matters and the wider Middle East peace process. The Jordanian track offered Netanyahu, to a certain degree, an opportunity to present himself as a moderate man in favour of the peace treaty.[11] However, there were much deeper mutual incentives for both himself and the Jordanians for developing relations with each other.[12] In essence, Netanyahu and the King shared many common beliefs: first, a deep mistrust of Yasser Arafat's PLO; second, opposition to a strong Palestinian state; and third, acceptance of a Jordanian role in administering the holy sites in Jerusalem.[13] Consequently, even after the death of Rabin and the bringing forward of the Israeli election to May 1996 by Peres, King Hussein was happy to meet Netanyahu in the middle of the protracted Israeli campaign. The effect of the meetings although largely superseded by Peres's anti-terrorism summit of world leaders should not be underestimated. In short, the King's message that he could do business with Netanyahu was not missed by Israeli voters who were being pressurised (indirectly or in some cases more directly – see Chapter 11) by almost every Arab and world leader to support Peres and his vision of the Middle East.[14]

As a result of the passive support of King Hussein, it was generally presumed that Netanyahu, after assuming office, would place a strong priority on developing relations with Jordan and maintaining a strong

---

10 See B. Rubin, 'More moderate than it looks', *Jerusalem Post*, 9 August 1996.

11 In the Knesset debate on ratification of the peace treaty, Netanyahu made it a free vote for Likud members and personally supported the treaty. The treaty was ratified by 105 to 3 votes on 25 October 1994.

12 See Steinberg, 'The impact of the peace process and terror', p. 230.

13 In addition to the meetings with Netanyahu, King Hussein refused to accept a visit by Peres to Amman during the campaign, and the Jordanian ambassador to Israel, Omar Rifai, met with Netanyahu some two weeks before the election and declared that his government would work with an elected government in Israel. See Inbar, 'Netanyahu takes over', p. 44.

14 On the importance of King Hussein's position on Netanyahu and the Likud during the Israeli elections, see Steinberg, 'The impact of the peace process and terror', p. 220.

personal relationship with the King and other Jordanian leaders. Moreover, Netanyahu decided to personally control ties with Jordan, largely bypassing the foreign ministry and the foreign minister, David Levy. In analysing the subsequent relations with Jordan, three specific periods can be defined: the first nine months up to the end of February 1997; March–October 1997; and post-October 1997. It should be stated that these periods refer to events and developments in the relationship. It is argued later that strategic interests between the two countries have remained relatively unchanged and these are discussed later in the chapter.

Disenchantment and Jordanian economic woes: June 1996 to the end of February 1997

This period can be characterised on two levels: first, on a political level a feeling of disenchantment by King Hussein with the Netanyahu administration; and second, on an economic level growing economic problems in Jordan that were illustrated by a serious outbreak of rioting over the price of bread and which threatened not only the stability of Jordan but also its relationship with Israel.

By October 1997, King Hussein was stating in public that Netanyahu's policies could lead the region to war.[15] This was a reflection of a Jordanian belief that Netanyahu had offered nothing to move the wider Middle East peace process forward and had violated Israel's pledges about safeguarding the Muslim holy sites in Jerusalem. Much of the Jordanian anger was aimed at two events and Netanyahu's rather insensitive handling of them. The government's decision to expand Jewish settlement in the West Bank taken in September and the decision to open the new entrance to the Hasmonean Tunnel in Jerusalem both damaged the relationship. (For a full account of the opening of the tunnel entrance, see Chapter 6.) The latter was particularly difficult for the King with Jordan's special status in protecting the Muslim holy sites in Jerusalem. However, both events had been coincidentally preceded by meetings between King Hussein and Netanyahu's adviser of foreign affairs, Dore Gold, in Amman. During both visits, Gold had failed to inform the King of either of the decisions that had already been taken in

---

15 Reported in D. Makovsky, 'Netanyahu needs to keep King Hussein in mind', *Jerusalem Post*, 10 October 1996.

Jerusalem and were to be implemented soon thereafter. In response to the opening of the tunnel an angry King stated that if Netanyahu was telling the world that he could do whatever he wanted then this was totally unacceptable.[16]

In essence, the King's comments reflected annoyance at Netanyahu, and importantly although Israeli–Jordanian relations were damaged by the actions of Netanyahu the long-term effect on the relationship was less significant. Put simply, the strategic mutual interests between Israel and Jordan had not been radically altered. King Hussein's comments, although reflecting genuine anger, can be viewed as addressing two key audiences: Jordanians and the wider Arab world. Regarding the first, during this time there was growing opposition in Jordan towards normalisation of ties with Israel, especially from the Palestinian part of society, until a final settlement of the Israeli-Palestinian track. Regarding the latter, King Hussein was acutely aware of the need not to isolate Jordan in the Arab world. Moreover, there was a danger that as Arab hostility towards the Netanyahu-led government's polices grew, Jordan's influence in the Arab world would be under threat. Put simply, King Hussein had to balance carefully the needs of Jordan for good relations with Israel against its similar requirements for good relations with Egypt and its neighbours, and therefore could not afford to be dramatically out of sync with the Arab world.

In economic terms this period was characterised by increasing tensions as the government tried to implement an IMF-supported structural reform package in August, which aimed to stabilise the Jordanian economy. The resulting riots over an increase in the price of bread were successfully dealt with by the government, but the deep-rooted nature of Jordan's economic problems remained unchanged. These can be summarised as the failure of a much-needed peace dividend from Israel and the loss of trade with Iraq following the end of the Persian Gulf War, and the cutting of aid to Jordan from the Gulf States for its pro-Iraq position during the war. Consequently, the failure, for whatever reasons, of the development of strong economic ties with Israel has sent Jordan, and in particular its major cities, into a deep recession.

However, the period ended on a more optimistic note with the widely acknowledged role of King Hussein in helping bring Netanyahu

---

16   Interview with King Hussein in *Asharq al-Awsat*, 9 October 1996.

and Arafat closer together in order to sign the Hebron Accords. Moreover, Netanyahu was keen to try to repair some of the damage done between his administration and Jordan by allowing the King to take a large share of the crisis for bridging the gaps between himself and Arafat, and securing the deal.

The Road from Har Homa to the Mossad: March 1997 to October 1997

This period was dominated by three major events: the decision of the Netanyahu government to build new housing for Jewish families on Har Homa in East Jerusalem; the killing of seven Israeli schoolgirls by a deranged Jordanian soldier; and a bungled assassination attempt by Mossad on a leader of Hamas in Amman in September 1997. In addition, in the summer of 1997 Jordan raised doubts over whether Israel was interested in keeping its commitments made in the peace treaty on the question of water. A major crisis over the water issue was only averted through the intervention of the Israeli Minister of National Infrastructure, Ariel Sharon.

The decision of Netanyahu to start work at Har Homa, although taken for mainly domestic reasons (as a pay-back to his right-wing partners and supporters for the Hebron Accords and subsequent troop redeployments), led to a fierce exchange of letters between the King and the Israeli prime minister. In his correspondence, King Hussein was reported to have said that he had not a trace of trust in Netanyahu and that he feared the lives of Israelis and Arabs were fast sliding towards an abyss of bloodshed and disaster brought about by fear and despair.[17] Although the comments contained much rhetoric there could be no mistaking the feelings of the King. However, within the Netanyahu administration there was a great deal of consternation over the fact that the King had decided to go public at the same time that officials in the Netanyahu administration were trying to convince the US to increase economic aid to Jordan.

Some three days after King Hussein's comments, a deranged Jordanian soldier shot and killed seven Israeli schoolgirls who were on a

---

17 Open letter from King Hussein to the Israeli prime minister reported in 'I have not a trace of trust in you', *Ma'ariv*, 11 March 1997, p. 1.

visit to Nayarayim in the Jordan Valley. Although the shooting was not directly related to the comments made by King Hussein, it shocked Israelis who had perceived the border with Jordan to be a quiet safe zone. In the short term the visit by King Hussein to Israel (including a personal visit to all the families of the bereaved) once more highlighted the King's unique position in Israeli politics as the only Arab leader to be seen as having crossed the divide. The tragic events at Nayarayim demonstrated the need for security cooperation between Jordan and Israel to prevent such attacks. The sight of the Israeli chief of Staff conferring with his Jordanian opposite number at the scene was a clear illustration of how far this security cooperation had developed.

The crisis over the water issue had its roots in the original peace treaty with Jordan – in which many (including Shimon Peres) believed that Rabin had been over-generous to Jordan on the water question. Before examining the details of the crisis that arose, it is worth recalling the article of the peace treaty that dealt with water.

In essence, the problem was based on Jordan's continued water shortage and its belief that Israel was not committing enough resources to parts 3 and 4A of the article, which called for developments in new water resources for use by both countries. In addition, and not mentioned in this part of the treaty, was the amount of water that Israel would allow to be transferred to Jordan. The Israeli prime minister called in Ariel Sharon to deal with the situation and this led to a significant development in Israeli–Jordanian relations – Sharon's first meeting with King Hussein. For many years Sharon had subscribed to the typical viewpoint of the right in Israel that Jordan was Palestine and that he did not recognise the Hashemite Kingdom. Two important factors emerged from the meeting and subsequent negotiations: first, Israel accepted almost all the Jordanian requests, thus in the short term defusing the crisis; and second (and important in the longer term), Sharon and King Hussein developed a close personal chemistry reminiscent of that which the King had enjoyed with Rabin and which was much warmer than the King's relationship with Netanyahu.[18]

---

18 There was a great deal of speculation in the Israeli media at the time over Sharon's relationship with King Hussein. What was clear was that Sharon and the King were united by a common distrust of Arafat and the concern that this man would be the leader of a Palestinian state in the West Bank. Sharon's generous

Relations between the King and Netanyahu worsened with the bungled assassination attempt by the Israeli Mossad on Khaled Mashaal (a leader of Hamas) on 25 September 1997 in Amman.[19] The attack represented Israel's biggest botched intelligence operation since Mossad agents had been caught red-handed in Lillehammer, Norway in 1973.[20] Moreover this action, which was fully authorised by the Israeli government, provided the biggest test of Israeli–Jordanian relations to date. The attack amounted to a direct and clear violation of the security agreement which was an integral part of the peace accord signed by the two countries in 1994.[21] The detailed events surrounding the attack were chronicled in the Israeli and international media and therefore here the discussion is limited to the effects of the attack on Israeli–Jordanian relations in both the short and long terms.[22] In the short term, relations were badly damaged. King Hussein extracted a high price from Netanyahu for the release of the two Mossad agents who had been captured in Amman by securing the release of the spiritual leader of Hamas, Sheikh Ahmed Yassin, from an Israeli jail and allowing his return to Gaza.[23] In addition, Israel agreed to release around 40 Palestinian security prisoners from its jails.[24] The King once more managed to turn a potentially disastrous

---

gift of the water was intended as a message to the King that he (Sharon) was a man of his word. On this, see A. Eldar, 'The Mossad old-boy network: up to the King', *Ha-Aretz*, 9 October 1997.

19 For more details on the background to the attack, see A. Eldar, 'John F. Kennedy and Danny Yatom', *Ha-Aretz*, 6 October 1997.

20 Editorial, *Yediot Ahronot*, 6 October 1997.

21 Article 4 in point 4c of the treaty entitled "Security" stated: "The parties undertake in accordance with the provisions of this article, the following: to take necessary and effective measures to ensure that acts or threats of belligerency, hostility, subversion or violence against the other party do not originate from, and are not committed within, their territory."

22 See, for example, the following: Editorial, "A victory for Hamas", and S. Rodan, 'Diplomats: Israel, Jordan need time to restore the relationship', both in *Jerusalem Post*, 7 October 1997; J. Bushinsky, B. Tsur, and L. Collins, 'Netanyahu: I won't fire Mossad chief', *Jerusalem Post*, 13 October 1997.

23 On the consequences of the failed attempt for Israel, Jordan and the wider Middle East peace process, see Y. Marcus, 'The only better of this disgrace', *Ha-Aretz*, 7 October 1997.

24 There appeared widespread support in Israel for the release of the prioress as part of a deal. Israel has always had to pay a high price in such issues. See, for example, Editorial, *Ma'ariv*, 7 October 1997.

affair to his advantage by forcing these concessions on Israel at a time when there was widespread anger on the streets of Arab capitals about Israel's actions.[25] Moreover, Jordan with its large Islamic groupings had to be seen to be taking a very tough line over the actions of the Mossad in order to avoid potential social unrest against King Hussein and the peace treaty with Israel.[26] In addition, the King's actions in securing the release of Yassin put Arafat in an uncomfortable position for two reasons: first, the release itself of the major opposition grouping to Arafat among the Palestinians; and second, the fact that King Hussein took all the credit for the release. Indeed, the extent of Arafat's unease was shown by his unscheduled summit meeting with Netanyahu which directly followed the release of Yassin.[27]

Israeli–Jordanian security contacts, in particular in the field of intelligence contacts, were thought to have been badly damaged and would take a period of time to recover. However, there needs to be a clear distinction made between political and military contacts at high levels and operational contacts on the ground. At the top level the Jordanian trust in Netanyahu was further eroded on security affairs as it became clear that he had personally authorised the operation. This was also the case with Danny Yatom, the head of Mossad, and there was widespread consternation in Amman that Yatom was not sacked by Netanyahu. Moreover, the Jordanian authorities (publicly) ordered the closing down of all Israeli intelligence operations that were based in the Israeli Embassy in Amman. However, at an operational level there was strong evidence that both the Israeli and Jordanian armies were still actively cooperating on the ground despite reports that Jordan had frozen such contacts. For example, on 10 October the IDF reported killing a Jordanian infiltrator and in the subsequent report the Israelis stressed that during and after the incident effective and positive cooperation

---

25　King Hussein originally demanded the release of hundreds of Hamas prisoners and only after negotiations with Sharon did the numbers decline. On this see, for example, J. Bushinsky, 'Probe into assassination fiasco', *Jerusalem Post*, 7 October 1997.

26　On the issue of the Islamic forces in Jordan and their effect on Jordanian foreign policy, see S. Al-Khazendar, *Jordan and the Palestine Question: The Role of Islamic and Left Forces in Foreign Policy Making* (Reading, Ithaca Press, 1997), Chapter 6.

27　In essence, the failed operation strengthened Hamas against the PA. On this, see M. Benvenisti, 'Reality is not a thriller', *Ha-Aretz*, 9 October 1997.

took place between the Jordanian and Israeli armies.[28] From this it can be deduced that even though only two weeks had passed since Israel's assassination attempt in Amman, on the ground security cooperation remained high despite the public differences of the King and the Israeli prime minister.

Finally, in a postscript to the event Danny Yatom was forced to resign over other matters in early 1998 and was replaced by Israel's ambassador to the European Union, Ephraim Halevy, who had prior to his entry into the diplomatic core served as deputy head of Mossad. The ambassador had been heavily involved with the negotiations over the peace treaty with Jordan and enjoyed an excellent personal relationship with the King. Moreover, Halevy was one of the main negotiators in striking the deal for the release of the captured Mossad agents. (Israeli security sources confirmed Halevy's involvement which extended to him personally driving the agents back to Israel in his car after securing their release.) Consequently, Halevy's appointment was viewed in Israel as, in part, an attempt by Netanyahu to both build bridges with the King and to reassure Jordan about future Israeli intelligence operations. (Netanyahu was widely perceived to have preferred to appoint another candidate, Major-General Amiram Levine, but after consulting widely he chose to appoint Halevy with Levine as his deputy who would take over after Halevy's retirement.)

Maturing and downgrading of expectations: post-October 1997

During this period Jordan has largely down-scaled its attempts at mediating between the Israeli government and Arafat's PA over issues such as settlements and Israeli troop redeployments. The United States moved back to centre stage with Special Envoy Dennis Ross and Secretary of State Albright heavily engaged in preventing a breakdown of the Israeli–Palestinian track. Furthermore, any Arab attempts at mediation have come from President Mubarak with Jordan playing a much more secondary role. However, on the Israeli side this period has been characterised by an increased sensitivity towards Jordan, and King Hussein in

---

28 Statement issued by IDF, 12 October 1997, Tel Aviv.

particular. The appointment of Efraim Halevy as head of Mossad serves as a good illustration of this seemingly new awareness in the Netanyahu administration. On the Jordanian side, King Hussein's major fear remains the prospect of a renewed Palestinian Intifada in the West Bank, and its potential knock-on effect on Jordan's large Palestinian population. Such a scenario would force the King to further down-scale public moves towards normalisation with Israel, and consequently further erode the prospects for Jordan's fragile economy.

In summary, the period since October 1997 has not been dominated by the dramatic events that defined the previous periods of the Netanyahu administration. What has emerged from all the difficulties can be defined as a neutral peace – neither warm (as many on both sides had intended), nor cold (as defined by the Israeli-Egyptian peace). This neutral peace is based not on expectations of building a new Middle East, but rather on mutual interests and strategic realities. In essence, Netanyahu's vision of the future of the Middle East based on realpolitik has superseded Peres's grand vision of a common market of states in which Israeli–Jordanian relations were to play a central role.

Neutral peace: mutual interests and strategic realities in the Middle East

It is important first to define the basic mutual self-interests of Israel and Jordan. The basic interests can be defined as follows.

Israeli interests
1. The prevention of Jordan being used by a third party to launch attacks against Israel.
2. Strategic depth of land to prevent a lightning attack of land forces on its eastern borders.
3. Cooperation in the fight against radical regimes in the area such as Iran.
4. The potential for Israel to use Jordan as means of attracting other Middle East counties into strategic alliances (particularly in the long term Turkey).

Jordanian interests
1. Feels threatened by Iran, Iraq and radical Islamic groups.

2.   Suspects Syria of carrying out terrorist attacks against it and needs support against Syrian hostile action.
3.   Opposition to a powerful Palestinian state on the West Bank.

These interests are enshrined in points 1(a) and 4(c) and (b) in Article 4: Security. The clear intention of these articles was to prevent any hostile foreign forces being stationed or crossing lands. In practical terms this means that should Iraq move into Jordan (as appeared possible in 1990–1) it is highly likely that Israel would respond considering such actions as an attack on itself. In addition, it tied the two countries together in terms of strategic alliances. Jordan, for example, would not be allowed (should it wish to) to sign a strategic alliance with a country that had not reached a peace accommodation with Israel.

Furthermore, it is clear the mutual interests between Israel and Jordan have not been radically altered by the difficulties in the relationship between King Hussein and the current Israeli government. Consequently, it is argued that these realities bind Israel and Jordan as close together in the Netanyahu era as during Rabin's period of office. As a result, although as previously outlined, the relationship between Israel and Jordan has been put under strain since 1996, it has shown itself to be extremely resilient. In short, the state of neutral peace in relations between Israel and Jordan remains a peace where these overall interests and strategic needs of each country can withstand growing pressures from short-term events and miscalculated actions.

The absence of a full warm peace between Israel and Jordan has prevented the full integration of Jordan into formal alliances with Israel and its major regional strategic partner Turkey (see Chapter 10). Despite these problems Israeli military planners still retain the long-term aim of a regional alliance comprised of Israel, Turkey and Jordan with military and economic support from the United States. Such an alliance is viewed as a means of checking the power of Syria, and the increase of Iranian and Russian influence in the Middle East. However, with the other tracks of the peace process stagnating, Jordan feels uncomfortable about moving forward too quickly by undertaking joint military exercises with Israel and Turkey. This said, Jordan has shown that by sending senior observers to monitor a joint Israel–Turkish naval search and rescue operation in early 1998 it does not intend to be sidelined totally in such matters. Moreover, intelligence cooperation between Israel and Jordan is thought to have been largely resumed following its suspension after the bungled Mossad assassination attempt in Amman. This form of cooperation away from the public eye is vital for both sides, and crucially because of its nature does not require the type of public commitment that a formal strategic pact between the two counties would demand.

Finally, it should be stressed that the military establishment in both Israel and Jordan are eager to develop and deepen ties between the two countries. Moreover, military planners in Israel are keen on the idea of Jordan serving as something more than simply a buffer state. In essence, it is hoped that after a period of time Jordan will play a more active role in the fight against radical regimes and groups in the region. In carrying out such a role it is presumed that the Jordanian armed forces will take a much more active role in both defensive and offensive actions against such extremists. However, in the short term Israeli planners retain a degree of concern over the stability of the Hashemite Kingdom, and consequently IDF plans for scenarios involving military confrontations with Jordan have not, to date, been significantly modified.

Conclusions

Returning to the central theme of the book it is clear that the Netanyahu government has complicated relations with Jordan. Much of the blame for this must go to the prime minister himself and his failure to build successfully on his relationship with King Hussein, which had first developed while Netanyahu was the opposition leader. Moreover, events such as the opening of the tunnel in Jerusalem and the expansion of Jewish settlements in East Jerusalem were not helped by Netanyahu's failure to consult privately with, or even simply inform, the King prior to announcing the decision. The King's understandable anger at these unilateral actions and the lack of progress in other tracks of the peace process have led to a situation where Jordan, although honouring the 1994 peace treaty, has not developed relations with Israel to the extent that was originally intended.

However, King Hussein seems to make a distinction between the Netanyahu government and Israel in general. Regarding the latter he has maintained his place in Israeli society as the one Arab leader to cross the divide, and therefore occupies an almost unique position of influence in Israel for an Arab leader. When the King stated that he was worried that the peace process between Jordan and Israel was at the point of collapse there was widespread concern both within the government and in Israel as a whole. Eventually, but only after the failed Mossad operation in Amman, the Israeli prime minister revised his strategy towards dealing with the King and has tried to avoid any actions that would place the King in a difficult position. To a certain extent this has been made easier by a downgrading of Jordanian involvement in the peace process and the lack of major attempts of mediation by the King.

Having charged Netanyahu with a failure to develop his relationship with Jordan and for, at times, damaging Israeli–Jordanian relations two additional points need to be stressed.

First, had the Labour government of Shimon Peres been re-elected there is a strong likelihood that Israeli relations with Jordan would have come under additional strain with the Labour Party's concentration on the Palestinian track, and in particular its support for a Palestinian state in the West Bank together with its acceptance of a PA role in the holy sites in Jerusalem. Under a Peres administration it would have been likely (though as Chapter 3 outlines, not certain) that the Palestinians would have been given control of the vast majority of territory in the West Bank, therefore making a potential state stronger than under the Likud. The extent of Jordanian unease at such prospects is illustrated by the development of a strong working relationship between King Hussein and Ariel Sharon, both of whom share a deep distrust of the PLO and Arafat, and oppose a strong PLO-dominated state in the West Bank. In addition, Peres's vision of a new Middle East (summarised in this chapter from one of his speeches) seemed to ignore Arab, and in this case Jordanian, reluctance towards full normalisation with Israel until all remaining issues in the peace process had been resolved. In essence, it would still have been difficult for a Labour-led government in Israel to overcome opposition in Jordan over deepening economic ties with Israel and developing joint infrastructure projects. Indeed, much of Peres's vision was seen in the Arab world as an Israeli attempt at economic colonialism.

Second, the emergence of what this chapter has termed a neutral peace between Israel and Jordan (which is based on mutual interests and strategic needs) would appear to offer the best opportunity for medium- to long-term stability in relations. In addition, because it is based on mutuality and needs it has shown that this type of relationship can withstand pressures from both developments in other tracks of the peace process and difficulties caused by events and unilateral actions by either side. There are signs that Jordan, after initial difficulties with strategic cooperation with Israel, is starting to play a more active role under the auspices of the United States – both in terms of public military exercise and private intelligence work. As Israeli–Jordanian reactions stabilise and develop over the coming years such strategic cooperation is set to increase greatly.

Finally, the fear that the Israeli and Jordanian relationship will, in the long run, develop into a cold peace along the same lines as the Israeli–Egyptian model needs to be addressed. To a certain extent this depends on regional developments and the outcome of the remaining tracks of the peace process. However, as strongly argued earlier, the strong mutual interests and strategic needs between Israel and Jordan show little sign of eroding. Furthermore, King Hussein has shown himself to be robust in standing up to pressure both from within Jordan and the wider Arab world (mainly from Syria and to a lesser extent Egypt) to isolate Israel in the region. In doing so Jordan has shown that it cannot afford to turn back the clock. In short, Jordan needs to maintain its ties with Israel just as Israel needs a friendly regime on its eastern borders.

8

An Israeli–Syrian peace on the Golan Heights

In providing an understanding of the dynamics involved in any potential Israeli–Syrian peace it is essential to discuss the central role of the disputed Golan Heights, which Israel captured from the Syrians in the 1967 Six Day War. Syria has stated that its price for making peace with Israel is a full return of the Arab lands which Israel conquered in 1967 and specifically all of the Golan Heights. However, since 1967 the Golan has been of vital strategic value to Israel with its commanding views overlooking Syria and its importance in helping secure Israel's north-eastern border and towns.[1] In addition, since conquering the land Israel has developed a strong physical presence on the Golan Heights. It has settled the land and today there are some 13,000 Jewish residents living in 32 communities on the Golan in kibbutzim, moshavim and in the town of Katzrin.[2] Moreover, Israel has developed a large agricultural sector there as well as the area becoming a major tourist attraction for Israelis. Finally, the Golan Heights contains vast reserves of water resources over which Israel is extremely reluctant to give up control.

On 14 December 1981 the Israeli Knesset passed the Golan Heights Law (63-21), which applied Israeli law to the Golan Heights. The law states the following.

1. The law, jurisdiction and administration of the State of Israel will apply in the territory of the Golan Heights as described in the Appendix (map).

---

1 For a detailed account of the Golan Heights' strategic value to Israel see, for example, D. Eshel, 'The Golan Heights: a vital strategic asset for Israel' in E. Karsh (ed.), *From Rabin to Netanyahu: Israel's Troubled Agenda* (London and Portland, Frank Cass, 1997), pp. 225–38.
2 Figures from *The Statistical Abstract of Israel* (various editions), The Central Bureau of Statistics, Jerusalem.

2.   The law goes into effect on the day it is approved by the Knesset. The Interior Ministry is in charge of executing the law.[3]

The then prime minister, Menahem Begin, cited historical, political and security factors which had led to the decision to extend Israeli law to the area.[4] In historical terms he claimed that the land was an inseparable part of the Land of Israel. In political terms, Begin claimed that on several occasions Israel had urged Syria to enter into negotiations but that it had refused. Moreover, it had stated that it would never recognise the Zionist state even if the Palestinians eventually did. In security terms, Begin stated that there was a national consensus that in order to preserve Israeli security Israel would never be able to step down from the Golan Heights.

Of the three areas cited by Begin it is the security issue that dominates the debate over the future of the Golan Heights and this chapter examines the developments on this issue in terms of the overall framework of achieving peace between Israel and Syria. As well as providing an account of the security options for both sides, and the potential problems with the various plans, the role of internal politics in determining the outcome of the process is highlighted. The other major issue involved in securing peace between these countries, Israel's presence in a self-declared security zone in southern Lebanon, is discussed in detail in Chapter 9.

In assessing how the process with Syria has developed under Netanyahu it is important to analyse first the developments that took place under Rabin and Peres between 1993 and 1996. In essence, both Rabin and subsequently Peres appeared willing to take larger gambles on the Syrian track than any of the other tracks of the peace process by secretly offering to return all of the Golan Heights to Syria. Indeed, the Syrian track was the initial priority for the previous Labour-led government with Rabin who felt that if he could secure peace with Syria then the rest of the Arab world would follow suit, thus ending the Arab–Israel conflict and securing Israel's long-term security. This chapter will chronicle the details of Rabin's and Peres's proposals to Syria as well

---

3   From the Laws of the State of Israel, Government Press Office, Jerusalem. See also background paper: 'The Golan Heights', Government Press Office, Jerusalem, 8 February 1994, p. 4.

4   For more details on this, see A. Shalev, *Israel and Syria: Peace and Security on the Golan*, pp. 82–3.

as examining the reasoning behind President Assad's reluctance to accept them. In addition, explanations of why the process has continued to stagnate under Netanyahu (see Chapter 2) are examined together with frameworks for maintaining a peace process between Israel and Syria with limited aims or with the intention of more dramatic progress.

The Golan Heights issue under Rabin and Peres, 1993–1996

Yitzhak Rabin and the Labour Party were returned to power in 1992 on the platform that the Golan Heights was a vital part of Israel's security and that, as Rabin himself said himself, Israel must never come down from the Golan. At this time Israel's overall position could be defined as follows.

1. Israel saw the Golan Heights as a vital strategic area, and even if there were to be a peace accord signed with Israel, then Israel would wish to retain control of all the area.
2. Israel saw the settlements on the Golan as helping protect Israeli control over the area and utilising the productive farm land in the area.
3. Israel wished to retain control over the water resources in the Golan Heights.

The Syrian position was equally clear and was as follows.

1. Syria demanded the return of all of the Golan Heights to Syrian sovereignty. It saw an Israeli withdrawal in terms of months rather than years.
2. It demanded the right of return for Syrians who had fled the Golan during the 1967 Six Day War.
3. Syria wanted control over the water resources and for Israel settlements to be immediately dismantled.
4. Only after the Golan Heights were returned to Syria would it consider ending the state of war and recognising the state of Israel.

However, between 1992 and 1993 there were wide-ranging secret changes made by Rabin to Israel's position. The recently published minutes of meetings between Rabin and the US Secretary of State, Warren Christopher, confirm that Rabin was willing to consider the idea of a full-scale withdrawal from the Golan. However, Rabin with his typical caution was concerned that Assad, even if Israel met his major demand, would find a way of rejecting peace with Israel. Consequently, Rabin enquired in a key meeting on the issue with Christopher on 4 August 1993:

> Assuming their needs on full withdrawal are met, are they ready for a peace deal with open borders, diplomatic relations and so on? We are giving the tangible assets. As was the case with Egypt, there are elements of peace we must get before completion of withdrawal: and it also depends on security arrangements . . . You can tell him it is your [Christopher's] understanding, but that he will not get it if he does not fulfil our needs.[5]

According to Ze'ev Schiff, Christopher returned to Israel the next day from a meeting with President Assad in Damascus with an encouraging response from Assad to Rabin's offer which although not direct at this stage would have been clear to Assad what the US and Israel were putting on the table.[6] At the meeting on 5 August 1993 Rabin told Christopher that if they (Israel and Syria) agreed on a package, he would fight for it and that Israel needed four or five years.[7] He stated once more that security arrangements were the key, and that he wanted American early warning stations on the Golan Heights plus a physical American presence there as well as part of an overall security package.[8]

In subsequent conversations in early 1993, Christopher informed Rabin that President Assad had asked for a clear commitment of an Israeli withdrawal to the 4 June 1967 borders[9] and would halt the talks

---

5 Minutes of the meeting between Prime Minister Rabin and Secretary of State Warren Christopher on 4 August 1993. The Israeli Ambassador to the United States, Itamar Rabinovich, was also present.
6 Schiff, 'What did Rabin promise the Syrians?'.
7 The lack of something more positive from Assad to this initiative led Rabin to go with Peres and the Oslo channel with the Palestinians rather than the Syrian option. Interestingly, Peres knew nothing of Rabin's secret pledges to Assad and was only informed of them when he was briefed by President Clinton on the day of Rabin's funeral.
8 Minutes of the meeting between Prime Minister Rabin and Secretary of State Warren Christopher on 5 August 1993.
9 The 4 June 1967 borders are open to interpretation. For a detailed assessment of Assad's intentions here and what he considered to be the 4 June 1967 borders, see Z. Schiff, 'June 4 1967: in three acts', *Ha-Aretz*, 2 September 1997.

if he did not receive this from Rabin.[10] The next key meeting between Rabin and Christopher took place on 18 July 1994 where the Secretary of State made a plea that it was essential that if Assad agreed to the conditions then he could state things clearly at the end of the line, but that it was not a formal commitment to Syria. In response Rabin said:

> You can tell him that he has every reason to believe, but that the Israelis will not spell it out before our needs are met.[11]

In response Christopher summarised and confirmed Rabin's position stating that he had it (Rabin's proposal) in his pocket, but that it wasn't on the table. An understanding of Rabin's position was provided by the US Special Envoy, Dennis Ross, in a subsequent meeting with the Israeli Ambassador to the US, Itamar Rabinovich. As Ross put it:

> At the end of the day, as part of a package in which Israel's needs would have to be met, the US understands that your needs would be met and therefore the meaning of full withdrawal in these circumstances would be to 4 June 1967. This is only when they meet your need on everything. In any event it's not on the table. It is in our pocket, not yours. It is our understanding, not a commitment. And we will only get to it when we have agreed on everything.[12]

The Americans were not happy with Rabin's verbal commitments and tried in vain to persuade him to put it down on paper. However, Rabin heeded the advice of Ambassador Rabinovich not to do so. Indeed, there is some evidence that Rabin by this stage, while still maintaining his offer in the presence of the Americans, was less enthusiastic to pursue the Syrian option following his concessions on the Palestinian track with the signing of the Declaration of Principles and recognition of the PLO in the autumn of 1993.

In addition to these secret commitments, Rabin continued to order the army to plan and conduct negotiations for only a partial withdrawal from the Golan Heights in which the Israel army would retain some positions on the Golan. Although this could be construed to be normal

---

10 See Schiff, 'What did Rabin promise the Syrians?'.
11 Minutes of the meeting between Prime Minster Rabin and Secretary of State Warren Christopher on 18 July 1994.
12 Reported in Schiff, 'What did Rabin promise the Syrians?'.

negotiation behaviour it appeared to confuse the Syrians over Rabin's real intentions.[13] Consequently, the mixed signals coming out of Jerusalem at this stage unsettled Assad who, with his refusal for direct face-to-face negotiations, was reliant on the US to pass messages between himself and Rabin.

There are a number of potential possibilities as to why Assad did not embrace the Rabin initiative and these can be divided into two frameworks: a technical explanation and a deeper, more ideological reluctance. The first deals with specific problems about the content and timing of Rabin's initiative while the second is of more significance in the long term. In addition, it is perfectly possible that Assad's rejection was based on a combination of factors from each of the frameworks.[14]

The first explanation of Assad's rejection offers two possibilities: first, Assad did not believe that he had a commitment from Rabin – only a promise to conduct negotiations over 4 June 1967 borders; and second, Assad did accept that he had a commitment from Rabin but that the security arrangements demanded by Rabin were too high. The deeper, more ideological reluctance explanation suggests that Assad fears a peace deal with Israel, and consequently it does not matter what any Israeli leader offers. The rationale behind the latter explanation can be divided into external (international) and domestic reasons and is as follows: the absence of Israel as a threat would make it more difficult for Syria to obtain aid, influence Arab consuls and maintain its control over Lebanon. In addition, any diplomatic solution would increase US influence in the region, and Syria feels that the US favours Egypt, Israel and Jordan over it, would block Syrian influence on the Palestinians and strengthen Syria's regional rival Israel. In domestic terms enemies of the regime within Syria could portray the peace as treachery, it could raise popular demands for democracy and higher living standards. Finally, Assad's regime does not wish to reduce the size of its armed forces which help sustain its rule.[15]

---

13 The Israeli–Palestinian negotiations proceeded along two simultaneous tracks (Washington and Oslo) with very different positions being offered in each of the separate negotiations. However, at the time (1993–4) this approach of, in essence, providing a cover or type of safety net for secret negotiations with more formal ones was quite new in the Arab–Israeli talks.

14 For a critical account of Assad's action and the missed opportunities, see D. Makovsky, 'Assad: the great miscalculator', *Jerusalem Post*, 4 June 1996.

15 A similar framework is provided in more detail in, for example, G. Bechor, 'Syria's shadow enemies', *Ha-Aretz,* 4 December 1996, p. 3. See also B. Rubin, 'External

In employing this framework it should be noted that Assad's rejection of Israel's overtures did not mean that he had opted for a military option.[16] On the contrary, Assad preferred the status quo of "no peace – no war". Syria had previously lost three wars against Israel (with only superpower pressure preventing Israel forces from rolling on towards Damascus). In essence this explanation argues that Assad is playing a long-term game and is hoping that Syria's relatively weak current position will improve in the future (see part two of Chapter 10 for an account of Assad's strategic moves to alter this and in particular relations with Russia). In the meantime, Assad is employing tones of cooperation and reasonableness with the US in negotiations to maintain a process of sorts.[17]

It goes beyond the scope of this chapter to consider the merits of these frameworks of explanations. Moreover, experts on Assad argue that he keeps his cards very close to his chest and consequently it is mere speculation in claiming to understand fully his exact motives.[18] However, it is important to stress that Assad's position, if based to some degree on the later framework, is rational (though not necessarily correct) and reflects a long-term strategic plan for Syria. Within the scope of this study, this strategy has important ramifications for the conduct of the Syrian track of the peace process by the Netanyahu-led government which are discussed later.

---

influences on the Israeli election' in D. Elazar and S. Sandler (eds), *Israel at the Polls 1996* (London and Portland, Frank Cass, 1998), p. 164. For a critical account of Assad's intentions, see also E. Karsh, 'What on earth is Assad up to?', *Jerusalem Post*, 20 September 1996.

16 Assad has himself stated that a stalemate in the peace process need not necessarily lead to war. Interview with Assad, broadcast on CNN, 28 September 1996.

17 Israeli intelligence was split on Assad's reasons for not agreeing to a peace treaty. The IDF Intelligence Branch accepted that Assad had made a strategic choice of going for peace. However, Mossad was more sceptical as confirmed in comments made by the outgoing Mossad head Shabtai Shavit: "I am still not completely convinced that he has actually made the necessary turning to reach a true and sincere peace, which includes full normalisation. I believe the Syrian president's real intentions must be subjected to a very, very careful and fundamental examination. I think the assessments about strategic departures were premature, and we must still search for signs and evidence of Assad's real desire for peace with Israel." Interview in *Yediot Ahronot*, 6 June 1996.

18 The established Western source on Assad and his thinking is P. Seale, *Assad of Syria: The Struggle for the Middle East* (London, I.B. Tauris, 1988).

In the end, Rabin grew impatient with the Syrians after the failure of the May 1994 initiative and Assad's reluctance for whatever reasons to make peace with Israel. Subsequently, he turned his attention towards King Hussein and the stronger potential for making peace with Jordan. The US tried to persuade Rabin that King Hussein would not move the Israeli–Jordanian process forward without the Syrians' prior approval. However, the Americans were proved wrong, and Rabin right, as he moved quickly to secure a full peace treaty with Jordan by the end of October 1994.[19] Finally, Rabin handed control of the Syrian channel to Peres to see if he could break the deadlock with Assad. Importantly, Rabin did not authorise Peres to make any commitment along the same lines that he himself had suggested in August 1993 and July 1994.[20] Moreover, by passing the track to Peres, Rabin was indicating that he no longer saw the potential for a breakthrough with the Syrian track in the near future.

Following Rabin's death Peres, now prime minister, went a stage further than Rabin's initiative, and against the advice of Itamar Rabinovich, formally adopted the position of a withdrawal from the Golan Heights in return for full peace. Moreover, Peres sent his now famous message to Assad through the Americans asking him to fly high and fast, and to hold a summit with him to negotiate a treaty. Peres correctly sensed that in the immediate period following Rabin's death the consensus in Israel had swung, temporarily, in favour of exchanging land for peace. The right and its leadership were in a state of a near disarray with Netanyahu charged by many from the left as having stoked the violent debate that culminated in Rabin's death. Unfortunately for Peres, the Syrians did not give the positive response to the plan that he had anticipated. As previously described in the Assad strategy framework, the Syrians still held reservations about making full peace with Israel. Added to this was the naturally cautious nature of Assad who after years of slow progress with Israel may have been suspicious of an Israeli desire to move quickly. Moreover, Assad may also have had concerns as to whether or not Peres

19 On this issue, see M. Zak, 'Syria's missed chances', *Jerusalem Post*, 3 September 1997.
20 In true cautious Rabin style he was already working on the deniability of the so-called "hypothetical exercise" and his offer of a return of all the Golan Heights to the Syrians in case US officials saw fit to leak it to the international press.

could deliver on any commitments he made on the question of an Israeli withdrawal from the Golan Heights.[21]

From this it is clear that despite the fact that Peres was now officially giving the Syrians their major demand Assad did not want to move as fast as Peres had hoped. Consequently, the talks that did eventually open in Maryland were conducted by Israeli and Syrian officials rather than at ministerial or leadership level. In addition, the Syrians insisted on conducting the negotiations through a third party (the Americans) and not as Israel had hoped in direct talks between the two parties (as in the Oslo process).[22] In the end, the suicide bombing campaign of Hamas and Islamic Jihad in February and March 1996 led to the Israeli delegation being recalled from the talks which were further put on hold by the decision of Peres to call early elections in Israel May 1996. A lack of progress in the talks with Syria and the diminishing prospects for a peace deal in the short term were one of the major factors that led Peres to his decision to risk early elections which he subsequently lost to Netanyahu and the right.[23]

The Golan Heights issue under Netanyahu: change and continuity, 1996–1998

Since the election of the Netanyahu-led government in 1996 formal negotiations with the Syrians have not restarted. After assuming office Netanyahu was asked by the Americans to accept the Rabin and Peres undertakings about a withdrawal from the Golan. However, Netanyahu argued that he would only honour formal written undertakings by the previous government such as the Oslo Accords. Moreover, the prime minister discussed the issue with Itamar Rabinovich, who argued against

---

21 The author found in 1996 that Syrian officials did not have a detailed understanding of the Israeli domestic political game. Their tendency was to view Israel as a single entity and realise the importance of PR gestures and of appealing to different sectors of Israeli society. If the Syrians had been better informed they might have realised that the window of opportunity was not as long as they presumed.

22 For an account of the talks see, for example, Chapter 7 in A. Bregman and J. El-Tahri, *The Fifty Years War: Israel and the Arabs* (London, Penguin Books, 1998), pp. 256–66.

23 On the issue of Syria and Israeli electoral politics see, for example, G. Steinberg, 'Peace, security and terror in the 1996 elections' in D. Elazar and S. Sandler (eds), *Israel at the Polls 1996*, pp. 224–5.

accepting the American request.[24] Consequently, the Syrians refused to return to the negotiations until Netanyahu accepted that they would start off from the position where the Maryland talks finished – that is, discussion of a full Israeli withdrawal from the Golan Heights. Moreover, the United States which is central to any set of negotiations appears under Secretary of State, Madeleine Albright, to be more preoccupied with saving the Israeli–Palestinian track of the peace process and has not devoted the same energy and resources towards the Israeli–Syrian track as her predecessor Warren Christopher. This may have been tactical or simply a reflection of US concerns over the Palestinian talks.

However, as outlined in Chapter 2, the lack of formal negotiations between the Israelis and Syrians has not led to a lack of engagement between the two sides. On the political front there have been groups of intermediaries shuttling between Jerusalem and Damascus attempting to maintain a line of communication between the two parties with the long-term intention of restarting more formal talks. In addition, as Chapter 2 also suggests, there is strong evidence that senior figures in Netanyahu's administration may have met in Europe with their Syrian counterparts.

On the military front between 1996 and 1998 there have been no overt moves by Syria to attempt to secure the Golan by military means. At various times senior Syrian commanders and defence officials have talked up such an eventuality but evidence on the ground suggests that at no stage have preparations been made for a major offensive. From this it can be deduced that Assad is content to wage a proxy war with Israel through the Syrian-controlled Hizbollah in southern Lebanon (see Chapter 9). However, Israel military planners suggest that Syria has the strategic balance of forces to be able to make a limited strike of the Golan to regain control of part of the territory for political victory. Consequently, Assad retains the option of a limited surprise attack in order to pressure Israel further into political concessions over the Golan. However, this would lead to an increase in reluctance within Israel of Israeli society and within the political and military élites to return the Golan in the foreseeable future.[25] Such an action by Assad, who is well aware of its consequences, would therefore largely confirm his reluctance

---

24 On Netanyahu's consultations with Rabinovich, see Zak, 'Syria's missed chances'.
25 On this see, E. Sivan, 'Danger from the north?', *Ha-Aretz*, 24 August 1997.

to strike a peace deal with Israel. A more viable option for Assad would be to instigate an armed confrontation with Israel in southern Lebanon involving Hizbollah with Syrian forces in support. This could gain Syria a limited victory while limiting the damage of the possibility of getting the Golan back in the long term.

Since assuming office Netanyahu has tried to find a formula to move the talks with Syria forward without committing himself to a total withdrawal from the Golan Heights. The official position of the Netanyahu government on the Golan Heights and the Likud as stated in its 1996 election manifesto is as follows:

> Israel will conduct peace negotiations with Syria, while maintaining Israeli sovereignty over the Golan Heights and its water resources.[26]

However, in private the prime minister's overall position bears a strong resemblance to Rabin's proposal of 1993–4. In essence, Netanyahu's formula is based on tying the depth of withdrawal (Israeli concessions) from the Golan Heights to the depth of security arrangements provided by Syria. It is logical that such a formula could conceivably lead to a total Israeli withdrawal from the Golan in return for total peace.[27] What is markedly different from the Rabin and Peres administrations is the tone of government statements directed towards Syria and some of its actions.

Rabinovich cites three of these that have sent the opposite signal to Syria:[28] first, the Golan Entrenchment Law, which would have meant that a special Knesset majority would be required to repeal the 1981 extension of Israeli law to the Golan, gained the support of the prime minister and the Cabinet (they had initially opposed the bill); second, the decision of Ariel Sharon to site a proposed dam in the southern foothills of the Golan Heights was confrontational as Syria claims the land is part of the area of the Golan Heights and therefore its territory (conversely, Israel argues that it is part of Mandatory Palestine and belongs to Israel; however, the Syrians view the project as an attempt by Israel to create a *fait accompli* in the disputed area); and third, in his keynote speech to the graduates of the National Defence College on 14 August 1994,

---

26 Chapter One: Peace and Security, 1996 *Likud Party Platform*, Likud Party Headquarters, Tel Aviv, p. 2.
27 For more on this, see Rabinovich, 'Commotion without motion'.
28 Ibid.

Netanyahu, while discussing the Israeli–Syrian track, questioned the value of full normalisation and spoke openly about the need for Israel to hold on to vital territory. As the prime minister put it:

> As long as our area is characterised by non-democratic regimes, we will have to pursue a policy that will preserve our ability to deter and will not give up strategic assets that are vital for our security. I believe that these principles can guide us also in obtaining a peace settlement with Syria.[29]

These seemingly contradictory approaches towards Syria by the prime minister could have two explanations. The first is that they merely reflect Netanyahu's relatively weak domestic position, which is largely covered in the opening chapters of this book. The strategy behind this approach would be that of talking tough in order both to develop his security credentials within Israeli society and to please his party, cabinet and wider coalition. Such a scenario would not rule out significant compromise at a later date if Assad were willing, or interested, in providing Israel with the necessary security commitments that its military establishment require.

The second explanation is that Netanyahu's position outlined in speeches such as the above accurately reflects his positions and intentions. This would largely rule out the possibility of a peace settlement with Syria before the next Israeli election, and Netanyahu would have to rely on progress on the other tracks of the peace process in order to present himself to the Israeli electorate as the man capable of delivering peace with security. Such a strategy would be a huge gamble for Netanyahu's chances of re-election in elections scheduled for the year 2000. A more likely explanation for the prime minister's actions and speeches is that they represent his beliefs and lines of thinking but are not cast-in-stone policy statements.[30]

Unfortunately, President Assad has tremendous difficulties in understanding what Netanyahu's intentions are and this has been reflected in

---

29 Address by Binyamin Netanyahu to Graduates of the National Defence College, 14 August 1997.

30 Netanyahu has himself hinted that this is the case. In a speech delivered in September 1997 he appeared to indicate his flexibility when discussing the Syrian track when he said: "The result will probably be very different for the both of us (Israel and Syria) from the initial starting position." Speech by Binyamin Netanyahu, Jerusalem, 15 September 1997.

Syria's strategy towards Israel since the election of Netanyahu in 1996. On the one hand, Syria has continued to talk up the possibility of war with Israel, but on the other hand, its forces have not moved from their defence positions in Syria and Lebanon. During times of tension senior Israeli military officials have charged that Syria is preparing for a partial retake of the Golan. However, even such assessments have been qualified with the fact that Assad would prefer a political solution.[31] During a visit by Israeli Arabs to Syria in August 1997, Assad remarked that he felt he could have made peace with Rabin or Peres but was not sure if he could reach a settlement with Netanyahu.[32] In addition, he is thought to have replied to a letter carried by the delegation from the Israeli Labour Party leader, Ehud Barak, who promised to continue the negotiations from the point they had left off in Maryland during Peres's government. Indeed, he told the delegation that he hoped he would be able to reach a settlement with Barak.[33] Such comments from Assad are highly significant as they indicate a new thinking in Damascus not to view Israel as a single entity in which the leadership are one and the same. Further evidence of this new thinking was apparent in Syrian radio commenting on the debate in Israel over the maintenance of its security zone in Lebanon. Moreover, such steps, although small, could nevertheless be of significance in the future. Conversely, it may prove to be simply a Syrian tactic designed to attempt to divide the Israeli political leadership.

In analysing Assad's overall strategy towards Israel since 1996 it is important to return to the two frameworks that were employed to provide an understanding of his reluctance to take up Rabin's offer in 1993 and 1994.[34] If Assad did indeed not accept Rabin's proposals because he believed that Israeli security demands were too great, then there is a

---

31 For an example of this, see the testimony of a senior Israeli Intelligence Officer to the Knesset Foreign Affairs and Defence Committee in September 1997 and reported in B. Tsur 'IDF: Syria preparing for partial retake of the Golan', *Jerusalem Post*, 16 September 1997.

32 Assad stated to this group that: "Thus far Netanyahu has made strange statements. He proposed exchanging peace for peace and later he proposed exchanging peace for security. Afterwards he announced that he is for UN Resolutions 242 and 338 according to his own interpretation of them." Comments by President Assad to a delegation of Israeli Arabs, Damascus, August 1997.

33 S. Rodan, 'What does Assad want?', *Jerusalem Post*, 21 August 1997.

34 For a highly critical account of Assad's strategy towards Israel in 1996, see S. Yerushalmi, 'Syrian landmine', *Ma'ariv*, 25 November 1996.

possibility that following intensive negotiations an agreement could be reached that would suit both Israeli and Syrian security arrangements. However, if Assad fears a peace deal with Israel (the second framework) then it is unlikely that whatever Netanyahu offers will be accepted by the Syrians. Moreover, the natural assumption in this framework is that Assad was pleased by the election of Netanyahu who has pulled the rug from a set of negotiations that were going to present Assad with some difficult choices. However, it is not inconceivable that Assad, even if employing the long-term wait-and-see strategy, will shift away from it at a later date, but he wishes to strengthen Syria's position both economically and militarily before doing so.

Netanyahu's options on the Golan and plans for peace with Syria, 1996–1998

In studying Netanyahu's options, a brief examination will be made of the Lebanese question, the Dore Gold Plan, the peace formula and unilateral withdrawal from Lebanon.

Lebanon First Plan: summer 1996

It is important to examine the specific proposals that Netanyahu has put forward towards Syria which have at times seemed like public relations exercises, but nevertheless when examined in more detail do reveal a line of thinking which is far detached from the rhetoric and bluster of much of the prime minister's public pronouncements. The first of these proposal became known as the Lebanon First Plan which, in simple terms, meant a separation of the Lebanese question from Syria. In essence, Israel was to withdraw from Lebanon with security guarantees from Syria, which would subsequently be used as a confidence-building measure for a potential withdrawal from the Golan. This plan and Assad's forthright rejection of it are discussed in Chapter 9 within the context of Israel's involvement in southern Lebanon.[35]

---

35 One of Assad's clearest rejections of "Lebanon First" came at a press conference with President Mubarak in Alexandria on 7 August 1996. As President Assad put it: "Syria and Lebanon first, at the same time, in the same steps. No one who read the invitation sent by Netanyahu gets the feeling that it is the road to peace and that those who wrote it are committed to peace."

The Dore Gold Plan: August 1996

The next Netanyahu initiative came in August 1996 in the form of a wide-ranging set of proposals by the prime minister's political adviser, Dore Gold, the details of which were never made fully public.[36] The central aim of the plan was twofold: first, to avoid the issue of normalisation which Gold believed to be the Syrian problem in the negotiations under Rabin and Peres (put simply, Gold charged that Syria had reservations about full normalisation ties such as embassies, trade links and tourism); and second, to attempt to develop relations between the two countries on a wide range of issues that would be able to withstand, and indeed prevent, a total breakdown on the issue of returning territory to Syria. In other words an alternative, or an addition, to set piece International Peace Conferences and bi-lateral negotiations.

The plan was largely based on the Helsinki Accord, a model devised by Henry Kissinger in the 1970s as a means of ensuring a sort of regional security in Europe during the years of the Cold War. Gold argued that the state of the Israeli–Syrian relationship was very similar to the East–West relations of the Cold War era. Consequently, the intention was to build a similar security establishment in the Middle East with channels of communications being developed between Israel and Syria in order to try to prevent any escalation into violence. Such examples include notification in advance of manoeuvres involving brigade level or higher or major tank exercises; and the installation of a hot line between Jerusalem and Damascus.

In essence, Gold saw the Israeli–Syrian relationship as being in a state of transition – peace had not been secured, but there was a peace process that had produced some tangible results. Consequently, he foresaw a common interest between Israel and Syria in maintaining, and securing, the process with in effect a series of safety nets so when the negotiations got difficult there would be other channels open. The groups (or as Gold termed them "baskets") would include the following areas: security, economic, water and human resources (Gold knew that human rights, which was in Kissinger's original model, would be vetoed by Syria). Moreover, other countries were to be encouraged to join in order to build fully this super-regional security system. The United

---

36 Many of the details were discussed in N. Levitzky, 'Netanyahu's Syrian paper', *Yediot Ahronot*, 16 August 1996, weekend supplement, pp. 6–7.

States was proposed to chair "the baskets" in alternation with France. The inclusion of the latter was aimed to please the Syrians whom Gold knew would not accept sole American chairmanship.

On a more specific level the plan included the following six aspects.

1. The IDF to leave Lebanon, with security arrangement guarantees by the Syrians.
2. The withdrawal to be both military and political and Israel to tell Assad that Lebanon is his.
3. Israel accepts the formula that peace in Lebanon is conditional upon comprehensive peace with Syria.
4. Israel accepts the formula that comprehensive peace in the region is conditional upon comprehensive peace with Syria.
5. Israel is prepared to discuss the future of the Golan Heights at the Maryland talks (to be resumed). The future status of the Golan is open to discussion.
6. Israel to offer Syria the option to expand the basis of the Maryland talks to include regional meetings and sub-committee working groups, mechanisms to address everyone's immediate interests.

In addition when the talks resumed, Israel would declare publicly that it would not withdraw from all of the Golan Heights. However, the plan, which dealt more with form than substance, was never taken up by the Syrians who viewed it simply as a mechanism for preventing a complete Israeli withdrawal from the Golan Heights. The standard response of the Syrians is that they want the Golan first, and only then will they discuss the issues with which this plan deals. Despite its failure, Gold's plan does nevertheless serve as an interesting framework for future cooperation in the Middle East, and provides an interesting insight into the thinking of Netanyahu who appeared to have adopted a carrot and stick approach in negotiations with Syria. This plan, with its absence of references to normalisation, was a first step which, had Assad accepted it, would have led to Netanyahu encouraging foreign aid for Syria from the US and Europe. The stick was to be Syrian regional and international isolation and a more robust IDF approach to dealing with southern Lebanon.[37]

---

37 Comments by Avraham Tamir, Security Advisor to President Weizman and involved with the Gold Plan reported in Levitzky, 'Netanyahu's Syrian paper'.

Overall, the plan marked a step forward from the Lebanon First Plan, which the prime minister presented and adopted in the first months of his administration. Although the Dore Gold Plan *does* contain an Israeli withdrawal from Lebanon with Syrian guarantees, it went much further in attempting to allay Syrian fears of breaking the link between withdrawal from Lebanon and the Golan Heights.

Netanyahu's comprehensive peace formula: September 1997

Following the Syrian rejection of the Dore Gold Plan it was more than a year before Netanyahu proposed a new formula for dealing with the Syrian track in September 1997. This plan was based on the formula that both sides would be free to raise any negotiating demand they wished. Moreover, this included the insistence of Assad that Israel withdraw to 4 June 1967 lines. The proposals, which were communicated to Secretary of State Albright, included an assurance from Netanyahu that the joint Israeli–Jordanian dam project, which was to be sited in disputed land, would not complicate negotiations.[38] In seemingly abandoning the Dore Gold Plan the prime minister now stated that he wanted a comprehensive peace treaty between Israel and Syria (thus including normalisation). In addition, Netanyahu stated that Israel was prepared to acknowledge all the agreements reached in Maryland under the previous Labour administration, pledging that he would not ignore them. However, the Syrians remained unimpressed and still demanded that Netanyahu unequivocally accept that negotiations would restart from the point they had finished in Maryland.

In private, and more frequently since the start of 1997, Netanyahu has maintained informal contacts with the Syrians (as chronicled in Chapter 2) and it is more likely that any potential progress will be made in these negotiations rather than in any semi-public forum. However, the Syrians remain sceptical about the Israeli government and prefer the United States to serve as a messenger between the two partners or at least be present in talks. Consequently, although private negotiations provide the best opportunity for success it is far from clear whether the Syrians are prepared to negotiate a comprehensive peace in such a forum without assurances from the Israelis that they will get all of the Golan.

---

38 On Netanyahu's new formula, see Z. Schiff, 'Netanyahu proposes new Syrian formula', *Ha-Aretz*, 21 September 1997.

Unilateral withdrawal from Lebanon: spring 1998

Netanyahu's most recent initiative (spring 1998), which had the principal aim of increasing the pressure on Syria, was to accept a UN resolution calling for an Israeli withdrawal from south Lebanon. The intention was clear: to disentangle an Israeli withdrawal from Lebanon from talks over the future of the Golan Heights. In addition, the move reflected the increasing debate with Israel on the merits of maintaining the security zone in Lebanon as a means of securing its northern border. The issues resulting from this move are discussed in detail in Chapter 9.

Conclusions

Despite Menahem Begin's wide-ranging set of reasons for annexing the Golan Heights in 1981 the central question in any Israeli–Syrian peace accord remains security, and in particular who controls the disputed Golan Heights. The late Yitzhak Rabin concluded that it would be possible to maintain Israeli security and come down from the Golan Heights, but there remain deep divisions in Israel on this question. Additional factors such as the presence of Israeli settlements and its development of industrial and tourist infrastructure in the area complicate the future of the Golan but are unlikely to present intractable problems if the security question can be successfully addressed.

Under the Netanyahu-led government the Syrian track of the peace process has returned to the status quo of no war but no peace. Much of the blame for this has to be apportioned to President Assad who did not embrace the initiatives of Rabin in 1993 and 1994, which would have most probably led to an Israeli withdrawal from the Golan Heights to 4 June 1967 borders. Consequently, the central demand of the Syrians would have been met and even the election of Netanyahu in 1996 would have been unlikely to alter the signed agreement.

Crucially, the current Israeli prime minister has repeatedly stated that he would honour all international commitments that the previous governments had signed. Moreover, not only did Assad *not* embrace Rabin's plan, he subsequently failed to accept a similar proposal put forward in early 1996 by Rabin's successor, Shimon Peres. Indeed, although politics is overburdened with hypothesis it is clear that Assad's actions helped lead to the eventual electoral defeat of Peres in the 1996 Israeli elections. If Assad had embraced the Israeli commitment to withdrawal, Peres would not have gone for early elections but would have opted for elections in October with a peace treaty with Syria to show for his brief term in office. In addition, the subsequent rush of other Middle Eastern countries to make formal peace with Israel following such a move by the Syrians would have provided Peres with tangible evidence that his vision of a new Middle East based on cooperation was more relevant than Netanyahu's viewpoint with its emphasis on suspicion and fear.

This chapter has detailed two frameworks to explain why Assad did not agree to a peace deal with Israel. To a large degree two key points can be deduced from Assad's actions: first, even if he had misinterpreted Rabin's signals in 1993 and 1994 it is inconceivable that the Syrians could also have misread Israeli signals in direct negotiations at Maryland in 1996; and second, Syrian foreign policy (which is centralised under Assad's control) would appear to be content with the current status quo, which it believes merely postpones the return of the Golan to Syria. Moreover, in the long term Assad clearly hopes that the Syrian economic and military position will improve to such an extent that it would be more prudent for him to wait to this time and negotiate from a stronger position.

On the Israeli side, Netanyahu, after initially consulting with Itamar Rabinovich, declined the American invitation to accept informal agreements made by the previous government as a basis for restarting the negotiations. Consequently, this move has allowed the Syrians to boycott any initiative to restart formal negotiations in Maryland, either from the Israelis or the US. In addition, Netanyahu has adopted different strategies to try to reduce the prospect of a total Israeli withdrawal from the Golan Heights such as the Dore Gold Plan outlined in this chapter, but in private he appears willing, albeit reluctantly, to pay the price of full withdrawal in order to secure a peace deal with Syria.

The additional factor of Israel's presence in southern Lebanon has complicated the negotiations with Syria in presenting Assad with the opportunity to fight a proxy war with Israel, but in the long term it is not considered likely that it would derail any potential peace agreement between Israel and Syria. These issues are dealt with more fully in Chapter 9, which outlines the mechanisms for an Israeli withdrawal from Lebanon – with or without Syrian security guarantees.

It remains to be seen what mechanisms can be employed to persuade a Syria that appears to have grave reservations about making a comprehensive peace with Israel to return to negotiations. As outlined in this chapter (and in Chapter 2) for domestic reasons a new formula of holding secret talks (probably away from the Middle East) would appear to present the best potential for achieving success. However, the Syrians remain wary of such talks on substantive issues and prefer to have at least one third party involved in the negotiations. Finally, due to Assad's total dominance over Syrian foreign policy a private summit between himself and an Israeli leader would appear to offer a sensible method of conducting diplomacy, but also the least likely to happen in the short term.

9

Israeli–Lebanese peace: Netanyahu's no-win options in Lebanon

The potential for peace between Israel and Lebanon lies in the signing of a comprehensive peace deal by the Israelis and Lebanon's masters Syria. Put simply, there appears little prospect that a Lebanese government would be willing or able to sign a separate bi-lateral deal with Israel. Consequently, this chapter concentrates on Israel's last active conflict on its borders and the responses of the Netanyahu government to the war in southern Lebanon. Moreover, it will assert that Netanyahu has been much more proactive in trying to find a way of removing Israeli forces from Lebanon than in other areas of the peace process.

Since the withdrawal of the majority of Israeli forces from Lebanon in 1985, Israel has maintained a ten-mile wide security zone in southern Lebanon. The ongoing conflict that has resulted from this occupation with the Iranian- and Syrian-backed Hizbollah has claimed the lives of around two dozen Israeli soldiers a year. Despite this, it is only in recent times that the political consensus in Israel on maintaining the security zone has shown signs of breaking down.

The rationale behind Israel's occupation of a security zone in Lebanon has been to secure Israel's northern border and towns from rocket attacks and terrorist infiltrations across the border into Israel itself. In essence, Israeli military planners view the area as a buffer zone between anti-Israeli forces in southern Lebanon and Israel's northern border. Consequently, around 2,000 Israeli troops together with the local pro-Israel Christian militia, the Southern Lebanese Army (SLA) patrol the area. However, the effectiveness of the zone in preventing rocket attacks has diminished as Hizbollah has acquired over the years more modern longer-range rockets from Iran that can hit Israel's northern settlements from a firing position outside the security zone.

The occupation of part of south Lebanon was originally viewed as a short-term measure until a comprehensive peace settlement could be reached with the Lebanese government and its Syrian power broker, which would include permanent security arrangements for the area. However, events in recent years have indicated that occupation may not be the most prudent method of achieving security along the border. This chapter also chronicles the recent history of the conflict and examines how it has become embroiled in the wider Arab–Israeli conflict. In addition, the merits and problems of each of the three Israeli options for resolving the conflict are discussed in detail. Before examining these options it is important to clarify the four central Israeli aims and intentions in the area.

1. Israel makes no territorial claim over the land in the security zone and wishes to be able to withdraw providing the Lebanese government (and in reality the Syrians) can provide security guarantees.
2. Israel wishes to see the Lebanese army assume control over the area when Israel withdraws and disarm Hizbollah.
3. Israel does not want to intervene in Lebanese internal political affairs and recognises the legitimacy of the Lebanese government to govern over all Lebanese sovereign lands.
4. Israel accepts the special role which Syria plays in Lebanon and does not actively call for the withdrawal of Syrian troops from Lebanon.

Historical background

The current conflict in Lebanon is a product of Israel's original invasion in June 1982 when it successfully removed the PLO from Beirut and the south of the country.[1] However, Israel has found it far more difficult to extricate itself from Lebanon than it did to mount a successful invasion. In the south of the country Israel developed infrastructure required to service its armed forces in the area such as military bases, new roads and prisons. Such actions, together with Israel's intense security operations

---

1 For the most detailed analysis of Israel's war in Lebanon in English, see Z. Schiff and E. Ya'ari, *Israel's Lebanon War* (London, George Allen and Unwin, 1985). See also D. Bavly and E. Salpeter, *Fire in Beirut: Israel's War in Lebanon with the PLO* (New York, Stein and Day, 1984). For a military account, see C. Herzog, *The Arab–Israeli Wars* (New York, Vintage Books, 1984).

in the area, led to the local mainly Shi'a population many of whom had originally welcomed the IDF as a liberating force turning against Israel. In essence, the Shi'a population started to perceive the IDF to be the army of occupation, and this coincided with an increase in the politicisation of the Shi'a population and the rise of Shi'a organisations such as Amal and Hizbollah. These developments had been largely overlooked by Israeli planners who had placed too much emphasis on the Palestinian aspect of southern Lebanon at the expense of understanding the needs of Amal and Hizbollah. Consequently Hizbollah, which was funded by Iran and controlled to a large degree by Syria, started offensive actions against Israel to force it to evacuate Lebanese territory.

Consequently, the Lebanon problem has dogged every Israeli administration from 1982 onwards. The partial withdrawal of Israeli forces and the setting up of the security zone by the then Minister of Defence, Yitzhak Rabin, in 1985 did not solve the problem. To the contrary, it led to fears among the local population of a permanent Israeli presence in Lebanon and an intensification of the conflict with Hizbollah. In the past, there was a deep-rooted consensus among the Israeli political élite and within Israeli society that the security zone and the cost to human life caused by these Hizbollah attacks were a price worth paying in order to secure Israel's northern border.[2]

Since 1985 there have been several dangerous escalations in fighting which have led to international intervention in order to secure a temporary cease-fire or, more recently, agreements designed to limit the nature of the conflict. The government led by Yitzhak Rabin launched "Operation Accountability" against Hizbollah in 1993 with intention of cutting Hizbollah's supply lines, destroying its camps and forcing Lebanese civilians to flee northwards. The aim of the latter was to encourage the government in Beirut to put pressure on the Syrians to use its influence to stop attacks by Hizbollah on Israel. The most recent major military operation took place between 11 April and 27 April 1996 in what was termed "Operation Grapes of Wrath" by the then Israeli prime minister

---

2 Mark Heller of the Jaffee Centre for Strategic Studies writing in early 1996 stated that the Israeli public debate about Lebanon centred around the best way to manage the security zone policy rather than on whether Israel should abandon it. See M. Heller, 'Weighing Israel's option now', in R. Hollis and N. Shepadi (eds), *Lebanon on Hold: Implications for Middle East Peace* (London, Royal Institute of International Affairs, 1996), p. 52.

Shimon Peres.[3] Moreover, in general terms there has been a marked increase in the attacks by Hizbollah (see Figure 8.1) from 1990 onwards against Israeli targets and in turn this has brought more retaliatory attacks from the IDF. "Operation Grapes of Wrath" was instigated by a Labour-led government but it enjoyed the support of the Likud and its leader Binyamin Netanyahu. Moreover, Netanyahu was critical of Peres for agreeing to a cease-fire under international pressure, claiming that Israel had not achieved its security goals with the operation.[4] In reality, both "Operation Accountability" and "Operation Grapes of Wrath" failed to bring about an end to the conflict or to fully achieve their respective goals, and in many ways served only to further turn the local Lebanese population against Israel.

FIGURE 8.1
The rise in Hizbollah attacks, 1990–1995

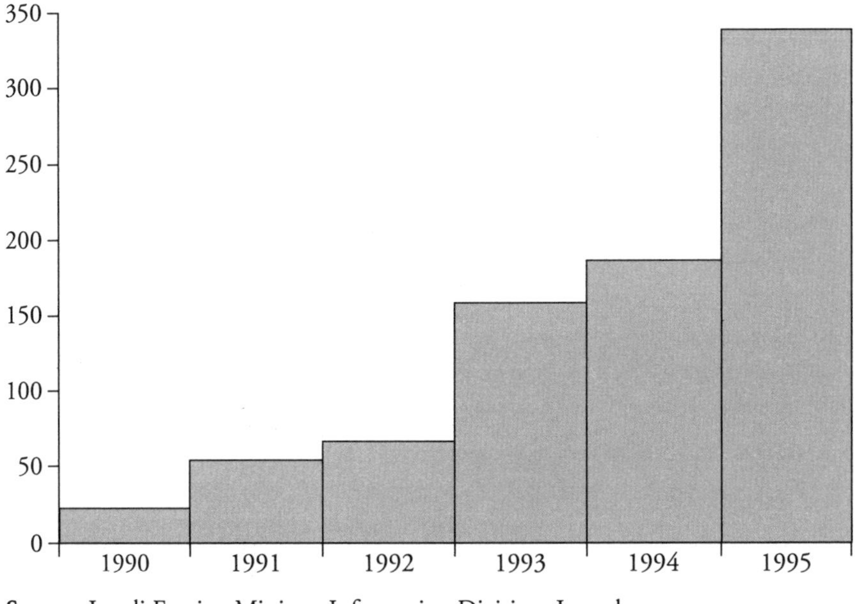

Source: Israeli Foreign Ministry Information Division, Jerusalem

---

3 The final casualty figures from the operation were 165 Lebanese killed, 401 wounded with 23,500 shells fired and 600 air raids in 16 days. Figures from the introduction to R. Hollis and N. Shepadi (eds), *Lebanon on Hold: Implications for Middle East Peace* (London, Royal Institute of International Affairs, 1996), p. xii.
4 See for example, Inbar, 'Netanyahu takes over'.

Under the premiership of Netanyahu little has changed in the security zone despite the prime minister's attempts to separate the Lebanon question from the wider Arab–Israeli conflict. The prime minister is acutely aware that his "peace with security" election promises (see Chapter 2) limit his scope for adopting high-risk strategies. More specifically, Israel's response to the Lebanon conflict since Netanyahu's election can be divided into four clear time phases: the Lebanon First Plan – summer and autumn 1996; the return to the status quo – end of 1996 up to the collision of two Israeli helicopters in February 1997; the re-examination of security zone policy and ways of leaving the security zone – March 1997 until March 1998; and the acceptance of UN Resolution 425 in March 1998 onwards.

Lebanon First: summer and autumn 1996

After assuming office in June 1996, Netanyahu moved quickly to try to alter the status quo with regards to Israel's maintenance of the security zone in Lebanon. In proposing what became known as a Lebanon First solution the prime minister hoped that he could entice the Syrians to help secure Israel's withdrawal. This plan called for a phased withdrawal from Lebanon by Israeli forces with security agreements signed between Israel and Syria to secure Israel's northern border.[5] The plan was to serve as a confidence-building measure for future talks with Syria over the future of the Golan Heights.[6] Such hopes and plans appeared simplistic

---

5 The Lebanon First Plan called for an Israeli withdrawal with three conditions: first, the disarming of Hizbollah; second, the redeployment of the Lebanese army southward to the international border with Israel; and third, the protection of the South Lebanese Army. Address by Binyamin Netanyahu to Graduates of the National Defence College, 8 August 1996. In his speech the prime minister also warned of problems between Israel and Syria, which could ignite into a larger confrontation. Netanyahu added that he found himself in a strange situation, since both Israel and Syria wanted the IDF out of Lebanon. "I find myself in a Kafkaesque situation, an almost unbelievable situation. Here is a situation where the prime minister of Israel announces he wants to get out of the territory of an Arab state Lebanon. And the Syrian government, together with the Lebanese, are opposing this withdrawal. The Middle East has seen a lot of strange things, but this I've never seen before," Netanyahu said. "I hope that President Assad agrees to our proposal. I intend to advance with him the negotiations on peace." Source as above.

6 For more details about the evolution of the plan, see H. Kuttler, 'Gold: plans developing for a withdrawal from Lebanon', *Jerusalem Post*, 4 August 1996.

and were unlikely to be accepted by a sceptical Assad but nevertheless indicated that Netanyahu was willing to try new ways of thinking about the IDF presence in the security zone is south Lebanon.[7]

Return to the status quo: end of 1996 until February 1997

Once the prime minister's proposals had been rejected by the Syrians to the extent that there seemed little point in pursuing them any further, Netanyahu returned to the position of the previous Labour-led governments of Rabin and Peres. The cornerstone of this position in simple terms was that the only way to withdraw successfully from Lebanon was through a comprehensive peace deal with Syria. In the absence of such an agreement, Israel would have to remain in the security zone. At the same time, events on the ground necessitated a concentration on the Palestinian track and the question of Lebanon was placed further down the agenda by the prime minister's increasing domestic difficulties.

Moreover, during this period Netanyahu was having to make difficult concessions for his party, Cabinet and right-wing constituency over the future of Hebron and troop withdrawals from the West Bank. The prime minister was well aware of the need to balance the concessions on the Palestinian track with a more hawkish tone on the future of the Golan Heights, which inflamed Syrian feelings and made it more unlikely that it would help Israel in any withdrawal.[8]

---

7 For an account of the Syrian rejection of Netanyahu's proposals, see the leader in *Tishreen* (official Syrian daily newspaper), 6 August 1996. The official response was also reported in the above publication and came from foreign minister Farouk al-Shara, who stated that Israel was still refusing to continue the peace process on the basis of land for peace and UN resolutions. Al-Shara was reported as saying at the meeting of the Syrian Cabinet on 5 August 1996 that: "If Israel is serious about reviving the peace process, it is required to affirm its commitments and respect its pledges without any disguise." The Lebanese President Elias Hrawi publicly also rejected the "Lebanon First" proposal stating: "Lebanon supports a just and comprehensive peace." He also said: "It will be the last country to sign a peace treaty with Israel." Speech on 1 August 1996.

8 The balancing act of making concessions by Israeli prime ministers on different tracks is an important issue. Rabin felt unable to make difficult concessions at the same time on the Palestinian and Syrian tracks between 1993 and 1995. For more details of this dilemma for Israeli prime ministers, see Bregman and El-Tahri, *The Fifty Years War: Israel and the Arabs*, p. 261.

Post-helicopter crash: March 1997 to March 1998

The collision of two helicopters on 4 February 1997, which claimed the lives of nearly 80 Israeli soldiers who were on their way to Lebanon, led to an intensification of the debate in the Israeli media and society over Israel's maintenance of the security zone. (The effect of the helicopter disaster cannot be over-estimated. The military casualties that resulted from the collision were the highest in a single day since the 1973 war. Helicopters had been employed to transport soldiers in and out of Lebanon in order to avoid Hizbollah's roadside bombs.) In addition, during this period there was an increase in the number of Israeli casualties in Lebanon caused by attacks from an increasingly confident Hizbollah, special operations that went wrong or accidents such as in bushfires. Consequently, the first major signs of division appeared in the Israeli political and military leadership over Israel's best course of action. Netanyahu, while concerned about the increased number of casualties, could do little to alter the status quo. In military terms the government changed the rules of engagement in Southern Lebanon, which meant that for the first time the IDF could open fire on the Lebanese army if it felt under threat. Moreover, there was an increase in air strikes mounted by the Israeli Air Force (IAF), but these appeared to have limited effect. To some degree, the government was limited by the agreements which Israel had made following the "Grapes of Wrath" operation in 1996 and the subsequent setting up of an international monitoring group to limit and control the extent of the fighting.[9]

During this time the Lebanon issue was near the top of the Israeli political agenda, but there appeared little chance of progress without the engagement of the Syrians. However, there was still a reluctance by the Israeli government to accept President Assad's requirement for re-starting negotiations with the Syrians – namely that they start from the point where they finished with Shimon Peres's government. As a consequence, there was little public movement from Netanyahu despite the growing splits and divisions in Israeli society.

---

9 There is evidence to suggest that Netanyahu did call for a more robust approach to policing the security zone from the IDF in an attempt to seize the initiative from Hizbollah. For details of this see, for example, S. Rodan, 'Shaky soloist: part two', *Jerusalem Post,* 15 November 1996.

UN Resolution 425: March 1998

The Cabinet, in accepting Resolution 425 which called for Israel's withdrawal from Lebanon with the necessary foreign assurances, meant that Netanyahu's government had moved further than any of the previous Israeli governments on the issue. To a certain extent this move was performed for international and domestic public relations reasons. In early 1998 there was stalemate in the talks with the Palestinians which showed worrying signs of escalating into a total collapse of the Oslo process. Consequently, the government needed to be seen to be active in another track, both to please the United States and to indicate to the Palestinians that perhaps Israel would start to concentrate more on the Syrian and Lebanon track. Nevertheless, this decision marked a clear change of intentions from the government which, for much of the previous year, had accepted the policy of maintaining the status quo. In many ways the decision reflected a domestic need for the government to be seen doing something to get the IDF out of Lebanon. However, pressure from the Israeli public on the government was not on the surface strong: there were no mass rallies in Tel Aviv calling for such a decision; deeper, there was a growing feeling of senselessness about the continued occupation of the security zone. One of Netanyahu's great strengths is that he generally accurately reflects Israeli centre-ground opinion on such issues and his initiative was clearly designed to remain in control of the political agenda on Lebanon. The prime minister's biggest fear was that pressure from Israel's crucial centre voters to get out of Lebanon would weaken his hand in the negotiations with Syria. More succinctly, the more desperate the Israeli government is to leave Lebanon, the higher the price President Assad will demand in the direct negotiations between Israel and Syria for allowing this to happen.

Netanyahu's difficult choices

The decision of the Israeli Cabinet on 1 March 1998 to accept UN Resolution 425 calling for Israeli withdrawal from Lebanon was in the short term primarily designed to put the Arabs, and Syria in particular, on the back foot. It did not mean that Israel would be able to get itself out of its Lebanon mire in the short to medium term. Indeed, Netanyahu told the meeting of the Israeli Cabinet, which adopted the resolution, that he had no intention of unilaterally withdrawing from Lebanon and leaving a security vacuum on Israel's northern border.[10]

Currently, there are three short-term options on the security zone from which Netanyahu can choose. All have major drawbacks, which could actually lead to a worsening of the security situation on Israel's northern border. The first is to maintain the current occupation, second unilaterally withdraw with no prior agreement with Syria or Lebanon, and third, a gradual withdrawal with security assessments made at each stage as to the effects of the withdrawal. A long-term option would be for Netanyahu to sign a peace deal with Syria and Lebanon, which would no doubt involve the return of the Golan Heights to Syria and a withdrawal from southern Lebanon.

1. Maintain the current occupation

One of the great paradoxes of the current debate is that one of the key opponents of Israel's original invasion of Lebanon in 1982, Yossi Sarid, now supports maintaining the current occupation, while Ariel Sharon, who was Minister of Defence in 1982 and most responsible for the invasion, now actively calls for a unilateral withdrawal.[11] Indeed, Sarid who left the Labour Party in disgust at its support of the war and who spent much of the 1980s campaigning with Peace Now for a withdrawal has clearly articulated the arguments for maintaining the occupation in the Israeli media. The arguments proceed along the following lines: any unilateral withdrawal would allow terrorist infiltration into northern settlements and make it easier to target those settlements.[12] In addition,

---

10 Cabinet Communiqué, Prime Minister's Office, Jerusalem, 1 March 1998.

11 For an account of Ariel Sharon's evolving position, see A. Eldar, *Ha-Aretz*, 7 September 1997. Sharon wishes to see Israel leave Lebanon without an agreement with Syria, as any withdrawal from the security zone as part of an overall deal including both Lebanon and Syria would involve Israel also leaving the Golan Heights. In essence, Sharon sees the battle over the Golan as more important in the long term. He is afraid that Israel's wish to get out of Lebanon will push it in the direction of a deal with Syria and the subsequent abandonment of the Golan. See also Ariel Sharon, *Yediot Aharonot*, 7 September 1997.

12 A lucid account of this argument was provided in a leader article in *Ha-Aretz*, 1 September 1997. In the article it stated that there was no way of knowing what the price would be in terms of civilian casualties in the north if the Hizbollah attempted to operate on the Israeli side of the fence . . . Israel clearly needed an

the security zone prevents Katyusha rocket launchers from getting too close thus projecting Israel's northern towns such as Kiryat Shemona. This line of argument has been followed by the current Minister of Defence, Yitzhak Mordechai and the majority of the Israeli defence establishment.[13]

In summarising the arguments against unilateral withdrawal it is clear that it would go against traditional Israeli security doctrine of controlling the majority of the variables during a conflict. In simple terms, this means that Israel would, in effect, be sub-contracting the security of its northern border to a Lebanese army that may not have the motivation or strength to prevent attacks on Israel. Moreover, it is argued that despite the pain inflicted by Israeli casualties it would set a dangerous precedent if Israel was seen as being chased out of Lebanon by a victorious Hizbollah. Such a precedent could be interpreted by Palestinian groups such as Hamas and Islamic Jihad as a signal to increase attacks on Israel in the hope of persuading Israel to relinquish control of more land in the West Bank and abandon vulnerable Jewish settlements.

Critics of this explanation argue that Israeli intelligence has noted that Hizbollah has now recently taken delivery from Iran of new range of super-Katyushas, which can hit the outskirts of the northern city of Haifa from the group's current positions in Lebanon. Consequently, it is argued that the security zone is preventing rocket attacks is folly. Indeed, some Israel leaders aware of this have suggested that Israel should expand its security zone, but Mordechai has stated that any advance into areas containing a hostile population would not be advisable.[14] An additional

---

enforcer in South Lebanon . . . and only President Assad of Syria was up to the task . . . As long as there was no certainty that the north would not be threatened in the wake of an Israeli withdrawal from the security zone – no prime minister, whether Labour or Likud, would take the risk. A summary of this article and an account appears in D. Gillis, 'Valley of slaughter', *Israel Business Arena,* 9 September 1997.

13 See, for example, interview with Yitzhak Mordechai, S. Rodan and A. O'Sullivan, 'National defence must rest on a solid base', *Jerusalem Post,* 5 October 1997.

14 Following an increase of Katyusha rocket attacks in August 1997 Rafael Eitan, the leader of Tsomet and government minister, called for an enlargement of the security zone. Eitan had served as Chief of Staff in the army during the initial Lebanon war in 1982. In addition, at this time the Minister of Defence during the Lebanon War in 1982, Ariel Sharon, stated that he favoured extending the security zone to the Litani River. However, as described later, Sharon now supports some form of unilateral withdrawal.

argument put forward by Major-General (Ret.) Oren Shahor, a former Co-ordinator IDF Activities in the Territories, for maintaining the security zone is that any unilateral withdrawal would quickly lead to a massacre of Southern Lebanese Army (SLA) members who would be accused of collaboration with the enemy.[15] He argues that only a formal agreement with Syria would prevent such a massacre from happening and consequently there must be no withdrawal until this is achieved.

2. Unilateral withdrawal with no formal guarantees of security

Most supporters of unilateral withdrawal qualify their position by stating that "unilateral" need not mean "without any guarantees". The major difference between this group and supporters of other formulas is that they would be willing to withdraw with minimal informal agreements. These vary, depending on the individuals concerned, from basic guarantees not to attack the IDF while it withdraws to longer-term measures aimed at keeping the border area quiet. Moreover, they are keen to point out that the IDF could return to Lebanon if further trouble broke out along Israel's border. In terms of securing Israel's northern border, this group favours a concentration on tightening of border security. Measures recommended include an increase in mine fields, strengthening of the electronic fence and the installation of more early warning stations. Such measures, they assert, would make it difficult for infiltrations across the border. Moreover, many supporters of unilateral withdrawal claim that it is unlikely that Hizbollah would cross the border, citing previous attacks by the group in 1997 when they launched attacks within a few hundred metres of the border fence but made no attempts to cross the border.

A unilateral withdrawal would bring the highest risks, but also the biggest potential security gain for Israel. Supporters of unilateral withdrawal argue that it would achieve three major political gains: call the bluff of Hizbollah; disentangle Lebanon from the negotiations with Syria; and provide Israel with a higher degree of international legitimacy to mount lightning raids across the border into Lebanon if Hizbollah continued attacks after the withdrawal.

---

15 O. Shahor, 'The immediate effect would be a massacre of SLA people and shooting at our settlements', *Ma'ariv*, 8 September 1997.

Eyal Zisser chronicled the intra-organisational politics of Hizbollah in a recent article and concluded that it remained unclear what action Hizbollah would undertake against Israel if it were to leave Lebanon.[16] On the one hand, in interviews with the international media Hizbollah leaders have stated that if Israel were to leave Southern Lebanon then Hizbollah would refrain from attacks on what it terms the Zionist entity. On the other hand, in addresses and interviews for domestic consumption the leadership has categorically stated that the battle will continue until all the land of Palestine is liberated from the Zionists.[17] Supporters of unilateral withdrawal are gambling on the first of these explanations being the most accurate.[18] However, on a regional level it is difficult to see Hizbollah backers – Iran and Syria, not encouraging Hizbollah to continue its attacks against Israel, especially in the absence of any permanent peace agreement between Syrian and Israel.[19]

The disentangling of the Lebanon issue from Israeli–Syrian negotiations would in itself be a major short-term boost to Netanyahu. In essence, it would remove the stick with which Assad had been beating Israel whenever he felt the need to remind Israel of his presence.[20] As Yossi Beilin often argues, the present situation is like something out of a

---

16 See E. Zisser, 'Hizbollah in Lebanon: at the crossroads', *Middle East Review of International Affairs*, no. 3 (3 September 1997).

17 For an account of these seemingly contradictory statements, see T. O'Dwyer, 'Nasrallah: Hizbollah's ruthless realist', *Jerusalem Post*, 22 September 1997.

18 Giles Trendle provides more details on the argument that Hizbollah will stop its war with Israel at the international border and not attempt to liberate Jerusalem. See G. Trendle, 'Hizbollah: pragmatism and popular standing', in R. Hollis and N. Shepadi (eds), *Lebanon on Hold: Implications for Middle East Peace* (London, Royal Institute of International Affairs, 1996), p. 64.

19 The argument that the Syrians would almost certainly continue to press Hizbollah to continue attacks against Israel in a bid to force it to withdraw from the Golan Heights as well was the decisive factor in Mordechai's decision that a unilateral pull out from Lebanon was impossible. Mordechai had commissioned a secret IDF review of possible alternatives to the current occupation of the security zone. The findings of the report and its conclusions were brought before the secret Inner Security Cabinet (probably in January or February 1997), which agreed with the recommendations made in the report. On this issue, see D. Makovsky, 'Mordechai rejected Lebanon withdrawal after policy review', *Ha-Aretz*, 8 September 1997.

20 On the leverage that Israel's continued presence in Lebanon gives to President Assad in being able to exert pressure on Israel, see L. Eisenberg, 'Israel's Lebanon policy', *Middle East Review of International Affairs*, 3 September 1997, p. 6.

Fellini movie with Israel wanting to leave Lebanon and Syria saying that it demands that Israel leaves Lebanon and then prevents it from doing so.[21] However, Assad robbed of his Lebanese card may look in other directions to exert pressure on Israel. These would likely include increased Syrian sponsorship of international terrorism, and in particular elements of Hizbollah who wished to continue attacks against Israel as well as Palestinian rejectionist groups, many of whom are based in Damascus.[22] Such moves by Assad would prompt closer ties between Syria and Iran and potentially Iraq in a new regional alliance. The visit of Assad to Tehran last year indicates that such moves are already underway although experts on Syria have indicated that Assad is reluctant to alienate the US. In addition, if Assad saw no short- to medium-term chance of a return of the Golan Heights, and with no Lebanon card to turn the heat up on Israel, then this could potentially push him towards direct armed confrontation with Israel on the Golan Heights.

The third argument submitted – that Israel would gain a higher degree of legitimacy for attacks across the border – is of questionable merit.[23] Such actions would still lead to civilian deaths, and the fighting with the Lebanese army based in the area as well as the various local militias would likely be of a higher intensity than at present. Moreover, Israeli intelligence has learnt from its withdrawals from the West Bank and Gaza about the problems of black holes in intelligence information. In Lebanon, where intelligence has proved to be of significant importance to the Israelis, it is easy to see the potential difficulties Israel would have in organising effective cross-border raids. Those such as Major-General (Ret.) Shlomo Gazit, a former head of Military Intelligence, largely ignore the intelligence question concentrating instead on the positive security

---

21 Yossi Beilin, Address to the Royal Institute of International Affairs, Chatham House, London, 11 July 1997.
22 As in note 8. The findings of the IDF report would appear to confirm this conclusion. In addition, a similar point is made by Ze'ev Schiff in suggesting that in the event of a unilateral withdrawal Syrian interests should not be overlooked. See Z. Schiff, 'Three withdrawals', *Ha-Aretz*, 12 September 1997.
23 Interestingly, even strong supporters of unilateral withdrawal such as Yossi Beilin openly talk about the possibility that if violence continued then Israel would always be able to take action in Lebanon or even return to the south of Lebanon if necessary. See, for example, Y. Beilin, 'The case for withdrawal', *Jerusalem Post*, 23 September 1997.

aspects of withdrawing to the international boundary.[24] Moreover, he accepts that there will be incursions across the border from terrorists from time to time but Israel's hands will be freer to respond wherever its choices and not, as he puts it, simply within an area of a few kilometres of the border. Consequently, even if Israel did not enjoy an increased level of international legitimacy for its military responses to attacks, on an operational level its withdrawal would reduce the current limitations placed on Israeli forces.

In response to a potential massacre of SLA personnel, the SLA personnel most at risk could easily be absorbed into Israel or more likely repatriated to a third country, probably France.[25] Current arrangements to ensure the loyalty of the SLA to Israel mean that many families and close friends of SLA members already work in Israel where the minimum salary is considerably higher than that of Lebanon. Consequently, the analysts argue that such a relocation would prove feasible, and indeed desirable, in economic terms for the SLA personnel most at risk. In the wake of recent Lebanese history Israel needs to consider the possibility of revenge against the SLA very seriously. The leader of Hizbollah, Sheikh Nasrallah, has promised an amnesty to SLA members who lay down their weapons prior to an Israeli withdrawal, but in reality it is not clear what this would mean on the ground.[26]

3. Gradual withdrawal, or the Jezzine First Plan

The Jezzine First plan was first put forward by the Israelis at the Madrid Conference in 1991. Jezzine is a small enclave situated outside Israel's security zone but controlled by an SLA group that is under the command of SLA leader General Lahad. The talks in 1991 progressed rapidly with the idea being that Jezzine would serve as a test case for a phased withdrawal by the IDF and SLA from Lebanon. In simple terms, if the withdrawal was deemed successful by the Israelis – that is, SLA personnel were successfully evacuated, the Lebanese army took control of the area and proceeded to disarm Hizbollah and other militia groups – then

---

24 S. Gazit, 'The security zone has served us faithfully but its time has passed', *Ma'ariv,* 8 September 1997.
25 For more background on the complication of defending the SLA, see L. Eisenberg, 'Israel's Lebanon policy', p. 8.
26 Nasrallah's promise of amnesty quoted in ibid.

Israel would continue with the next stage of the pull back. This process of withdrawal would last for years rather than months. However, the Syrians, concerned that they would lose one of their most important bargaining chips with Israel before a deal over the Golan Heights was agreed, intervened and put pressure on the Lebanese government. Subsequently, the government in Beirut rejected the Jezzine First formula and has consistently done so every time it has been put forward.

In September 1997 the Israeli Labour Party leader, Ehud Barak, a former Chief of Staff of the army, joined a group calling for the Jezzine First Plan.[27] This plan was partially embraced by Mordechai in September 1997. He suggested publicly for the first time that he was prepared to discuss a withdrawal from Jezzine and that the depth of withdrawal would match the depth of peace.[28] However, in an interview conducted in October 1997 he again re-emphasised the need for international elements to help secure Israel's withdrawal and help the Lebanese government provide adequate security arrangements in the south following Israel's departure.[29] The apparent shift in the Minister of Defence's position was, to a large extent, due to the remaining difficulties in securing even informal deals involving the Lebanese, brokered by the US, in providing these necessary security guarantees to Israel.

The main problem with this plan is, like the Oslo Accords which contain interim stages designed as confidence-building measures, it allows rejectionists the opportunity to derail the process with violent attacks. In this instance these could take the form of increased attacks on IDF and SLA personnel who remained in Southern Lebanon. If such a scenario were to happen then it is inevitable that Israel would respond with massive retaliation and this would lead to a new dangerous escalation of the conflict. However, it would at least provide an end to the occupation of Lebanon and would prove popular with an Israeli population which on the one hand is becoming ever more sceptical about the merits of the occupation, but on the other, opinion polls have shown that no large majority exists for a unilateral withdrawal.

---

27 The evolution in Barak's thinking is chronicled in L. Galili, 'The Lebanese mess is still with us', *Ha-Aretz,* 8 September 1997.
28 See D. Rudge, 'Mordechai ready to discuss Jezzine First proposal', *Jerusalem Post,* 4 September 1997.
29 Interview with Mordechai, *Jerusalem Post,* 5 October 1997.

Netanyahu's window of opportunity

The breaking of consensus among the Israeli political élite over the maintenance of the occupation of the security zone has provided Netanyahu with one of his first opportunities to free himself of coalition shackles and demonstrate real leadership. Within the Cabinet the leadership of one of the seven parties, the Third Way, is formally in favour of a unilateral pullout. In addition, at least two Cabinet members from the prime minister's own Likud party, Ariel Sharon and Minister of Science Michal Eitan, both favour withdrawal. (Privately, many more Likud members of the Cabinet support a withdrawal but are afraid to be seen to be abandoning the northern towns and settlements to terrorist attacks. It should be stated that the vast majority of the populations on Israel's towns in the north are against a withdrawal. Moreover, their respective mayors are among some of the most vocal supporters of maintaining the security zone.) In public, between assuming office in June 1996 and March 1998, Netanyahu adopted a rigid "no withdrawal" position until security guarantees are provided by Lebanon (post-March 1998 he asserts it now could be informal and not the previously required formal peace treaty). In addition, he has been heavily critical of the ongoing debate suggesting that it breaks with Israeli norms of not discussing such matters publicly while the IDF is in action. Indeed in a tersely worded Cabinet communiqué he argued:

> We all want to leave Lebanon under the appropriate conditions, but the rash statements about a hasty departure from Lebanon under pressure only encourage Hizbollah and its cohorts like fuel in the engines of Hizbollah's rockets. I have demanded that government ministers hold firm to government decisions. The question of the conditions for a departure from Lebanon and how to achieve it, is a question which must be clarified in the cabinet and not in public. I also request that members of the cabinet show solidarity.[30]

Netanyahu's latter remarks were clearly aimed at Cabinet members such as Michael Eitan who had been actively calling for a unilateral withdrawal – though Eitan later clarified this arguing that he merely wanted an exhaustive review of Israel's policy in Southern Lebanon.[31]

---

30 Cabinet communiqué, the Prime Minister's Office, Jerusalem, 7 September 1997.
31 See M. Dudkevitch and S. Honig, 'Netanyahu raps talk of Lebanon pullout', *Jerusalem Post*, 8 September 1997.

However, in private Netanyahu was said to have presented to the US mediators a revamped version of his original Lebanon First proposal, which was one of his first diplomatic initiatives after coming to power in May 1996. The proposal called for the Israeli withdrawal from Lebanon to serve as a confidence-building measure between Israel and Syria. Unsurprisingly, Assad rejected the move and is likely to do so again unless Netanyahu commits himself to returning the Golan Heights to Syria as the conclusion of the process. At this stage it is worth summarising Syrian motivations for rejecting the Lebanon First proposal and why it opposes any Israeli unilateral withdrawal. These can be outlined in three points.

1. Syria seeks the return of all Arab land that Israel occupies (the Golan Heights and Southern Lebanon).
2. President Assad views Lebanon as a means of applying pressure on Israel with the conduct of a limited proxy war.
3. Syria will not tolerate any agreement between Israel and Lebanon (even informal) as any such deal would suit Israeli interests of seeking a separate peace with Lebanon. In essence, the price Israel must pay for extracting itself from Lebanon is a peace deal with Syria.

In early 1998 there were signs that Netanyahu was considering ways of reopening negotiations with the Syrians. The formal talks between the two sides stopped when Israel recalled its delegation from Maryland after the spate of suicide bombings by Islamic extremists in February 1996.[32] Indeed, the American administration is reported to be extremely concerned that the PM will use such a move in order to stall further the implementation of the Oslo process with the Palestinians. US Secretary of State, Madeleine Albright, voiced these very fears during her visit to Israel. In late 1997 and the first half of 1998 the Israeli media has been full of stories of secret meetings in Europe between Netanyahu's adviser on foreign affairs, Uzi Arad, and Syrian officials. Although the Prime Minister's Office has denied the contacts, leading members of the Likud are convinced that the meetings took place and that the prime minister put forward a new formula to restart negotiations with the Syrians on

---

32 For a highly critical account of these talks, how they were conducted and why they ultimately failed from a Syrian point of view, see Interview with Ambassador Walid al-Moualem, *Journal of Palestinian Studies*, 26–2, pp. 81–94.

the basis of an exchange of land for peace. Moreover, it is highly likely that Netanyahu has reached several informal understandings with Assad through intermediaries (a group of American Jewish businessmen or official US state department channels) on controlling the Lebanon situation.[33] In addition, Israel has made it clear that it will try to reintroduce the Lebanese question at the start of more formal contacts between the two sides.

Conclusions

Returning to Netanyahu's no-win options the prime minister may decide that he does not have enough confidence in the alternative security arrangements to alter the status quo. Moreover, much of the advice Netanyahu is getting from the IDF itself suggests that the current option of maintaining the status quo while seemingly offering more to deflect domestic and international pressures is the best of a highly limited range. Netanyahu's major hope must be that Assad will seize any initiative from him to bring about a peace treaty in the short to medium term.

Comments made by the Lebanese prime minister, Rafik Hariri, that Israel could reach peace with Lebanon and Syria within three months if it were ready to give up territory seem somewhat optimistic, but events in the Middle East do have a habit of developing at lightning speed.[34] However, the central question of what actions Hizbollah will undertake if Israel leaves Lebanon remains uncertain. Even if Syria were to exert its authority over the organisation and the Lebanese army were to be successful at disarming it, there remains a possibility that breakaway factions would continue the struggle against what it terms the Zionist entity on Israel's northern border and throughout the world.

Hizbollah's unknown long-term aims and intentions present a large uncontrollable variable for the decision-making process in Israel. In reality, the much-hyped security establishment, which has grown up over the years in Israel, is very conservative in nature and in the past the

---

33 For an example of the role of official US mediators, see D. Gardner, 'US steps in to halt further Lebanon fighting', *Financial Times,* 12 September 1997 and Israel Radio News report on 13 September 1997.
34 'Lebanon says peace is possible in three months', *Jerusalem Post,* 10 September 1997.

presence of such variables would have led to a deep reluctance by the Israeli leadership to take a gamble. It should be remembered that the key players in the government are all a product of this establishment and security decision-making doctrine. Netanyahu served as an officer in an élite commando unit, Mordechai was Deputy Chief of Staff until a few months before the 1996 election and Ariel Sharon was a senior figure in developing the IDF and its strategies in the 1970s and 1980s. However, the fact that the government has taken some moves in the direction of withdrawal with the adoption of UN Resolution 425 indicates that the Israeli military establishment is at the very least split on the issue of the security zone.

In essence, Israel's decision to accept a withdrawal with some kind of security guarantees has succeeded in opening splits between the Lebanese (who are keener on the idea) and the Syrians (who oppose it for the previously outlined reasons). However, the Cabinet's move has not necessarily brought the day of Israel's withdrawal any closer. In reality, Israel has only succeeded in illustrating to the world the restraints that it has been placed upon it to prevent a withdrawal from an area on which it makes no territorial claim.

10

Israel and Turkey: deepening ties and strategic implications, 1995–1998

This chapter charts one of the most important developments in the peace process under Netanyahu – the continued development of ties between Israel and Turkey. The relationship originally grew closer under the premiership of Rabin and Peres between 1992 and 1996. However, relations have not been adversely effected by the coming to power of Netanyahu and the subsequent slow-down of other tracks of the peace process.

For many years Israeli strategists have sought to find suitable partners to construct a coalition of minority states in the Middle East or simply a partner with which to develop a strong bi-lateral alliance.[1] The post-Madrid and Oslo era in the Middle East offers new possibilities for Israel to become an attractive ally to non-Arab states in the region and potentially in the long term to ruling élites in moderate Arab states.[2] Furthermore, Israel's high level of military sophistication and its willingness

---

1 Shai Feldman provides a lucid account of the rationale behind the role of alliances in Israel's grand strategy of national security policy. He asserts that such alliances were designed to help overcome Israel's numerical disadvantage, but were not a substitute to the cornerstone of security strategy, namely self-reliance. Israel tried to create three kinds of alliances to help its security: with a superpower (mainly the US); with states on the periphery of the Middle East; and with minorities in the region. Turkey and Iran serve as examples of the second kind of alliance partners with which Israel has at different times enjoyed close ties and the Maronite Christians in Lebanon are an example of the third type of alliances with minorities. See, for example, Feldman and Toukan, *Bridging the Gap*, pp. 14–15.

2 For a more detailed explanation of this concept see, for example, E. Cohen, M. Eisenstadt and A. Bacevich, 'Israel's revolution in security affairs', *Survival*, vol. 40, no. 1 (1998), p. 48.

(and need) to develop arms sales with allies make this attractiveness even greater, especially to the military establishments of these countries.[3]

Turkey would appear to be the natural choice of ally for Israel. It is a secular country with close ties through its participation in the North Atlantic Treaty Organization (NATO) with the United States. Though not a member of the European Union (EU) it enjoys close political and trade links with many European governments and still maintains ambitions about becoming a full member early in the next century. Israel has long looked for friends in Europe which though a major trading partner for Israeli companies has seen EU institutions often taking political positions that were hostile to Israeli interests. In addition, Turkey is viewed by Israel as the gateway to the newly formed Central Asian Republics, and more specifically to helping Israel develop political and economic ties with these countries.[4] Moreover, Turkey, like Israel, shares a border with Syria and has not enjoyed good relations with President Assad over a number of issues. Indeed, in the realm of mutual interests it is difficult to see two better suited countries in the region for fostering closer ties.

As a result of all the above factors, Israel's rapidly developing political, military and economic relationship with Turkey is as important a development in the Middle East region as any of the peace treaties it has signed with the Arabs.[5] Although the recent moves towards closer cooperation started in earnest as recently as late 1995, this is not the first time that Israel and Turkey have had close political and military ties.[6] Indeed, during the 1960s the Israeli and Turkish armed forces drew up joint military plans against an Arab nation. Both the Israelis and Turks were concerned about the rise of the Ba'th party in Iraq and Syria, and the Israeli and Turkish Chief of Staffs went as far as meeting to formulate operational plans.[7] Once tension eased in the region the Israeli–Turkish relationship did not develop any further.

---

3 For a description of the development of Israel's Defence (Military) Industrial Complex, see Y. Shichor, 'Israel's military transfers to China and Taiwan', *Survival*, vol. 40, no. 1 (1998), pp. 75–7.

4 For further explanation of the background to this assessment, see D. Menashri, 'Introduction: is there a new Middle East?' in D. Menashri (ed.), *Central Asia Meets the Middle East* (London and Portland, Frank Cass, 1998), pp. 12–13.

5 See E. Inbar, 'Peace is a mirage', *Jerusalem Post*, 2 March 1998.

6 See Z. Schiff, 'Keeping the romance quiet', *Ha-Aretz*, 2 January 1998.

7 Ibid.

Before chronicling the development of the relationship and its consequences for the Middle East, it is worth summarising the potential gains and losses to Israel and Turkey of fostering closer ties. The current benefits to Israel are: first, in terms of contracts for military hardware; second, easier access to the new Central Asian Republics (particularly economic markets for high-tech and agricultural equipment); third, the use of Turkish airspace for pilot training and perhaps (as Turkish officials have quietly hinted at), a staging post for air strikes on Iraq which is highly appealing to the IDF;[8] and fourth, in military terms splitting the deployment of the Syrian army onto two fronts in case a coordinated attack by Israel and Turkey reduces the threat of a major Syrian attack on the Golan (although it is likely that such wartime cooperation involving Israel and Turkey is still a long way off).[9] The Israelis have provided the military equipment it requires to modernise Turkey's armed services at very competitive prices. Indeed, it is the well-documented speciality of the Israeli Military Industrial Complex (MIC) to modernise ageing and obsolete equipment. Israeli–Turkish intelligence cooperation, although still a sensitive issue, is thought to have helped Turkish operations and military planning. In addition, more than a quarter of a million Israelis visited Turkey during 1997 and have become an integral part of Turkey's tourist trade.

The negative factors that the parties need to consider are (for Israel) an over-concentration on developing ties with a country that has a high degree of political instability and where there are strong forces that reject closer links with Israel, notably the Islamists. In addition, there must be a question mark over whether pressure from Arab capitals on Turkey will make the Turks slow down the process of normalisation with Israel, thus forcing it to renege on deals it has signed or to cancel

---

8 Moshe Zak's account of Yitzhak Shamir's secret agreement with King Hussein of Jordan not to use Jordanian airspace to launch an attack against Iraq during the Persian Gulf War in 1991 makes fascinating reading. It is likely that if hostilities between Israel and Iraq started in the future there would once more be intense Jordanian pressure on any Israeli prime minister not to violate Jordanian airspace. Consequently, the Turkish northern air route would be both politically and militarily favourable for use during potential Israeli air strikes on Iraq. For details of Shamir's private agreements with King Hussein, see Zak, 'Israel and Jordan: strategically bound', pp. 39–60.

9 See A. Barzilai, 'Allies with Ankara', *Ha-Aretz*, 8 December 1997.

potential joint projects with Israel. Naturally, such pressures are likely to increase if the Middle East peace process remains stalled. Moreover, Turkey needs to consider the possibility of Arab economic sanctions against it if the situation in the Middle East deteriorates further into open conflict and it continues to develop its ties with Israel. Consequently, not only does this chapter chronicle and explore the development of this new relationship in the political, security and economic fields, but also it examines its effects on strategic alliances in the Middle East region as a whole.

It is only in recent months that both Israel and Turkey have become more open about their relationship. The previously outlined fear of Arab hostility towards Turkey for its dealings with Israel was enough to ensure that the majority of cooperation remained secret. However, the signing of the Declaration of Principles and Cairo Accords between the Israeli government and the PLO in 1993–4 has lent a far higher degree of legitimacy to Turkish contacts with Israel both within Turkish society and in the Arab world than otherwise would have been the case. Moreover, had the aforementioned agreements not been reached, it is difficult to envisage Israeli–Turkish ties having developed at the pace they have. Consequently, it is ironic that to some degree the current Netanyahu-led government in Israel is reaping the rewards of the peace process initiated by its predecessor and to which it is at best only partially committed. Having stressed the linkage between progress in resolving the Arab–Israeli conflict and the Israeli–Turkish relationship, it should be noted that such deals were merely an excuse for Israel and Turkey to more openly pursue their mutual agenda of self-interests and not the *raison d'être* for the relationship. In examining the recent Israeli–Turkish ties, three distinct time periods reflect the dynamic development of the relationship which largely correspond to the formation and fall of the three Turkish governments of recent years.

The first period: October 1995 to July 1996

The first period was marked by a rapid improvement in relations between Israel and Turkey. This clearly reflected the centre-ground pragmatic foreign policy, which the Turkish government pursued. Moreover there was a realisation in Jerusalem that Turkey was at this time ready to deepen economic, military and political ties. The political élite in Israel, and in particular the Ministry of Foreign Affairs, saw this as a natural progression of the Madrid peace process. The decision of Yitzhak Shamir to talk directly with the Palestinians (in a Jordanian–Palestinian delegation) meant that Ankara could start the process of normalisation with Israel.[10] The appointment of an Israeli Ambassador to Turkey was the first stage together with the opening of the new embassy. The next step in this logical process was more progress in the negotiations between the Israelis and the Arabs (especially the Palestinian track) so visible ties would deepen. The final outcome of the process was to be a full normalisation of relations between the two countries. The fundamental measure of the success of the relationship using this criterion was good bi-lateral trade relations, together with the accompanying high-level political contacts by politicians and government officials.

The military establishments of Israel and Turkey were following the same path to normalisation as their political counterparts, but had their own additional agenda, which went further than the one outlined by the political élite. In the first instance, the military élites of both countries date the increased cooperation as far back as 1985, when Israel decided to withdraw from the majority of Lebanon. The Israeli withdrawal led to a change in thinking among senior Turkish officers who no longer viewed Israel as a threat to Turkey's borders. Consequently, secret ties and contacts were formed between the two military élites, which included visits and joint briefing sessions.

These ties developed into the close relationships that are apparent between the military establishments today.[11] In essence, the military in both Israel and Turkey have, for some considerable time, viewed the potential for a strategic alliance between their countries (either informal understandings or formal agreements). In general terms, they view such an alliance as vital to both countries in terms of mutual interest in military trade and in dealing with the growing threat of radical states in the region. Part of the formal strategic plan of Israel and Turkey was revealed with the agreements signed during this period. It should be stressed

---

10 Yitzhak Shamir saw the fact that many countries that, prior to Madrid, had not had official diplomatic links with Israel started a process of normalisation following the conference as one of the historic achievements of the Madrid Conference. Author's interview with Yitzhak Shamir, Tel Aviv, 17 August 1994.

11 See Barzilai, 'Allies with Ankara'.

that, as the subsequent agreements illustrate, the paths of political and military were mutually inclusive in that one would not have developed without the other.

In October 1995 Israel and Turkey signed a three-part military cooperation agreement. The agreement included the setting up of a Strategic Assessment Working Group (which Jordan was eventually supposed to join), increased intelligence cooperation and Israeli aid in organising and training Turkish army units.[12] Parts of the agreement remain secret, but official Turkish sources acknowledged that joint air exercises took place in May and early June 1996 over Turkey and Israel. Indeed, it is reported that the Israeli Air Force (IAF) discovered a new Syrian chemical gas factory in the mountains near the Turkish border.[13] Counter-terrorism cooperation between Israel and Turkey was included in the agreement, but remains a secret. Some sources suggest that this went as far as to include Israeli support for Turkey's attempt to deal with the PKK, the Kurdish Workers' Party, which Syria has supported in its campaign to destabilise Turkey. Such a scenario would almost inevitably lead to a heightening of tension between Syria and Turkey.[14]

Israel and Turkey signed a treaty on 16 March 1996 dealing with the setting up of a free trade zone between the two counties, together with support of capital investments and the prevention of double taxation in key areas of trade.[15] This deal reflected the continuation of the deepening economic ties between the two countries by making existing trade cheaper and attracting potential new trade.

Overall, this period was marked by a rapid development of ties between the Peres-led government in Israel and the Vilmaz-led secular Turkish government. Not only were there visible results of the cooperation such as the agreements mentioned above but also there were growing contacts between senior figures in Israel's military élite and their counterparts in Turkey. The closeness of these relationships was to prove of great significance following the collapse of Mesut Yilmaz's government

---

12 See Barzilai, 'Allies with Ankara'.
13 Reported in S. Rodan, 'Ties with Turkey: the most important story of the decade', *Jerusalem Post*, 14 June 1996.
14 Ibid.
15 See O. Koren, 'Israel and Turkey sign treaty concerning free trade, capital, investments support and prevention of double taxation', *Israel Business Arena*, 18 March 1996.

in Turkey and its replacement by a coalition, which included for the first time an Islamic fundamentalist prime minister, Necmettin Erbakan, in July 1996.

The rise of the Islamic fundamentalists in Turkey was of great concern to Israel with their anti-Israel dogma, which had been most visible during its local and national elections campaigns.[16] In a development that astonished many in Turkey, the Islamic Welfare Party (WP) formed a coalition to secure a parliamentary majority with the centre-right True Path Party (TPP), which was led by the ex-prime minister Tansu Çiller. During the election campaign of 1995, Çiller had compared the WP to Maoists and its economic platform to that of Castro's Cuba.[17] In addition, Çiller had promised that she would never form a coalition with the WP who in turn had slated the TPP as evil corrupt pro-Westerners. The coalition marriage of convenience was largely instigated to help the Islamists into power while they supported Çiller and her officials in parliamentary commissions investigating cases of corruption.[18] However, it was not long until the WP itself became embroiled in several similar cases in which the TPP reciprocated the gesture by supporting them. (Allegations soon arose that Erbakan had registered party property in his name and that some 25 per cent of funds raised in a Bosnian relief appeal had ended up in the Welfare Party coffers.)

---

16 Israeli concerns over the growing appeal of the Islamists in Turkey were clearly articulated at the time by Efraim Inbar, who stated that if an Islamic regime were to emerge in Turkey it would have tremendous regional and international destabilising repercussions. See E. Inbar, 'Israel's security in a new international environment', *Israel Affairs*, vol. 2, no. 1 (1995), pp. 35–6.

17 More specifically worrying to Israel was that Erbakan had previously referred to Çiller as an "Israeli puppet" and threatened that the WP would cut all contacts with Israel when in power. In addition, he told voters in election campaigns that the choice was between supporting "Greater Israel" or "Greater Turkey" and included Jerusalem in a list of Moslem areas he would liberate.

18 The WP's support for Çiller was somewhat ironic given the fact that Erbakan had helped bring down the previous government by starting parliamentary enquires into some of Çiller's financial dealings. The allegations included illegal profiting from car and electric utility contracts, and a charge that $6 million had not been accounted for. If Çiller had been indicted she would have been temporarily suspended from politics, and if convicted, permanently banned. For full details see, for example, G. Gruen, 'Relations with Ankara: crisis of cooperation', *The Jerusalem Post*, 5 July 1996.

The second period: June 1996 to June 1997

The period of office of Prime Minister Erbakan (July 1996 to June 1997) was characterised by continued good relations between Israel and the secular elements of the government in Ankara as well as the Turkish economic and military élite. However, relations between Israel and the Islamic Fundamentalist elements of the government were less warm.[19] In many ways relations with Israel became one of the key divisive issues that split Turkey's rulers and led to the eventual downfall of Erbakan's government in June 1997.

The change of government in Israel on 29 May 1996 with the victory of Binyamin Netanyahu and his subsequent formation of a centre-right government in June 1996 did not alter the deepening ties between Israel and Turkey from an Israeli perspective. Netanyahu made it clear that he placed great value on Israel's relationship with Turkey. However, the growing Arab pressure on Israel following Netanyahu's election was mirrored by increasing pressure on Turkey not to deepen its ties with Israel.

A prime example of both the deepening ties and the complications introduced by Erbakan's premiership can be seen when on 29 August 1996 Israel and Turkey signed a further military cooperation agreement. The principal aim of this agreement was to further extend security ties between the two countries and to develop cooperation between their military industries. More specifically, it was signed to enable the implementation of a $600 million deal (later costed at nearer to $800 million) between Israel Aircraft Industries (IAI) and the Turkish Ministry of Defence to upgrade Turkey's ageing Phantom jet fighters.[20] However, Erbakan opposed the deal and in particular the decision to use IAI to upgrade the Phantoms.[21]

---

19 Difficulties in relations between the Likud-led government and the Islamists in Turkey were unsurprising. The Israeli prime minister, Binyamin Netanyahu, writing in 1994 cited the Welfare Party in Turkey as an example of the dangerous spread of Islamic Fundamentalism which challenged the West and Israel. Despite this, Netanyahu, now in office, sent a letter to Erbakan congratulating him on his appointment as Turkish prime minister. For Netanyahu's reference to the WP in 1994, see B. Netanyahu, *Fighting Terrorism: How Democracies Can Defeat Domestic and International Terrorists* (London, Allison and Busby, 1996), p. 93.

20 See D. Marom, 'Irvy signs Israel–Turkey defence cooperation agreement', *Israel Business Arena*, 29 August 1996.

21 See D. Marom, 'Phantom jet deal won't be cancelled despite Turkish PM's opposition', *Israel Business Arena*, 2 December 1996.

Erbakan argued that the deal should be cancelled because in economic terms the project would cost $800 million and not the original $600 million quoted by Israel. (Part of the deal required Turkey to obtain credit from Israeli banks and the reason for the increased costing of the project was that the interest rates set by the Israeli banks turned out to be higher than first thought.) Moreover, he went as far as instructing members of his Islamic Social Welfare Party not to ratify the deal with Israel.

Evidence of the growing tension between the prime minister and the Turkish military was made obvious with the statement by the Commander of the Turkish Airforce. In his statement, the Commander argued that Turkey had no option but to make use of the Israelis to upgrade the aircraft which were vital for Turkey to maintain the high technological level of its airforce.[22] Eventually, under such pressures Erbakan relented and signed the ratification of the deal along with the other 17 Cabinet ministers from his party. However, in a related development the ratification of the trade agreement between Israel and Turkey was delayed and consequently the day of its commencement, 1 January 1997, was not met. This led to fears in Israel that the deal would not be ratified by the Turkish parliament.[23]

The Turkish military, never happy with the participation of the Islamic Welfare Party in the government, became increasingly uneasy with the foreign policy of the governing coalition. The military establishment was particularly concerned about the government's move towards rapprochement with Iran, which it viewed as a threat to the political stability of Turkey. A series of demonstrations, which called for an Islamic revolution in Turkey, and which were organised by local leaders of the Welfare Party, increased the tension. In addition, these rallies were characterised by anti-Israeli sentiments and the honouring of dead Hizbollah and Hamas fighters as well as including calls to liberate Jerusalem. Such sentiments clearly worried the military, which saw its developing ties with Israel being placed in danger.

Turkey's internal political dynamics became more complicated when the National Security Council (NSC) met on 28 February 1997. The NSC advised the government that the biggest threat to national solidarity

---

22 Statement reported in 'Phantom jet deal'.
23 See O. Koren, 'Fears that free trade ratification with Turkey may be torpedoed', *Israel Business Arena*, 9 February 1997.

no longer came from the PKK, but rather from Islamic Fundamentalists and their foreign backers. Moreover, it recommended several measures to deal with this situation, which Prime Minister Erbakan had obvious difficulties in implementing. In addition, there were growing strains on the coalition and a general sense of political inertia (the Cabinet rarely met, let alone agreed on anything). This climate of crisis was added to by pressure from the military leadership and economic élite, as well as the parliamentary opposition, to bring down the ruling coalition.[24]

At the same time as the political crisis in Turkey worsened, the relationship between the military élite of Israel and Turkey deepened considerably. The contacts included a meeting between the Israeli Minister of Defence, Yitzhak Mordechai, and his Turkish counterpart, Turhan Tayan, in Tel Aviv in May. During this meeting the idea was muted of joining Israeli–Turkish production of the Popeye II air-to-ground missile for the Turkish airforce.[25]

Overall, this short-term self-interest coalition government was paradoxically both worrying to Israel and at the same time to some degree beneficial. Clearly, there was no mistaking the hostility of the Islamists towards Israel but the effects of inter-Turkish politics on the relationship were more complex. These were precisely outlined by the outgoing Israeli Ambassador to Turkey, Zvi Elpeleg, in September 1997:

> Erbakan did not actively do any harm to those relations [Israel and Turkey], and I would even venture to say that Israel has a vital interest in seeing a Turkish regime that is not hostile to its neighbours. If Turkey were hostile towards Iran, Iraq or Syria, what benefit would Israel derive from such a situation? . . . It was not ideal [the coalition], but given the present reality in Turkey, where its leaders were competing with each other for the pot of gold, Erbakan as prime minister was a preferable option. If the secular leadership promotes nepotism and social polarization, Turkey will have a problem.[26]

---

24 For more details of this crisis, see E. Kalaycioglu, 'The logic of contemporary Turkish politics', *Middle East Review of International Affairs*, no. 3 (September 1997).

25 See R. Dagoni, 'Israel and Turkey set to produce Popeye missile', *Israel Business Arena*, 28 May 1997.

26 Interview with Ambassador Zvi Elpeleg, 'It might not have been ideal, but it was not all that bad', *Ha-Aretz*, 30 September 1997.

The Ambassador went on to highlight the argument that it was better to have a submissive Erbakan in the government than an unruly anti-Israel and anti-West Islamic element outside the administration.[27] In addition, he cited the fact that with all Turkey's socio-economic problems Erbakan's WP, with its commitment to the poor, increased the legitimacy of an administration within these key constituency groups. Consequently, the WP's participation brought a degree of stability to a government having to make difficult economic choices. (When the Islamists joined the government, inflation in Turkey was running at around 80 per cent and unemployment was around 10 million people. Moreover, there was a rapidly growing budget deficit and a large increase in the population. Taken together with the economic costs of fighting a ten-year campaign against the PKK, this left the Turkish economy in deep trouble.)

The third period: June 1997 to March 1998

The resignation of Erbakan on 18 June 1997 and his replacement by the TPP leader, Tansu Çiller, did little to stem the pressure on the coalition. Eventually, President Demirel named Mesut Yilmaz as the new prime minster and he subsequently won a vote of confidence in parliament in July 1997. The new coalition included secular, nationalist and liberal conservative right-wing parties. In typical Turkish style this grand coalition was viewed as a short-term administration with a limited mandate to carry out political reforms and call early elections for 1998. In addition, it was clearly designed to help restore confidence in central government, not least from the military and economic élites. One of the first actions of the Yilmaz government was to introduce a progamme of anti-religious measures such as closing down of religious schools. Such actions were designed to help restore the religious status quo in Turkey, which the Islamists had sought to alter. However, in the long term it remains to be seen if such actions will stem the rise of Islamic forces.

Israel greeted the change of government in Turkey with some relief. The clear short-term signal from Ankara was that this broad-based new coalition, together with the support of the Turkish military establishment, would ensure that Turkey would not slide into an Islamic anti-Israel and anti-West state in the near future. Consequently, this period saw an

---

27 Interview with Elpeleg.

accelerated development of relations between the two countries in the fields of political ties, trade and strategic links.

Evidence of a further deepening of ties was provided with the visit of the Israeli Chief of Staff, Amnon Shahak, to Turkey at the beginning of October 1997 for talks on strategic coordination and cooperation in the defence industries.[28] As a result of the visit, Turkish sources reported that it was agreed that Israel and Turkey would consider joint manufacture of a new long-range cruise missile entitled "Delilah".[29] In addition, the Turks agreed to purchase some 40 Popeye air-to-air missiles from Israel.[30] Significantly, a consortium of Israeli defence companies submitted a bid to the Turks for supplying the Merkava Mark 3 tank to Turkey in response to a Turkish tender for its battle tank for the next decade. The Merkava is Israel's most advanced tank and the bids approval by the Israeli Ministry of Defence was an indication of the depth of military ties between the two countries.[31] In addition, the Chief of Staff discussed the next step in cooperation – joint naval exercises to be held in January 1998, and a strengthening of intelligence ties and sharing of information.[32] Shahak's visit resulted in the most detailed discussion to date between Israel and Turkey over long-term strategic planning. Indeed, it is unlikely that Israel had previously ever held such discussions on security issues with any country apart from the United States.

Shahak's trip laid the groundwork for the visit of the Israeli Minister of Defence, Yitzhak Mordechai, to Ankara on 8 December 1997. During the visit Mordechai met with his Turkish counterpart, the prime minister, Chief of Staff, the speaker of parliament and senior figures in the defence establishment.[33] In a joint press briefing with his Turkish hosts, Mordechai summed up the overall Israeli aim of the relationship with Turkey by saying:

28 See A. Barzilai, 'Israel and Turkey to build new missile', *Ha-Aretz*, 15 October 1997.
29 Reported in *Turkish Daily News*, 14 October 1997.
30 Reported in *Turkish Daily News*, 20 October 1997.
31 See D. Marom and R. Dagoni, 'IMI led Israeli consortium offers Turkey Merkava Mark 3 Tank', *Israel Business Arena*, 21 October 1997.
32 See Z. Bar'el, 'A double edged sword', *Ha-Aretz*, 19 October 1997.
33 See A. Barzilai, 'Mordechai trip aims to deepen ties with Turkey', *Ha-Aretz*, 7 December 1997.

> When we lock hands we will form a powerful fist . . . These relations will help us defend ourselves against any threat . . . and help establish peace in the region.[34]

The main outcome of the meetings was the decision of Israel and Turkey to work together on research into military space projects. In addition, the Turkish prime minister, Mesut Yilmaz, invited his Israeli counterpart to visit Turkey.[35] This was highly significant because Yilmaz had been critical of Netanyahu's policies towards the Palestinians. Consequently, the invitation sent a clear signal that Turkey was more confident of deepening its ties with Israel irrespective of progress on the peace process.

It was not coincidental that Mordechai's visit to Turkey should take place at the same time as the meeting of the 55-member Organization of the Islamic Conference (OIC) in Tehran. A draft resolution at the conference called for the ending of the process of normalisation of ties with Israel because of the policies of the Netanyahu government. More specifically, the relationship between Israel and Turkey was addressed in a clear attempt to exert pressure on the Turks to freeze its ties with Israel. Despite calls by the Syrian foreign minister, Farouq al-Shara, to adopt more critical resolutions Turkey was not specifically named in the resolution that was eventually adopted. It simply urged Muslim states that have military cooperation with Israel to reconsider.[36] The conference was seen as a victory for Turkey and Jordan, which had worked hard to ensure that the Turks would not be isolated because of its relations with Israel. The major loser was Syria, which had lobbied hard for stronger actions to be taken against Israel and Turkey.[37] The growing sense of confidence in Turkey over its relations with Israel was illustrated by the Turkish reaction to the OIC resolution. The Turkish Minister of Defence, Ismet Sezgin, stated that Turkey respected the Islamic Conference: "We

---

34 Yitzhak Mordechai, comments reported in, *Ha-Aretz*, 9 December 1996.
35 See A. Barzilai, 'Israel and Turkey look to the stars as strategic ties deepen', *Ha-Aretz*, 10 December 1997.
36 Draft Resolution of Organisation of the Islamic Conference, 7 December 1997.
37 The Jordanian Foreign Minister, Fayez al-Tarawneh, summarised Jordan's position stating that Jordan wanted Turkey to feel that it was on its side, rather than alienate it. This is not the purpose of the OIC. Interview with Fayez al-Tarawneh, reported in 'Muslim countries call for an end to normalization with Israel', *Ha-Aretz*, 8 December 1997.

belong to it, but we cannot allow it to dictate our relations." He went on to argue that the resolution wasn't binding for Turkey.[38]

Mordechai's visit led to a further deepening of military ties between the two countries. The visit to Israel of the Turkish Deputy Minister of Defence, General Toncher Killinch, starting on 21 December 1997, was seen as a sign that not only were the Turks ignoring the Islamic Conference's resolution but also they were actively looking to further deepen military ties with Israel. Moreover, a high-level meeting was held in Ankara on 22 December 1997 between an Israeli delegation led by the special adviser to the Minister of Defence, David Ivri and the Turkish Deputy Chief of Staff, General Cevic Bir.[39] The Israeli delegation included members of the army's planning branch and senior airforce commanders. The fact that these individuals were included was a clear signal of the long-term strategic planning nature of the agenda of the meeting. Such meetings, although commonplace in the past, were now held more openly and reported in both the Turkish and Israeli media. Indeed, there was a fear among some of the Israeli members of the delegations who attended such meetings that Turkey was becoming too open about its military contacts with Israel. The Israelis were not used to such openness about sensitive security issues and they feared that such publicity could lead to renewed Arab pressure on Turkey to downgrade its deepening strategic links with Israel.[40]

Further evidence of these deepening ties was provided by the joint US–Israeli–Turkish naval exercise, which took place on 7 January 1998 in the form of a practice search and rescue mission off the coast of Israel and Lebanon. The operation, relatively small by modern standards, involved some five ships, several helicopters and search aircraft. Eventually, Jordan decided to send an observer, which indicated that King Hussein

---

38 Comments by Turkish Minster of Defence, Ismet Sezgin, reported in 'Turkey pledges to deepen ties', *Ha-Aretz*, 9 December 1997.

39 See A. Barzilai, 'Israel and Turkey accelerate dialogue', *Ha-Aretz*, 21 December 1997.

40 See Schiff, 'Keeping the romance quiet'. In this article Schiff argues, correctly, that both press attention being given to the alliance and the desire of officials to leak details of talks and agreements to the media was "feeding the flames of anger" of the Arab states and Iran. In addition, he states that this inadvertently helped to create the climate where King Hussein of Jordan was reluctant to join the partnership.

was willing to make a stand against Arab protests about the drills.[41] The hostility of Syria and Iran in particular was an indication of the fear of the new alliances starting to emerge of the naval exercise participants and the United States.[42] Though the exercises were small scale and designed simply to practise coordination of rescuing stranded boats in the area, they none the less were a foretaste of more openly military exercises involving Israel, Turkey and the US.

The period following the naval exercises saw a deepening of the relationship with the visit to Israel of the general commander of the Turkish army, General Ismail Kardai, at the start of February.[43] General Kardai's visit was aimed at securing a deal with Israel over a proposal by Israeli Military Industries to upgrade Turkey's existing tanks at a cost of between $500 million to $1.5 billion depending on which upgrade package the Turks accepted. This deal, large scale even by military terms, indicated both the economic potential of selling to Turkey for Israel and, for the Turks, the opportunity to modernise its entire armoured division by putting state-of-the-art technology into existing equipment. However, it should be stressed that this remains a relatively short-term measure. The Turks will soon have to decide which new tank to purchase, and Israel is again top of its list with the previously mentioned Merkava Mark 3 tank.

In a related development at the start of 1998, Turkey's growing concern that trade with Israel was becoming too one-sided became more vocal.[44] Turkish Ministry of Defence officials started to call openly for Israel to make large-scale reciprocal investments in Turkey. Such calls

---

41 Reported in 'Jordan to observe controversial US–Turkey–Israel naval drills', *Ha-Aretz*, 4 January 1998.

42 Iraqi fears were articulated by its foreign minister, Mohammed Saeed al-Sahaf, who urged Turkey to withdraw from the drill, which he called a provocative act against the Arab nation. The Syrian vice-president, Abdel Halim Khaddam, on a visit to Paris discussed the risks of the manoeuvres not only to the surrounding countries but also on the world's peace and security. Both reactions reported in A. Harel, 'Mermaid exercise draws Arab protest', *Ha-Aretz*, 8 January 1998. The Egyptian foreign minister, Amr Moussa, noted that Turkey must know that any alliance with Israel would trigger the establishment of a counterbalance. Reported in A. Barzilai and A. Harel, 'Reliant mermaid runs into rough seas', *Ha-Aretz*, 7 January 1998.

43 See A. Barzilai, 'The Turkish knight', *Ha-Aretz*, 11 January 1998.

44 See R. Dagoni, 'Turkey asks Israel to increase reciprocal trade after defence deal', *Israel Business Arena*, 14 January 1998.

opened up what is likely to become a medium- to long-term problem for the Turks in that Israel has little intention of making purchases from it on the scale that the Turks are clearly hoping for.[45] An alternative, which is a more probable prospect, is that Israel and Turkey will undertake more joint research and development projects as well as joint production of key new weapons.

Consequences for Middle East strategic alliances

The speed and scale of the development of ties between Israel and Turkey have meant that the ramifications of the relationship have not only been felt in Jerusalem and Ankara but also throughout the Middle East region and beyond. This study does not argue that such ties have themselves transformed the Middle East, but rather that the Israeli–Turkish relationship has contributed significantly to a process of realignment and potential change in the region.

The strategic alliances and conflicts following the Persian Gulf War (1991) and the Madrid Peace Conference (1991) in the Middle East became more complex.[46] In general terms the players in the region could be divided into the following areas: Israel; the moderate Arab states (willing to seek an accommodation with the Jewish state); the radical states (not willing to reach a deal with Israel); and greater Middle Eastern countries such as Iran and Turkey. In addition, there was a growing increase in inter-Arab conflict, particularly between the radical and moderate states not only about dealings with Israel but also concerning either land disputes, conflict over the increasingly limited natural resources or support for nationalist causes such as the Palestinians and the Kurds. It should be remembered that the decade started with the Persian Gulf War – a war where Arab nation fought Arab nation essentially over the fear that the military strength of one Arab army would threaten other Arab and Gulf states; a war in which Israel played no active part.

---

45 Turkey claimed that Israel had agreed to the purchase of up to 50 Scorpion armoured vehicles from it for $10 million. Such small-scale purchases are likely to be as far as Israel goes in acquiring arms from Turkey. Report from Dagoni, 'Turkey asks Israel to increase reciprocal trade after defence deal'.

46 For a comprehensive account of the post-Persian Gulf War security and strategic situation in the Middle East, with special reference to Israel's position, see Inbar, 'Israel's security in a new international environment'.

In a deeper sense it became abundantly clear that Israel was first, no longer an isolated country in the region (nor conversely, was it fully integrated) and second, that it was not the sole source of tension in the Middle East.[47] Consequently, Israel's gradual entry into the Middle East has taken place at a time when other conflicts in the region are becoming more serious and widespread. In essence, these other problems are not superseding the Arab–Israeli conflict but are on a comparable level to it. Added to these developments is the fact that since the demise of the Soviet Union, the US has been the hegemonic superpower in the region. All these factors added together have meant that all the inter-related dynamic strategic relationships are shifting to produce a more uncertain picture of the future of the Middle East.

The effects of the Israeli–Turkish ties can be seen across the Middle East. The partial (at present) rapprochement between Syria and Iraq (enemies at the start of the 1990s) is the first direct result of these ties. The Israeli Chief of Staff, Amnon Shahak, addressing the Knesset Foreign Affairs and Defence Committee, argued that the opening of the Syrian–Iraqi border to allow some trade was a clear sign that the Syrians were becoming increasingly concerned over the peace process and Israel's links with Turkey.[48] Furthermore, the reopening of the border will in all likelihood lead to limited political contacts in the short term and possibly full, more comprehensive relations in the medium to long term between Syria and Iraq.

President Assad of Syria also hoped to deepen strategic ties with Iran as an additional counterfoil to the Israeli–Turkish ties. His extremely rare foreign sortie to Tehran on 31 July and 1 August 1997 illustrated the importance to Syria of such ties.[49] The fundamental Syrian fear lies with the potential formation of a formal alliance of Israel and Turkey with the blessing and support of the US. Such an alliance, Syria asserts, would

---

47 For a detailed presentation of the argument that Israel is becoming more integrated into the Middle East systems see, for example, E. Podeh, 'Rethinking Israel in the Middle East' in E. Karsh (ed.), *From Rabin to Netanyahu: Israel's Troubled Agenda* (London and Portland, Frank Cass, 1997), pp. 280–95.

48 Shahak announced that Syria had reopened its borders with Iraq at three crossings. He went on to state that the Syrians were giving these contacts an economic guise but he doubted this. Lt. General Amnon Shahak, Address to the Foreign Affairs and Defence Committee, The Knesset, 24 June 1997.

49 See G. Bechor, 'Syrian leaders take high stand against Israel', *Ha-Aretz*, 1 August 1997.

attempt to destabilise the Syrian regime and force it into concessions to Israel and in other border disputes. President Assad needs close relations with Iran, and perhaps in the longer term Iraq as well, to show the US that Syria still has partners despite the attempts of the US to isolate it in the region. Consequently, the replacement of President Rafsanjani with the more moderate Muhammed Khatami in August 1997 was a cause of great concern to President Assad – the major Syrian fear being that Khatami will open a dialogue with the US and move away from the Iranian–Syrian alliance. Obviously, such moves would leave Syria weakened and highly isolated in the region.

In practical terms Syria is using the Israeli–Turkish alliance as a way of gaining Iranian assistance in purchasing arms, many of them from Russia. In return the Syrians are allowing Iran the greater role in Middle East affairs that Tehran has sought for many years.

Iranian influence was also highly visible in Turkey during the period of the WP's participation in the government. The Iranian Ambassador was present at some of the previously described rallies, which called for an Islamic revolution in Turkey. The Iranian strategy was, in addition to the usual call for an Islamic revolution, to encourage the WP to weaken Turkey's links with Israel.

However, such a strategy was doomed to failure in the short term for a number of reasons. First, Turkey is a key member of NATO and has developed close ties with the US military. The Turkish military establishment is a powerful element of the ruling élite and has shown itself to be a strong upholder of Turkey's secular traditions. Moreover, the military has historically shown itself willing to step in and prevent what it termed as unpatriotic elements from seizing power. The actions of the military, both in the National Security Committee and in behind-the-scenes manoeuvrings, to remove the Islamists forces from the government in 1997 show that it remains willing to exercise its influence. Turkey's alliance with Israel is to a large degree the product of the military's assertion that Israel is its best partner in the region, and as a consequence any Iranian attempts to fracture this alliance in political terms are likely to prove problematic.

The second key consequence of Israeli–Turkish ties is the re-emergence of Russia as an active player in the region.[50] Though economic

---

50 See E. Inbar, 'Peace is a mirage', *Jerusalem Post*, 2 March 1998, which provides a deep understanding of the effects on Russia's growing influence in the Middle East in the late 1990s.

constraints currently prevent Russia from challenging the US hegemony in the region. Russia has responded to the Israeli–Turkish links by itself developing closer relations with Iran and Syria. Regarding the latter this has included help in updating and rearming the Syrian armed forces. Moreover, in response to the naval exercises conducted by Israeli–Turkey and the US, the Russians called for joint exercises between itself, Iran and Syria.

The potential for deeper ties between Russia and Iran may prove to be limited – this, despite the growing cooperation of military spheres and economic deals between the two countries. Tehran has always feared what it sees as imperialist Russia and has historically sided with the opponents of Russia in the "Great Game" of Central Asia. Today, Russia and Iran compete for influence in the new Central Asian Republics both politically and for economic markets. Consequently, Syria may find it difficult to reconcile the growing relationship between Syria and Russia and the links with Iran. Moreover, Iran and Turkey have been cooperating in recent times to limit the sphere of Russian influence in the Central Asia area. The fact that this has happened in spite of Turkey's relations with Israel is an illustration of Iranian suspicion of Russian intentions.

Although relations between the US and Iran remain almost non-existent, there have been signs from Tehran of a more moderate stance towards the US. A further shift in the direction of a more pragmatic foreign policy by Iran could lead to serious revisions of the US policy towards it in the medium to long term. In essence, simple mutual self-interest could bring Iran and the US closer together if the latter truly understands Russian intentions and opposes Russian attempts at major re-entry into Middle East affairs.

Both Iran and the US know that the way to each other is through Israel. However, such is the hostility between Israel and Iran there is unlikely to be any substantial shift in the near future of public positions or indeed high-level direct contacts.[51] Instead, indirect contacts through

---

51 There have been the usual spate of reports in the Israeli media concerning the opening of channels between Israel and Iran in an effort to reduce military tensions and settle Israel's debt of up to $1 billion to Tehran. See, for example, a detailed account in S. Rodan, 'Iran, Israel reportedly forging contacts', *Jerusalem Post*, 9 September 1997. However, it should be remembered that it is only the presidency in Iran that has changed and not the regime, and therefore the potential for change to Iran's attitude to the West, and to Israel in particular, may prove to be limited.

Turkey, and probably of, at first, an economic nature, are a more likely prospect. Interestingly, one of the few foreign policies that Israel's prime minister, Binyamin Netanyahu, initially modified from the previous Labour-led administration was towards Iran. Israeli commentators noted that during the first months of the administration there was a clear playing down of the Iranian threat that Rabin had talked up so much, in part to help secure continued US military support for Israel. However, once Israeli intelligence had unveiled the extent of the Iranian arsenal, the Israeli government has returned publicly to reminding the world of the threat that Iran poses.

The intended effects of the Israeli–Turkish relationship on the politics of Central Asia have been less successful for both participants. This has been caused by a number of factors. Initial Israeli enthusiasm for the new economic markets in the these countries has receded in the wake of problems dealing with extensive bureaucracies and other unforeseen costs which have yet to be resolved.[52] In addition, being closely linked to Turkey has done little for Israel as many of the Central Asian Republics are deeply suspicious of Turkish intentions in the region.[53] Initially, Israel had hoped that itself and Turkey would be able to pave the way into Central Asia for the US. This would have proved useful as an additional strategic use of Israel to the US. However, it has transpired that many large-scale companies from the US are making direct contact with the new republics, and consequently negating the value of Israel and Turkey in this area to the US.[54] Consequently, this area of Israel–Turkish relationships has not been as successful as Israel had hoped. Though there is little evidence to suggest that Israel's close

---

52 See D. Menashri, 'Introduction: is there a new Middle East?', pp. 15–16.

53 For a detailed history of the difficulties with Turkey's relations with the Central Asian Republics, see P. Robins, 'Turkey's Ostpolitik: relations with the Central Asian states' in D. Menashri (ed.), *Central Asia Meets the Middle East* (London and Portland, Frank Cass, 1998), pp. 129–49.

54 Although this is the general rule there have been notable exceptions where Israel and the US have cooperated in the region. These have usually been in the field of agriculture where Israel has been able to offer technical assistance together with investments (which included funds from both leading Israeli industrialists such as the late Shaul Eisenberg and the US). For more details of such actions, see P. Clawson, 'The disintegration of the Soviet Union: economic consequences for the Middle East', in D. Menashri (ed.), *Central Asia Meets the Middle East* (London and Portland, Frank Cass, 1998), p. 206.

links with Turkey have actually harmed its prospects of strategic and economic influence in the Central Asia it is clear that it has not enhanced its prospects either.

Conclusions

In assessing Israel's relationship with Turkey it is necessary to explore its importance in the short term and the medium to longer term. Moreover, it should be remembered that alliances are no substitute for a comprehensive peace settlement in the region. However, the potential for such a settlement remains limited at the end of the twentieth century. The complexity of the issues involved makes it likely that conflict will sadly continue to play an active part in the Middle East for the foreseeable future. In addition, growing competition between states for the limited natural resources makes it more likely that conflicts will actually intensify during the first part of the twenty-first century.

Accepting the assertion that it is likely to be necessary for Israel to maintain strategic alliances as part of its national security policy for the foreseeable future, then it is important that Israel chooses sensible and reliable partnerships. Currently, there are few countries in the region willing and able to develop such ties with Israel that Turkey has so carefully nurtured over the past few years. However, the absence of such candidates does not mean that Turkey is necessarily an ideal choice for Israel to court. The case against Turkey is that although it appears to offer the best short-term alliance there remain important questions over its longer-term value to Israel.

Israel's choice of strategic partners has itself been dominated in the past by short-termism over a more long-term view. Such a concentration on the first to some degree at the expense of the latter is hardly surprising given the nature of the threat that Israel has faced during the first 50 years of its existence. In addition, the decision in the 1970s to develop Israel's Military Industrial Complex together with the financial difficulties this sector of the economy has faced, has made it imperative that Israel exports arms. Consequently, this in turn has re-emphasised the concentration on finding strategic partners who will purchase weapons and to whom Israel feels able to sell. In this case the Turkish alliance is ideal given the Turkish military's eagerness to undertake a programme of modernisation of its large armed services using primarily Israeli companies.

In simple terms, orders placed by the Turks have prevented job losses and helped to secure projects that otherwise might have been in jeopardy. Moreover, in this capital-intensive research and development-dominated economic sector there are clear possibilities for jointly funded projects to share the burden of costs.

On a strategic and political level, Turkey does apparently suit Israeli objectives of putting pressure on Syria, proving, to a limited degree, a bridge to Central Asia and offering new options for potential air strikes on Iraq. Turkish links with the US through its participation in NATO also tie in well with Israel's close relationship with the US. Moreover, as was outlined earlier, the Turkish military has shown itself willing to intervene in Turkey's domestic politics in order to check destabilising influences that threaten the alliance in the short term.

However, in the medium to longer term, Israel's ties with Turkey may not prove to be so beneficial to it as first appeared for a number of reasons. First, the purchase of military hardware from Israel is not unlimited. Indeed, there are growing signs from Turkey that it expects Israel to make reciprocal purchases. Unsurprisingly, Israel has little desire to do so given its highly developed MIC and this could lead to a scenario where Turkey downgrades Israel's current "favoured status" in tendering competitions. In addition, the extent to which Israel and Turkey will pursue joint research and development projects is unclear. Israel has shown a strong tendency to favour the US with all its experience and capital for such schemes.

Second, although it is possible to argue that it is important for Israel to put pressure on Syria in the short term, it would be prudent not to do so to the extent that it excludes any future peace deal with Syria. In simple terms, there is a need to strike a fine balance between exerting pressure on Assad and at the same time still holding out an olive branch to tempt him to conduct meaningful negotiations with Israel. Consequently, this partially explains growing unease among some Israeli officials that Turkey is courting too much publicity for its links with Israel.

Third, Turkey remains politically, economically and socially highly unstable. In the long term it is difficult to foresee the Islamist challenge reducing and it is more than likely that economic hardship will actually intensify the threat from the Islamists. Though Turkey's deep-rooted secular nature may prove strong enough to withstand such a challenge, the internal compromises reached may well include a downgrading of its links with Israel.

Such factors are worrying to Israel which, to date, has not secured a long-term alliance of countries in the region, or on the periphery or with minorities, but which has managed only short-term deals that have subsequently cooled or broken down completely. The ex-prime minister, Shimon Peres, in stating that "governments change but basic interests remain" should note that self-interest can quickly change in the rapidly shifting sands of Middle East politics.[55] Consequently, Israeli planners need to be aware of the limitations of closer ties with Turkey in terms of both the difficulties within the relationship itself and the effects it has on the strategic balance of the Middle East.

---

55 Interview with Shimon Peres, CNN, 1 July 1996.

PART IV

EXTERNAL ACTORS IN THE PEACE PROCESS: THE CASE OF THE UNITED STATES

11

The development of the role of the United States in the peace process, 1991–1998: is there room at the table for new mediators?

Since the end of the Cold War and the demise of the Soviet Union the United States has been the major superpower operating in the Middle East. This has brought increased responsibilities for US administrations as they attempt to act as both mediator and at times policeman in the region. In essence, in the era of the so-called new world order the Middle East continues to require a great deal of attention from the US both to secure existing peace treaties and to pursue the ultimate goal of securing a comprehensive peace in the region.

Following the election of the Netanyahu-led government in Israel the normally close relationship between Israel and the US would appear to have come under enormous strain. However, these tensions do not represent a totally new development. Indeed, under the Shamir government (1990–2), relations between the Bush administration and Israel deteriorated to the point where President George Bush withheld some $10 billion in loan guarantees from Israel in order to punish the Israeli government for its continued settlement programme in the West Bank and the Gaza Strip.[1] To date the Netanyahu government has not encountered any financial penalty from the US, but increasing difficulties in relations have led to various diplomatic snubs by the Clinton administration towards the Israeli prime minister. (The most apparent diplomatic snub was Clinton's refusal to meet with Netanyahu during one of the Israeli prime minister's visit to the US. In addition, the Clinton administration

---

1 On the loan guarantee issue see, for example, L. Hadar, 'The 1992 electoral earthquake and the fall of the second Israeli republic', *Middle East Journal*, vol. 46, no. 4 (1992).

has been quick to issue invitations to the Israeli president, Ezer Weizman, who is well known for his dovish views on the peace process.)

Consequently, in analysing the role of the US in the peace process since 1996, and in particular its special relationship with Israel, this chapter provides an understanding of the complex inter-dependent nature of the relationship between the US and Israel. In addition, it examines how US administrations have favoured the Israeli Labour Party with its apparent willingness to trade land for peace over the Likud with its ideological reluctance to do the same, and the role of the US in recent Israeli elections.[2] Subsequently, the events and tactics of the US towards the peace process since 1996 are discussed. This period includes the end of Warren Christopher's term as Secretary of State and the first years of Madeleine Albright's tenure.

One of the major tactics employed by the US during the second Clinton administration has been to withdraw from the process at points of stalemate between the sides and to encourage other third parties to attempt to mediate and break the impasse. As a result, this chapter also examines the role of the European Union (EU) and Egypt in the peace process and considers whether there is indeed room for an additional influential third party in the negotiations. Finally, the re-emergence of Russia as a new regional power is discussed in the context of its potential to become involved in the negotiations, thus helping to balance the Arab perception of US pro-Israel bias.[3]

Background to the US and Israeli relationship

Before analysing the role of the US in the peace process since the defeat of Shimon Peres and the Israeli Labour Party in 1996, it is important to provide first an understanding of the inter-related nature of the Israeli–US relationship, which has developed in full since the 1973 Arab–Israeli war. Following the war, the Nixon administration took the decision that Israel's "qualitative edge" in military hardware was vital to

---

2 On US relations with both the Likud and the Labour Party in Israel, see J. Rynhold, 'Labour, Likud, the special relationship and the peace process' in E. Karsh (ed.), *From Rabin to Netanyahu: Israel's Troubled Agenda* (London and Portland, Frank Cass, 1997), pp. 239–62.

3 The re-emergence of Russia in the Middle East is discussed in Chapter 10 and in Inbar, 'Peace is a mirage'.

ensure the continued existence of its closest ally in the Middle East.[4] To put it more succinctly, Israel's regional position during the American–Soviet Cold War was of great strategic value to the successful pursuit of American foreign policy objectives.[5] Consequently, this fact alone was enough for American policy makers to forge close ties with Israel. However, the additional factor of the large Jewish constituency in the American electorate meant that most national political leaders, either in the Congress or in the White House, adopted a strong pro-Israel stance. In addition, the Jewish lobby in Washington was among the best funded and strongest lobby group in Capitol Hill.[6] For the above reasons no president, prior to George Bush, had attempted to challenge this powerful group.

The inter-dependent nature of the relationship is clearly illustrated in practical terms not only in Israel's strategic value to the US but also in the dependence of parts of the American Military Industrial Complex (MIC) on orders from the Israeli military establishment.[7] In essence, what occurred was that the Israelis were presented with around 50 per cent of the $3 billion aid in the form of a credit note, which was subsequently spent on buying American military hardware. Without this large annual order from Israel parts of the American MIC, based largely in the key electoral state of California, would have found it difficult to survive. Therefore it is clear that the large proportion of American aid to Israel was self-sufficing in two ways: first, to help support a regional ally in the Middle East theatre of the Cold War; and second, to ensure orders for the American MIC. The latter of these clearly helped to prevent job losses – particularly in the high-tech sector, which was located in a politically sensitive state for any presidential administration.

---

4 On the policy of maintaining Israel's military qualitative edge in the Middle East, see D. Gold, 'US policy towards Israel's qualitative edge', *JCSS Memorandum*, 36, 1992.

5 For a detailed account of the history and development of strategic relations between Israel and the US during the Cold War, see E. Luttwak, 'Strategic aspects of US–Israeli relations' in G. Sheffer (ed.), *US–Israeli Relations at the Crossroads* (London and Portland, Frank Cass, 1997), pp. 198–211.

6 On American support for Israel and an assessment of the role of Jewish lobby in US domestic politics, see C. Lipson, 'American support for Israel: history, sources, limits' in G. Sheffer (ed.), *US–Israeli Relations at the Crossroads*, pp. 128–46.

7 For more details on the dependency relationship that existed between the US and Israel, see G. Abed, 'Israel in the orbit of America: the political economy of a dependency relationship', *Journal of Palestine Studies*, vol. 16, no. 1 (1986).

However, the inter-dependent nature of the relationship has not prevented points of conflict. In recent times these have been centred around the opposition of US administrations to the Israeli settlement programme in the territories.[8] This has led to a situation where the US, although not wishing directly to intervene in Israeli domestic politics, has none the less tried to create a set of conditions that favours the parties in Israel which are considered to be more conducive to continuing the peace process. As a result, both the 1992 and 1996 Israeli elections were marked by unprecedented attempts by external powers to influence the eventual results in favour of the Labour Party-led block. The Bush presidency (1988–92) and the Clinton administration (1992 onwards) clearly favoured the Israeli Labour Party with its greater willingness to trade land for peace, which the US considered to be vital if the peace process was to succeed.

The battle over the loan guarantees in 1991–2 marked the first concerted attempt by an American administration to exercise overt influence over the foreign policy of Israel. Moreover, evidence will be presented, which aims to show that the agenda of President Bush went further than merely attempting to influence the then Likud-led government of Prime Minister Yitzhak Shamir. In short, it aimed to intervene directly in the Israeli election campaign by employing a carrot and stick approach to the Israeli electorate in terms of the granting of loan guarantees ($10 billion) from America, which were needed by Israel to absorb the Aliyah of ex-Soviet Jews.

In essence the American administration attempted to illustrate to the Israeli electorate that it would no longer accept the continuation of the Likud government's settlement programme in the West Bank and the Gaza Strip. Yitzhak Rabin, the new leader of the opposition Labour Party was viewed, by the Americans, as more ideologically flexible regarding the settlement programme in these areas. Consequently, Rabin was seen by the Americans as the most likely Israeli personality who was capable and willing to the further the peace process. Interestingly, at the time Rabin supported Shamir's decision to stand up to the Americans and argued that he himself would have been unwilling to impose the freeze that the Americans were demanding before granting the loan guarantees. However, it was clear that Rabin's short-term position of support did

---

8 See Lochery, *The Israeli Labour Party*, pp. 191–2.

not conceal his greater flexibility with regard to the future status of the territories than that of Shamir and his right-wing allies in the government.

There were additional reasons that led to the feeling of exasperation of President Bush and his Secretary of State, James Baker, with the Israeli government – namely the lack of progress in the Washington peace talks where Israel offered little or no concessions. There was a suspicion in the American administration that Shamir was content to ensure the continuation of the talks while he pressed ahead with the settlement programme in the West Bank and the Gaza Strip. (Incidentally, after the 1996 election in Israel the defeated Shamir was reported to have stated that he had intended to keep the talks going for ten years while continuing with the settlement programme. Shamir denied making such comments.) If this was the strategy of the Israeli government, then it was clear that the talks could continue until the end of the century. In addition, there was a natural reluctance by both the Israeli and the Arab participants to walk out of the talks for fear of offending the Americans.

Such a fear was mainly based on the question of economic punishments that the Americans might have imposed on any country viewed as responsible for destroying the process. This would likely have taken the form of reductions in the level of aid to the offending country or countries. It is true that from time to time during the talks there were crises, but all the parties eventually returned to the negotiating table. Consequently, the Americans were pressed into sponsoring a process that gave little or no indication of making substantive progress, but which in turn did not collapse allowing the Americans to modify or change its strategy. In essence, the Bush administration was forced to work within the framework set up at the Madrid Peace Conference (1991) and did not feel able to consider alternatives due to the absence of a total breakdown of the original framework.

It became apparent that the American administration through the frequent visits to the Middle East by Secretary Baker was trying to exert more and more pressure on Shamir's government to announce a suspension of its settlement activities.[9] In turn, Shamir was coming

---

9 Accounts of this pressure were provided by Likud leaders in interviews conducted by the author in 1994 – for example, interview with Yitzhak Shamir on 17 August 1994 and Moshe Arens 26 September 1994. The most lucid published account remains Arens, *Broken Covenant: American Foreign Policy and the Crisis between the US and Israel*.

under intra-party and inter-party block pressure to increase the pace of settlement. Indeed, the Sharon plan, proposed by the Minister of Housing and Construction, Ariel Sharon, called for a doubling of the number of settlements as well as a major expansion programme to existing ones. In addition, Shamir's room for manoeuvre was, in any event, restricted by the coalition partners in his administration, the ultra-right wing parties. These parties, Tsomet, Moledet and Tehiya, were strong supporters of the settlement in the territories that they saw as a definitive right of the Jewish people and the best way of preserving long-term Jewish sovereignty over these areas.

The role of the US in Shamir's eventual election defeat in 1992 is difficult to quantify; there were a number of domestic and international issues leading to his and the Likud's downfall.[10] However, the fact that soon after Rabin came to power in Israel the US reversed the decision and granted the full guarantees to Israel was an illustration of how party politicised US involvement in Israel had become.

In 1996, the Clinton administration responded favourably to requests from the then prime minister, Shimon Peres, for indirect help in his election campaign following the series of suicide bombings in February and March 1996. The US responded by organising and participating in a high-level anti-terror summit and by arranging a visit to Israel by President Clinton on 14 March 1996 prior to the main part of Israel's election campaign. However, Clinton was careful not to make any statements that could be directly construed as an indication of support for one party or another.[11] Indeed, Rubin argues that Clinton, while clearly preferring a Peres victory, went out of his way to be seen as remaining neutral in public. Consequently, Peres and the Labour Party gained little in electoral terms from Clinton's preference, although the effect of the perception of Clinton's support for Peres on the Israeli electorate is more difficult to measure. In addition, it is worth considering that Clinton was somewhat restrained by a staunchly pro-Israel Congress, many of whom enjoyed good relations with Netanyahu and the Likud.[12]

---

10 On the 1992 elections and the defeat of the Likud, see Lochery, *The Israeli Labour Party*, Chapter 10.

11 On this issue, see Rubin, 'External influences on the Israeli elections', p. 154.

12 Netanyahu had learnt many lessons from Shamir, one of which was the need to develop closer ties with Congress, and in particular the Republican leaders in both houses. As a consequence, Congress has, at times, helped to check the power

The so-called perception of Clinton favouring Peres irritated the Likud and in particular the actions of the US ambassador to Israel, Martin Indyk, who senior Likudniks charged with trying to create the conditions to assure that Peres was re-elected.[13] In summary, it is clear that the (direct or indirect) intervention of the Clinton administration in the Israeli election of 1996 was not as great as the attempt of the Bush administration in 1992 against Shamir. And even if Clinton's intervention had been overt it was unlikely to have altered the result of the vote. However, what the latter did achieve was a feeling of suspicion on the part of the incoming Netanyahu government towards elements of the Clinton administration.[14] The new prime minister was afraid that the US would push Israel further than it was willing to go by threatening the special relationship that existed between the two countries. Consequently, Netanyahu made it clear that his priority was Israeli security interests over relations with the US. As he put it:

> Although relations with the United States are a strategic asset of utmost importance, it is not the supreme asset of the State of Israel. The supreme asset is our security. The supreme asset is things holy to us, like Jerusalem. If an administration of the US comes and says give all this up in exchange for relations with the US, I will not give them up . . . I will make our work with the United States fit our interests, and do not adapt our interests to fit our ties with the US.[15]

Subsequently, this unease has added to the problems as the peace process has not developed along the lines that the US had previously mapped

---

of President Clinton on Israeli issues. Evidence of Netanyahu's close relationship with Congress was provided by the reception he received when delivering a speech to a special joint session of the two houses soon after assuming office.

13 In 1997, Martin Indyk was appointed to head the Middle East desk at the State Department in Washington and has continued to play a central role in the peace process.

14 Netanyahu, having spent a great deal of time in the US serving in the Israeli Embassy in Washington and as ambassador to the UN, knew many of Clinton's team personally prior to coming to office in Israel. Of Clinton's team, the US Special Envoy to the Middle East, Dennis Ross, was perhaps the only official in whom the new prime minister had total trust. However, and probably as a result of this, Dennis Ross was the US official in whom the Palestinians had least faith, thus illustrating the problems for US officials in the area.

15 Interview with Binyamin Netanyahu, Israel Radio, 15 September 1996.

out during the era of Rabin and Peres in Israel. In short, since 1996 there has existed a varying degree of mutual suspicion from both the Israeli and US administrations towards each other and these are examined in chronicling the various stages of development of the US role in the peace process since 1996.

Israel, the US and the peace process 1996 onwards

Following Netanyahu's victory there was no change in US aims and interests in the Middle East peace process, although the possibility of securing these aims would appear in the short term to have become more complex. These can be defined as the following.

1. To help secure a comprehensive and just peace in the region based on a return of some lands to the Arabs which were captured by Israel in 1967.
2. To find a solution to the Palestinian problem through a negotiated solution.
3. To maintain and develop relations with Israel and to help ensure its short- and long-term security.
4. To develop relations with the moderate Arab states as a potential foil against radical anti-US regimes in the area.

Consequently, the Clinton administration has continued to fill all the roles that its position in the Middle East demands. It has organised and hosted top-level (crisis) summits between Netanyahu and Arab leaders, acted as a messenger (between Israel and Syria), helped to maintain a degree of momentum to the process (the Hebron agreement) and, most importantly, has continued to attempt to fill the role of mediator between the various parties. Although Netanyahu's term in office has placed a strain on US–Israeli relations these have not led to a substantial re-evaluation of the long-term commitment of the US to the process. In examining the role of the US in the Middle East since Netanyahu's election there are three distinct time periods: first, June 1996 to end of January 1997; second, February 1997 to August 1997; and third, from September 1997 onwards.

From crisis to Hebron: the end of Christopher's era, June 1996 to January 1997

The opening of the tunnel entrance in Jerusalem in September 1996 and the resulting violence marked the first real crisis of the Netanyahu era. The US response to the events was twofold: first, as described in Chapter 6, President Clinton was publicly indirectly highly critical of Netanyahu's action; and second, the Clinton administration decided to gamble on a full-scale diplomatic summit in Washington on 1 October with the participation of the Israeli prime minister, Chairman Arafat, King Hussein and President Mubarak.[16] However, President Mubarak refused to attend the summit citing reasons of lack of preparation time, but in reality reflecting his belief that any progress at this time was highly unlikely.

Despite an intensive two days of discussions – some directly involving Clinton and others without the participation of any third party – no significant progress was made on any of the major issues. In addition, Arafat and Netanyahu, despite a marked improvement in their personal relationship, failed to agree on anything other than setting a date for negotiations to continue over the Israeli redeployment in Hebron.[17] Unsurprisingly, at the post-summit press conference Clinton defended the decision to hold the meetings by questioning where the region would have been without them and stating that the discussions had improved trust between the parties. (A more interesting comment on the talks came from King Hussein who stated that he understood why President Mubarak had stayed away.) In reality, there was no mistaking the failure of the American intervention and in private senior US officials acknowledged the fact. This was reflected in a marked rise in the belief that the US should tactically withdraw from trying to arrange peace in the region and let the various sides try to find an agreement between themselves. Although, the US did not at this stage take such a formal decision, the Middle East peace process was clearly moved down the US political agenda in favour of more politically profitable areas. In essence, there

---

16 The meeting, which came only five weeks before the presidential election in the US, was an indication of how concerned the Clinton administration was that the Middle East peace process was on the point of collapse. On the diplomatic gamble, see 'Agreeing to disagree', *The Economist*, 5 October 1996, p. 73.

17 For an interesting inside account of the meetings in the White House, see B. Nelan, 'Inside the summit', *Time*, 14 October 1996, pp. 28–32.

was a realisation in the White House that there was little prospect of significant progress in the short term and that it would continue to employ a lower key mediation effort to "keep the lid on" the region and move the protracted negotiations over Hebron forward.

However, this sceptical climate in Washington was matched by a realisation that there was a need for the US to continue to use what little momentum that had been obtained from the summit to pressurise the parties into a deal over Hebron. Consequently, Warren Christopher made another trip to the region on 6 October in order to hold meetings with Netanyahu and Arafat as well as addressing the negotiators at the resumed talks between the Israeli government and the PA over Hebron.[18] In addition, Dennis Ross continued his shuttle diplomacy between the parties in the Middle East and was present during the protracted negotiations over Hebron.

Following Clinton's successful re-election in November there was no immediate marked change in US strategy towards the Middle East, and the Netanyahu government in particular. However, two longer-term changes were thought likely to have an impact. The first was the appointment of the US Ambassador to the United Nations, Madeleine Albright, as the new Secretary of State from the end of January 1997 onwards. Albright had a reputation as a tough negotiator, but with little knowledge of the Middle East and it was assumed (initially correctly) that she would not devote the same amount of attention or travel towards the Middle East. Second, now that the president was serving his final term in office he would not be so concerned about attracting the Jewish vote, which remains important in securing office in the US. As a result of this, Clinton would be in a stronger position to pressurise, and if necessary confront, the Netanyahu government in order to force it into concessions.

Unsurprisingly, both changes were considered by Arab governments as vital if the US were to push the peace process forward, but were viewed with concern in Jerusalem. In reality, neither change has had the impact on the process that was originally thought. The question of Albright is dealt with later, suffice to say that she has not had the impact

---

18 Christopher once more attempted to inject some urgency into talks, warning that both sides needed to reach an agreement as quickly as possible in order to avoid fresh bloodshed. In addition, he reiterated the US position that the Oslo Accords must be implemented. Comments by Warren Christopher at Press Conference, 6 October 1996.

many thought. Indeed, the Palestinians have accused Albright of being a very pro-Israel Secretary of State, and to date she has enjoyed much better personal relations with the Likud-led government than James Baker did with the previous Likud government of Shamir. In addition, President Clinton, weakened and embroiled in a number of sex scandals, has proven somewhat reluctant to risk offending the Jewish vote in the US in case his opinion poll rating drops, thus increasing pressure on him to resign.

Finally, the end of Christopher era was marked by the signing of the Hebron Accords between Netanyahu and Arafat on 15 January 1997. However, the US could not claim sole responsibility for this breakthrough. The deadlock was not finally broken until King Hussein intervened and held separate meetings with Arafat in Gaza and Netanyahu in Tel Aviv. Indeed, the King only stepped in when American efforts seemed once more to have failed and there was a potential for a return to the scale of violence witnessed after the opening of the tunnel in Jerusalem. Moreover, this continued the pattern of recent times that any deals that were signed in the region were brokered directly by the parties: the Oslo and Cairo Accords and the Israel–Jordanian peace.

Increased tension and new agendas: the start of the Albright era, February to August 1997

The US role in the Middle East peace process during the first months of the Albright tenure was extremely limited. There were five major reasons for this. First, the US realised that the fact it had been forced to act as a guarantor of the implementation of the Hebron agreement was not a good sign. In short, it had been drawn in much deeper than it wanted and was trying to extricate itself from this position. However, to a degree this proved impossible because the reciprocal obligations that were tied into the Hebron agreement and guaranteed by the US were not met by either side.[19] Second, other issues such as the delicate negotiations over the expansion of NATO into Eastern Europe were higher on the US foreign policy agenda. This was viewed by the US as left-over business from the end of the Cold War and required a great deal of time from members of

---

19 See J. Dempsey, 'Ross rides back to the rescue', *Financial Times*, 27 March 1997.

the administration. Third, there was a feeling from Albright that she did not wish to become immersed in a process that the administration viewed as having limited opportunity for short-term successes. Fourth, Albright was also keen to illustrate that she represented a change in style from Christopher and his frequent visits to the region and seemingly endless one-to-one meetings with the various key players in the peace process.[20] Finally, as events developed, further tensions arose between the US and Israel, a fact that led the US administration to take a strategic decision to withdraw temporarily from the process. (This was not a new strategy. It was employed by James Baker in 1991, when he told the Middle East leaders that they had his phone number and to call him when they were ready to enter serious negotiations.) The major events that led to the Israeli withdrawal were the decision to build at Har Homa (see Chapter 6) in February 1997, which infuriated Clinton and led to an impasse in the peace process with the Palestinians and the threat of further regional isolation for Israel. In addition, Netanyahu's future prospects of political survival were in deep trouble with what became known as the Bar-On scandal dominating the Israeli domestic agenda. US officials presumed (correctly) that the prime minister would not do anything to anger his right-wing coalition partners at this time, and consequently any new initiatives from the US would have been met with limited enthusiasm in Jerusalem.

As a result of the above factors the Clinton administration employed the following levels of engagement to prevent the Middle East peace process from an irreversible collapse. It should be stressed that these engagements were designed primarily for the Israeli–Palestinian track while other tracks were placed even further down the agenda. At the first level were regular meetings of officials from the State Department with officials from the specific parties (mainly Israeli and Palestinian) in Washington. At the second level, and less regular, one-to-one meetings at leadership level – such as those between Clinton and Mubarak (10 March), Clinton and King Hussein (1 April) and Clinton and Netanyahu (7 April). The third level was the crisis shuttle diplomacy of Dennis Ross which was employed when the cycle of violence in the region increased and where there appeared the possibility of the violence getting out of control.

---

20 For a highly critical analysis of Albright's tactics during this period see A. Eldar, 'And who didn't come?', *Ha-Aretz*, 6 August 1997.

The aim of the first level was to maintain communication with the parties and explore new or revised proposals for moving the various tracks of the peace process forward. Instances of such meetings producing major developments included the visit by Netanyahu's adviser of foreign affairs, Dore Gold, to the State Department on 24 March in which Gold outlined Netanyahu's plan of 20 March, which proposed completing accelerated Final Status talks within six months and a by-passing of the interim stages of the Oslo Accords. Such meetings were held in private with the Clinton administration using them to make assessments if the time was ripe for another US-led initiative in the region.

The rationale behind the second level, Clinton's meetings with Middle East leaders, was twofold: first, maintain and develop America's bi-lateral relations with its allies in the region; and second, to explore any new formula for overcoming the difficulties in the peace process. For the US president this was a low-risk strategy; he was seen to be continuing his personal involvement in the process, but without the risks attached to a major summit of regional leaders. In essence, as Clinton himself suggested after the meeting with Netanyahu on 7 April, he would remain personally involved in the peacemaking, but made it clear he would not launch any new initiative unless the parties cooperated. In addition, he went on to rule out a Camp David peace conference, similar to the framework used in Israeli–Egyptian negotiations in 1978, and in lowering his sights called for the parties to re-establish the confidence necessary for further progress.[21]

At the third level, there were two major aims behind the shuttle diplomacy of US officials in the Middle East. The first was in response to a major crisis of a series of damaging events. The major instance of this occurred following a worsening of violence in the West Bank, a suicide bomb attack in Tel Aviv on 21 March and the subsequent Israeli closures of the West Bank and the Gaza Strip. The US envoy, Dennis Ross, arrived in Israel on 27 March to attempt to defuse the situation, listen and report back to Clinton.[22] Second, the shuttle diplomacy of

---

21 Remarks by President Clinton to the White House press on 7 April 1997.

22 Ross also used his visits to help arrange meetings between key personnel on various sides. For example he was heavily involved in arranging the Ariel Sharon (Israeli Minister of National Infrastructure) meeting with Abu Mazen (the no. 2 in the PA) in June 1997. This was important because it represented Sharon's first

Ross was used as a means of preparing the ground for the high profile visit of the Secretary of State in August. In short, Ross's mission was to help create a favourable climate so the results of such a visit would be deemed positive. Interestingly, throughout this period Albright did not visit the region, and State Department officials hoped the longer her absence went on, the greater impact her first visit was likely to have.

Albright's takes centre stage: August 1997 onwards

The period from early August onwards saw the resurrection of the US diplomatic campaign in the region. Following the suicide bomb attack at Mahane Yehuda, Dennis Ross arrived in Israel and started an intensive series of meetings aimed at restoring the Israeli–Palestinian track negotiations.[23] With neither side by this stage talking directly to each other Ross was forced to shuttle between Jerusalem and Ramallah in the hope of securing a short-term deal which could lead to the resumption of formal negotiations.[24] However, this time Ross's visit served an additional purpose of preparing the ground for a visit to the region by Albright. The visit by the Secretary of State did not reflect any major new US initiative, but rather a feeling that she could no longer put off a visit to the area. As a result, she arrived in Israel on 10 September with no dramatic breakthrough on the horizon, and in the hope that her personal involvement could help secure a restart to the Israeli–Palestinian and Israeli–Syrian tracks of the peace process.[25] In essence, Albright had to reconcile Israeli demands that the PA do more to prevent terrorist attacks against Israel with Palestinian demands for a freeze of the building of Jewish settlements in the West Bank.[26] In addition, the

meeting with a senior member of the PLO. On this, see Eldar, 'Dennis Ross helped set up Sharon-Abu Mazen meeting', *Ha-Aretz,* 30 June 1997.

23 For a detailed account of Ross's visit see, J. Bushinsky and J. Immanuel, 'Ross begins Jerusalem–Ramallah shuttle', *Jerusalem Post,* 11 August 1997.

24 An interesting perspective on US mediation at this stage is provided by A. Eban, 'No more room for American ambiguity', *Jerusalem Post*, 8 August 1997.

25 US officials fearing total failure were deliberately pessimistic about the visit. James Rubin, the State Department spokesman, declared that Albright was not a magician. On the problems facing Albright's visit, see Y. Tal, 'Albright faced toughest challenge', *Ha-Aretz*, 10 September 1997.

26 On the issues facing Albright and potential implications for Israeli–US relations, see Z. Schiff, 'Confrontation at home or in Washington', *Ha-Aretz,* 15 August 1997.

US was once more central to maintaining security cooperation between Israel and the PA, and Albright wanted this cooperation developed more fully, in part to allow the US to concentrate on other longer-term aspects of the process.[27]

Albright's comments at the press conference that followed her meeting with Netanyahu on the 10th clearly illustrated the dual approach of the US to persuade Arafat to act on terrorism and Netanyahu on settlements. As she put it:

> I will be seeing Chairman Arafat tomorrow, and my message will be clear. It is essential that Israeli–Palestinian security cooperation be serious, sustained and effective. At the same time, the PA must take unilateral steps and actions to root out terrorist infrastructure. If we are able to create and sustain an invigorated and accelerated negotiating process, there simply is no other way . . . Achieving this peace turns fundamentally on a political process which meets through a genuine process of give and take the needs of both sides. Clearly Israel also has a responsibility to shape an environment which will give the process a chance to succeed. This means that Israel should be taking steps that build confidence and to refrain from actions that undermine confidence and trust. As I said in my speech last month, it is very difficult to create a serious environment for negotiations when unilateral actions are taken that prejudge or pre-empt issues reserved for Final Status negotiations.[28]

In short, the US strategy was clear that there could be little progress until Arafat acted on the terrorism issue, but once the US considered he was doing this then it would apply pressure on Israel on the political issues such as expansion of Jewish settlements.[29] Furthermore, there was an additional modification to US policy during Albright's trip when she publicly, and implicitly, called for a settlement freeze by Israel.[30] The

---

27 See D. Makovsky, 'Albright will press Arafat, but Israel must respond', *Ha-Aretz*, 11 September 1997.

28 Address by Madeleine Albright at joint press conference with Binyamin Netanyahu, Jerusalem, 10 September 1997.

29 For an American perspective on this, see T. Lippman, 'Albright visit bares US–Israel division over peace', *Washington Post*, 11 September 1997.

30 Albright's comments were made in Ramallah after meeting with Arafat on 11 September and subsequently reiterated in a speech at the Jerusalem Academy of Arts and Science on the same day. See D. Makovsky, 'Albright urges a time out

outcome of Albright's visit was viewed by the Netanyahu government as quite successful; they had largely avoided any major confrontation with the Secretary of State, and Netanyahu had not been pressurised into conceding anything new.[31] Conversely, there was concern from the Palestinian side that Albright had proved unwilling to exert any real pressure on the Netanyahu government, nor in their opinion showed any sign of doing so in the near future.[32] From the US perspective Albright's visit in the short term was viewed as a qualified success, but Albright claimed as she departed the region that she would not return until there were real signs of progress. Upon leaving the region she summarised her intentions:

> If the region's leaders are not prepared to make the hard choices required to achieve peace, I have other things to do and will not allow the Middle East to dominate my attention. If I can make a difference, I will be there. If there is not enough happening for me to make a difference, I'm going to concentrate on Cambodia or our upcoming summit with the Chinese or on Bosnia and NATO expansion and meeting with the Russians . . . The United States' responsibilities are so large, I can't be occupied with this full time.[33]

In reality, Albright's visit drew her and the US closer into the peace process, and despite her threats she has subsequently become engaged in regular meetings with Middle East leaders (mainly in Europe). In addition, Dennis Ross returned to his intensive shuttle diplomacy as he attempted to find a formula to gain agreements on Israeli redeployments from the West Bank.

Throughout the first part of 1998, the US strategy was once more modified presenting its own detailed plans to restart the Israel–Palestinian track. These plans, which were made public in June 1998, dealt specifically with the problem of delayed Israeli troop redeployments in the West

---

on settlements if Arafat acts against terror', *Ha-Aretz*, 12 September 1997. For an American perspective on the comments, see Samar Assad, 'Albright urges settlement time out', *Washington Post*, 11 September 1997.

31 For more details on the short-term effect of Albright's visit of Netanyahu, see Yoel Marcus, 'She left her stick at home', *Ha-Aretz*, 12 September 1997.

32 On this fear see, for example, C. Shalev, untitled piece, *Ma'ariv* and A. Golan, untitled piece, *Yediot Aharonot*, both 11 September 1997.

33 Reported by T. Lippman, 'Albright pessimistic as Mideast trips end', *Washington Post*, 16 September 1997.

Bank, the lack of Permanent Status negotiations (due to have started in May 1997), Israeli–Palestinian security cooperation, amending the PLO charter calling for the destruction of Israel, and a freeze on Israeli settlement building. The presence of this detailed US plan illustrated two points: first, that with a near-complete breakdown of trust between the participants of the peace process the short-term dependency on US involvement and mediation was extremely high; and second, that Albright had become as entrenched in dealing with the affairs of the region as her predecessor, Warren Christopher, and that US policy, though having gone through a cycle of temporary withdrawal, was once again as active in the region as it had been since the end of Persian Gulf War in 1991.

Room at the table for other mediators

There is a potential for the involvement of three other international mediators in the region, the EU, Egypt and Russia. At present, it would appear that these three countries can only play a secondary role to the US in the so-called new world order in the Middle East. This chapter, while largely agreeing with this argument, will outline the existing roles played by these nations and analyse the opportunities for increased involvement.

A European role in the Middle East

In economic terms the EU is the largest donor of aid to the PA, but to date has secured only a secondary political role in the peace process. There are a number of reasons for this: an Israeli feeling that the Europeans are pro-Arab and therefore not honest brokers; Europe's inability until recent times to speak with one voice; and the reluctance of the US to coordinate and cooperate fully with the EU. Of these factors the first is clearly the biggest problem and there would appear to be limited possibilities of changing. However, the Netanyahu government has shown itself to be more inclined to involve single European countries, and specifically their leaders, in the process as a means of checking the influence of Clinton. The major example of this to date has been the Israeli involvement of the British prime minister, Tony Blair, in attempts to break the deadlock with the Palestinians. (At the time Britain held the presidency of the EU, but for Netanyahu this was not the major reason for inviting Blair to become involved. In short, the Israeli prime minister viewed Blair as a strong supporter of Israel and wished to cultivate this support.) However, these attempts have been limited in nature and the Israeli feeling of suspicion towards the EU prevents it from a full role in the process.[34]

This said, the EU has played an important part in preventing a total collapse of the process in recent times. The EU special envoy to the region, Miguel Moratinos, has been active as both a channel of communication between the parties and in playing a secondary role to the US in shuttle diplomacy (often working in tandem with Dennis Ross).[35] However, at a higher-level events such as Robin Cook's ill-fated trip to Israel in early 1998 again highlighted the difficulties that the Europeans have in the process. (The visit of Robin Cook to Israel culminated in the Israeli prime minister cancelling a joint dinner engagement with Cook claiming that he had broken an agreement over his visit to Har Homa. At the time Cook was head of the Council of Foreign Ministers and was visiting Israel in his European capacity.) In essence, such visits merely reinforce Israeli sentiments of an Arab bias in European governments.

Two facts have become apparent over the European role in the Middle East peace process: first, that its role is clearly secondary to that of the US, as a result of which the Europeans would not take any major political initiative that the US administration had strong reservations about nor would it attempt to conduct a process without full consultations with the US; and second, that the Europeans present an additional option when the US, as previously outlined, decides to withdraw partially from the process as part of its long-term strategy. In such circumstances the EU can fill the hole for a period of time and help to prevent a total breakdown of the peace process.

---

34 A poll published by the Tami Steimetz Centre for Peace Research at Tel Aviv University in June 1998 found that the majority of Israelis perceived the EU to be more supportive of the Palestinians. The findings were as follows. Asked about their opinion of the Europeans as mediators in the peace process 60 per cent thought they were more supportive of the Palestinians, 31 per cent considered them to be neutral and 4 per cent more supportive of Israelis. When asked a similar question about the US, 24 per cent considered it more supportive of Israel, 50 per cent neutral and 20 per cent more supportive of the Palestinians. In addition, 77 per cent of the respondents favoured an increased US involvement in the process with 21 per cent opposed, and 43 per cent supported greater European involvement with 53 per cent opposed to it.

35 For more details, see interview with Moratinos published in *Ha-Aretz*, 19 September 1997 under the heading 'Model of mediators'.

However, it is difficult to foresee any role for the EU above and beyond that of a secondary mediator that plays an important political part, but whose influence is limited through the pre-eminence of the US in the minds of the major players in the peace process. Furthermore, the perceived Arab bias of the EU makes it unlikely that even with the Netanyahu government in Israel, and its strained relationship with the US administration, any Israeli government would encourage a deeper European involvement.

An Egyptian role in the peace process

As Israel and Egypt have had a stable if cold peace since 1978 a detailed analysis of relations goes beyond the scope of this study on the current Middle East peace process.[36] However, during the first years of the Netanyahu government the Egyptians have attempted, at times, to mediate between Israel and the PA. It should be stressed (and is outlined in Chapter 2) that at other times the Egyptians have also acted to slow down the process such as during the negotiations over Hebron in late 1996. In terms of mediation the major instance of this occurred when the US had withdrawn from the process and gave Egypt the green light to attempt to break the impasse. President Mubarak arranged a summit meeting in Sharm e-Sheikh with Netanyahu at the end of May 1997. Subsequently, a new Egyptian initiative emerged from this summit with the Egyptians appointing Dr Osama el-Baz (a national security adviser to Mubarak) to shuttle back and forth between the sides. However, after six weeks it became clear that the Egyptian effort was doomed to failure. As the Egyptian foreign minister, Amr Moussa, confirmed in an interview with the Hebrew daily, *Ha-Aretz,*

> Let me put it you frankly: after six weeks of effort, the Egyptian initiative has not made any progress at all. The Israeli government refuses to budge from its position. Without results, there is no point in going on. After all, we didn't come here to dispense smiles. And then Israel wonders why the situation is so tense in Hebron.

---

36 Two interesting examples of recent studies on Israeli–Egyptian are: K. Stein, 'Continuity and change in Egyptian–Israeli relations, 1973–1997' in E. Karsh (ed.), *From Rabin to Netanyahu: Israel's Troubled Agenda* (London and Portland, Frank Cass, 1997), pp. 298–320, and S. Pine, 'Myopic vision: whither Israeli–Egyptian relations?', as above, pp. 321–34.

Israel is the guilty party . . . There is nothing to hinder any of us from visiting Israel, but we must have a good reason for doing so. There must be purpose.[37]

Following this, the Egyptian effort came to an end, in part due to this lack of progress, but also because of the return of the US to the peace process. However, even though the initiative failed it reflected two factors: first, the concern of Mubarak about the peace process and the potential de-stabilising effects its collapse would have for the region; and second, an acceptance in Jerusalem that Egypt can play a positive role in the peace process. Regarding the latter, previously under Rabin and Peres, relations between Israel and Egypt had not developed as hoped. This was caused to a large degree by Egypt's reluctance to allow Israel to integrate fully in the region, both politically and economically. In many ways the arrival of Netanyahu with his publicised commitment to continue the peace process, but at a slower pace, was less threatening to the Egyptians than Rabin and Peres's dramatic rapid peace making. Moreover, Netanyahu was careful to court Mubarak during the initial stages of his period in office, and as a consequence Mubarak refrained from making bitter personal attacks on Netanyahu. Interestingly, even during the protracted Hebron negotiations when it was clear that the Egyptians were pressuring Arafat not to sign up, criticism of Egypt came more from the Israeli media circles rather than from the government itself.[38]

However, following Netanyahu's decision to build at Homa, the increased violence in the West Bank and the resulting impasse in the peace process, Mubarak has become much more critical of the Netanyahu government even claiming that Israel's peace treaty with Egypt is at risk.[39] In addition, Egypt has been a leading force in attempting to isolate Israel in the region. As a result of this, in the long run it is difficult to see a deeper role developing as a mediator for Egypt. It is more likely that

37 Interview with Amr Moussa in G. Bechor, 'Giving peace a chance', *Ha-Aretz*, 15 July 1997.
38 Criticism of Egypt, and Mubarak in particular, continued throughout late 1996 and 1997. For a good example, see Editorial: 'Mubarak's new Middle East', *Jerusalem Post*, 22 September 1997.
39 On this, see D. Makovsky, 'Mubarak says Netanyahu wrecking peace process', *Ha-Aretz*, 9 September 1997.

Mubarak will attempt to intervene in times of crisis when the cycle of violence threatens to move out of control. In addition, if the Israeli–Palestinian track were to collapse totally then Mubarak would come under intensive domestic pressure to intervene militarily if the IDF were to re-enter the Palestinian autonomous areas. Consequently, it is clear that Mubarak and the Egyptians are too closely involved in the process themselves to be in a position to serve as convincing central mediators.

Russia as a mediator

The re-emergence of Russia back into the Middle East was considered in Chapter 10, but it would appear that at present there is not a strong potential for it to play a major role as a mediator in the Middle East. As Chapter 10 outlined there is a great deal of suspicion concerning Russian attempts to re-arm the Syrian military and other Russian intentions in the region. However, Russia could play a role in other areas of the Middle East peace process, which need to be addressed if there is to be any chance of a comprehensive peace settlement in the future. These include dealing with Saddam Hussein and the ongoing conflict over UN weapons inspections where Russia was heavily involved at the start of 1998 in successfully preventing a return to military action by the US and its allies.

However, increasing Israeli concerns over Russian arms sales to Iran mean that it is highly improbable that Israel would permit any Russian mediation in the Arab–Israeli conflict. As a consequence, Russian efforts are more likely to develop along dealing with secondary disputes in the region and not on the central areas of the peace process.

Conclusions

Following the end of the Cold War and the Persian Gulf War the US has emerged as the sole superpower in the region. Consequently, its involvement in the Middle East peace process since 1991 has been central to maintaining and developing the peace process. Moreover, the fact that the deals signed between Israel and the Arabs during this time have been negotiated directly without a third party should not diminish the role of the US in maintaining some sort of process first, in Washington, and subsequently with its concentration on shuttle diplomacy, when it appeared that the process was close to collapse.

Central to US involvement in the Middle East is its close relationship with Israel. This chapter has outlined the development of this relationship since the 1973 Arab–Israel war and argued that the relationship is of a complex inter-dependent nature. However, the relationship has been put under strain as both Republican and Democratic administrations have attempted to move Israel towards agreeing peace accords with the Palestinians and their Arab neighbours. Consequently, the strains in this relationship with the Netanyahu-led government in power in Israel are not new developments but represent a continuation of the difficulties that the Bush administration encountered with the Israeli government of Yitzhak Shamir. In addition, such strains would seem to be quite natural as the US calls on Israel to make the difficult territorial concessions it needs to in order to have a chance of securing a permanent peace in the region. Unfortunately, the strained relations have not been helped by the apparent lack of personal chemistry between President Clinton and Binyamin Netanyahu, and the latter's unilateral actions such as the opening of the tunnel and the Har Homa project, which have been undertaken without prior warning or consultation with the US.

During the Netanyahu era the US has adopted various strategies towards the peace process ranging from attempts at summit diplomacy to shuttle diplomacy, including periods where it has tactically withdrawn from the process. Moreover, the prospect that the US will attempt to impose a solution on the region would appear not as improbable as a few years ago. Clearly, the absence of any Final Status agreement between the Israelis and the Palestinians, and the failure of Israel and Syria to reach agreement on a peace treaty could lead the US to frame its own detailed Final Status plans and seek agreement from the parties on them. However, Israel's friends, and in particular Netanyahu's allies, on Capitol Hill would be mobilised to attempt to block any US administration-sponsored plan, which Congress felt asked too much of Israel. Currently, President Clinton, weakened by sex scandals, has shown little appetite for such a confrontation with Congress over Israel. In addition, the vice-president, Al Gore, aware that he will almost certainly seek to follow Clinton in 2000, is being deliberately careful to distance himself from any US efforts to exert pressure on Israel.

Finally, it is apparent that there is limited room at the table for other mediations, but the other parties need to coordinate their efforts with the US. The EU has started to exert itself more in the process with the appointment of a special envoy and its increased diplomatic activity in the Middle East. In addition, it has developed close ties with the PA and Arafat, which views Europe as a more neutral party than the US. However, it is also apparent to Arafat that the US is the only power which can, if it so desires, attempt to pressurise Israel into concessions. In short, the dominant role of the US in the process is likely to continue in the foreseeable future with other parties such as the EU and, to a lesser degree Egypt and Russia, participating in the mediation, but at a secondary level.

PART V

APPLICABLE LESSONS OF THE MIDDLE EAST PEACE PROCESS FOR OTHER CONFLICTS

12

Lessons of the Middle East peace process for other conflicts

The central aim of this chapter is to examine the lessons (to date) that can be learnt from the Middle East peace process and applied to other conflicts. It should be stressed that each of the areas on the list below merits separate studies in their own right but are used in this context as a mechanism to illustrate the lessons of the Middle East peace process. These lessons, both positive and negative, are applied mainly to the Northern Irish peace process, which culminated in the Good Friday Agreement in 1998.[1] For the purpose of conducting this study the potential lessons are divided into the following areas.

1. The role of secret diplomacy.
2. The use and problems of interim stages in agreements.
3. Rejectionist groups: framework of methods for dealing with them.
4. Partners for peace.
5. Creation of an atmosphere of trust.
6. The role of personalities in peace making over ideology.
7. Role of external parties: active (mediators), passive (messenger) and guarantor (political and economic) of agreement.
8. Democracy: security of agreements when governments change.
9. Peace-making methodology: maintenance of a gradual process versus radical change (gambling).
10. The importance of peace dividends.
11. Reconstruction: building a new society and region.

---

1 For background reading on the Irish peace process, see the following which together provide a comprehensive account of the process: A. Aughey and D. Morrow (eds), *Northern Ireland Politics* (London and New York, Longman, 1996); P. Bew, H. Patterson and P. Teague, *Between War and Peace: The Political Future of Northern Ireland* (London, Lawrence and Wishart, 1987); N. Collins and T. Cradden, *Irish Politics Today* (Manchester, Manchester University Press, 1997); H. Patterson, *The Politics of Illusion: Political History of the IRA* (London,

Two points should be noted about the above categories: first, many of the topics are inter-related; and second, the list is not exhaustive but the 11 topics constitute the major areas where lessons from the Middle East peace process can be deduced and applied to other areas. Finally, the chapter will include an assessment of what the Netanyahu government has learnt from these lessons derived from the recent history of the peace process.

The role of secret diplomacy

The Middle East peace process has illustrated both the success of secret diplomacy and some of its shortcomings. First, from a positive perspective, the use of a secret channel was deemed by both parties to be a vital component in helping to secure an initial peace treaty between the Israeli government and the PLO which included statements of mutual recognition. In the case of Israel and the PLO there were four major advantages of the secret channel. First, it provided a mechanism for direct negotiations to take place when the legal position of Israel remained that such contacts were in breach of Israeli law which prevented direct contacts with the PLO. Second, as both sides agreed to complete deniability about the talks there were more opportunities to put forward ideas and discuss positions and potential for trading one issue against another. Third, and as discussed in detail in several chapters of this book, the secret channel prevented the need for public posturing and playing for domestic audiences which has characterised the formal multi-lateral talks in Washington. Finally, the secret nature of the talks encouraged the participants to have more private and direct contact with each other and subsequently helped to develop a degree of personal chemistry, which was vital in helping creative problem solving of previously intractable issues.

However, the Middle East peace process has also illustrated the potential pitfalls of secret diplomacy. As Chapters 2 and 8 chronicled, the breakdown of previous attempts to open a secret channel between Israel and Syria were caused, to a large extent, by leaks to the press (mainly from the Israeli side) aimed at gaining political advantage in the

---

Serif, 1997); N. Porter, *Rethinking Unionism* (Belfast, Blackstuff Press, 1996); M. Ryman, *War and Peace in Ireland* (London, Pluto, 1994); J. Tonge, *Northern Ireland: Conflict and Change* (London, Simon and Schuster, 1998); T. Henessey, *A History of Northern Ireland, 1920–1996* (London, Macmillan, 1997); K. Pipe, *The Origins of the Present Troubles in Northern Ireland* (London, Addison Wesley, 1997); and *The Good Friday Agreement* (London, Northern Ireland Office, 1998).

negotiations. There were two major results of such actions: first, the formal public negotiations were themselves damaged by the leak; and second, the lack of trust that resulted from the actions has prevented any further high-level direct contact without the presence of third parties at the table. (The highest level contact to date under Netanyahu has involved his adviser on foreign affairs; Uzi Arad, meeting with Syrian officials in Europe in an effort to find a formula to restart the formal negotiations.)

In general terms, secret channels can provide a direct mechanism for negotiations away from the public and media scrutiny for a limited period of time. One of the major problems that surrounded the Oslo channel was maintaining the secrecy once details slowly started to emerge of the clandestine meetings. Moreover, the limited time period attached to secret channels means that there would have to be a strong desire on both sides of a conflict to secure an agreement and a willingness (and ability) to make concessions in order to secure such a deal. In addition, accepting that such channels have a limited time scale to secure success, then they are clearly more appropriate in conflicts where there are two directly involved parties and not in more complex ones such as in the former Yugoslavia.

The use and problems of interim stages in agreements

It was the Palestinian side that insisted on the interim stages in the agreement with the idea of increasing the strength of the Palestinian Authority (PA) in terms of the amount of territory it controlled (as discussed in Chapter 3) and developing the Palestinian economy (see Chapter 4) before Final Status talks.[2] In essence, the PA wanted to go into these Final Status negotiations in a stronger position than it held at the time of the Oslo negotiations in 1993. Moreover, within this context it should be remembered that the original Oslo negotiations were not government-to-government talks but rather government-to-revolutionary movement negotiations. Consequently, the PLO wanted time to develop the prerequisites for what it saw as the Palestinian State that would emerge at the end of the process.

In theory, the idea of interim stages of negotiations contained several advantages for both sides. These included the postponement of

---

2 For more details on this, see U. Savir, *The Process* (New York, Random House, 1998).

difficult compromises until the latter part of the process and providing time to develop internal support for the deal (both in Israeli and Palestinian society). In reality, the interim stages have not proved very successful in the Israeli–Palestinian peace process. Moreover, the failure of the interim agreements (see Chapters 3 and 4) is connected to another of the potential lessons of the Middle East peace process for other conflicts – namely, the effects of the attempts of rejectionist groups to wreck the process. In essence, the interim stages have allowed a period of time for the rejectionists to attempt to derail the process through suicide bomb attacks against Israeli cities by the Islamic fundamentalist groups such as Hamas and Islamic Jihad and, in Israel, the assassination of the prime minister, Yitzhak Rabin, by a right-wing fanatic opposed to the Oslo process.

As a result of these attacks (and other failings) the interim stages have not served their purpose. The suicide bomb attacks damaged (in the short term) the level of support in Israeli society for the accords. Crucially, the attacks brought about the kind of economic and security response from the Israeli government that damaged the prospects of further transfer of land to the PA, and closures of borders that damaged the already weak Palestinians economy (see Chapter 4). In returning once more to the central theme of the book it is clear that the responses of the Israeli government have been very similar to such attacks from either a Likud-led or Labour-led governments.

The final major failing of the interim stages is that the Palestinians perceived them to be the one way that the PA would be able to strengthen its position while not enough consideration was given to Israeli attempts to create facts on the ground for Final Status talks. Chapter 6 chronicled Israeli efforts at Har Homa and in greater Jerusalem to create such conditions on the ground that could not be altered. Moreover, these Israeli efforts were also apparent in its renewed programme of expanding certain key settlements in the West Bank. Indeed, there is a strong case for arguing that Israel has benefited much more from the interim agreements than the Palestinians who have not gained the amount of territory in the West Bank that they originally believed they would control by Final Status talks.

In attempting to apply the value of interim agreements to other conflicts three key points need to be remembered. First, such agreements are a sign of weakness in that they illustrate the failure of the two parties to agree and implement a deal immediately. Second, if there are large rejectionist forces, as in the Arab–Israeli conflict and as in Northern Ireland, then interim agreements can offer an invitation for these forces to destabilise and even destroy the process. (The size of the rejectionist forces in Northern Ireland was shown by the performance of these parties and individuals in the elections to the Assembly in June 1998 where they almost won a blocking majority.) Third, such agreements are of more use when one of the parties is so politically weak that it does not possess the necessary cards to negotiate a deal that would satisfy some of its people's aspirations. In the Middle East context this was true of the position of the PLO in 1993, but could also apply to several other fading revolutionary/terrorist organisations, which need time to convert from such movements into government of entities (states).

Rejectionist groups: a framework of methods for dealing with them

As discussed earlier within the contest of interim agreement there is a need to devise frameworks to deal with rejectionist groups whose aims are to wreck a peace process. In the Israeli–Palestinian case there are several important negative lessons for peace making in other conflicts. The central lesson concerns the fact that careful consideration needs to be given to methods for dealing with rejectionist groups who resort to violent attacks. In this respect one of the major charges of the Israeli right against the Oslo Accords is that successive Israeli governments have had to transfer the job of preventing such attacks from its own security forces to PA forces which, due to structural problems and political restraints imposed by Arafat, have not been effective. Indeed, a common accusation of the Rabin–Peres and Netanyahu governments in Israel has been that Arafat has not done enough to dismantle the infrastructure of such groups.

Despite the fact that both Arafat and Israel share a common objective in weakening Hamas and Islamic Jihad, Arafat has appeared, to date, unwilling to move against these groups for fear of a potential backlash in Palestinian society. Though there are no easy solutions to the problems of dealing with such groups, there needs to be a more concerted attempt by Arafat to address this problem, backed with increased security cooperation with Israeli security forces (particularly in the area of intelligence gathering). However, in the climate of a lack of trust between the two parties (which has emerged in recent times) such cooperation is not easy to develop or maintain. In essence, the enemies of peace (those not involved in the process and who resort to violent means such as suicide bombs to express their opposition) need to be dealt with forcibly by the parties involved in the peace making. Furthermore, failure to do this will present groups such as Hamas and Islamic Jihad with the opportunity either to directly destroy the process or, through the retaliatory measures, closures and economic sanctions by Israel against the PA areas, indirectly derail the process.

Transferring such thinking to the Irish peace process, at the time of writing it is abundantly clear that there are still several prominent Republican splinter groups from the Provisional Irish Republican Army (PIRA) who possess the ability to destabilise the peace process through bombing and shooting campaigns. (At the time of writing – summer 1998 – all Loyalist paramilitary groups would appear to be observing cease-fires of some sort.) Consequently, the new Northern Irish Assembly, together with the governments of Great Britain and Ireland, will need to intensify their security efforts to destroy the infrastructure of such groups. Moreover, such moves need to be carried out regardless of the political sensitivities of Republican political groups such as Sinn Fein if the long-term success of the peace process is to be secured. Failure to do so could lead Northern Ireland to a similar position as the Israeli–Palestinian process where the violent rejectionist groups have succeeded in creating a vacuum in the political process, which has led in the short term to a derailing or impasse in the peace process.

Finally, in addition to attempts to destroy the infrastructure of such groups there is a need to try and attract any semi-moderate leaders of factions within these groups to embrace the peace process. In the Israeli–Palestinian context it should be remembered that Israel initially encouraged Hamas as a moderate alternative to the PLO. Moreover, the Israeli government has shown that it is perfectly possible to attempt to destroy the infrastructure of an organisation such as Hamas while at the same time appealing to so-called moderate elements in the organisation to join the peace process. However, such tactics of the fist and olive branch are of limited value when (as in the case of Hamas) the more moderate elements have no control over the more militant military wing of the organisation (responsible for organising and carrying out the attacks).

Partners for peace, the creation of an atmosphere of trust, and the role of personalities in peace making over ideology

It was Yitzhak Rabin who said that you cannot choose your partners for peace and that he would much rather have shaken the hand of almost anyone else in the world on the White House lawn in 1993 than Arafat's. In addition, he cited that you make peace with enemies not friends.[3] However, once partners for peace making have been chosen and accepted, there is a need for a sea change in political thinking and education to secure the partnership. Two points are directly related to this sea change: first, the creation of an atmosphere of mutual trust between the two parties; and second, the importance of the role of personal relations between the respective leaderships in finding pragmatic solutions to old ideology problems.[4]

Regarding the issue of trust, the peace process in the Middle East has highlighted the importance of this when peace agreements contain a degree of constructive ambiguity designed to allow both sides slightly different interpretations on various points. Under the government of Rabin in Israel, this degree of trust was at an acceptable level to make the process work. However, a central argument of this book has been that this was based on somewhat false assumptions (particularly by Arafat) that the PA would be able to obtain the majority of its goals in Final Status talks. Under Netanyahu, Israel's positions have not radically altered towards to the peace process but the element of trust between the two sides has collapsed as Netanyahu has attempted to lower Palestinian aspirations making the Oslo process seemingly unworkable.

Consequently, the central lesson of this aspect of the Israeli–Palestinian track for other conflicts is the need to develop and maintain a degree of trust between the partners for peace. Furthermore, this is

---

3 Rabin stated this on many occasions – for example, as he put it to the Labour Knesset faction: "You don't make peace with friends. You make peace with enemies who are not at all nice. I will not try to prettify the PLO; the PLO was an enemy, it's still an enemy, but you negotiate with the enemy." Address by Yitzhak Rabin to Labour Party Knesset faction on 9 September 1993.

4 Rabin, when asked whether or not he trusted Arafat the day before signing the agreement stated: "We give him the benefit of the doubt that he intends to fulfil what he or his representative signs. We need a Palestinian partner. This is an entirely different PLO, at least in terms of what they declare on paper . . . This government must take this calculated risk for peace." Interview with Rabin on CNN on 12 September 1993.

of even greater importance if the potential peace agreement contains ambitious clauses that are open to interpretation by both sides.

In the context of the Irish peace process the negotiations to date have been characterised by an almost total lack of trust between the two parties. Interestingly, the level of mistrust between the Unionists and Sinn Fein (the political wing of PIRA) was so great that the former called for special letters of assurance form the British prime minister, Tony Blair, on central parts of the agreement concerning the decommissioning of weapons.

A more positive lesson from the Middle East peace process has been the role of personalities (leaders) in peace making, which has helped overcome old ideological problems and physical obstructions to peace. As Chapter 7 outlined, the personal relationship between King Hussein and Yitzhak Rabin played a significant role in securing the peace agreement between Israel and Jordan. In addition, their strong personal chemistry offered the opportunity for: first, the solving of seemingly intractable territorial disputes between the two countries; and second, the development of a warm peace. However, under Netanyahu the relationship with Jordan has been put under renewed strain. Once more, it was the personal chemistry between King Hussein and (this time) Ariel Sharon that helped to avert a crisis over the water issue, and with Efraim Halevy over the botched Mossad asssassination attempt in Amman during the summer of 1997.

As Chapter 8 outlined, President Assad of Syria has been aware of successive Israeli prime ministers' attempts to negotiate at the highest level with him (or as Peres put it in 1996, high and fast). Assad's reluctance to meet an Israeli leader (even when he was offered the Golan Heights by Rabin) is an illustration that he views the negotiations with Israel differently than King Hussein. Central to Assad's thinking is the maintenance of a process rather than any progress in the peace process, and he therefore does not want to develop personal relations with Israeli leaders for two reasons: first, such relations would undermine his position as the bastion of Arab nationalism; and second, such relations may break a psychological barriers, which once removed could lead to arguably one of Assad's biggest fears – a rapid process of normalisation between Israel and Syria. (See Chapter 8 for the evidence and arguments behind Assad's fears.)

In the Irish context the realisation of the importance of personal chemistry in a peace process led to the decision of the Social and

Democratic Labour Party (SDLP) to put forward its deputy leader, Shamus Mallon instead of its leader, John Hume, for the post of deputy first minister of Northern Ireland in June 1998. Shamus Mallon was said to have enjoyed a better chemistry and working relationship with the leader of the Ulster Unionist Party (UUP) and first minister, David Trimble. In essence, the SDLP acknowledged the lessons of the importance of such partnerships in helping to secure and develop peace following the initial agreement.

Role of external parties: active (mediators), passive (messenger), and guarantor (political and economic) of agreement

The role of the United States as the primary external party in the Middle East peace process was outlined in Chapter 11 in which the three inter-related elements of mediator, messenger and guarantor were discussed in detail. From the recent role of the US during the era of the Netanyahu government in Israel there are three major lessons for other peace processes, as outlined below.

The first is to recognise the fact that the need for mediation is a sign of weakness and should not lead to an over-involvement of the external party if there is little potential for such attempts enjoying a degree of success. At times, there is an over-concentration on the shuttle diplomacy of the US in the area that, in reality, is really masking the distance between the parties concerned and the lack of potential breakthroughs. For example, between 1992 and 1996 each time the US Secretary of State, Warren Christopher, shuttled back and forth between Damascus and Jerusalem was little more than a reflection on the lack of willingness of one of the parties (Syria) to enter into direct negotiations. Furthermore, it was not until direct negotiations started between Syria and Israel in Maryland in 1996 that any limited progress was made (admittedly these talks were hosted by the US). The current Secretary of State, Madeleine Albright, was aware of this fact and tried to remain more distant from the process, not visiting the region until it was unavoidable and not indulging in shuttle diplomacy during her first year.

Second is the key question of the impartiality of the external party. Moreover, once more this is also of particular relevance to the Irish peace process where the US has been perceived as supporting one side (the Republicans) over the other (the Loyalists). Within the Middle East context the US support of Israel is viewed by some (mainly Arab and

Third World countries) as disqualifying it from carrying out a primary mediation role. However, as Chapter 11 concluded, there is currently a lack of viable of alternatives to the US to play such a role in the region, and the other willing parties such as the EU are largely viewed by Israel as biased in favour of the Arab side. Accusations of US bias towards Israel have been compounded in recent times by the actions of the Clinton administration, which has not been willing to exert enough pressure on the Netanyahu government. In addition, certain US officials such as Dennis Ross have been targeted by the PA as being personally biased towards the Israelis, which has further complicated their already difficult missions. The US has shown signs of learning in this respect and Secretary of State Albright has been keen to adopt a more even-handed approach with strong public criticisms of the Netanyahu government.

Third, the problems of acting as guarantor to an agreement were illustrated by the Hebron Agreement and the attached commitments by both sides which the US was to guarantee. However, neither the Israelis nor the Palestinians have maintained commitments that were made and, consequently, the US has been drawn in ever deeper as it attempts to act as referee in the endless disputes, accusations and counter-accusations from each side.

In attempting to draw more global conclusions from the US efforts in the Middle East, it is clear that the US has attempted to fulfil its role as the sole superpower in the region, but has not been successful in securing a comprehensive peace. Indeed, the two major peace deals of recent times, the Israeli–Palestinian Oslo Accords and the formal Israeli–Jordanian Peace Treaty, were negotiated directly between the parties with little or minimal external intervention. As a result it is clear that if there is a strong desire to reach agreement between the parties, then an external agent or mediator is largely superfluous. However, for much of the time in the Middle East conflict, and other conflicts throughout the world, this mutual desire does not exist, nor is it blocked by political difficulties and it is at this time that external parties such as the US play a vital role. Since the start of the current Middle East peace process at Madrid in 1991, the US has acted to maintain some sort of a process even when there was little chance of major breakthrough. This role should not be under-estimated, as by helping maintain a degree of momentum, however small, it helped to create the conditions that eventually pushed the parties together. Consequently, the central lesson of this for mediation efforts and the role of external parties in other conflicts is the need to maintain a peace process of sorts in the short term in the hope that in the long term the dynamics of the conflict will alter and encourage the parties to come together.

Democracy: security of agreements when governments change

The election of Netanyahu in Israel in 1996 was thought to put the Oslo Accords at risk. As Chapter 1 outlined, there was grave international concern as to whether the new prime minister would carry out the international commitments that his predecessors had agreed to and, significantly, had signed up for. However, Netanyahu's statement during the election campaign that he would carry out Israel's binding commitments seemed to allay these fears. Subsequently, during the first years of his period of office, the prime minister has carried out a withdrawal from Hebron and further redeployments from the West Bank and released Palestinian prisoners. However, Netanyahu has attempted to re-negotiate parts of the accords which he feels are not in Israel's interest, and has reminded the world in speeches and interviews that the Oslo Accords are, in his view, flawed and in places dangerous for Israel.

As a result of Netanyahu's actions the Oslo Accords would appear to have survived a change of government in the only Western-style democracy in the region, and a party and personality that led the original fight against ratifying the original agreement in Israel have offered a degree of continuity to the process. From a Palestinian perspective, Arafat stated that he made peace with Israel and not with a particular Israeli government. Such thinking was rather naïve when nearly 50 per cent of the Israeli Knesset voted against the Oslo Accords – including almost the entire centre-right and religious parties. In the long run it remains to be seen if the Oslo Accords prove successful in ending the conflict between the Israelis and Palestinians, but in many ways the Accords have passed the biggest test of surviving (in the short term) the change of government in Israel.

However, it remains to be seen if the Oslo Accords will survive a change of leadership in the PA when Arafat departs the scene. In addition, there are question marks over whether Israel's peace treaty with Egypt would survive if Mubarak were to be overthrown and likewise in Jordan with King Hussein. In short, the continued presence of radical groups in the region means that though the peace agreements involving Israel can survive changes of government it is not clear that they could withstand changes of leadership in the other non-democratic states in the region.

The biggest lesson other conflicts can learn from the experience of the Oslo Accords in this area is the need for both parties to build as wide a base of support as possible for the agreement. Critics of the Oslo Accords argued that they were a private agreement between the Israeli Labour Party (supported by big business) and the right-wing part of the Fatah movement (also with large business interests). Clearly, the failure to expand the basis of support for the agreement on the Israeli side almost led to its downfall. In addition, on the Palestinian side there are similar risks, especially given the decline of the economy since the Oslo Accords were signed (see Chapter 4). Arafat's position could come under threat from hardliners both from within the PA-controlled areas and those who have remained abroad.

The Israeli–Syrian track of the peace process has illustrated another side of the influence of changes in governments on the peace process. As Chapter 8 chronicled, Netanyahu has refused (to date) to accept to continue the negotiations with Syria from the point where they were left off under the Peres government in 1996. His rationale is that, unlike the Oslo Accords, these negotiations were based only on verbal undertakings and nothing had been agreed or signed by either party. Moreover, Netanyahu's right to do this is supported by many of the Israeli left (as well as the right) who argue that Assad missed his chance and that Netanyahu is within his democratic rights to take such a course of action.

In applying this to other conflicts there is a need for the parties concerned to understand the nature of democracy and the fact that it can lead to a change of government that will have a very different platform from the original negotiating partners. Conversely, this can work the other way with one side holding out in the hope of a potential change of government in one of the other parties that they perceive would benefit them. Perhaps the most obvious recent example of this was Sinn Fein's realisation that they would not be able to reach a satisfactory agreement with the governments of John Major and John Bruton in power in London and Dublin, respectively. As a result, Sinn Fein chose to wait until both these administrations had been replaced by more sympathetic governments before fully engaging in the negotiations that culminated in the Good Friday Agreement.

Peace-making methods: maintenance of a gradual process vs radical change (gambling)

Another key lesson of the peace process in the Middle East concerns the type and style of peace making. The region has seen examples of both a gradual process (under the Madrid framework and including the multi-laterals in Washington) and the radical change agreements (the Oslo Accords).[5] There are two key conclusions that can be reached from an analysis of peace-making methods in the region. First is the need for both types to be present to complement each other or for the maintenance of a process to act as a safety net for a potential failure of radical change negotiations. Moreover, this need is shown in peace plans submitted by Israelis such as Yossi Beilin who called for fast track Final Status negotiations with the multi-laterals in Washington acting as a safety net in the event of failure.[6]

The second relates to radical change negotiating, which is often a reflection of the failure of a gradual process to achieve the type of breakthroughs that would lead to a final settlement. For example, the decision of the Rabin government to go with the Oslo channel was largely due to Rabin's frustration at the slow pace of the multi-lateral negotiations in Washington. However, Rabin illustrated the importance of maintaining the multi-laterals by refusing to proceed with the Oslo channel if the

---

5 For a detailed account of what is termed here as radical peace making and its advantages and the failings within the context of the Oslo Accords, see Y. Bar-Siman-Tov, 'Peacemaking with the Palestinians: change and legitimacy' in E. Karsh (ed.), *From Rabin to Netanyahu: Israel's Troubled Agenda* (London and Portland, Frank Cass, 1997), pp. 170–86.

6 The Beilin Peace Plan was submitted in summer 1997 and included the following points: 1. Move to a six months so-called fast track final status solution; 2. The second and third Israeli troop withdrawals from Area C to be postponed for the duration of the fast track talks; 3. A halt to building at Har Homa for the period of the talks agreed by the Israeli government; 4. The PA to agree to fight terrorism and resume top level security contacts; 5. The multi-laterals in Washington to continue with more effort from all sides with the aim of these talks acting as a safety net for fast track; 6. The fast track negotiations to produce a Declaration of Principles on final status. This is to include competed and signed maps; 7. If agreement is reached then no Israeli troop withdrawals from areas under Oslo agreements, but rather a move to withdrawal in accordance with the newly agreed document; 8. If no agreement is reached then the original Israeli troop withdrawals to take place at the end of the six month period.

Palestinian delegation did not continue with the talks in Washington.[7] As a result of having two twin negotiating processes, if the high risk Oslo channel had failed to achieve a satisfactory agreement then there would have been a possibility of reverting back to the multi-laterals. Moreover, it should be remembered that the Oslo channel was just one of many secret channels that were attempted during the early 1990s and that the others did not prove successful. Consequently, the need for a safety net is important if such channels are to be explored without the restrictive extreme pressures of the consequences of their potential failure over-burdening the negotiators.

In applying the lesson of a safety net to other regions it is clearly more relevant in conflicts where there is a formal negotiation framework in place and where the results of these negotiations have not succeeded in ending the conflict, but have also not totally broken down.

The importance of peace dividends and reconstruction: building a new society and region

Chapters 4 and 7 outlined the failure of first, the Oslo peace process to provide a peace dividend for the Palestinians living in PA-controlled areas and for Israelis, and second, the Israeli–Jordanian peace agreement to significantly improve the economy of Jordan. Clearly, a central negative lesson of the Middle East peace process has been the need to transfer political advancements in the peace process into visible economic improvements in the lives of the majority of the populations. This failure to provide any peace dividend has given the rejectionist groups an opportunity to further their radical agendas by stressing the limitations of the current process. This is particularly true of PA-controlled areas where the radical Islamic groups are funded by the Gulf States (and by private groups with bases in the US) and can attract local support by investing these resources into infrastructure such as Hamas hospitals. Crucially, it is vital for Israel and the PA to help create the kinds of condition that are likely to attract investment into this area. For Israel this means not using closures of the border as a political weapon and for the PA developing a

---

7 At the time of Rabin's decision the Palestinian delegation was boycotting the talks in Washington following Rabin's expulsion of some 450 Hamas activists from Israeli-controlled territory into Southern Lebanon. For more details on Rabin's decision, see Makovsky, *Making Peace with the PLO*.

modern system of government and successfully addressing the problem of corruption.

Consequently, there are two lessons from the Middle East peace process on the issues of peace dividends: first, the need to develop a peace dividend to underpin support for peace agreements; and second, the importance of educating populations about the linkage of any improvement in the economy to the peace process. The Irish peace process has already shown that it is aware of the need to produce a peace dividend for its population if the process is to prove successful in the long term. In addition, both official government sources and international investors have made it clear that the future economic development of Northern Ireland is directly related to a permanent ending of political violence.[8] In addition, in Bosnia the international community has been quick to rebuild the infrastructure destroyed in the war and has consequently encouraged the increase in levels of foreign investment.

In terms of building a new society and region the central lessons of the Middle East are twofold. First, in addressing the problem of building a new society it is important to educate populations about the benefits of peace and to encourage points of contact between the various populations in the conflict through the development of educational, cultural and social exchange programmes. For instance, the Cold Peace that exists between Israel and Egypt, and potentially in the long term between Israel and Jordan, is characterised by a lack of contact between the two populations except for an ever-declining number of Israeli tourists who make brief trips to Egypt to see the sites. However, a more encouraging area has been the increase in the number of educational exchanges involving young Israeli and Palestinian school children – for example, where they attend joint classes during summer vacations.

Second, the Israeli agenda on building a new region has been dominated by Shimon Peres's vision of a new Middle East which has been outlined and analysed in several chapters in the book.[9] Moreover, the Netanyahu government has moved quickly to downgrade expectations in this area arguing that such a system would not work in a region that is characterised by non-democratic regimes. The argument against

---

8 For more details on the importance of a peace dividend in Northern Ireland, see W. Hopkinson, 'Peace dividend?', *The World Today*, vol. 54, no. 7, July 1998, pp. 193–4.

9 On this, see Peres, *The New Middle East*.

Peres's vision is that he is putting the horse in front of the cart or, to put it another way, there are a number of difficult obstacles to be overcome before such a vision could be anything more than a political dream – the central requirement being a comprehensive peace agreement in the region which, as the conclusion to Chapter 10 argued, is not likely to happen in the near future.

Conclusions

As this chapter has outlined, there are many lessons for other conflicts from the Middle East peace process. The majority of these lessons are of a negative nature, a reflection of the recent history of the peace process in the Middle East which has not delivered a comprehensive peace to the region and, as Chapter 10 argued, is unlikely to do in the foreseeable future. Moreover it is important that these lessons are absorbed first, by the current Israeli government and Arab leaders and second, by leaders involved in other peace processes in the world.

Within Israel and in the context of this study, Netanyahu has shown himself to be partially aware of the lessons that he and the government need to learn from the recent peace process. First, he has embraced the idea of secret diplomacy. Indeed, as outlined in the first part of this study, Netanyahu's close advisers see it as a near-essential part of negotiating a peace deal with Syria. Second, the current government is acutely aware of the problems of the interim stages in the Oslo Accords and has sought to change this with the proposal to bypass these stages and move directly to Final Status talks. Furthermore, his government has been fully aware of the need to attempt to deal with the rejectionist groups on both sides.

However, in other areas Netanyahu has proved not as successful in absorbing lessons such as in the lack of his understanding of the relationship between Israel's improved economic position and the peace process, the link between the problems of the PA economy and the peace process, and in the failure to develop strong personal relations with Arab leaders which could encourage and not hinder positive developments in the peace process.

On a wider level, there are six general lessons that need to be stressed about the lessons for other conflicts.

1. Secret diplomacy offers the best opportunity for the most rapid advancement of a particular track of a peace process, proving the

will and means are forthcoming from both sides. However, it possible that a safety net of official public negotiations can help to reduce the consequences of the potential failure of a secret channel.

2. Deals that involve interim stages need to be clearly defined and at the very least provision needs to be made for dealing with rejectionist groups who are likely to use the period of the interim stages to destabilise, and eventually destroy, the agreements.

3. The importance of chemistry between negotiators and leaders cannot be over-stressed. However, such chemistry does not in itself secure the peace agreement which is, after all, between two countries (peoples) and not between two governments or individuals.

4. There is a need to develop a degree of personal trust (this can be partial as in the case of Rabin and Arafat) between the parties involved in the peace making. This does not have to take the form of official confidence building measures (CBMs), but could simply involve keeping promises made in agreements. Such trust is even more significant when agreements (such as the Oslo Accords) contain varying degrees of constructive ambiguity.

5. The role of external parties in the peace process needs to be clearly defined. In short, are they acting as mediators, as messengers or as guarantors of agreements?

6. As argued in Chapter 4, there is a strong need for an economic peace dividend to help underpin any political deal. This is increasingly important if one side is living under, or the near, the poverty line and in a situation where its leaders have had to make significant political compromises.

Returning to the Irish peace process, the most appropriate lessons from the Middle East are the need to develop personal relationships and a degree of trust between the various sides, and the development of a significant peace dividend. Regarding the latter, there are major economic disparities in Northern Ireland as there are in PA-controlled areas, which need to be dealt with through investment, the creation of jobs and improved long-term conditions for the less well off.

Finally, one aspect of the Oslo Accords chronicled in the first part of the book is the relative robust nature of the Accords, which have survived predominantly because the central figures in the process see them as the only game in town. Consequently, perhaps this represents the central lesson of the Middle East peace process – namely that only when there is a lack of viable alternatives will the parties make an agreement (to some degree) workable.

General conclusions

In examining the various tracks of the peace process, this book has found that the peace process although in trouble is not dead. On the one hand, it is clear that the peace process has not developed with the same impetus as it did during the period of the Rabin–Peres governments in Israel between 1992 and 1996. Furthermore, negotiations in certain areas have been totally suspended or are being conducted through a third channel (the USA) which characterised the period prior to the breakthrough at Oslo and the negotiations between Israel and Jordan. On the other hand, the peace process has shown itself to be remarkably resilient, and able to survive difficult periods and traumatic events; this is because all parties appear committed to the process itself – if not to actually securing agreements themselves. In essence, all the parties are afraid of the consequences of a total breakdown of the peace process, and in particular of being viewed as the cause of the collapse with all the economic and political penalties which would follow such a verdict. As a result, even at times of deep crisis no party has walked away from the process itself, but has merely acted to suspend the negotiations.

A central theme of this study has been that many (but not all) of the difficulties that have arisen in the peace process since 1996 would have occurred whether Netanyahu had been elected or not. (This argument, incidentally, does not suggest that Netanyahu has not made many mistakes that have added to the problems, but rather that the substantive problem issues would have arisen under any leader.) In defending this argument Netanyahu's network of beliefs and views was explored and it was concluded that he is essentially a pragmatist interested in achieving office and retaining his position. This is in contrast to his predecessors as leader of the Likud, Menahem Begin and Yitzhak Shamir, both of whom were more inclined towards ideological politics over and above power. Critics of Netanyahu argue that there is no real difference in the views of Netanyahu and his predecessors in the Likud and that Netanyahu's eventual goal is to destroy the peace process with the Arabs. However, such thinking ignores several key points that have been highlighted in the book.

Netanyahu, as Chapters 3 to 6 outlined, has embraced the Oslo Accords and has attempted to move the peace process with the Palestinians forward despite a large amount of opposition from within the Likud, other parties of the Israeli right and extra-parliamentary pressure groups such as the settlers movement, Gush Emunim. The signing of the Hebron Accord in January 1997, the subsequent troop withdrawal from parts of the West Bank and the release of Palestinian prisoners all illustrate that his government has to some degree met Israeli obligations under the Oslo Accords. In addition, Chapter 7 highlighted Netanyahu's support for the peace accord with Jordan, and despite his blunders with various actions such as the botched Mossad assassination attempt in Amman, the Israeli government has found ways of defusing problems with the Hashemite Kingdom and at least maintaining peace with Jordan. Chapter 8 outlined Netanyahu's reluctance to restart negotiations with Syria from the point where they were left off by the previous Labour-led governments in Israel, but as the chapter illustrated (along with Chapter 2), he appears willing to exchange land for peace – put simply, to return the Golan Heights to Syria in exchange for a comprehensive peace treaty between Israel and Syria. Finally, as Chapter 10 argued, the deepening ties between Israel and Turkey have not been affected by Netanyahu who has continued to develop this relationship as a foil against the radical regimes in the area.

In reality, Binyamin Netanyahu has more in common with the late Yitzhak Rabin than generally noted by local political commentators. Both were outsiders in their own political parties, both relied on popular support within the country as a whole rather than from within their own party institutions, both were seen as reluctant partners with Arafat and the PLO, but crucially they saw the peace process as the only option. In addition, both (as Chapter 3 mentioned) can be referred to as security hawks rather than ideological or religious hawks in terms of their rationale for retaining parts of the West Bank. Indeed, as Chapter 3 argued, Netanyahu's opening position for Final Status talks on the West Bank bore a strong resemblance to Rabin's likely opening gambit because their respective positions were based on similar views on Israeli security and water requirements in this area. As a result, although it is uncomfortable for many in Israel to accept (particularly on the left), Netanyahu is in many respects the natural successor to Rabin. Furthermore, the above evidence suggests at the very least a large degree of continuity in terms of policy and basic principles.

Finally, within the Israeli domestic arena, there were signs prior to and during the 1996 Israeli election campaign that the Labour Party leader, Shimon Peres, was shifting his position back to the centre ground in Israel and therefore hardening his negotiating positions with the Arabs – for example, with actions such as the Grapes of Wrath Operation in Southern Lebanon (Chapter 9) and the decision to postpone negotiations over Hebron (Chapter 2). As a result, had he been narrowly elected, and in all likelihood without a Jewish majority, then the highly pragmatic Peres would have pursued policies not to dissimilar to those of Netanyahu.

The study has also attempted to highlight the push and pull factors on Netanyahu in the area of policy formation and management of the peace process. Clearly there are a number of variables that have affected his actions.

First, it has been strongly argued that Israel's new electoral system which was designed to increase the power of the prime minister has, in fact, had the opposite effect. Although the system played a role in securing his actual election in 1996 it has imposed strong internal restraints on Netanyahu (or indeed any other leader) with its fragmentation of the Knesset and the subsequent coalition management problems for a prime minister. This has been most apparent in the negotiations with the Palestinians where the majority of Netanyahu's Cabinet retain (at best) grave reservations about the very concept of Oslo and negotiating with the PLO and Arafat. In addition, these feelings are reflected throughout the wider ruling coalition where Netanyahu is often derided for giving away too much to the PA.

Second, the shift in Israeli public opinion, which although still supportive of the Oslo Accords, is becoming increasingly reluctant to make the difficult compromises required for the process to work. Moreover, it is becoming more apparent that much of the Israeli public support for Oslo was based on ignorance of the exact compromises that the agreement implied. For instance, it was only in the summer of 1996 that the real debate broke out in the Israeli media on what exactly Israeli transfer of land to PA control meant in physical terms for Israel.[1]

Netanyahu's major domestic strength lies in the fact that his policies largely reflect the mainstream views of most centre-ground Israelis (the key voting constituency in any Israeli election). The views of this group are defined in the following general terms: a growing sense of scepticism towards the Oslo Accords; a feeling that Arafat and the Palestinians are not interested in peaceful co-existence; and in a general sense a return to the siege mentality which largely defined Israel of the late 1980s. Moreover, Netanyahu's pragmatic instincts tell him that his chances of re-election depend on reflecting these views and that this group, despite all its misgivings about the peace process, would not tolerate a total breakdown of the process and a return to a Palestinian Intifada or widespread Palestinian terrorism.

In overall terms, the over-concentration on Netanyahu as the fundamental reason for the slowing down of the peace process ignores the arguments outlined in the various studies in this book. First, the problems and complications in the Israeli–Palestinian track have been caused by a large number of reasons: the structure of the Oslo Accords and especially the interim stages which leave the difficult issues to the end of the process; the seemingly unbridgeable gap between Palestinian aspirations for a state in the West Bank and Gaza, and Israeli security and water needs in the same areas; the weak Palestinian economy which has not allowed PA infrastructure to develop to the planned levels; the complications over the refugees and the right of return; and the issue of the future status of Jerusalem. All these issues, when taken together, illustrate the problems of arriving at a Final Status agreement between the Israelis and Palestinians. Concepts such as mutual recognition and Palestinian autonomy in Gaza and Jericho (important at the time) appear in retrospect somewhat less complex and easier to secure.

---

1 The debate surrounded the question of whether Netanyahu should return 9 per cent or 13 per cent as requested by the US of the West Bank to PA control and the publication of a series of maps by Dr Chaim Gvirtzman from the Hebrew University which showed exactly the consequences of the various transfer of lands for Israeli settlements and Israeli control over water sources would be. On this, see D. Makovsky, 'Nine per cent? Thirteen per cent?: what does it all mean?', *Ha-Aretz*, 21 May 1998 and D. Makovsky, 'US rejects Netanyahu's combined pullback plan', *Ha-Aretz*, 21 May 1998.

On the Israeli–Syrian and Lebanese tracks there has been little movement for a number of reasons: the failure of Assad to embrace the original offers of an Israel withdrawal from the Golan Heights made by both Rabin and Peres; Assad's fear of making peace with Israel for the future prospects of his regime, both domestically and internationally; the absence of direct (face to face) negotiations between the two parties; and a lack of positive initiatives from the Israeli government.

In the wider Middle East there are signs that Israel is no longer isolated in the region but, as Chapter 10 argued, nor is it integrated into regional political and economic systems. Consequently, at the end of the twentieth century is clear that the Middle East in a state of transition. The peace process has not produced a comprehensive peace settlement in the region, but there is a lack of desire to turn the clock back to old days of open confrontation with Israel. Essentially, the status quo can be defined as "no peace – no war", but needless to say in a region that houses a large number of radical regimes and groups such a situation is not a particularly satisfactory nor safe one.

In looking to the future it is clear that the threat of major war has not been removed by the peace process. As Chapter 10 concluded, there is unlikely to be a comprehensive peace settlement in the region in the foreseeable future, and indeed there is likely to be an intensification of smaller-scale conflicts over competition for the declining natural resources in the region such as water. Moreover, although some progress in specific areas of the peace process can be expected, there would appear to be a strong possibility that the other issues will remain unresolved and within the Israeli–Palestinian framework postponed once more to a post-Final Status period which is likely to take the negotiations well into the next century.

APPENDICES

Protocol concerning the redeployment in Hebron

(as initialled on 15 January 1997)

In accordance with the provisions of the Interim Agreement and in particular of Article VII of Annex I to the Interim Agreement, both Parties have agreed on this Protocol for the implementation of the redeployment in Hebron.

Security arrangements regarding redeployment in Hebron

1. Redeployment in Hebron

The redeployment of Israeli Military Forces in Hebron will be carried out in accordance with the Interim Agreement and this Protocol. This redeployment will be completed not later than ten days from the signing of this Protocol. During these ten days both sides will exert every possible effort to prevent friction and any action that would prevent the redeployment. This redeployment shall constitute full implementation of the provisions of the Interim Agreement with regard to the City of Hebron unless otherwise provided for in Article VII of Annex I to the Interim Agreement.

2. Security powers and responsibilities

(a) (i) The Palestinian Police will assume responsibilities in Area H-1 similar to those in other cities in the West Bank; and

(ii) Israel will retain all powers and responsibilities for internal security and public order in Area H-2. In addition, Israel will continue to carry the responsibility for overall security of Israelis.

(b) In this context – both sides reaffirm their commitment to honour the relevant security provisions of the Interim Agreement, including the provisions regarding – Arrangements for Security and Public Order

(Article XII of the Interim Agreement); Prevention of Hostile Acts (Article XV of the Interim Agreement); Security Policy for the Prevention of Terrorism and Violence (Article II of Annex I to the Interim Agreement); Guidelines for Hebron (Article VII of Annex I to the Interim Agreement); and Rules of Conduct in Mutual Security Matters (Article XI of Annex I to the Interim Agreement).

3. Agreed security arrangements

(a) With a view to ensuring mutual security and stability in the City of Hebron, special security arrangements will apply adjacent to the areas under the security responsibility of Israel, in Area H-1, in the area between the Palestinian Police checkpoints delineated on the map attached to this Protocol as Appendix 1 (hereinafter referred to as "the attached map") and the areas under the security responsibility of Israel.

(b) The purpose of the above mentioned checkpoints will be to enable the Palestinian Police, exercising their responsibilities under the Interim Agreement, to prevent entry of armed persons and demonstrators or other people threatening security and public order, into the above mentioned area.

4. Joint security measures

(a) The DCO will establish a sub-office in the City of Hebron as indicated on the attached map.

(b) JMU [Joint Mobile Units] will operate in Area H-2 to handle incidents that involve Palestinians only. The JMU movement will be detailed on the attached map. The DCO will coordinate the JMU movement and activity.

(c) As part of the security arrangements in the area adjacent to the areas under the security responsibility of Israel, as defined above, Joint Mobile Units will be operating in this area, with special focus on the following places.
    (i)   Abu Sneinah
    (ii)   Harat A-Sheikh
    (iii) Sha'aba
    (iv)   The high ground overlooking new Route No. 35.

(d) Two Joint Patrols will function in Area H-1:

(i)   a Joint Patrol which will operate on the road from Ras e-Jura to the north of the Dura junction via E-Salaam Road, as indicated on the attached map; and

(ii) a Joint Patrol which will operate on existing Route No. 35, including the eastern part of existing Route No. 35, as indicated on the attached map.

(e) The Palestinian and Israeli side of the Joint Mobile Units in the City of Hebron will be armed with equivalent types of weapons (Mini-Ingraham submachine guns for the Palestinian side and short M16s for the Israeli side).

(f) With a view to dealing with the special security situation in the City of Hebron, a Joint Coordination Centre (hereinafter the "JCC") headed by senior officers of both sides, will be established in the DCO at Har Manoah/Jabel Manoah. The purpose of the JCC will be to coordinate the joint security measures in the City of Hebron. The JCC will be guided by all the relevant provisions of the Interim Agreement, including Annex I and this Protocol. In this context, each side will notify the JCC of demonstrations and actions taken in respect of such demonstrations, and of any security activity, close to the areas under the responsibility of the other side, including in the area defined in Article 3(a) above. The JCC shall be informed of activities in accordance with Article 5(d)(iii) of this Protocol.

5. The Palestinian Police

(a) Palestinian Police stations or posts will be established in Area H-1, manned by a total of up to 400 policemen, equipped with 20 vehicles and armed with 200 pistols, and 100 rifles for the protection of the police stations.

(b) Four designated Rapid Response Teams (RRTs) will be established and stationed in Area H-1, one in each of the police stations, as delineated on the attached map. The main task of the RRTs will be to handle special security cases. Each RRT shall be comprised of up to 16 members.

(c) The above mentioned rifles will be designated for the exclusive use of the RRTs, to handle special cases.

(d) (i)   The Palestinian Police shall operate freely in Area H-1.

(ii)   Activities of the RRTs armed with rifles in the Agreed Adjacent
       Area, as defined in Appendix 2, shall require the agreement of
       the JCC.
(iii) The RRTs will use the rifles in the rest of Area H-1 to fulfil
       their above mentioned tasks.

(e) The Palestinian Police will ensure that all Palestinian policemen,
prior to their deployment in the City of Hebron, will pass a security
check in order to verify their suitability for service, taking into account
the sensitivity of the area.

6. Holy sites

(a) Paragraphs 2 and 3(a) of Article 32 of Appendix 1 to Annex III of
the Interim Agreement will be applicable to the following Holy Sites in
Area H-1:
(i)   The Cave of Othniel Ben Knaz/El-Khalil;
(ii)   Elonei Mamre/Haram Er-Rameh;
(iii) Eshel Avraham/Balotat Ibrahim, and
(iv)   Maayan Sarah/Ein Sarah.

(b) The Palestinian Police will be responsible for the protection of the
above Jewish Holy Sites. Without derogating from the above responsibility
of the Palestinian Police, visits to the above Holy Sites by worshippers
or other visitors shall be accompanied by a Joint Mobile Unit, which
will ensure free, unimpeded and secure access to the Holy Sites, as well
as their peaceful use.

7. Normalization of life in the old City

(a) Both sides reiterate their commitment to maintain normal life
throughout the City of Hebron and to prevent any provocation or friction
that may affect the normal life in the city.

(b) In this context, both sides are committed to take all steps and measures
necessary for the normalisation of life in Hebron, including:
(i)   the wholesale market – Hasbahe – will be opened as a retail
       market in which goods will be sold directly to consumers from
       within the existing shops
(ii)   the movement of vehicles on the Shuhada Road will be gradually
       returned, within four months, to the same situation which existed
       prior to February 1994.

8. *The Imara*

The Imara will be turned over to the Palestinian side upon the completion of the redeployment and will become the headquarters of the Palestinian Police in the City of Hebron.

9. *City of Hebron*

Both sides reiterate their commitment to the unity of the City of Hebron, and their understanding that the division of security responsibility will not divide the city. In this context, and without derogating from the security powers and responsibilities of either side, both sides share the mutual goal that movement of people, goods and vehicles within and in and out of the city will be smooth and normal, without obstacles or barriers.

Civil arrangements regarding the redeployment in Hebron

10. *Transfer of civil powers and responsibilities*

(a) The transfer of civil powers and responsibilities that have yet to be transferred to the Palestinian side in the city of Hebron (12 spheres) in accordance with Article VII of Annex I to the Interim Agreement shall be conducted concurrently with the beginning of the redeployment of Israeli military forces in Hebron.

(b) In Area H-2, the civil powers and responsibilities will be transferred to the Palestinian side, except for those relating to Israelis and their property, which shall continue to be exercised by the Israeli Military Government.

11. *Planning, zoning and building*

(a) The two parties are equally committed to preserve and protect the historic character of the city in a way which does not harm or change that character in any part of the city.

(b) The Palestinian side has informed the Israeli side that in exercising its powers and responsibilities, taking into account the existing municipal regulations, it has undertaken to implement the following provisions.

    (i)   Proposed construction of buildings above two floors (6 metres) within 50 metres of the external boundaries of the locations specified in the list attached to this Protocol as Appendix 3 (hereinafter referred to as "the attached list") will be coordinated through the DCL.

(ii) Proposed construction of buildings above three floors (9 metres) between 50 and 100 metres of the external boundaries of the locations specified in the attached list will be coordinated through the DCL.

(iii) Proposed construction of non-residential, non-commercial buildings within 100 metres of the external boundaries of the locations specified in the attached list that are designed for uses that may adversely affect the environment (such as industrial factories) or buildings and institutions in which more that 50 persons are expected to gather together will be coordinated through the DCL.

(iv) Proposed construction of buildings above two floors (6 metres) within 50 metres from each side of the road specified in the attached list will be coordinated through the DCL.

(v) The necessary enforcement measures will be taken to ensure compliance on the ground with the preceding provisions.

(vi) This Article does not apply to existing buildings, or to new construction or renovation for which fully approved permits were issued by the Municipality prior to 15 January 1997.

12. Infrastructure

(a) The Palestinian side shall inform the Israeli side, through the DCL, 48 hours in advance of any anticipated activity regarding infrastructure which may disturb the regular flow of traffic on roads in Area H-2 or which may affect infrastructure (such as water, sewage, electricity and communications) serving Area H-2.

(b) The Israeli side may request, through the DCL, that the Municipality carry out works regarding the roads or other infrastructure required for the well-being of the Israelis in Area H-2. If the Israeli side offers to cover the costs of these works, the Palestinian side will ensure that these works are carried out as a top priority.

(c) The above does not prejudice the provisions of the Interim Agreement regarding the access to infrastructure, facilities and installations located in the city of Hebron, such as the electricity grid.

13. Transportation

The Palestinian side shall have the power to determine bus stops, traffic arrangements and traffic signalisation in the city of Hebron. Traffic signalisation, traffic arrangements and the location of bus stops in Area H-2 will remain as they are on the date of the redeployment in Hebron. Any subsequent change in these arrangements in Area H-2 will be done in cooperation between the two sides in the transportation sub-committee.

14. Municipal Inspectors

(a) In accordance with paragraph 4c of Article VII of Annex I of the Interim Agreement, plainclothes unarmed municipal inspectors will operate in Area H-2. The number of these inspectors shall not exceed 50.

(b) The inspectors shall carry official identification cards with a photograph issued by the Municipality.

(c) The Palestinian side may request the assistance of the Israel Police, through the DCL of Hebron, in order to carry out its enforcement activities in Area H-2.

15. Location of offices of the Palestinian Council

The Palestinian side, when operating new offices in Area H-2, will take into consideration the need to avoid provocation and friction. Where establishing such offices might affect public order or security the two sides will cooperate to find a suitable solution.

16. Municipal services

In accordance with paragraph 5 of Article VII of Annex I of the Interim Agreement, municipal services shall be provided regularly and continuously to all parts of the city of Hebron, at the same quality and cost. The cost shall be determined by the Palestinian side with respect to work done and materials consumed, without discrimination.

Miscellaneous

17. Temporary International Presence

There will be a Temporary International Presence in Hebron (TIPH). Both sides will agree on the modalities of the TIPH, including the number of its members and its area of operation.

18. Annex I
Nothing in this Protocol will derogate from the security powers and responsibilities of either side in accordance with Annex I to the Interim Agreement.

19. Attached appendices
The appendices attached to this Protocol shall constitute an integral part hereof.

Done at _____ this _____ day of _____ 1997.

_____   _____

Dan Shomrom   **Saeb Erekat**
For the Government of   For the PLO
the State of Israel

Appendices

Appendix 2, Article 5: Agreed Adjacent Area
The Agreed Adjacent Area ("AAA") shall include the following.
1. An area defined by a line commencing from AAA Reference Point (RP) 100, proceeding along old Route No. 35 until RP 101, continuing by a straight line to RP 102, and from there connected by a straight line to RP 103.
2. An area defined by a line commencing at RP 104, following a straight line to RP 105, from there following a line immediately westward of checkpoints 4, 5, 6, 8, 9, 10, 11, 12 and 13, and from there connected by a straight line to RP 106.
3. An area defined by a line connecting RPs 107 and 108, passing immediately northward of checkpoint 15.

Appendix 3, Article 12: List of locations
• The area of Al Haram Al Ibrahimi/the Tomb of the Patriarchs (including the military and police installations in its vicinity)
• Al Hisba/Abraham Avinu

- Osama School/Beit Romano (including the military location in its vicinity)
- Al Daboya/Beit Hadasseh
- Jabla Al Rahama/Tel Rumeida
- The Jewish Cemeteries
- Dir Al Arbein/the Tomb of Ruth and Yishai
- Tel Al Jaabra/Givaat Avot Neighbourhood (including the police station in its vicinity)
- The Road connecting Al Haram Al Ibrahimi/the Tomb of the Patriarchs and Qiryat Arba

Note for the Record

The two leaders met on 15 January 1997, in the presence of the US Special Middle East Co-ordinator. They requested him to prepare this "Note for the record" to summarise what they agreed upon at their meeting.

Mutual undertakings

The two leaders agreed that the Oslo peace process must move forward to succeed. Both parties to the Interim Agreement have concerns and obligations. Accordingly, the two leaders reaffirmed their commitment to implement the Interim Agreement on the basis of reciprocity and, in this context, conveyed the following undertakings to each other.

Israeli responsibilities
The Israeli side reaffirms its commitments to the following measures and principles in accordance with the Interim Agreement.

Issues for implementation
1. Further redeployment phases
The first phase of further redeployments will be carried out during the first week of March.

2. Prisoner release issues
Prisoner release issues will be dealt with in accordance with the Interim Agreement's provisions and procedures, including Annex VII.

Issues for negotiation

3. Outstanding Interim Agreement issues

Negotiations on the following outstanding issues from the Interim Agreement will be immediately resumed. Negotiations on these issues will be conducted in parallel:

  (a) safe passage
  (b) Dahaniya Airport
  (c) Gaza port
  (d) passages
  (e) economic, financial, civilian and security issues
  (f) people-to-people.

4. Permanent status negotiations

Permanent status negotiations will be resumed within two months after implementation of the Hebron Protocol.

Palestinian responsibilities

The Palestinian side reaffirms its commitments to the following measures and principles in accordance with the Interim Agreement.

1. Complete the process of revising the Palestinian National Charter.
2. Fighting terror and preventing violence.
    (a) Strengthening security cooperation.
    (b) Preventing incitement and hostile propaganda, as specified in Article XXII of the Interim Agreement.
    (c) Combat systematically and effectively terrorist organisations and infrastructure.
    (d) Apprehension, prosecution and punishment of terrorists.
    (e) Requests for transfer of suspects and defendants will be acted upon in accordance with Article II(7)(f) of Annex IV to the Interim Agreement.
    (f) Confiscation of illegal firearms.
3. Size of Palestinian Police will be pursuant to the Interim Agreement.
4. Exercise of Palestinian governmental activity, and location of Palestinian governmental offices, will be as specified in the Interim Agreement.

The aforementioned commitments will be dealt with immediately and in parallel.

[268]

Other issues

Either party is free to raise other issues not specified above related to implementation of the Interim Agreement and obligations of both sides arising from the Interim Agreement.

Prepared by Ambassador Dennis Ross
at the request of Prime Minister Binyamin Netanyahu
and Ra'ees Yasser Arafat

Letter to be provided by US Secretary of State Christopher to Binyamin Netanyahu at the time of signing of the Hebron Protocol

Dear Mr Prime Minister

I wanted personally to congratulate you on the successful conclusion of the "Protocol Concerning the Redeployment in Hebron". It represents an important step forward in the Oslo peace process and reaffirms my conviction that a just and lasting peace will be established between Israelis and Palestinians in the very near future.

In this connection, I can assure you that it remains the policy of the United States to support and promote full implementation of the Interim Agreement in all of its parts. We intend to continue our efforts to help ensure that all outstanding commitments are carried out by both parties in a co-operative spirit and on the basis of reciprocity.

As part of this process, I have impressed upon Chairman Arafat the imperative need for the Palestinian Authority to make every effort to ensure public order and internal security within the West Bank and Gaza Strip. I have stressed to him that effectively carrying out this major responsibility will be a critical foundation for completing implementation of the Interim Agreement, as well as the peace process as a whole.

I wanted you to know that, in this context, I have advised Chairman Arafat of US views on Israel's process of redeploying its forces, designating specified military locations and transferring additional powers and responsibilities to the Palestinian Authority. In this regard, I have conveyed our belief, that the first phase of further redeployments should take place as soon as possible, and that all three phases of the further redeployments should be completed within 12 months from the implementation of the first phase of the further redeployments but not later than mid-1998.

Mr Prime Minister, you can be assured that the United States' commitment to Israel's security is ironclad and constitutes the fundamental cornerstone of our special relationship. The key element in our approach to peace, including the negotiation and implementation of agreements between Israel and its Arab partners, has always been a recognition of Israel's security requirements. Moreover, a hallmark of US policy remains our commitment to work co-operatively to seek to meet the security needs that Israel identifies. Finally, I would like to reiterate our position that Israel is entitled to secure and defensible borders, which should be directly negotiated and agreed with its neighbours.

Primary violations of the
Israeli–Palestinian agreements

March 1997

Overview

In the "Note for the record" attached to the Hebron Protocol, the Israeli and Palestinian sides both reaffirmed undertakings made in the Interim Agreement. For its part, Israel undertook to implement the first phase of the further redeployment process, to release women prisoners who had not yet been released, and to re-open negotiations on a range of issues including safe passage, Dahaniya Airport, Gaza Port etc. Israel has complied with its undertakings in all these respects.

For its part, the Palestinian Council undertook to complete the process of revising the Palestinian charter, to take strengthened measures to fight terrorism and prevent violence – including the transfer of suspects, confiscation of illegal firearms, and reduction of the size of the Palestinian Police to that permitted in the Interim Agreement, and to conduct Palestinian Council activity in the areas of Palestinian jurisdiction – and not in Jerusalem. In respect of every one of these commitments the Palestinian side has failed to demonstrate its intention or will to comply with its undertakings.

To the contrary, the Palestinian side has instead chosen to focus its energies on generating political pressure within and outside the region, and to avoid the direct bilateral talks that are the very basis of the Israeli–Palestinian negotiations, and its only hope for progress.

This document lists the most significant violations of the Israeli–Palestinian agreements, with regard to which Israel is still awaiting compliance from the Palestinian side. It does not purport to be a comprehensive list. It focuses only on the most prominent violations, which appear to be a result of deliberate and continuous activity on the part of the Palestinian leadership.

Primary violations

1. Failure to take sufficient measures to combat terrorist activity

The Interim Agreement (Annex I, Article II) obliges the Palestinian Council to act against all expressions of violence and terror. This obligation was restated and strengthened in the "Note for the record" attached to the Hebron Protocol in which the Palestinian side undertook both to combat systematically and effectively terrorist organisations and infrastructure, and to apprehend, prosecute and punish terrorists. Notwithstanding these clear obligations, recent months have seen a marked decline in the extent of Palestinian activity directed against terrorists. Not only has the Council ceased to arrest individuals suspected of terrorist activity and to take measures against the terrorist infrastructure, but it has continued to release members of terrorist groups, many of who have been actively involved in the organisation and perpetration of acts of terror.

2. Incitement to violence

The Interim Agreement contains a specific provision (Article XXII) which not only requires the Palestinian leadership to abstain from violence and hostile propaganda, but also obliges it to take legal measures to prevent any incitement taking place under their jurisdiction. None the less, the Palestinian leadership frequently calls for *jihad* (holy war) against Israel and praises prominent terrorists such as Yihye Ayash ("the Engineer"). A document issued by the Palestinian leadership, purporting to list Israeli violations of the Interim Agreement threatened that if Palestinian demands are not met this "will bring the region and its people back to violent confrontation and disasters, an outcome that will be the sole responsibility of the Government of Israel". The current peace process is based on the resolution of differences by peaceful means and the renunciation of violence. Veiled threats of violence such as these undermine the foundations of dialogue between the two sides. Moreover, as the September Riots tragically demonstrated, the language of incitement rarely remains in the realm of words alone.

3. Failure to comply with obligations in the legal sphere – including transfer of terrorist suspects

The Palestinian side has failed to comply with the provisions of the legal annex of the Interim Agreement in such matters as notifying Israel of

Palestinian legislation, and cooperating in the field of legal assistance. Even more significant in this area is the repeated refusal of the Palestinian side, in direct contradiction to the express provisions of the Legal Annex, to transfer requested terrorist suspects to Israel. Israel has to date submitted 19 transfer requests (relating to 23 individuals) to the Palestinian side and none has been complied with.

4. Failure to amend the PLO charter

The Palestinian side undertook to amend the PLO charter, which advocates the use of violence and calls for the destruction of the State of Israel, in the Arafat–Rabin exchange of letters in September 1993. Following the failure of the Palestinian side to comply with this under-taking, the obligation was restated in the exchange of letters annexed to the Gaza–Jericho agreement and then again in the Interim Agreement. Most recently, the Palestinian side undertook to complete the process of changing the PLO charter in the "Note for the record" attached to the Hebron Protocol. Recent comments by the Palestinian leadership that the charter will only be changed "after Israel has a constitution" raise doubts about the sincerity of Palestinian intentions in this regard.

5. Palestinian Council activity in Jerusalem

The Declaration of Principles and the Interim Agreement provide that the Palestinian Council shall have no authority in Jerusalem during the interim period. Furthermore, the "Note for the record" attached to the Hebron Protocol, restated the Palestinian undertaking that all Palestinian Council offices and activity would be within the areas under Palestinian jurisdiction – that is, outside Jerusalem. Notwithstanding these provisions, the Palestinian Council continues to exert efforts to establish a presence in Jerusalem both by establishing offices and by making independent Palestinian institutions subject to its authority. Such activities include attempts to make hospitals and schools subject to Palestinian Council officials, meetings with foreign diplomats at the Orient House and the operation of Palestinian police in Jerusalem.

6. Conduct of foreign relations

Article IX of the Interim Agreement provides that the Palestinian Council will not have powers and responsibilities in the sphere of foreign relations.

Notwithstanding this prohibition, the Palestinian Council continues to conduct foreign relations. In particular:

(a) it has entered into numerous international agreements with foreign states or international organisations in such spheres as air transport, telecommunications, and postal arrangements

(b) it has sought to have individuals abroad recognised as diplomatic representatives of the Council (To date, Israel is aware of seven countries in which PLO representatives have sought admission as ambassadors of the Palestinian Council or of "Palestine")

(c) it has permitted representatives of foreign states to establish diplomatic representations within the areas under its jurisdiction

(d) it has attempted to prejudice the Final Status negotiations by presenting the Palestinian areas as a state in international fora.

7. Size of Palestinian Police

Under the terms of the Interim Agreement, the Palestinian Police at this stage should comprise no more than 24,000 policemen (a further 6,000 may be recruited at a later stage). The obligation to comply with these restrictions on the size of the police was restated in the "Note for the record" attached to the Hebron Protocol. Despite this, in practice the Palestinian police consists of over 30,000 policemen.

In addition, the Interim Agreement provides that every candidate for recruitment to the police must be notified to Israel, which has the right to object. In practice, only 18,000 Palestinian policemen have been notified to and approved by Israel. In other words, the employment of over 10,000 Palestinian policemen is in breach of the Agreement. Many of those recruited to the Palestinian police without Israel's approval are individuals who have been wanted for terrorist activity in the past. Over the last year, over 20 Hamas fighters involved in terrorist activity were recruited into the Palestinian forces.

In the Hebron area, in which the Hebron Protocol permits a maximum of 400 policemen, some 1,500 Palestinian police are operating, many of them armed with rifles which both in type and quantity violate the provisions of the Hebron Protocol.

8. Failure to confiscate illegal arms

The Interim Agreement (Annex I, Article II) provides that the Palestinian Council is obliged to confiscate all illegal arms. This provision was restated as a Palestinian obligation in the "Note for the record" attached to the Hebron Protocol. Notwithstanding these provisions, the Palestinian Council has only confiscated a token number of arms from among the tens of thousands of illegal weapons in the areas under its authority. This problem has become even more acute since the September Riots in which members of the Palestinian police gave police weapons to Palestinian civilians.

9. Arrest and interrogation of Israelis
The Palestinian Police frequently arrest and interrogate Israelis situated in the areas under the jurisdiction of the Palestinian Council. In 1996 over 100 Israeli citizens were arrested by the Palestinian Police. It will be recalled that the Declaration of Principles and the Interim Agreement provide that the Palestinian Council will not have any authority in relation to permanent status issues – including Israelis. The only situation in which the Palestinian Police are permitted to take any action in respect of Israelis is where an Israeli in the territory under Palestinian jurisdiction is committing a crime against a person or property. In such a case the police may detain him in place pending the arrival of the Israeli police, and are required to notify the Israeli authorities immediately.

10. Abuse of VIP privileges
Palestinian VIPs continue to abuse their privileges and use their vehicles to transport individuals whose entry into Israel is prohibited. In addition, despite numerous Israeli protests, Palestinian VIPs continue to bring bodyguards with unlicensed weapons into Israel.

11. Movement of Palestinian Police outside Area A without prior coordination
Notwithstanding the provisions of the Security Annex of the Interim Agreement, the Palestinian Police continue to operate outside Area A without prior coordination in Israel. In 1997 there have been some 35 occurrences of unauthorised police activity every month.

12. Unauthorised construction of Dahaniya Airport
The Palestinian side continues to establish facts on the ground with regard to the construction of an airport. Such construction has been effected in direct violation of the Interim Agreement and subsequent

agreements between the two sides. In addition, the Palestinian side continues to refuse to accept the provision in the Interim Agreement that the airport will be subject to the same arrangements, including security arrangements, as other international passages. Furthermore, in direct contravention of the Interim Agreement the Palestinian side has concluded a number of international agreements with foreign states in the field of aviation. Notwithstanding these violations, the issues relating to the airport are currently under negotiation between the two sides.

13. Unauthorised construction of Gaza Port

The Interim Agreement provides that all aspects relating to the establishment of a port in the Gaza Strip are to be discussed and agreed between the two sides. Notwithstanding this proviso, the Palestinians have commenced construction work on an old wharf in the Gaza Strip with the declared intention of making this into a port. Only after an order issued by Israel prohibited the entry of construction materials to this area, did the Palestinian side refrain from acting in violation of the agreement. Pursuant to the "Note for the record" attached to the Hebron Protocol, the two sides have resumed negotiations on the issue.

14. Failure to enforce visitor permit requirements

Contrary to the provisions of the Interim Agreement the Palestinian side has not taken any steps to expel from the areas under its jurisdiction visitors who have exceeded the period of their visitor's permit. It is estimated that the failure to expel such unlawfully present individuals has resulted in some 31,000 individuals currently remaining in the territories. Moreover, in two recent cases it was discovered that such unlawfully present individuals were employed by the Palestinian Council.

15. Breaches of Agreement provisions in civilian spheres

The Palestinian Council continues to breach the provisions of the Civil Annex of the Interim Agreement. Among the most frequent violations are the failure to enforce building permits, unauthorised activity in Area C, particularly in relation to garbage and sewage disposal, and the exercise of enforcement procedures outside the jurisdiction of the Council.

Source: Israeli Prime Minister's Office, Jerusalem, March 1997

Appendix 3

Beilin-Eitan agreement
National agreement regarding the negotiations on permanent settlement with the Palestinians, 1996

The central objective of the Zionist movement, from the day of its founding, was the establishment of sovereign state in the Land of Israel. The Jewish state was established in 1948, but it was not until 1977 that the first Arab state, Egypt, recognised and later signed a peace treaty with the State of Israel.

The Camp David Agreements, the Oslo Accords, the Mutual Recognition between the Israeli government and the Palestine Liberation Organization (PLO) and the projects of the settlements in the territories under Israeli control since 1967 have created a reality from which none of the involved parties can escape.

Both danger and opportunity are concealed in the dialogue between the Israeli and Palestinian leadership. The last two Israeli governments made the strategic decision to take calculated risks with the goal of pursuing every possible chance for attaining peace and a relationship of good neighbours between Jews and Arabs in the Land of Israel.

Against the backdrop of a readiness to find a means of historic compromise between Jews and Arabs, a bitter controversy has developed within the Jewish nation: giving up parts of the homeland.

In addition to the prevalent ideological controversy, there are bitter differences of opinion about the degree of security risk that it is acceptable to assume given the risks and threats from the Arab side. There are those who are suspicious that a secure peace is nothing but an illusion, a deceptive vision that will lead Israel into a trap that will, in the end, exact a heavy price of blood. Opposing them are those who claim fervently that the process has potential and that a lasting peace is essential to ensure the security of the State of Israel for generations.

This grave political polarisation reached its climax towards the end of 1995. In September the Israeli government signed Oslo II, which was understood to be a step towards the transfer of the territories of the West Bank to the Palestinians. Protest demonstrations intensified and many saw the signing of the Accord as fundamental heresy. This climate of intense polarisation lead to the political assassination, several weeks later, of the late Yitzhak Rabin.

Despite the fact that the murder and the murderer were condemned unequivocally by the high-ranking leadership in Israel, there were more than a few who identified with the nefarious act and in their identification made clear that a real risk of civil war existed. It was as if we had not learned the historical lesson of what was bound to happen in the aftermath of the use of terror as a means of internal political disagreement between Jews and other Jews in the face of an "enemy besieging the city".

Members of the Knesset from the Likud-Gesher-Tsomet faction and from the Labour faction came together with the common objective of clarifying the areas of agreement and disagreement between them regarding the future negotiations with the Palestinians on a permanent settlement. Following a series of discussions and clarifications they have arrived at the conclusion that it is necessary to reach a national consensus on the basis of the following three principles.

1. It is necessary to continue the dialogue with the Palestinian representatives and to pursue exhaustively every opportunity to achieve a permanent agreement with them. In the framework of such an agreement it is necessary to permit the establishment of a Palestinian entity whose status will be determined in negotiations between the parties and the limits on the sovereignty of which will be discussed in the following sections.

2. Under conditions of peace and following the achievement of an agreement on the issue of the permanent settlement, the State of Israel must preserve its ability to prevent every attack or risk of an attack on its territorial integrity, the safety of its citizens and their property and in its vital interests in Israel and in the world.

3. No agreement signed by the Israeli government can include a commitment to uproot Jewish settlements in the Western Land of Israel nor will any agreement compromise the rights of the residents to keep their Israeli citizenship and their ties as individuals and as a community with the State of Israel.

[278]

A. Borders

The position of Israel on every issue relating to the question of borders will be based on the following principles.

1. There will be no return to the 1967 borders.
2. The majority of settlers will live on their settlements under Israeli sovereignty, in order to preserve territorial continuity between the settlements and the State of Israel.
3. The residents of the Israeli settlements that will exist outside of the area that will be annexed by the State of Israel will receive special, agreed upon, arrangements within the framework of which their Israeli citizenship and their ties with the State of Israel, as individuals and as a community, will be preserved. Thus their right of free and safe passage to the territories under full Israeli sovereignty will be preserved.
4. The Jordan Valley will be a special security zone and Israeli army forces will be posted along the Jordan. The residents of the area will be permitted to remain where they are, according to point 3, above. Another version insists upon an Israeli sovereignty over the Jordan valley.

B. Security components

1. The Palestinian entity will be demilitarised and it will have no army.
2. The Jordan River will be the security border of Israel. Secure crossing conditions will be regulated by IDF forces in proportion to need and to the changing conditions within the Palestinian entity, affecting the estimated need for the IDF on the borders.
3. The Palestinian entity will establish a strong police force to meet the needs of internal security.
4. No foreign army may be stationed within the boundaries of the Palestinian entity.
5. The security forces of Israel and the Palestinian entity will work to deter and foil acts of terrorism aimed against Jews and Arabs.
6. The Palestinian entity will not sign any military agreement or any other agreement that includes a threat to the territorial integrity of the State of Israel, the security of its citizens or the integrity of their property. It will not sign any agreement regarding boycott or any

other illegal steps against the Israeli economy nor any agreement involving negative propaganda against the State of Israel or against the Jewish people.

7. The commitment of the two parties to the agreement regarding the permanent settlements will be strengthened by the fulfilment of all of their other commitments.

8. Any basic violation of the commitments presented in this section will allow the violated party to regard the whole agreement as annulled and will grant the assailed the right to act freely to right the violations and to prevent further violations.

C. Status of the Palestinian entity and limits on its sovereignty

If the Palestinian entity subjects itself to the limits presented in this document, its self-determination will be recognised. According to an alternative opinion it will be regarded as an enlarged autonomy, and according to another opinion, as a state.

D. Jerusalem

1. Jerusalem, the capital of Israel, with its existing municipal borders, will be a single unified city within sovereign Israel.

2. The Palestinians will recognise Jerusalem as the capital of Israel and Israel will recognise the governing centre of the Palestinian entity which will be within the borders of the entity and outside the existing municipal borders of Jerusalem.

3. Muslim and Christian holy places in Jerusalem will be granted special status.

4. Within the framework of the municipal government the Palestinian residents of Arab neighbourhoods in Jerusalem will receive a status that will allow them to share in the responsibility of the administration of their lives in the city.

E. Refugees

1. The right of the State of Israel to prevent the entry of Palestinian refugees into its sovereign territory will be recognised.

2. The administration of the entrance of refugees into the Palestinian entity and the limits to that entry will be decided upon during the negotiations of the permanent settlement, within the larger discussion of Israel's security issues.

3. An international organisation will be founded, in which Israel will play an important role, with the goal of financing any carrying out of projects for compensation and rehabilitation of the refugees in their places. The organisation will also address Israeli claims for reparations for Jewish refugees from Arab countries.

4. Israel and the Palestinian entity, each within its own boundaries, will rehabilitate the refugees on the basis of the disengagement of the UNRWA, the repealing of the refugee status and the arrangement of housing and employment and housing with international aid. (For Israel this refers to the Shoafat and Kalandia refugee camps in Jerusalem.)

5. Israel will continue its policy of family reunification on the basis of existing criteria.

F. Water

The agreement on the issue of water usage, as it was signed in the framework of the interim agreement, will remain in effect. The water authorities of Israel and the Palestinians will establish shared control over its usage.

Any future change of anything related to the issue of division of water, modes of production or means of protection of water purity must be made with the agreement of both parties. In the absence of such an agreement the status quo will remain.

Israel and the Palestinian entity will act together in regards to everything pertaining to desalination and regional water enterprises.

G. Economy and trade

The economic sphere is one of the cornerstones in the relationship between Israel and the Palestinian entity, with the goal of strengthening their interests in achieving a just, lasting and comprehensive peace. The two parties will cooperate in this arena in order to create a solid economic basis for these relations, which will be grounded in the different economic spheres on the values of mutual respect of each party for the economic interests of the other, mutuality, justice and protection. The parties will invite the Kingdom of Jordan to participate in this economic cooperation.

H. Education, culture and good neighbours
The Israeli leadership and the Palestinian leadership must create a fitting environment for the development of peaceful relations between Jew and Palestinians. It is necessary to encourage educational initiatives, cultural connections and to foster models of Jewish–Arab cooperation as a basis for relations as good neighbours. A true peace between Jews and Arabs in the Land of Israel will be attained when both of the populations will accept the existence of its counterpart on a basis of mutuality and equality.

I. The interim agreement and the permanent settlement
1. There will be a special effort to conclude the talks of the issue of the Permanent Settlement and especially to finalise the borders between Israel and the Palestinian entity before the intended date for further redeployment.
2. If the borders are not finalised before the third redeployment Israel will redeploy so that up to 50 per cent of the West Bank will be designated as territories A and B.

Source: Knesset Records, Jerusalem

The Palestinian national charter:
Resolutions of the Palestine National Council

1–17 July 1968

Author's note: In his letter of 9 September 1993 to Prime Minister Rabin, Yasser Arafat stated that those articles which deny Israel's right to exist or are inconsistent with the PLO's new commitments to Israel following their mutual recognition, are no longer valid. The articles to be amended are in *italics*.

Text of the Charter:

Article 1: Palestine is the homeland of the Arab Palestinian people; it is an indivisible part of the Arab homeland, and the Palestinian people are an integral part of the Arab nation.

Article 2: Palestine, with the boundaries it had during the British Mandate, is an indivisible territorial unit.

Article 3: The Palestinian Arab people possess the legal right to their homeland and have the right to determine their destiny after achieving the liberation of their country in accordance with their wishes and entirely of their own accord and will.

Article 4: The Palestinian identity is a genuine, essential, and inherent characteristic; it is transmitted from parents to children. The Zionist occupation and the dispersal of the Palestinian Arab people, through the disasters which befell them, do not make them lose their Palestinian identity and their membership in the Palestinian community, nor do they negate them.

Article 5: The Palestinians are those Arab nationals who, until 1947, normally resided in Palestine regardless of whether they were evicted from it or have stayed there. Anyone born, after that date, of a Palestinian father – whether inside Palestine or outside it – is also a Palestinian.

Article 6: The Jews who had normally resided in Palestine until the beginning of the Zionist invasion will be considered Palestinians.

Article 7: That there is a Palestinian community and that it has material, spiritual, and historical connection with Palestine are indisputable facts. It is a national duty to bring up individual Palestinians in an Arab revolutionary manner. All means of information and education must be adopted in order to acquaint the Palestinian with his country in the most profound manner, both spiritual and material, that is possible. He must be prepared for the armed struggle and ready to sacrifice his wealth and his life in order to win back his homeland and bring about its liberation.

Article 8: The phase in their history, through which the Palestinian people are now living, is that of national (watani) *struggle for the liberation of Palestine. Thus the conflicts among the Palestinian national forces are secondary, and should be ended for the sake of the basic conflict that exists between the forces of Zionism and of imperialism on the one hand, and the Palestinian Arab people on the other. On this basis the Palestinian masses, regardless of whether they are residing in the national homeland or in Diaspora* (mahajir) *constitute – both their organizations and the individuals – one national front working for the retrieval of Palestine and its liberation through armed struggle.*

Article 9: Armed struggle is the only way to liberate Palestine. This is the overall strategy, not merely a tactical phase. The Palestinian Arab people assert their absolute determination and firm resolution to continue their armed struggle and to work for an armed popular revolution for the liberation of their country and their return to it. They also assert their right to normal life in Palestine and to exercise their right to self-determination and sovereignty over it.

Article 10: Commando action constitutes the nucleus of the Palestinian popular liberation war. This requires its escalation, comprehensiveness, and the mobilisation of all the Palestinian popular and educational efforts and their organization and involvement in the armed Palestinian revolution. It also requires the achieving of unity for the national (watani) *struggle among the different groupings of the Palestinian people, and between the Palestinian people and the Arab masses, so as to secure the continuation of the revolution, its escalation, and victory.*

Article 11: The Palestinians will have three mottoes: national (*wataniyya*) unity, national (*qawmiyya*) mobilisation, and liberation.

Article 12: The Palestinian people believe in Arab unity. In order to contribute their share toward the attainment of that objective, however, they must, at the present stage of their struggle, safeguard their Palestinian identity and develop their consciousness of that identity, and oppose any plan that may dissolve or impair it.

Article 13: Arab unity and the liberation of Palestine are two complementary objectives, the attainment of either of which facilitates the attainment of the other. Thus, Arab unity leads to the liberation of Palestine, the liberation of Palestine leads to Arab unity; and work towards the realisation of one objective proceeds side by side with work towards the realisation of the other.

Article 14: The destiny of the Arab nation, and indeed Arab existence itself, depends upon the destiny of the Palestine cause. From this interdependence springs the Arab nation's pursuit of, and striving for, the liberation of Palestine. The people of Palestine play the role of the vanguard in the realisation of this sacred (*qawmi*) goal.

Article 15: The liberation of Palestine, from an Arab viewpoint, is a national (qawmi) duty and it attempts to repel the Zionist and imperialist aggression against the Arab homeland, and aims at the elimination of Zionism in Palestine. Absolute responsibility for this falls upon the Arab nation – peoples and governments – with the Arab people of Palestine in the vanguard. Accordingly, the Arab nation must mobilise all its military, human, moral and spiritual capabilities to participate actively with the Palestinian people in the liberation of Palestine. It must, particularly in the phase of the armed Palestinian revolution, offer and furnish the Palestinian people with all possible help, and material and human support, and make available to them the means and opportunities that will enable them to continue to carry out their leading role in the armed revolution, until they liberate their homeland.

Article 16: The liberation of Palestine, from a spiritual point of view, will provide the Holy Land with an atmosphere of safety and tranquillity, which in turn will safeguard the country's religious sanctuaries and guarantee freedom of worship and of visit to all, without discrimination of race, colour, language or religion. Accordingly, the people of Palestine look to all spiritual forces in the world for support.

Article 17: The liberation of Palestine, from a human point of view, will restore to the Palestinian individual his dignity, pride and freedom. Accordingly the Palestinian Arab people look forward to the support of all those who believe in the dignity of man and his freedom in the world.

Article 18: The liberation of Palestine, from an international point of view, is a defensive action necessitated by the demands of self-defence. Accordingly the Palestinian people, desirous as they are of the friendship of all people, look to freedom-loving, and peace-loving states for support in order to restore their legitimate rights in Palestine, to re-establish peace and security in the country, and to enable its people to exercise national sovereignty and freedom.

Article 19: The partition of Palestine in 1947 and the establishment of the state of Israel are entirely illegal, regardless of the passage of time, because they were contrary to the will of the Palestinian people and to their natural right in their homeland, and inconsistent with the principles embodied in the Charter of the United Nations, particularly the right to self-determination.

Article 20: The Balfour Declaration, the Mandate for Palestine, and everything that has been based upon them, are deemed null and void. Claims of historical or religious ties of Jews with Palestine are incompatible with the facts of history and the true conception of what constitutes statehood. Judaism, being a religion, is not an independent nationality. Nor do Jews constitute a single nation with an identity of its own; they are citizens of the states to which they belong.

Article 21: The Arab Palestinian people, expressing themselves by the armed Palestinian revolution, reject all solutions which are substitutes for the total liberation of Palestine and reject all proposals aiming at the liquidation of the Palestinian problem, or its internationalisation.

Article 22: Zionism is a political movement organically associated with international imperialism and antagonistic to all action for liberation and to progressive movements in the world. It is racist and fanatic in its nature, aggressive, expansionist, and colonial in its aims, and fascist in its methods. Israel is the instrument of the Zionist movement, and geographical base for world imperialism placed strategically in the midst of the Arab homeland to combat the hopes of the Arab nation for liberation, unity, and progress. Israel is a constant source of threat vis-à-vis peace in the Middle East and the whole world. Since the liberation of Palestine will destroy the Zionist and imperialist presence and will contribute to the establishment of peace in the Middle East, the Palestinian people look for the support of all the progressive and peaceful forces and urge them all, irrespective of their affiliations and beliefs, to offer the Palestinian people all aid and support in their just struggle for the liberation of their homeland.

Article 23*: The demand of security and peace, as well as the demand of right and justice, require all states to consider Zionism an illegitimate movement, to outlaw its existence, and to ban its operations, in order that friendly relations among peoples may be preserved, and the loyalty of citizens to their respective homelands safeguarded.*

Article 24: The Palestinian people believe in the principles of justice, freedom, sovereignty, self-determination, human dignity, and in the right of all peoples to exercise them.

Article 25: For the realisation of the goals of this Charter and its principles, the Palestine Liberation Organization will perform its role in the liberation of Palestine in accordance with the Constitution of this Organization.

Article 26: The Palestine Liberation Organization, representative of the Palestinian revolutionary forces, is responsible for the Palestinian Arab people's movement in its struggle – to retrieve its homeland, liberate and return to it and exercise the right to self-determination in it – in all military, political, and financial fields and also for whatever may be required by the Palestine case on the inter-Arab and international levels.

Article 27: The Palestine Liberation Organization shall cooperate with all Arab states, each according to its potentialities; and will adopt a neutral policy among them in the light of the requirements of the war of liberation; and on this basis it shall not interfere in the internal affairs of any Arab state.

Article 28: The Palestinian Arab people assert the genuineness and independence of their national (*wataniyya*) revolution and reject all forms of intervention, trusteeship, and subordination.

Article 29: The Palestinian people possess the fundamental and genuine legal right to liberate and retrieve their homeland. The Palestinian people determine their attitude toward all states and forces on the basis of the stands they adopt vis-à-vis to the Palestinian revolution to fulfil the aims of the Palestinian people.

Article 30: Fighters and carriers of arms in the war of liberation are the nucleus of the popular army which will be the protective force for the gains of the Palestinian Arab people.

Article 31: The Organization shall have a flag, an oath of allegiance, and an anthem. All this shall be decided upon in accordance with a special regulation.

Article 32: Regulations, which shall be known as the Constitution of the Palestinian Liberation Organization, shall be annexed to this Charter. It will lay down the manner in which the Organization, and its organs and institutions, shall be constituted; the respective competence of each; and the requirements of its obligation under the Charter.

Article 33: This Charter shall not be amended save by [vote of] a majority of two-thirds of the total membership of the National Congress of the Palestine Liberation Organization [taken] at a special session convened for that purpose.

English rendition as published in *Basic Political Documents of the Armed Palestinian Resistance Movement*, ed. Leila S. Kadi (Beirut: Palestine Research Centre, December 1969), pp. 137–41.

Extract from the protocol on economic relations between the Government of the State of Israel and the PLO, representing the Palestinian people (the Paris Agreement)

Paris, 9 April 1994

Preamble

The two parties view the economic domain as one of the cornerstones in their mutual relations with a view to enhance their interest in the achievement of a just, lasting and comprehensive peace. Both parties shall cooperate in this field in order to establish a sound economic base for these relations, which will be governed in various economic spheres by the principles of mutual respect of each other's economic interests, reciprocity, equity and fairness.

This protocol lays the groundwork for strengthening the economic base of the Palestinian side and for exercising its right of economic decision making in accordance with its own development plan and priorities. The two parties recognise each other's economic ties with other markets and the need to create a better economic environment for their peoples and individuals.

Article I

Framework and scope of this protocol

1. This Protocol establishes the contractual agreement that will govern the economic relations between the two sides and will cover the West Bank and the Gaza Strip during the interim period. The implementation will be according to the stages envisaged in the Declaration of Principles on Interim Self Government Arrangements signed in Washington DC on 13 September 1993 and the Agreed Minutes thereto. It will therefore begin in the Gaza Strip and the Jericho Area and at a later stage will also apply to the rest of the West Bank, according to the provisions of

the Interim Agreement and to any other agreed arrangements between the two sides.

2.   This Protocol, including its Appendixes, will be incorporated into the Agreement on the Gaza Strip and the Jericho Area (in this Protocol – the Agreement), will be an integral part thereof and interpreted accordingly. This paragraph refers solely to the Gaza Strip and the Jericho Area.

3.   This Protocol will come into force upon the signing of the Agreement.

4.   For the purpose of this Protocol, the term "Areas" means the areas under the jurisdiction of the Palestinian Authority, according to the provisions of the Agreement regarding territorial jurisdiction. The Palestinian Jurisdiction in the subsequent agreements could cover areas, spheres or functions according to the Interim Agreement. Therefore, for the purpose of this Protocol, whenever applied, the term "Areas" shall be interpreted to mean functions and spheres also, as the case may be, with the necessary adjustments.

Source: Israeli Ministry of Finance, Jerusalem

Treaty of peace between the State of Israel and the Hashemite Kingdom of Jordan

26 October 1994

The Government of the State of Israel and the Government of the Hashemite Kingdom of Jordan:

Bearing in mind the Washington Declaration, signed by them on 25 July 1994, and which they are both committed to honour;

Aiming at the achievement of a just, lasting and comprehensive peace in the Middle East based an Security Council resolutions 242 and 338 in all their aspects;

Bearing in mind the importance of maintaining and strengthening peace based on freedom, equality, justice and respect for fundamental human rights, thereby overcoming psychological barriers and promoting human dignity;

Reaffirming their faith in the purposes and principles of the Charter of the United Nations and recognising their right and obligation to live in peace with each other as well as with all states, within secure and recognised boundaries;

Desiring to develop friendly relations and cooperation between them in accordance with the principles of international law governing international relations in time of peace;

Desiring as well to ensure lasting security for both their States and in particular to avoid threats and the use of force between them;

Bearing in mind that in their Washington Declaration of 25 July 1994, they declared the termination of the state of belligerency between them;

Deciding to establish peace between them in accordance with this Treaty of Peace;

Have agreed as follows:

Article 1: Establishment of peace

Peace is hereby established between the State of Israel and the Hashemite Kingdom of Jordan (the "Parties") effective from the exchange of the instruments of ratification of this Treaty.

Article 2: Gene ral principles

The Parties will apply between them the provisions of the Charter of the United Nations and the principles of international law governing relations among states in times of peace. In particular:

1. They recognise and will respect each other's sovereignty, territorial integrity and political independence

2. They recognise and will respect each other's right to live in peace within secure and recognised boundaries

3. They will develop good neighbourly relations of cooperation between them to ensure lasting security, will refrain from the threat or use of force against each other and will settle all disputes between them by peaceful means

4. They respect and recognise the sovereignty, territorial integrity and political independence of every state in the region

5. They respect and recognise the pivotal role of human development and dignity in regional and bilateral relationships

6. They further believe that within their control, involuntary movements of persons in such a way as to adversely prejudice the security of either Party should not be permitted

Article 3: International boundary

1. The international boundary between Israel and Jordan is delimited with reference to the boundary definition under the Mandate as is shown in Annex I(a) on the mapping materials attached thereto and coordinates specified therein.

2. The boundary, as set out in Annex I(a), is the permanent, secure and recognised international boundary between Israel and Jordan, without prejudice to the status of any territories that came under Israeli military government control in 1967.

3. The parties recognise the international boundary, as well as each other's territory, territorial waters and airspace, as inviolable, and will respect and comply with them.

4. The demarcation of the boundary will take place as set forth in Appendix (I) to Annex I and will be concluded not later than nine months after the signing of the Treaty.

5. It is agreed that where the boundary follows a river, in the event of natural changes in the course of the flow of the river as described in Annex I(a), the boundary shall follow the new course of the flow. In the event of any other changes the boundary shall not be affected unless otherwise agreed.

6. Immediately upon the exchange of the instruments of ratification of this Treaty, each Party will deploy on its side of the international boundary as defined in Annex I(a).

7. The Parties shall, upon the signature of the Treaty, enter into negotiations to conclude, within nine months, an agreement on the delimitation of their maritime boundary in the Gulf of Aqaba.

8. Taking into account the special circumstances of the Naharayim/ Baqura area, which is under Jordanian sovereignty, with Israeli private ownership rights, the Parties agreed to apply the provisions set out in Annex I(b).

9. With respect to the Zofar/Al-Ghamr area, the provisions set out in Annex I(c) will apply.

Article 4: Security
1(a) Both Parties, acknowledging that mutual understanding and co-operation in security-related matters will form a significant part of their relations and will further enhance the security of the region, take upon themselves to base their security relations on mutual trust, advancement of joint interests and cooperation, and to aim towards a regional framework of partnership in peace.

(b) Towards that goal the Parties recognise the achievements of the European Community and European Union in the development of the Conference on Security and Cooperation in Europe (CSCE) and commit themselves to the creation, in the Middle East, of a CSCME (Conference on Security and Cooperation in the Middle East).

This commitment entails the adoption of regional models of security successfully implemented in the post-World War era (along the lines of the Helsinki process) culminating in a regional zone of security and stability.

2.   The obligations referred to in this Article are without prejudice to the inherent right of self-defence in accordance with the United Nations Charter.

3.   The Parties undertake, in accordance with the provisions of this Article, the following:
   (a)   to refrain from the threat or use of force or weapons, conventional, non-conventional or of any other kind, against each other, or of other actions or activities that adversely affect the security of the other Party
   (b)   to refrain from organising, instigating, inciting, assisting or participating in acts or threats of belligerency, hostility, subversion or violence against the other Party
   (c)   to take necessary and effective measures to ensure that acts or threats of belligerency, hostility, subversion or violence against the other Party do not originate from, and are not committed within, through or over their territory (hereinafter the term "territory" includes the airspace and territorial waters).

4.   Consistent with the era of peace and with the efforts to build regional security and to avoid and prevent aggression and violence, the Parties further agree to refrain from the following:
   (a)   joining or in any way assisting, promoting or cooperating with any coalition, organisation or alliance with a military or security character with a third party, the objectives or activities of which include launching aggression or other acts of military hostility against the other Party, in contravention of the provisions of the present Treaty
   (b)   allowing the entry, stationing and operating on their territory, or through it, of military forces, personnel or material of a third party, in circumstances which may adversely prejudice the security of the other Party.

5.   Both Parties will take necessary and effective measures, and will cooperate in combating terrorism of all kinds. The Parties undertake:
  (a)   to take necessary and effective measures to prevent acts of terrorism, subversion or violence from being carried out from their territory or through it, and to take necessary and effective measures to combat such activities and all their perpetrators
  (b)   without prejudice to the basic rights of freedom of expression and association, to take necessary and effective measures to prevent the entry, presence and cooperation in their territory of any group or organisation, and their infrastructure, which threatens the security of the other Party by the use of, or incitement to the use of, violent means
  (c)   to cooperate in preventing and combating cross-boundary infiltrations.

6.   Any question as to the implementation of this Article will be dealt with through a mechanism of consultations which will include a liaison system, verification, supervision, and where necessary, other mechanisms, and higher level consultation. The details of the mechanism of consultations will be contained in an agreement to be concluded by the Parties within three months of the exchange of the instruments of ratification of this Treaty.

7.   The Parties undertake to work as a matter of priority, and as soon as possible in the context of the Multilateral Working Group on Arms Control and Regional Security, and jointly, towards the following:
  (a)   the creation in the Middle East of a region free from hostile alliances and coalitions
  (b)   the creation of a Middle East free from weapons of mass destruction, both conventional and non-conventional, in the context of a comprehensive, lasting and stable peace, characterised by the renunciation of the use of force, reconciliation and goodwill.

Article 5: Diplomatic and other bilateral relations
1.   The Parties agree to establish full diplomatic and consular relations, and to exchange resident ambassadors within one month of the exchange of the instruments of ratification of this Treaty.

2. The Parties agree that the normal relationship between them will further include economic and cultural relations.

Article 6: Water

With the view to achieving a comprehensive and lasting settlement of all the water problems between them:

1. The Parties agree mutually to recognise the rightful allocations of both of them in Jordan River and Yarmouk River waters and Araba/Arava ground water in accordance with the agreed acceptable principles, quantities and quality as set out in Annex II, which shall be fully respected and complied with.

2. The Parties, recognising the necessity to find a practical, just and agreed solution to their water problems and with the view that the subject of water can form the basis for the advancement of cooperation between them, jointly undertake to ensure that the management and development of their water resources do not, in any way, harm the water resources of the other Party.

3. The Parties recognise that their water resources are not sufficient to meet their needs. More water should be supplied for their use through various methods, including projects of regional and international cooperation.

4. In light of paragraph 3 of this Article, with the understanding that cooperation in water-related subjects would be to the benefit of both Parties, and will help alleviate their water shortages, and that water issues along their entire boundary must be dealt with in their totality, including the possibility of trans-boundary water transfers, the Parties agree to search for ways to alleviate water shortage and to cooperate in the following fields:

    (a) development of existing and new water resources, increasing the water availability including cooperation on a regional basis as appropriate, and minimising wastage of water resources through the chain of their uses

    (b) prevention of contamination of water resources

    (c) mutual assistance in the alleviation of water shortages

    (d) transfer of information and joint research and development in water-related subjects, and review of the potentials for enhancement of water resources development and use.

5.   The implementation of both Parties' undertakings under this Article is detailed in Annex II.

Article 7: Economic relations

1.   Viewing economic development and prosperity as pillars of peace, security and harmonious relations between states, peoples and individual human beings, the Parties, taking note of understandings reached between them, affirm their mutual desire to promote economic cooperation between them, as well as within the framework of wider regional economic cooperation.

2.   In order to accomplish this goal, the Parties agree to the following:
    (a)   to remove all discriminatory barriers to normal economic relations, to terminate economic boycotts directed at each other, and to cooperate in terminating boycotts against either Party by third parties
    (b)   recognising that the principle of free and unimpeded flow of goods and services should guide their relations, the Parties will enter into negotiations with a view to concluding agreements on economic cooperation, including trade and the establishment of a free trade area, investment, banking, industrial cooperation and labour, for the purpose of promoting beneficial economic relations, based on principles to be agreed upon, as well as on human development considerations on a regional basis; these negotiations will be concluded no later than six months from the exchange of the instruments of ratification of this Treaty
    (c)   to cooperate bilaterally, as well as in multilateral forums, towards the promotion of their respective economies and of their neighbourly economic relations with other regional parties.

Article 8: Refugees and displaced persons

1.   Recognising the massive human problems caused to both Parties by the conflict in the Middle East, as well as the contribution made by them towards the alleviation of human suffering, the Parties will seek to further alleviate those problems arising on a bilateral level.

2.   Recognising that the above human problems caused by the conflict in the Middle East cannot be fully resolved on the bilateral level, the

Parties will seek to resolve them in appropriate forums, in accordance with international law, including the following:

(a) in the case of displaced persons, in a quadripartite committee together with Egypt and the Palestinians

(b) in the case of refugees:

(i) in the framework of the Multilateral Working Group on Refugees

(ii) in negotiations, in a framework to be agreed, bilateral or otherwise, in conjunction with and at the same time as the Permanent Status negotiations pertaining to the territories referred to in Article 3 of this Treaty

(c) through the implementation of agreed United Nations programmes and other agreed international economic programmes concerning refugees and displaced persons, including assistance to their settlement.

Article 9: Places of historical and religious significance

1. Each party will provide freedom of access to places of religious and historical significance.

2. In this regard, in accordance with the Washington Declaration, Israel respects the present special role of the Hashemite Kingdom of Jordan in Muslim Holy shrines in Jerusalem. When negotiations on the Permanent Status will take place, Israel will give high priority to the Jordanian historic role in these shrines.

3. The Parties will act together to promote inter-faith relations among the three monotheistic religions, with the aim of working towards religious understanding, moral commitment, freedom of religious worship, and tolerance and peace.

Article 10: Cultural and scientific exchanges

The Parties, wishing to remove biases developed through periods of conflict, recognise the desirability of cultural and scientific exchanges in all fields, and agree to establish normal cultural relations between them. Thus, they shall, as soon as possible and not later than nine months from the exchange of the instruments of ratification of this Treaty, conclude the negotiations on cultural and scientific agreements.

Article 11: Mutual understanding and good neighbourly relations

1. The Parties will seek to foster mutual understanding and tolerance based on shared historic values, and accordingly undertake:

(a) to abstain from hostile or discriminatory propaganda against each other, and to take all possible legal and administrative measures to prevent the dissemination of such propaganda by any organisation or individual present in the territory of either Party

(b) as soon as possible, and not later than three months from the exchange of the instruments of ratification of this Treaty, to repeal all adverse or discriminatory references and expressions of hostility in their respective legislation

(c) to refrain in all government publications from any such references or expressions

(d) to ensure mutual enjoyment by each other's citizens of due process of law within their respective legal systems and before their courts.

2. Paragraph 1(a) of this Article is without prejudice to the right to freedom of expression as contained in the International Covenant on Civil and Political Rights.

3. A joint committee shall be formed to examine incidents where one Party claims there has been a violation of this Article.

Article 12: Combating crime and drugs

The Parties will cooperate in combating crime, with an emphasis on smuggling, and will take all necessary measures to combat and prevent such activities as the production of, as well as the trafficking in, illicit drugs, and will bring to trial perpetrators of such acts. In this regard, they take note of the understandings reached between them in the above spheres, in accordance with Annex III and undertake to conclude all relevant agreements not later than nine months from the date of the exchange of the instruments of ratification of this Treaty.

Article 13: Transportation and roads

Taking note of the progress already made in the area of transportation, the Parties recognise the mutuality of interest in good neighbourly relations in the area of transportation and agree to the following means to promote relations between them in this sphere.

1. Each party will permit the free movement of nationals and vehicles of the other into and within its territory according to the general rules applicable to nationals and vehicles of other states. Neither party will impose discriminatory taxes or restrictions on the free movement of persons and vehicles from its territory to the territory of the other.

2. The Parties will open and maintain roads and border-crossings between their countries and will consider further road and rail links between them.

3. The Parties will continue their negotiations concerning mutual transportation agreements in the above and other areas, such as joint projects, traffic safety, transport standards and norms, licensing of vehicles, land passages, shipment of goods and cargo, and meteorology, to be concluded not later than six months from the exchange of the instruments of ratification of this Treaty.

4. The Parties agree to continue their negotiations for a highway to be constructed and maintained between Egypt, Israel and Jordan near Eilat.

Article 14: Freedom of navigation and access to ports

1. Without prejudice to the provisions of paragraph 3, each Party recognises the right of the vessels of the other Party to innocent passage through its territorial waters in accordance with the rules of international law.

2. Each Party will grant normal access to its ports for vessels and cargoes of the other, as well as vessels and cargoes destined for or coming from the other Party. Such access will be granted on the same conditions as generally applicable to vessels and cargoes of other nations.

3. The Parties consider the Strait of Tiran and the Gulf of Aqaba to be international waterways open to all nations for unimpeded and non-suspendable freedom of navigation and overflight. The Parties will respect each other's right to navigation and overflight for access to either Party through the Strait of Tiran and the Gulf of Aqaba.

Article 15: Civil aviation

1. The Parties recognise as applicable to each other the rights, privileges and obligations provided for by the multilateral aviation agreements

to which they are both party, particularly by the 1944 Convention on International Civil Aviation (The Chicago Convention) and the 1944 International Air Services Transit Agreement.

2. Any declaration of national emergency by a Party under Article 89 of the Chicago Convention will not be applied to the other Party on a discriminatory basis.

3. The Parties take note of the negotiations on the international air corridor to be opened between them in accordance with the Washington Declaration. In addition, the Parties shall, upon ratification of this Treaty, enter into negotiations for the purpose of concluding a Civil Aviation Agreement. All the above negotiations are to be concluded not later than six months from the exchange of the instruments of ratification of this Treaty.

Article 16: Posts and telecommunications
The Parties take note of the opening between them, in accordance with the Washington Declaration, of direct telephone and facsimile lines. Postal links, the negotiations on which having been concluded, will be activated upon the signature of this Treaty. The Parties further agree that normal wireless and cable communications and television relay services by cable, radio and satellite, will be established between them, in accordance with all relevant international conventions and regulations. The negotiations on these subjects will be concluded not later than nine months from the exchange of the instruments of ratification of this Treaty.

Article 17: Tourism
The Parties affirm their mutual desire to promote cooperation between them in the field of tourism. In order to accomplish this goal, the Parties – taking note of the understandings reached between them concerning tourism – agree to negotiate, as soon as possible, and to conclude not later than three months from the exchange of the instruments of ratification of this Treaty, an agreement to facilitate and encourage mutual tourism and tourism from third countries.

Article 18: Environment
The Parties will cooperate in matters relating to the environment, a sphere

to which they attach great importance, including conservation of nature and prevention of pollution, as set forth in Annex IV. They will negotiate an agreement on the above, to be concluded not later than six months from the exchange of the instruments of ratification of this Treaty.

Article 19: Energy

1. The Parties will cooperate in the development of energy resources, including the development of energy-related projects such as the utilisation of solar energy.

2. The Parties, having concluded their negotiations on the interconnecting of their electric grids in the Eilat-Aqaba area, will implement the interconnecting upon the signature of this Treaty. The Parties view this step as a part of a wider binational and regional concept. They agree to continue their negotiations as soon as possible to widen the scope of their interconnected grids.

3. The Parties will conclude the relevant agreements in the field of energy within six months from the date of exchange of the instruments of ratification of this Treaty.

Article 20: Rift Valley Development

The Parties attach great importance to the integrated development of the Jordan Rift Valley area, including joint projects in the economic, environmental, energy-related and tourism fields. Taking note of the Terms of Reference developed in the framework of the Trilateral Israel–Jordan–US Economic Committee towards the Jordan Rift Valley Development Master Plan, they will vigorously continue their efforts towards the completion of planning and towards implementation.

Article 21: Health

The Parties will cooperate in the area of health and shall negotiate with a view to the conclusion of an agreement within nine months of the exchange of instruments of ratification of this Treaty.

Article 22: Agriculture

The Parties will cooperate in the areas of agriculture, including veterinary services, plant protection, biotechnology and marketing, and shall negotiate with a view to the conclusion of an agreement within six months from the date of the exchange of instruments of ratification of this Treaty.

Article 23: Aqaba and Eilat

The Parties agree to enter into negotiations, as soon as possible, and not later than one month from the exchange of the instruments of ratification of this Treaty, on arrangements that would enable the joint development of the towns of Aqaba and Eilat with regard to such matters, *inter alia*, as joint tourism development, joint customs, free trade zone, cooperation in aviation, prevention of pollution, maritime matters, police, customs and health cooperation. The Parties will conclude all relevant agreements within six months from the exchange of instruments of ratification of the Treaty.

Article 24: Claims

The Parties agree to establish a claims commission for the mutual settlement of all financial claims.

Article 25: Rights and obligations

1.   This Treaty does not affect and shall not be interpreted as affecting, in any way, the rights and obligations of the Parties under the Charter of the United Nations.

2.   The Parties undertake to fulfil in good faith their obligations under this Treaty, without regard to action or inaction of any other party and independently of any instrument inconsistent with this Treaty. For the purposes of this paragraph each Party represents to the other that in its opinion and interpretation there is no inconsistency between their existing treaty obligations and this Treaty.

3.   They further undertake to take all the necessary measures for the application in their relations of the provisions of the multilateral conventions to which they are parties, including the submission of appropriate notification to the Secretary General of the United Nations and other depositories of such conventions.

4.   Both Parties will also take all the necessary steps to abolish all pejorative references to the other Party, in multilateral conventions to which they are parties, to the extent that such references exist.

5.   The Parties undertake not to enter into any obligation in conflict with this Treaty.

6.   Subject to Article 103 of the United Nations Charter, in the event of a conflict between the obligations of the Parties under the present Treaty and any of their other obligations, the obligations under this Treaty will be binding and implemented.

Article 26: Legislation
Within three months of the exchange of ratifications of this Treaty the Parties undertake to enact any legislation necessary in order to implement the Treaty, and to terminate any international commitments and to repeal any legislation that is inconsistent with the Treaty.

Article 27: Ratification
1.   This Treaty shall be ratified by both Parties in conformity with their respective national procedures. It shall enter into force on the exchange of instruments of ratification.

2.   The Annexes, Appendices and other attachments to this Treaty shall be considered integral parts thereof.

Article 28: Interim measures
The Parties will apply, in certain spheres, to be agreed upon, interim measures pending the conclusion of the relevant agreements in accordance with this Treaty, as stipulated in Annex V.

Article 29: Settlement of disputes
1.   Disputes arising out of the application or interpretation of this Treaty shall be resolved by negotiations.

2.   Any such disputes which cannot be settled by negotiations shall be resolved by conciliation or submitted to arbitration.

Article 30: Registration
This Treaty shall be transmitted to the Secretary General of the United Nations for registration in accordance with the provisions of Article 102 of the Charter of the United Nations.

Done at the Arava/Araba Crossing Point this day Heshvan 21st, 5775, Jumada Al-Ula 21st, 1415 which corresponds to 26 October 1994 in the Hebrew, English and Arabic languages, all texts being equally authentic. In case of divergence of interpretation the English text shall prevail.

For the State of Israel
Yitzhak Rabin, Prime Minister

For the Hashemite Kingdom of Jordan
Abdul Salam Majali, Prime Minister

Witnessed by: William J. Clinton
President of the United States of America

List of Annexes, Appendices and other Attachments

Annex I
(a) International Boundary
(b) Naharayim/Baqura Area
(c) Zofar Area

Appendices (27 sheets):
I.   Emer Ha'arava (10 sheets), 1:20,000 orthophoto maps
II. Dead Sea (2 sheets), 1:50,000 orthoimages
III. Jordan and Yarmouk Rivers (12 sheets), 1:10,000 orthophoto maps
IV. Naharayim Area (1 sheet), 1:10,000 orthophoto map
V.   Zofar Area (1 sheet), 1:20,000 orthophoto map
VI. Gulf of Eilat (1 sheet), 1:50,000 orthoimage

Annex II
Water

Annex III
Crime and Drugs Annex

Annex IV
Environment Annex

Annex V
Interim Measures Agreed Minutes

Text of cease-fire understanding

The following is the text of the "understanding" reached on 26 April 1996, for the cease-fire in Lebanon.
The United States understands that after discussions with the governments of Israel and Lebanon, and in consultation with Syria, Lebanon and Israel will ensure the following:

1. Armed groups in Lebanon will not carry out attacks by Katyusha rockets or by any kind of weapon into Israel.

2. Israel and those cooperating with it will not fire any kind of weapon at civilians or civilian targets in Lebanon.

3. Beyond this, the two parties commit to ensuring that under no circumstances will civilians be the target of attack and that civilian populated areas and industrial and electrical installations will not be used as launching grounds for attacks.

4. Without violating this understanding, nothing herein shall preclude any party from exercising the right of self-defence.

A Monitoring Group is established consisting of the United States, France, Syria, Lebanon and Israel. Its task will be to monitor the application of the understanding stated above. Complaints will be submitted to the Monitoring Group.

In the event of a claimed violation of the understanding, the party submitting the complaint will do so within 24 hours. Procedures for dealing with the complaints will be set by the Monitoring Group.

The United States will also organise a Consultative Group, to consist of France, the European Union, Russia and other interested parties, for the purpose of assisting in the reconstruction needs of Lebanon.

It is recognised that the understanding to bring the current crisis between Lebanon and Israel to an end cannot substitute for a permanent solution. The United States understands the importance of achieving a comprehensive peace in the region.

Towards this end, the United States proposes the resumption of negotiations between Syria and Israel and between Lebanon and Israel at a time to be agreed upon, with the objective of reaching comprehensive peace.

The United States understands that it is desirable that these negotiations be conducted in a climate of stability and tranquillity.

This understanding will be announced simultaneously at 1800 hours, 26 April 1996, in all countries concerned.

The time set for implementation is 0400 hours, 27 April 1996.

The Wye River Memorandum

23 October 1998

The following are steps to facilitate implementation of the Interim Agreement on the West Bank and Gaza Strip of 28 September 1995 (the "Interim Agreement") and other related agreements including the Note for the Record of 17 January 1997 (hereinafter referred to as "the prior agreements") so that the Israeli and Palestinian sides can more effectively carry out their reciprocal responsibilities, including those relating to further redeployments and security respectively. These steps are to be carried out in a parallel phased approach in accordance with this Memorandum and the attached time line. They are subject to the relevant terms and conditions of the prior agreements and do not supersede their other requirements.

I. Further Redeployments

A. Phase One and Two Further Redeployments

1. Pursuant to the Interim Agreement and subsequent agreements, the Israeli side's implementation of the first and second F.R.D. will consist of the transfer to the Palestinian side of 13% from Area C as follows:

    1% to Area (A)

    12% to Area (B)

The Palestinian side has informed that it will allocate an area/areas amounting to 3% from the above Area (B) to be designated as Green Areas and/or Nature Reserves. The Palestinian side has further informed that they will act according to the established scientific standards, and that therefore there will be no changes in the status of these areas, without prejudice to the rights of the existing inhabitants in these areas including Bedouins; while these standards do not allow new construction in these areas, existing roads and buildings may be maintained.

The Israeli side will retain in these Green Areas/Nature Reserves the overriding security responsibility for the purpose of protecting Israelis and confronting the threat of terrorism. Activities and movements of the Palestinian Police forces may be carried out after coordination and confirmation; the Israeli side will respond to such requests expeditiously.

2. As part of the foregoing implementation of the first and second F.R.D., 14.2% from Area (B) will become Area (A).

B. Third Phase of Further Redeployments
With regard to the terms of the Interim Agreement and of Secretary Christopher's letters to the two sides of 17 January 1997 relating to the further redeployment process, there will be a committee to address this question. The United States will be briefed regularly.

II. Security
In the provisions on security arrangements of the Interim Agreement, the Palestinian side agreed to take all measures necessary in order to prevent acts of terrorism, crime and hostilities directed against the Israeli side, against individuals falling under the Israeli side's authority and against their property, just as the Israeli side agreed to take all measures necessary in order to prevent acts of terrorism, crime and hostilities directed against the Palestinian side, against individuals falling under the Palestinian side's authority and against their property. The two sides also agreed to take legal measures against offenders within their jurisdiction and to prevent incitement against each other by any organizations, groups or individuals within their jurisdiction.

Both sides recognize that it is in their vital interests to combat terrorism and fight violence in accordance with Annex I of the Interim Agreement and the Note for the Record. They also recognize that the struggle against terror and violence must be comprehensive in that it deals with terrorists, the terror support structure, and the environment conducive to the support of terror. It must be continuous and constant over a long-term, in that there can be no pauses in the work against terrorists and their structure. It must be cooperative in that no effort can be fully effective without Israeli–Palestinian cooperation and the continuous exchange of information, concepts, and actions.

Pursuant to the prior agreements, the Palestinian side's implementation of its responsibilities for security, security cooperation, and other issues will be as detailed below during the time periods specified in the attached time line:

A. Security Actions

1. Outlawing and Combating Terrorist Organizations
(a) The Palestinian side will make known its policy of zero tolerance for terror and violence against both sides.

(b) A work plan developed by the Palestinian side will be shared with the U.S. and thereafter implementation will begin immediately to ensure the systematic and effective combat of terrorist organizations and their infrastructure.

(c) In addition to the bilateral Israeli–Palestinian security cooperation, a U.S.–Palestinian committee will meet biweekly to review the steps being taken to eliminate terrorist cells and the support structure that plans, finances, supplies and abets terror. In these meetings, the Palestinian side will inform the U.S. fully of the actions it has taken to outlaw all organizations (or wings of organizations, as appropriate) of a military, terrorist or violent character and their support structure and to prevent them from operating in areas under its jurisdiction.

(d) The Palestinian side will apprehend the specific individuals suspected of perpetrating acts of violence and terror for the purpose of further investigation, and prosecution and punishment of all persons involved in acts of violence and terror.

(e) A U.S.–Palestinian committee will meet to review and evaluate information pertinent to the decisions on prosecution, punishment or other legal measures which affect the status of individuals suspected of abetting or perpetrating acts of violence and terror.

2. Prohibiting Illegal Weapons
(a) The Palestinian side will ensure an effective legal framework is in place to criminalize, in conformity with the prior agreements, any importation, manufacturing or unlicensed sale, acquisition or possession of firearms, ammunition or weapons in areas under Palestinian jurisdiction.

(b) In addition, the Palestinian side will establish and vigorously and continuously implement a systematic program for the collection and appropriate handling of all such illegal items in accordance with the prior agreements. The U.S. has agreed to assist in carrying out this program.

(c) A U.S.–Palestinian–Israeli committee will be established to assist and enhance cooperation in preventing the smuggling or other unauthorized introduction of weapons or explosive materials into areas under Palestinian jurisdiction.

3. Preventing Incitement

(a) Drawing on relevant international practice and pursuant to Article XXII (1) of the Interim Agreement and the Note for the Record, the Palestinian side will issue a decree prohibiting all forms of incitement to violence or terror, and establishing mechanisms for acting systematically against all expressions or threats of violence or terror. This decree will be comparable to the existing Israeli legislation which deals with the same subject.

(b) A U.S.–Palestinian–Israeli committee will meet on a regular basis to monitor cases of possible incitement to violence or terror and to make recommendations and reports on how to prevent such incitement. The Israeli, Palestinian and U.S. sides will each appoint a media specialist, a law enforcement representative, an educational specialist and a current or former elected official to the committee.

B. Security Cooperation

The two sides agree that their security cooperation will be based on a spirit of partnership and will include, among other things, the following steps:

1. Bilateral Cooperation

There will be full bilateral security cooperation between the two sides which will be continuous, intensive and comprehensive.

2. Forensic Cooperation

There will be an exchange of forensic expertise, training, and other assistance.

3. Trilateral Committee

In addition to the bilateral Israeli–Palestinian security cooperation, a high-ranking U.S.–Palestinian–Israeli committee will meet as required and not less than biweekly to assess current threats, deal with any impediments to effective security cooperation and coordination and address the steps being taken to combat terror and terrorist organizations. The committee will also serve as a forum to address the issue of external support for terror. In these meetings, the Palestinian side will fully inform the members of the committee of the results of its investigations concerning terrorist suspects already in custody and the participants will exchange additional relevant information The committee will report regularly to the leaders of the two sides on the status of cooperation, the results of the meetings and its recommendations.

C. Other Issues

1. Palestinian Police Force

(a) The Palestinian side will provide a list of its policemen to the Israeli side in conformity with the prior agreements.

(b) Should the Palestinian side request technical assistance, the U.S. has indicated its willingness to help meet these needs in cooperation with other donors.

(c) The Monitoring and Steering Committee will, as part of its functions, monitor the implementation of this provision and brief the U.S.

2. PLO Charter

The Executive Committee of the Palestine Liberation Organization and the Palestinian Central Council will reaffirm the letter of 22 January 1998 from PLO Chairman Yasir Arafat to President Clinton concerning the nullification of the Palestinian National Charter provisions that are inconsistent with the letters exchanged between the PLO and the Government of Israel on 9/10 September 1993. PLO Chairman Arafat, the Speaker of the Palestine National Council, and the Speaker of the Palestinian Council will invite the members of the PNC, as well as the members of the Central Council, the Council, and the Palestinian Heads of Ministries to a meeting to be addressed by President Clinton to reaffirm their support for the peace process and the aforementioned decisions of the Executive Committee and the Central Council.

3. Legal Assistance in Criminal Matters

Among other forms of legal assistance in criminal matters, the requests for arrest and transfer of suspects and defendants pursuant to Article II (7) of Annex IV of the Interim Agreement will be submitted (or resubmitted) through the mechanism of the Joint Israeli–Palestinian Legal Committee and will be responded to in conformity with Article II (7) (f) of Annex IV of the Interim Agreement within the twelve week period. Requests submitted after the eighth week will be responded to in conformity with Article II (7) (f) within four weeks of their submission. The U.S. has been requested by the sides to report on a regular basis on the steps being taken to respond to the above requests.

4. Human Rights and the Rule of Law

Pursuant to Article XI (1) of Annex I of the Interim Agreement, and without derogating from the above, the Palestinian Police will exercise powers and responsibilities to implement this Memorandum with due regard to internationally accepted norms of human rights and the rule of law, and will be guided by the need to protect the public, respect human dignity, and avoid harassment.

III. Interim committees and economic issues

1. The Israeli and Palestinian sides reaffirm their commitment to enhancing their relationship and agree on the need actively to promote economic development in the West Bank and Gaza. In this regard, the parties agree to continue or to reactivate all standing committees established by the Interim Agreement, including the Monitoring and Steering Committee, the Joint Economic Committee (JEC), the Civil Affairs Committee (CAC), the Legal Committee, and the Standing Cooperation Committee.

2. The Israeli and Palestinian sides have agreed on arrangements which will permit the timely opening of the Gaza Industrial Estate. They also have concluded a "Protocol Regarding the Establishment and Operation of the International Airport in the Gaza Strip During the Interim Period."

3. Both sides will renew negotiations on Safe Passage immediately. As regards the southern route, the sides will make best efforts to conclude the agreement within a week of the entry into force of this Memorandum.

Operation of the southern route will start as soon as possible thereafter. As regards the northern route, negotiations will continue with the goal of reaching agreement as soon as possible. Implementation will take place expeditiously thereafter.

4.   The Israeli and Palestinian sides acknowledge the great importance of the Port of Gaza for the development of the Palestinian economy, and the expansion of Palestinian trade. They commit themselves to proceeding without delay to conclude an agreement to allow the construction and operation of the port in accordance with the prior agreements. The Israeli–Palestinian Committee will reactivate its work immediately with a goal of concluding the protocol within sixty days, which will allow commencement of the construction of the port.

5.   The two sides recognize that unresolved legal issues adversely affect the relationship between the two peoples. They therefore will accelerate efforts through the Legal Committee to address outstanding legal issues and to implement solutions to these issues in the shortest possible period. The Palestinian side will provide to the Israeli side copies of all of its laws in effect.

6.   The Israeli and Palestinian sides also will launch a strategic economic dialogue to enhance their economic relationship. They will establish within the framework of the JEC an Ad Hoc Committee for this purpose. The committee will review the following four issues: (1) Israeli purchase taxes; (2) cooperation in combating vehicle theft; (3) dealing with unpaid Palestinian debts; and (4) the impact of Israeli standards as barriers to trade and the expansion of the A1 and A2 lists. The committee will submit an interim report within three weeks of the entry into force of this Memorandum, and within six weeks will submit its conclusions and recommendations to be implemented.

7.   The two sides agree on the importance of continued international donor assistance to facilitate implementation by both sides of agreements reached. They also recognize the need for enhanced donor support for economic development in the West Bank and Gaza. They agree to jointly approach the donor community to organize a Ministerial Conference before the end of 1998 to seek pledges for enhanced levels of assistance.

IV. Permanent status negotiations

The two sides will immediately resume permanent status negotiations on an accelerated basis and will make a determined effort to achieve the mutual goal of reaching an agreement by May 4, 1999. The negotiations will be continuous and without interruption. The U.S. has expressed its willingness to facilitate these negotiations.

V. Unilateral actions

Recognizing the necessity to create a positive environment for the negotiations, neither side shall initiate or take any step that will change the status of the West Bank and the Gaza Strip in accordance with the Interim Agreement.

Attachment: Time Line
This Memorandum will enter into force ten days from the date of signature.
Done at Washington, D.C. this 23rd day of October 1998.

For the Government of the State of Israel:
Binyamin Netanyahu

For the PLO:
Yassir Arafat

Witnessed by:
William J. Clinton
The United States of America

Time Line

Note: Parenthetical references below are to paragraphs in "The Wye River Memorandum" to which this time line is an integral attachment. Topics not included in the time line follow the schedule provided for in the text of the Memorandum.

1. Upon Entry into Force of the Memorandum:
- Third further redeployment committee starts (I (B))
- Palestinian security work plan shared with the U.S. (II (A) (1) (b))

- Full bilateral security cooperation (II (B) (1))
- Trilateral security cooperation committee starts (II (B) (3))
- Interim committees resume and continue; Ad Hoc Economic Committee starts (III)
- Accelerated permanent status negotiations start (IV)

2. Entry into Force – Week 2:
- Security work plan implementation begins (II (A) (1) (b)); (II (A) (1) (c)) committee starts
- Illegal weapons framework in place (II (A) (2) (a)); Palestinian implementation report (II (A) (2) (b))
- Anti-incitement committee starts (II (A) (3) (b)); decree issued (II (A) (3) (a))
- PLO Executive Committee reaffirms Charter letter (II (C) (2))
- Stage 1 of F.R.D. implementation: 2% C to B, 7.1% B to A. Israeli officials acquaint their Palestinian counterparts as required with areas; F.R.D. carried out; report on F.R.D. implementation (I (A))

3. Week 2-6:
- Palestinian Central Council reaffirms Charter letter (weeks two to four) (II (C) (2))
- PNC and other PLO organizations reaffirm Charter letter (weeks four to six) (II (C) (2))
- Establishment of weapons collection program (II (A) (2) (b)) and collection stage (II (A) (2) (c)); committee starts and reports on activities.
- Anti-incitement committee report (II (A) (3) (b))
- Ad Hoc Economic Committee: interim report at week three; final report at week six (III)
- Policemen list (II (C) (1) (a)); Monitoring and Steering Committee review starts (II (C) (1) (c))
- Stage 2 of F.R.D. implementation: 5% C to B. Israeli officials acquaint their Palestinian counterparts as required with areas; F.R.D. carried out; report on F.R.D. implementation (I (A))

4. Week 6-12:
- Weapons collection stage II (A) (2) (b); II (A) (2) (c) committee report on its activities.

- Anti-incitement committee report (II (A) (3) (b))
- Monitoring and Steering Committee briefs U.S. on policemen list (II (C) (1) (c))
- Stage 3 of F.R.D. implementation: 5% C to B, 1% C to A, 7.1% B to A. Israeli officials acquaint Palestinian counterparts as required with areas; F.R.D. carried out; report on F.R.D. implementation (I (A))

5. After Week 12:
Activities described in the Memorandum continue as appropriate and if necessary, including:
- Trilateral security cooperation committee (II (B)(3))
- (II (A) (1) (c)) committee
- (II (A) (1) (e)) committee
- Anti-incitement committee (II (A) (3) (b))
- Third Phase F.R.D. Committee (I (B))
- Interim Committees (III)
- Accelerated permanent status negotiations (IV)

End of Attachment

Wye River Memorandum
Washington D.C., 23 October 1998

Side Letter from US Secretary of State Madeleine Albright to Israeli Prime Minister Binyamin Netanyahu

Dear Mr. Prime Minister,
The United States is pleased to have worked with you in achieving a successful outcome in the negotiations on "The Wye River Memorandum." We believe its parallel phased approach will help provide greater confidence to both sides in the implementation process, since actions in each stage of the time line are to be completed by both sides before moving to the next stage. I can confirm that the United States is prepared to play the role identified for it in the Memorandum.

The United States recognizes the importance of the security provisions of "The Wye River Memorandum" to the State of Israel. In this context, and given the role specified for the United States in the Memorandum, we wish to reiterate our ironclad commitment to Israel's security and to peace, and to stress that Palestinian security undertakings are a critical foundation of the Memorandum.

In this context, we wanted to confirm our understanding of assurances we have received from the Palestinians on several issues that you have indicated are of special concern to Israel. Regarding the Palestinian apprehension of terrorism suspects (II (A) (1) (d)), we have been assured that all the cases which have been identified will be acted upon. With respect to Palestinian decisions regarding the prosecution, punishment or other legal measures that affect the status of individuals suspected of abetting or perpetrating acts of violence or terror, there are procedures in place to prevent unwarranted releases. Furthermore, we will express our opposition to any unwarranted releases of such suspects, and in the event of such a release, we will be prepared to express our position publicly.

Regarding the Palestinian side's program for confiscation and disposition of illegal weapons under paragraph II (A) (2) (b), our assistance to the Palestinian side will help ensure that any retention of weapons is consistent with the relevant Interim Agreement provisions, including Article IV (5) of Annex I. The U.S. plans to inform Israel periodically of the progress of our assistance program. Finally, with respect to the Palestinian side's provision of its list of policemen to Israel (II (C) (1) (a)), the U.S. has been assured that it will receive all appropriate information concerning current and former policemen as part of our assistance program.

Sincerely,
Madeleine K. Albright

Bibliography

Documents

Agreement on the Gaza Strip and the Jericho Area, 4 May 1994.

Agreement on the Preparatory Transfer of Powers and Responsibilities (Israel–PLO), 29 August 1994.

Beilin–Eitan National Agreement Regarding the Negotiations on the Permanent Settlement with the Palestinians, 1996.

Camp David Accords, 17 September 1978.

The Golan Heights Law, 14 December 1981.

Interim Agreement between Israel and the Palestinians, 28 September 1995.

Israel–Jordan Common Agenda, 14 September 1993.

Israel–Lebanon Cease-fire Understanding, 26 April 1996.

Israel–Palestinian Declaration of Principles, 13 September 1993.

Israel–PLO Recognition, 9 and 10 September 1993.

The Jerusalem Law, 30 July 1980.

Palestinian National Charter, 17 July 1968.

Peace Treaty between Israel and Egypt, 26 March 1979.

Protocol Concerning the Redeployment in Hebron, 17 January 1997.

Separation of Forces Agreement between Israel and Syria, 31 May 1974.

Summit of Peacemakers – Final Statement, Sharm el-Sheikh, 13 March 1996.

Treaty of Peace between Israel and Jordan, 26 October 1994 – Preamble and Articles.

UN Security Council Resolution 338, 22 October 1973.

UN Security Council Resolution 425 (Withdrawal from Lebanon), 19 March 1978.

The Washington Declaration (Israel–Jordan–US), 25 July 1994.

Official publications

Central Bureau of Statistics, *Half Yearly Economic Survey*, Jerusalem, September 1997.

Central Bureau of Statistics, *Statistical Abstract of Israel*, Jerusalem, editions from 1990–1996.

Giza Group, 'Privatisation in Israel', prepared by *Israel Business Arena*, October 1996.

Government of the State of Israel, Background Paper: 'The Refugee Issue', Jerusalem, October 1994.

Government Press Office, Background Paper: 'The Golan Heights', Jerusalem, 8 February 1994.

Government Press Office, The Laws of the State of Israel, Jerusalem.

International Monetary Fund, *Recent Economic Developments, Prospects and Progress in Institution Building in the West Bank and Gaza Strip*, Middle Eastern Department, Washington, DC, 6 March 1997.

The Israel Labour Party's Peace and Security Platform for Elections to the 14th Knesset, Labour Party Headquarters, Tel Aviv, 1996.

Israeli Ministry of Foreign Affairs, Background Paper: 'Economic relations between Israel and the Palestinian Authority', Jerusalem, February 1998.

Israeli–Palestinian Economic Relations Update, Israeli Ministry of Foreign Affairs, 25 May 1998.

The Likud Party Platform 1996, Peace and Security, Likud Party Headquarters, Tel Aviv, 1996.

Ministry of Foreign Affairs, Israel's Basic Laws: *The Elections 1996*, Jerusalem.

National Religious Party Platform 1996: Peace and Security, NRP Headquarters, Jerusalem.

Principles of the Meretz Platform 1996, Meretz Headquarters, Tel Aviv.

Report of the Commissioner-General of the United Nations Relief and Works Agency for Palestine Refugees in the Near East, 1 July 1996 – 30 June 1997, General Assembly Official Records – Fifty-second Session, Supplement no. 13 (A/52/13).

Books, journal articles, papers, newspapers and magazines

Abadi, S. 'Investment by Palestinian banks', paper presented at conference on investment in the northern West Bank, Centre for Palestine Research and Studies, Nablus, July 1997.

Abdul Hadi, M. 'The ownership of Jerusalem: a Palestinian view' in G. Karmi (ed.), *Jerusalem Today* (Reading, Ithaca Press, 1996).

Abed, G. 'Israel in the orbit of America: the political economy of a dependency relationship', *Journal of Palestine Studies,* vol. 16, no. 1 (1986).

Alpher, J. 'Israel's security concerns in the peace process', *Journal of International Affairs*, vol. 70, no. 2 (1994).

—'Settlements and borders', *Final Status Issues: Israel–Palestinians, Study 3*, Jaffee Centre for Strategic Studies, Tel Aviv University, 1994.

Anat Kurz, A. and N. Tal, 'Hamas: radical Islam in a national struggle', *Jaffee Centre for Strategic Studies Memorandum 47*, Tel Aviv University, 1997.

Arafat, Y. *Al-Ayyam* (newspaper), 29 December 1997.

Arens, M. *Broken Covenant: American Foreign Policy and Crisis Between the US and Israel* (New York, Simon and Schuster, 1995).

Asa-El, A., D. Gerstenfeld and D. Harris, 'Frenkel to the defence', *Jerusalem Post*, 5 October 1997.

Assad, S. 'Albright urges settlement time out', *Washington Post*, 11 September 1997.

Aughey, A. and D. Morrow (eds), *Northern Ireland Politics* (London and New York, Longman, 1996).

Bar El, R. 'Growth from peace', *Israel Business Arena*, 29 March 1996.

Bar'el, Z. 'A double edged sword', *Ha-Aretz*, 19 October 1997.

Bar-Siman-Tov, Y. 'Peacemaking with the Palestinians: change and legitimacy' in E. Karsh (ed.), *From Rabin to Netanyahu: Israel's Troubled Agenda* (London and Portland, Frank Cass, 1997).

Barzilai, A. 'Israel and Turkey to build new missile', *Ha-Aretz*, 15 October 1997.

—'Mordechai trip aims to deepen ties with Turkey', *Ha-Aretz*, 7 December 1997.

—'Allies with Ankara', *Ha-Aretz*, 8 December 1997.

—'Israel and Turkey look to the stars as strategic ties deepen', *Ha-Aretz*, 10 December 1997.

—'Israel and Turkey accelerate dialogue', *Ha-Aretz*, 21 December 1997.

—'The Turkish knight', *Ha-Aretz*, 11 January 1998.

Barzilai, A. and A. Harel, 'Reliant mermaid runs into rough seas', *Ha-Aretz*, 7 January 1998.

Bavly, D. and E. Salpeter, *Fire in Beirut: Israel's War in Lebanon with the PLO* (New York, Stein and Day, 1984).

Bechor, G. 'Syria's shadow enemies', *Ha-Aretz,* 4 December 1996.

—'Giving peace a chance', *Ha-Aretz*, 15 July 1997.

—'Syrian leaders take high stand against Israel', *Ha-Aretz*, 1 August 1997.

Beilin, Y. *Israel: A Concise Political History* (London, Weidenfeld and Nicolson, 1992).

—'Principles for negotiations' *Ha-Aretz*, 10 August 1994.

—'The case for withdrawal', *Jerusalem Post*, 23 September 1997.

Benvenisti, M. 'Recycling injustices', *Ha-Aretz*, 24 July 1997.

—'Reality is not a thriller', *Ha-Aretz*, 9 October 1997.

Benziman, U. 'The gap between the final settlement and reality', *Ha-Aretz*, 21 September 1997.

Bew, P., H. Patterson and P. Teague, *Between War and Peace: The Political Future of Northern Ireland* (London, Lawrence and Wishcart, 1987).

Bregman, A. and J. El-Tahri, *The Fifty Years War: Israel and the Arabs* (London, Penguin Books, 1998).

Bushinsky, J. 'Arafat must make a choice', *Jerusalem Post*, 5 September 1997.

—'Probe into assassination fiasco', *Jerusalem Post*, 7 October 1997.

Bushinsky, J. and J. Immanuel, 'Ross begins Jerusalem–Ramallah shuttle', *Jerusalem Post*, 11 August 1997.

Bushinsky, J., B. Tsur and L. Collins, 'Netanyahu: I won't fire Mossad chief', *Jerusalem Post*, 13 October 1997.

Clawson, P. 'The disintegration of the Soviet Union: economic consequences for the Middle East' in David Menashri (ed.), *Central Asia Meets the Middle East* (London and Portland, Frank Cass, 1998).

Cohen, E., M. Eisenstadt and A. Bacevich, 'Israel's revolution in security affairs', *Survival*, vol. 40, no.1 (1998).

Collins, L. 'One person, two votes, many options', *Jerusalem Post*, 10 May 1996.

—'Riots are an eye opener', *Jerusalem Post*, 27 September 1996.

—'Assad: Netanyahu and enemy of peace', *Jerusalem Post*, 13 August 1997.

Collins, N. and T. Cradden, *Irish Politics Today* (Manchester, Manchester University Press, 1997).

Dagoni, R. 'Israel and Turkey set to produce Popeye missile', *Israel Business Arena*, 28 May 1997.

—'Turkey asks Israel to increase reciprocal trade after defence deal', *Israel Business Arena*, 14 January 1998.

Dallal, J. 'Colour blind', *Jerusalem Post*, 28 August 1996.

Dempsey, J. 'Israel waits for Netanyahu to deliver', *Financial Times*, 22 November 1996.

—'Israel eases bar on Palestinian workers', *Financial Times*, 2 September 1997.

—'Israeli tanks enter West Bank', *Financial Times*, 27 September 1996.

—'Ross rides back to the rescue', *Financial Times*, 27 March 1997.

Dempsey, J. and A. Machlis, 'Opening of a tunnel blocks the road to peace', *Financial Times*, 27 September 1996.

Diskin, A. *Elections and Voters in Israel* (New York, Praeger, 1991).

Dudkevitch, M. and S. Honig, 'Netanyahu raps talk of Lebanon pullout', *Jerusalem Post*, 8 September 1997.

Dumper, M. 'Demographic and border issues affecting the future of Jerusalem' in G. Karmi (ed.), *Jerusalem Today* (Reading, Ithaca Press, 1996).

Eban, A. 'No more room for American ambiguity', *Jerusalem Post*, 8 August 1997.

Eisenberg, L. 'Israel's Lebanon policy', *Middle East Review of International Affairs*, 3 September 1997.

Eisenstadt, N. *Israeli Society* (London, Weidenfeld and Nicolson, 1967).

Elazar, D. and S. Sandler (eds), *Israel at the Polls 1996* (London and Portland, Frank Cass, 1998).

Eldar, A. 'Dennis Ross helped set up Sharon–Abu Mazen meeting', *Ha-Aretz*, 30 June 1997.

—'And who didn't come?', *Ha-Aretz*, 6 August 1997.

—'John F. Kennedy and Danny Yatom', *Ha'-Aretz*, 6 October 1997.

—'The Mossad old-boy network: up to the King', *Ha-Aretz*, 9 October 1997.

Erez, Y. 'Arafat's last chance', *Ma'ariv*, 5 September 1997.

Eshel, D. 'The Golan Heights: a vital strategic asset for Israel' in E. Karsh (ed.), *From Rabin to Netanyahu: Israel's Troubled Agenda* (London and Portland, Frank Cass, 1997).

Feldman, S. and A. Toukan, *Bridging the Gap: A Future Security Architecture for the Middle East* (Lanham, Maryland and Oxford, Rowan and Littlefield, 1997).

Flamhaft, Z. *Israel on the Road to Peace: Accepting the Unacceptable* (Boulder, Colorado and Oxford, Westview Press, 1996).

Frankel, G. *Beyond the Promised Land: Jews and Arabs on the Hard Road to a New Israel* (New York, Simon and Schuster, 1996).

Galili, L. 'The Lebanese mess is still with us', *Ha-Aretz*, 8 September 1997.

Gardner, D. 'Peace crisis crushes hopes: survey of Jordan', *Financial Times*, 1 November 1996.

—'US steps in to halt further Lebanon fighting', *Financial Times*, 12 September 1997.

Gazit, S. ' The security zone has served us faithfully but its time has passed', *Ma'ariv*, 8 September 1997.

Gilbert, M. *Israel: A History* (London, Doubleday, 1998).

Gillis, D. 'Valley of slaughter', *Israel Business Arena*, 9 September 1997.

Gold, D. 'US policy towards Israel's qualitative edge', *JCSS Memorandum*, 36 (1992).

Gowers, A. and T. Walker *Behind the Myth: Yasser Arafat and the Palestinian Revolution* (London, W.H. Allen, 1990).

Gruen, G. 'Relations with Ankara: crisis of cooperation', *Jerusalem Post*, 5 July 1996.

Hadar, L. 'The 1992 electoral earthquake and the fall of the second Israeli republic', *Middle East Journal*, vol. 46, no. 4 (1992).

Haetzni, D. 'Netanyahu wants to give: Arafat does not want to take', *Ma'ariv*, 1 November 1996.

Harel, H. 'Mermaid exercise draws Arab protest', *Ha-Aretz*, 8 January 1998.

Harris, D. 'A closed economy', *Jerusalem Post*, 9 October 1997.

Hattis-Rolef, S. (ed.) *Political Dictionary of the State of Israel* (Jerusalem, Jerusalem Publishing House, 1994).

Hazan, R. 'Presidential parliamentarism: direct popular election of the Prime Minister, Israel's new electoral and political system', *Electoral Studies*, 15–1 (1996).

Heller, M. 'A policy of his own', *Jerusalem Post*, 22 August 1996.

—'Weighing Israel's option now' in R. Hollis and N. Shepadi (eds), *Lebanon on Hold: Implications for Middle East Peace* (London, Royal Institute of International Affairs, 1996).

Henessey, T. *A History of Northern Ireland, 1920–1996* (London, Macmillan, 1997).

Herzog, C. *The Arab–Israeli Wars* (New York, Vintage Books, 1984).

Hollis, R. and N. Shepadi (eds), *Lebanon on Hold: Implications for Middle East Peace* (London, Royal Institute of International Affairs, 1996).

Hopkinson, W. 'Peace dividend?', *The World Today*, vol. 54, no. 7 (July 1998).

Immanuel, J. 'Abu Mazen call for state at Final Status talks', *Jerusalem Post*, 6 May 1996.

—'Netanyahu warns Arafat: don't declare a state', *Jerusalem Post*, 24 November 1996.

—'Palestinian conference rejects compensation for refugees', *Jerusalem Post*, 22 September 1996.

—'Refugee talks could set precedent', *Jerusalem Post*, 7 March 1995.

Inbar, E. 'Israel's security in a new international environment', *Israel Affairs*, vol. 2, no. 1 (1995).

—'Netanyahu takes over' in D. Elazar and S. Sandler (eds.) *Israel at the Polls 1996* (London and Portland, Frank Cass, 1998).

—'Peace is a mirage' *Jerusalem Post*, 2 March 1998.

Inbari, P. 'Economics and the Palestinian question', *Jerusalem Post*, 12 June 1996.

—'Labour's Mashov Circle backs recognition of Palestinian state', *Jerusalem Post*, 11 September 1996.

Kalaycioglu, E. 'The logic of contemporary Turkish politics', *Middle East Review of International Affairs*, no. 3 (September 1997).

Kanovsky, E. 'Middle East economies and Arab–Israeli peace agreements', *Israel Affairs*, vol. 1, no. 4 (1995).

Karmi, G. (ed.), *Jerusalem Today* (Reading, Ithaca Press, 1996).

Karsh, E. (ed.), *From Rabin to Netanyahu: Israel's Troubled Agenda* (London and Portland, Frank Cass, 1997).

—'What on earth is Assad up to?', *Jerusalem Post*, 20 September 1996.

Al-Khazendar, S. *Jordan and the Palestine Question: The Role of Islamic and Left Forces in Foreign Policy Making* (Reading, Ithaca Press, 1997).

Kimmerling, B. and J. Migdal *Palestinians: The Making of a People* (Cambridge, Massachusetts, Harvard University Press, 1994).

Koren, O. 'Israel and Turkey sign treaty concerning free trade, capital, investments support and prevention of double taxation', *Israel Business Arena*, 18 March 1996.

—'Fears that free trade ratification with Turkey may be torpedoed', *Israel Business Arena*, 9 February 1997.

—'Israel imposes economic sanctions for the first time', *Israel Business Arena,* 31 July 1997.

Korn, D. 'The National Unity Years in Israel 1984–1990', Ph.D. thesis, London School of Economics, London (1991).

—*Time in Grey 1994–1990* (in Hebrew) (Tel Aviv, Zmona Bitan, 1994).

Kuttler, H. 'Gold: plans developing for a withdrawal from Lebanon', *Jerusalem Post,* 4 August 1996.

Levi, G. 'The time has come to face up to the fearsome right of return for refugees', *Shaml Newsletter,* no. 8 (October 1997).

Levitzky, N. 'Netanyahu's Syrian paper', *Yediot Ahronot,* 16 August 1996.

Levran, A. *Israeli Strategy After Desert Storm* (London and Portland, Frank Cass, 1997).

Libai, D., U. Lynn, A. Rubinstein and Y. Tsiddon. *Changing the System of Government in Israel: Proposed Basic Law; The Government, Direct Election of the Prime Minister* (in Hebrew), The Jerusalem Centre for Public Affairs and the Public Committee for a Constitution in Israel, Jerusalem, 1990.

Lippman, T. 'Albright visit bares US–Israel division over peace', *Washington Post,* 11 September 1997.

—'Albright pessimistic as Mideast trips end', *Washington Post,* 16 September 1997.

Lipson, C. 'American support for Israel: history, sources, limits' in G. Sheffer (ed.), *US–Israeli Relations at the Crossroads* (London and Portland, Frank Cass, 1997).

Lochery, N. 'Blocking Bibi's bid for power', *The World Today,* vol. 53, no. 6 (June 1996).

—*The Israeli Labour Party: In the Shadow of the Likud* (Reading, Ithaca Press, 1997).

—'Israel's political Houdini', *The World Today,* Royal Institute of International Affairs, vol. 54, no. 5 (May 1998).

—'The internal restraints on Netanyahu in Israel: the Middle East peace process, 1996-1997', unpublished working paper, University of Exeter.

Luttwak, E. 'Strategic aspects of US–Israeli relations' in G. Sheffer (ed.), *US–Israeli Relations at the Crossroads* (London and Portland, Frank Cass, 1997).

Makovsky, D. *Making Peace with the PLO: The Rabin Government's Road to Oslo* (Boulder, Colorado and Oxford, Westview Press, 1996).

—'Assad: the great miscalculator', *Jerusalem Post*, 4 June 1996.

—'Netanyahu needs to keep King Hussein in mind', *Jerusalem Post*, 10 October 1996.

—'Mordechai rejected Lebanon withdrawal after policy review', *Ha-Aretz*, 8 September 1997.

—'Mubarak says Netanyahu wrecking peace process', *Ha-Aretz*, 9 September 1997.

—'Albright will press Arafat, but Israel must respond', *Ha-Aretz*, 11 September 1997.

—'Albright urges a time out on settlements if Arafat acts against terror', *Ha-Aretz*, 12 September 1997.

—'Nine per cent? Thirteen per cent?: what does it all mean?', *Ha-Aretz*, 21 May 1998.

—'US rejects Netanyahu's combined pullback plan', *Ha-Aretz*, 21 May 1998.

Makovsky, D. and E. Rabin, 'PM's office: we are facing a propaganda war with the Palestinians', *Ha-Aretz*, 14 July 1997.

Marcus, Y. 'A Chief of Staff of their own too?', *Ha-Aretz*, 8 July 1997.

—'The robber of dreams', *Ha-Aretz*, 22 August 1997.

—'She left her stick at home', *Ha-Aretz*, 12 September 1997.

—'The only better of this disgrace', *Ha-Aretz*, 7 October 1997.

Margalit, D. 'Need a giant portion of mutual trust', *Ha-Aretz*, 11 August 1997.

Marom, D. 'Irvy signs Israel–Turkey defence cooperation agreement', *Israel Business Arena*, 29 August 1996.

—'Phantom jet deal won't be cancelled despite Turkish PM's opposition', *Israel Business Arena*, 2 December 1996.

Marom, D. and R. Dagoni, 'IMI led Israeli consortium offers Turkey Merkava Mark 3 Tank', *Israel Business Arena*, 21 October 1997.

Menashri, D. (ed.), *Central Asia Meets the Middle East* (London and Portland, Frank Cass, 1998).

Mendilow, J. 'The Likud's dilemma in the 1996 elections: between the devil and the deep blue sea', unpublished paper, Rider University.

Murphy, E. 'Structural inhibitions to economic liberalisation in Israel', *Middle East Journal*, vol. 48, no. 1 (1994).

Nelan, B. 'Inside the summit', *Time*, 14 October 1996.

Netanyahu B., *A Place Among Nations: Israel and the World* (New York, Bantam, 1993).

—*Fighting Terrorism: How Democracies Can Defeat Domestic and International Terrorists* (London, Allison and Busby, 1996).

Newman, D. 'The territorial politics of ex-urbanisation', *Israel Affairs,* vol. 3, no. 1 (1996).

O'Dwyer, T. 'Nasrallah: Hizbollah's ruthless realist', *Jerusalem Post,* 22 September 1997.

Patterson, H. *The Politics of Illusion: Political History of the IRA* (London, Serif, 1997).

Peres, S. *The New Middle East* (New York, Holt, 1993).

—*The Valley of Peace* (Jerusalem, Minister of Foreign Affairs, 1994).

—*Memoirs: Battling for Peace* (London, Weidenfeld and Nicolson, 1995).

Peretz, D. and G. Doron, 'Israel's 1996 elections: a second political earthquake?', *Middle East Journal,* 50–4 (1996).

—*The Government and Politics of Israel* (Boulder, Colorado, Oxford, Westview, 1997).

Peters, J. (1996) 'Israel's new government', The Royal Institute of International Affairs, *Briefing Paper* 33 (July 96).

Pine, S. 'Myopic vision: whither Israeli–Egyptian relations?' in E. Karsh (ed.), *From Rabin to Netanyahu: Israel's Troubled Agenda* (London and Portland, Frank Cass, 1997).

Pipe, K. *The Origins of the Present Troubles in Northern Ireland* (London, Addison Wesley, 1997).

Plotzker, S. 'Economists around the world say we're doing fine', *Yediot Aharonot,* 26 September 1997.

Podeh, E. 'Rethinking Israel in the Middle East' in Efraim Karsh (ed.), *From Rabin to Netanyahu: Israel's Troubled Agenda* (London and Portland, Frank Cass, 1997).

Porter, N. *Rethinking Unionism* (Belfast, Blackstuff Press, 1996).

Rabin, Y. *The Rabin Memoirs* (Bnei Brak, Steimatzky, 1994).

Rabinovich, A. 'Commotion without motion', *Jerusalem Post,* 29 August 1997.

—'A nasty storm fast brewing up' *Jerusalem Post,* 21 September 1997.

Robins, P. 'Turkey's Ostpolitik: relations with the Central Asian states' in D. Menashri (ed.), *Central Asia Meets the Middle East* (London and Portland, Frank Cass, 1998).

Rodan, S. 'Ties with Turkey: the most important story of the decade', *Jerusalem Post,* 14 June 1996.

—'Shaky soloist', *Jerusalem Post,* 15 November 1996.

—'Shaky soloist: part two', *Jerusalem Post*, 15 November 1996.

—'Crisis of confidence', *Jerusalem Post*, 17 July 1997.

—'Where terror lurks', *Jerusalem Post*, 8 August 1997.

—'What does Assad want?', *Jerusalem Post*, 21 August 1997.

—'Iran, Israel reportedly forging contacts', *Jerusalem Post*, 9 September 1997.

—'Diplomats: Israel, Jordan need time to restore the relationship', *Jerusalem Post*, 7 October 1997.

Rodan, S. and B. Hutman, 'Of talks and traps', *Jerusalem Post*, 3 May 1996.

Rodan, S. and A. O'Sullivan, 'National defence must rest on a solid base', *Jerusalem Post*, 5 October 1997.

Rubin, B. 'No prime minister: a melodrama in three acts', *Jerusalem Post*, 21 June 1996.

—'More moderate than it looks', *Jerusalem Post*, 9 August 1996.

—'Jordan's economic woes could threaten warm peace with Israel', *Jerusalem Post*, 18 August 1996.

—'External influences on the Israeli elections' in D. Elazar and S. Sandler (eds), *Israel at the Polls 1996* (London and Portland, Frank Cass, 1998).

Rubinstein, D. 'A renewed occupation or security measures?', *Ha-Aretz*, 4 August 1997.

Rudge, D. 'Mordechai ready to discuss Jezzine First proposal', *Jerusalem Post*, 4 September 1997.

Ryman, M. *War and Peace in Ireland* (London, Pluto, 1994).

Rynhold, J. 'Labour, Likud, the special relationship and the peace process' in E. Karsh (ed.), *From Rabin to Netanyahu: Israel's Troubled Agenda* (London and Portland, Frank Cass, 1997).

Samit, G. 'The bomb and the marvel', *Ha-Aretz*, 1 August 1997.

Savir, U. *The Process* (New York, Random House, 1998).

Schiff, Z. 'A Palestinian–Israeli military confrontation and its ramifications', *Ha-Aretz*, 4 July 1997.

—'Confrontation at home or in Washington', *Ha-Aretz*, 15 August 1997.

—'What did Rabin promise the Syrians?', *Ha-Aretz*, 29 August 1997.

—'June 4 1967: in three acts', *Ha-Aretz*, 2 September 1997.

—'Three withdrawals', *Ha-Aretz*, 12 September 1997.

—'Netanyahu proposes new Syrian formula', *Ha-Aretz*, 21 September 1997.

—'Keeping the romance quiet', *Ha-Aretz*, 2 January 1998.

Schiff, Z. and E. Ya'ari, *Israel's Lebanon War* (London, George Allen and Unwin, 1985).

Seale, P. *Assad of Syria: The Struggle for the Middle East* (London, I.B. Tauris, 1988).

Segal, A. 'What a Palestinian state would look like', *Wall Street Journal*, 31 January 1997.

Shahor, O. 'The immediate effect would be a massacre of SLA people and shooting at our settlements', *Ma'ariv*, 8 September 1997.

Shalev, A. *Israel and Syria: Peace and Security on the Golan*, JCSS Study no. 24, Tel Aviv University, 1994.

Shalev, C. 'Beneficial to peace opponents', *Ma'ariv*, 31 July 1997.

Sharkansky, I. 'The potential for ambiguity: the case of Jerusalem' in E. Karsh (ed.), *From Rabin to Netanyahu: Israel's Troubled National Agenda* (London and Portland, Frank Cass, 1997).

Sharon, A. *Yediot Aharonot*, 7 September 1997.

Shavit, A. 'The Prime Minister would like a few minutes of your time', *Ha-Aretz*, 22 November 1996.

Sheffer, G. (ed.), *US–Israeli Relations at the Crossroads* (London and Portland, Frank Cass, 1997).

Shichor, Y. 'Israel's military transfers to China and Taiwan', *Survival*, vol. 40, no. 1 (1998).

Shindler, C. *Israel, Likud and the Zionist Dream: Power, Politics and Ideology from Begin to Netanyahu* (London, I.B. Tauris, 1995).

Shragai, N. 'Meanwhile in the Jewish settlements', *Ha-Aretz*, 14 September 1997.

Sivan, E. 'Danger from the north?', *Ha-Aretz*, 24 August 1997.

Sprinzak, E and L. Diamond (eds), *Israeli Democracy under Stress* (London, Lynne Rienner, 1993).

Stein, K. 'Continuity and change in Egyptian–Israeli relations, 1973–1997' in E. Karsh (ed.), *From Rabin to Netanyahu: Israel's Troubled Agenda* (London and Portland, Frank Cass, 1997).

Steinberg, G. 'Peace, security and terror' in D. Elazar and S. Sandler (eds), *Israel at the Polls 1996* (London and Portland, Frank Cass, 1998).

Tal, Y. 'Albright faced toughest challenge', *Ha-Aretz*, 10 September 1997.

Tessler, M. *A History of the Israeli-Palestinian Conflict* (Bloomington and Indianapolis, Indiana University Press, 1994).

Tonge, J. *Northern Ireland: Conflict and Change* (London, Simon and Schuster, 1998).

Trendle, G. 'Hizbollah: pragmatism and popular standing' in R. Hollis and N. Shepadi (eds), *Lebanon on Hold: Implications for Middle East Peace* (London, Royal Institute of International Affairs, 1996).

Tsur, B. 'IDF: Syria preparing for partial retake of the Golan', *Jerusalem Post*, 16 September 1997.

Van-Hear, N. 'Reintegration of the Palestinian returnees', *Shaml Monographs*, no. 6 (February 1997).

Weissbrod, L. 'Gush Emunim and the Israeli–Palestinian peace process: moderate religious fundamentalism in crisis', *Israel Affairs,* vol. 3, no. 1 (1996).

Werter, R. 'Former ambassador says Assad missed his chance', *Jerusalem Post*, 29 August 1997.

Winter, E. 'Business in the Bibi era', *Jerusalem Post*, 25 June 1996.

Ya'ari, E. 'Neighbourhood watch: the formula', *Jerusalem Report*, 4 June 1995.

Yakan, M. 'From war to peace, prospects and implications of the Middle East peace process' in E. Karsh (ed.), *From Rabin to Netanyahu: Israel's Troubled Agenda* (London and Portland, Frank Cass, 1997).

Yerushalmi, S. 'Syrian landmine', *Ma'ariv,* 25 November 1996.

Zak, M. 'A friendship that conquered all', *Jerusalem Post*, 18 October 1996.

—'Israel and Jordan: strategically bound', *Israel Affairs,* vol. 3, no. 1 (1996).

—'Syria's missed chances', *Jerusalem Post*, 3 September 1997.

Zakheim, D. 'Economic security after a settlement: the prospects for Israel', *Israel Affairs*, vol. 2, no. 1 (1995).

Zilberfarb, B. 'The effect of the peace process on the Israeli economy', *Israel Affairs*, vol. 1, no. 1 (1994).

—'The Israeli economy in the 1990s: immigration, the peace process, and the medium term prospects for growth', *Israel Affairs*, vol. 3, no. 1 (1996).

Zisser, E. 'Hizbollah in Lebanon: at the crossroads', *Middle East Review of International Affairs*, no. 3 (September 1997).

Index